Dr. Weaver's examination of of David Edwin Harrell, Jr. des informative and historically seeks to explain causes of events and issues faced by Harrell and fellow Christians during his lifetime. Beyond that, however, it will almost certainly challenge the reader to introspectively evaluate influences upon his/her own thought patterns when approaching Bible study, living in the present as a Christian, and maintaining membership in the body of Christ.

C. G. "Colly" Caldwell
Past President & Professor Emeritus
Florida College

John Weaver's *Explorer in Search of Zion* is a biography of David Edwin Harrell, Jr. It resembles Harrell's own book, *The Churches of Christ in the 20th Century*, which chronicled the history of churches of Christ through about the third quarters of the 20th century intertwined the events that occurred with the life of Homer Hailey, a pilgrim who also sought to travel the New Testament pathway to "Mount Zion and to the city of the living God, the heavenly Jerusalem, and to myriads of angels, to the general assembly and church of the first-born who are enrolled in heaven, and to God, the Judge of all, and to the spirits of righteous men made perfect, and to Jesus, the mediator of a new covenant, and to the sprinkled blood, which speaks better than the blood of Abel" (Hebrews 12:23-24, NASB). Hailey and Harrell were very different men, but both were searching for the pathway to Zion.

Harrell understood that Jesus was the original "Pathfinder," who described himself as "the way" to Zion, and revealed through his ambassadors the twists and turns of his word that were to be followed by his disciples. Some of them received his instructions and tried to obey them; many did not. Throughout the centuries following the apostolic age, more and more weeds of human opinion obscured the way to Zion. Therefore, each generation has had to rediscover it through a study of the teachings of Christ and his apostles and the examples of how churches they founded followed their orders. Harrell called this quest a search for primitivism. Some readers will conclude from the pages of *Explorer in Search of Zion* that Ed found the right path to follow, while others will not. Instead, they will be convinced that both he and John have taken the wrong road.

Ed Harrell was a complex person, a common man with an uncommon mind. Some of his writings are simple and easy to understand, although others are agonizingly complex. As would be expected, therefore, Weaver's biography is characterized by the same duality. Parts of it are easy to understand, while others are difficult to follow, but he offers something to everyone. It is like a garden filled with a variety of produce.

Explorer in Search of Zion contains descriptions of events and statements about contemporary individuals, and some of them may inadvertently be incorrect. I personally know John Weaver to be a sincere and honest Christian. He is a humble disciple of Christ, who is both multi-talented and a well-trained scholar with impeccable credentials. Moreover, this biography reflects John's close association with Ed. It is carefully documented, using primary sources, including an enormous number of personal interviews both with Ed and others, and displays Weaver's familiarity with important secondary sources. I hope each person will read this labor of love with an eagerness to learn and a charitable mindset. God will judge us all.

Melvin Curry
Biblical Studies Professor Emeritus
Florida College

In academic circles, David Edwin Harrell, Jr. is known as an incisive historian of Southern Christianity, a prolific author, and a demanding professor and mentor. In church circles, he is known as a preacher, a defender of the faith as he understood it, and a missionary in India. Few, however, know the story of this gifted and driven man as John Weaver has masterfully told it. For those who dismiss Harrell's primitivist religious commitments as naïve, Weaver's sophisticated analysis reveals an intellectually robust rationale for his ideas.

When he cast his lot with non-institutional Churches of Christ in the 1950s, Harrell became doggedly committed to a view of the nature and function of scripture that to others was simplistic and wrongheaded. Even those who welcomed his defense of their views did not understand the complexity of his thought. And while Harrell's accusations of apostasy were often aimed at people like me, no honest observer can ignore the ideas that formed his commitments and drove his life.

Weaver's biography is a fascinating account of the formation, life, and thought of an imminent historian of marginalized southern Christian traditions and an enigmatic self-styled "legalistic fanatic" for a cause he truly believed.

Douglas A. Foster
Professor of Church History
Emeritus
Abilene Christian University

John Weaver's biography of Ed Harrell maintains a balance between erudite research and accessible prose to tell the story of one of the most influential historians from the Stone-Campbell Movement. Weaver uses personal interviews, local newspapers, archival materials, and many other sources to narrate a finely textured and personal story not only of a scholar's life and contributions but also of a mischievous youth, an indefatigable churchman who led through preaching and publishing, and an international missionary. Weaver's biography functions also as a historical and theological overview of the non-institutional Churches of Christ. Some readers will disagree with Weaver's interpretation of non-institutionalism, but he delivers a well-researched and creatively organized telling of Harrell's life, ministry, and scholarly historiographical contributions.

James L. Gorman
Professor of History
Johnson University

David Edward Harrell, Jr.—Ed Harrell—was equally at home in two worlds. He was an urbane university historian whose groundbreaking works on Southern religion challenged popular stereotypes of "sectarian" piety. But he was also a restorationist lay preacher, a biblical literalist, and self-described "legalist fanatic," celebrated (or condemned) for his sharp polemics against any Christian yearnings for cultural respectability. And yet, through it all, he had a marvelous sense of humor that permeated everything he did or said. Weaver's book brings to life an influential Southern religious conservative who knew how to laugh at himself.

E. Brooks Holifield
Charles Howard Candler Professor,
Emeritus
Emory University

Beautifully written and exhaustively researched, John Weaver's *Explorer in Search of Zion* is not only a first-rate biography, it is also a fitting tribute to Ed Harrell precisely because it reflects the kind of careful scholarship that marked everything that Harrell wrote. An exploration of Harrell's life as scholar and professor, it also explores his life as a preacher, a polemicist, and a Christian committed to a sectarian form of the Christian faith. In the end, *Explorer in Search of Zion* shows how Harrell's personal sectarian beliefs shaped a magnificent career of first-rate historical scholarship devoted to understanding a wide variety of sectarian Christian movements and placed Harrell among the best historians of American religion of his time.

Richard T. Hughes
Scholar in Residence at Lipscomb
University
Co-author, *Reviving the Ancient Faith: The Story of Churches of Christ in America*

Explorer in Search of Zion is the story of the life and legacy of David E. Harrell, Jr. Harrell left behind an enormous body of scholarly historical work that focused on American religious history. His studies of religion in the South called for broader appreciation of marginalized religious groups. His research contributed to a greater awareness of how the culture and society can impact the assumptions and faith of religious groups and individuals. Harrell brought particular attention to the theme of biblical primitivism—the restoration ideal—and its impact on history and culture, calling it one of the most persistently recurring and influential themes in history. This restoration ideal—the quest to restore Jesus' teachings and the church's purity as found in the New Testament—was ultimately the guiding principle of Harrell's life of faith and service to Christ. This book is the story of that life journey.

Professor Weaver's telling of the story is based on sound historical research and engaging narrative. As inspiring as it is informative, it should serve as a fitting tribute to Ed Harrell's legacy of learning and teaching others.

Dan Petty
Professor Emeritus, Florida College,
Author of *Our Help in Ages Past*

Ed Harrell was a unique figure among those of us committed to the restoration ideal of following the New Testament. He combined scholarly historical expertise with a plain-spoken respect for biblical authority. I didn't always agree with his conclusions but have come to recognize the debt we owe him for his ground-breaking work in warning against the growing influence of the social gospel and denominational mindsets within our ranks. John Weaver has done an outstanding job of introducing a fuller picture of this multifaceted brother to those of us who had only limited personal contact with him. *Explorer in Search of Zion* is an important contribution to the study of church history during this period and the life of a beloved disciple, preacher, and historian who lived it.

Kyle Pope
Chair, Publications Committee
Truth Publications, Inc.

Harrell ranked with Martin Marty as one of the tiny few professional historians who made as well as wrote history. He was brilliant, erudite, and distinguished by a prodigious publication record on a wide range of topics. Always impeccably attired, he was blessed with a wicked sense of humor, eager to extend a hand to younger academics, a polite yet intimidating force in academic meetings, and deeply committed to his populist version of church of Christ theology and ecclesiology.

In an era when academic biographers are prone to deconstruct their subjects, Weaver is unapologetically yet appropriately admiring of a person who merits admiration. His massively researched, fairly argued, and clearly written volume stands as an eloquent testimony to the capaciousness of Harrell's life and legacy. If Ed (as his friends knew him) were still with us, I am confident that he would have been slightly embarrassed but secretly pleased.

Grant Wacker
Gilbert T. Rowe Distinguished
Professor (Emeritus) of Christian
History
Duke Divinity School

EXPLORER IN SEARCH IN ZION

Explorer in Search of Zion

The Spiritual Journey of David Edwin Harrell, Jr.

John B. Weaver

FLORIDA COLLEGE
PRESS

Explorer in Search of Zion

© 2025 by Florida College Press

119 N. Glen Arven Avenue, Temple Terrace, Florida 33617

ISBN (paperback): 978-1-965356-02-9

ISBN (hardback): 978-1-965356-07-4

ISBN (digital): 978-1-965356-08-1

Printed in the United States of America.

ESV Text Edition: 2016

For my students
at Florida College

CONTENTS

ACKNOWLEDGMENTS

I first interviewed Ed Harrell in 2017 on the balcony of a New Delhi hotel with fledgling curiosity about his four decades of missionary work in India. Two years later in 2019, after his plan to write a memoir faltered because of his declining health, he and Deedee accepted my offer to write his biography, which I already sensed would illuminate many more lives than his own. I'm grateful to them both for the insights and trust that Ed and Deedee gave me. I have tried to relate fairly the path of Harrell's life, including the perspectives of various participants in Ed's life, including those that disagreed with him. I have sought not to surface my own beliefs at several points where I disagreed with him or his critics. Still, I suspect that he would firmly question some of the observations and conclusions that I allow, even though I have sought to write with the historical evenhandedness that he often modeled in his own biographical writings.

This project owes much to many people. Russ and Liz Roberts were instrumental in hosting my visits to Jacksonville, FL, and in making available archival materials. Now at the Brown Library of Abilene Christian University, the Harrell Archives benefit many through the expert stewardship of Mac Ice and his team, who assisted during multiple research trips to Abilene, TX, and countless requests for digital scans of primary materials. Shelly Jacobs, Archivist for the Disciples of Christ Historical Society, gave assistance and energizing hospitality during a key phase of research and writing in Bethany, WV. The librarians at Florida College—Jennifer Kearney, Brooke Ward, and Malachi Darling—have provided unflagging support.

Among those interviewed for this book, I'm especially grateful to Ron Halbrook, Sewell Hall, Mike Willis, and Steve Wolfgang for reading the manuscript and offering critical feedback. They were friends to me in their frank and challenging input. There are places in the biography where I will likely disappoint them, but I love and respect them all.

This biography benefited greatly from the gifts of David Holder of Ft Worth, TX. He read through the manuscript multiple times and provided much that improved it. I know I probably overlooked several of his corrections and insights, as well as those of Adam Shanks, director of the Florida College Press, to whom I credit the inclusion of appendices reprinting three of Ed's short and most impactful essays. I'm grateful to the original publishers of these works for the permission to reproduce them. Two of my former students, Jacob Black and Caleb Speer, read through an earlier version of this book, offering encouraging and formative input from their perspectives as young evangelists in the missionary fields of North America. It is to them and to all the students in my Bible and Church History courses at Florida College that I dedicate this book, with gratitude for the inspiration they provide to me every semester and a prayer that the story of Harrell's life will aid them and others along The Way.

A Brief Timeline of
Ed Harrell's Life

1930	Born in Jacksonville, Florida
1958	BA Lipscomb College
1961	Assistant Professor of History, East Tennessee State University
1962	PhD Vanderbilt University
	Pamphlet publication: "The Emergence of the Church of Christ Denomination."
1966	Associate Professor of History, University of Oklahoma
	Quest for a Christian America: Social History of the Disciples of Christ, Vol. I
1967	Associate Professor of History, University of Georgia
	"Peculiar People: The Rationale of Modern Conservative Disciples"
1970	Professor of History, University of Alabama
1971	*White Sects and Black Men in the Recent South*
1973	*The Sources of Division in the Disciples of Christ: A Social History of the Disciples of Christ, Vol. II*
1975	*All Things Are Possible: The Healing and Charismatic Revivals in Modern America*
1976	Senior Fulbright Lecturer, University of Allahabad, Allahabad, India
1976	University Scholar in History, University of Alabama
1980	Visiting Professor of Regional Studies, University of Arkansas

1981	Distinguished Professor of History, University of Arkansas
1984	First issue of *Christianity Magazine*
1985	University Scholar in History, University of Alabama
Oral Roberts: An American Life
1987	*Pat Robertson: A Personal, Religious and Political Portrait*
1989	First article on "The Bounds of Christian Unity" in *Christianity Magazine*
1990	Daniel F. Breeden Eminent Scholar in the Humanities, Auburn University
1993	Director, American Studies Research Centre, Hyderabad, India
1999	Last issue of *Christianity Magazine*
2000	*The Churches of Christ in the 20th Century: Homer Hailey's Personal Journey of Faith.*
2005	*Unto A Good Land: A History of The American People*
2007	"Christian Primitivism in the Twenty-first Century: Thinking 'Inside the Box' About Restoring New Testament Christianity"
2021	Passed away in Ponte Vedra Beach, Florida

CHAPTER ONE

Prologue

> "There is nothing petty or
> arbitrary about the enterprise of
> seeking to be primitive Christians
> in the twenty-first century."[1]

What does a true believer look like? This may evoke in your mind images of crazy-acting repulsive fanatics or beloved heroes living with conviction, of cult leaders and national reformers. But for me—and I think I am not alone—this question becomes increasingly pressing in the context of the fast-changing secular culture of early 21st century America. The demographic decline of Christian faith in the United States in the late 20th and early 21st centuries is much documented and discussed. This includes recognition that the reality is often complex and multidirectional. This complexity is especially seen within a broader historical and global frame. Christianity is not declining, even in the Western world, and is rapidly expanding in the Southern Hemisphere. In fact, there is good reason to think that we may see a broad revival of true belief in our lifetimes. Regardless of what happens, we can be sure that the past will be prologue to the

---

1. David Edwin Harrell, Jr., *Christian Primitivism in the Twenty-first Century: Thinking "Inside the Box" About Restoring New Testament Christianity* (Lakeland: Harrell/Lewis Publishing, 2007), 51.

This writing has been reprinted with permission in the appendices of this book. All future references to this material will refer to the reprint within this book. This reference is found on page 362.

future. We can learn from the lives of Christians who lived through difficult times. We gain insights from our near contemporaries who experienced with us the potentially faith-corroding influence of increased educational achievement and monetary affluence in the post-WWII United States. These believers maintained faith and grew in conviction and compassionate impact over the course of their lives. If such belief can thrive in our increasingly post-Christian age, might it also thrive for you and me? If so, how?

This is the story of a true believer who spent much of his life trying to show others what true Christian belief looked like throughout human history. This is not, however, a tale of hero worship. Like all humans and all accounts of history, Dr. David Edwin Harrell, Jr. was flawed and limited. His limitations were facts he would return to time and again both in his professional life as a distinguished church historian, as a husband and father to six children, and in his ministry as a beloved Christian preacher and missionary. The limitation of our religious commitments—not to know and do what we want to know and do—was a theme of Harrell's lifework especially in his accounts of Pentecostal leaders. Indeed, renowned church historians have penned essays on Harrell's ability to discern and describe the limitations of his and others' religious choices, especially how these choices resulted from both personal circumstances in life and the broader social conditions of shared history.[2] Less recognized about Harrell's life, and a special focus of this book, is the *prescriptive* nature of Harrell's historical descriptions and related prophetic proclamations of Christian faith. As a historian of Christianity in the American South, Harrell described how broader cultural forces impacted individual

---

2. B. Dwain Waldrep and Scott Billingsley, eds., *Recovering the Margins of American Religious History: The Legacy of David Edwin Harrell, Jr.* (Tuscaloosa: University of Alabama Press, 2012). This *Festschrift* was presented to Harrell at the 2012 Christian Scholars Conference.

Christians and distinctive Christian movements in repeated and often predictable ways: one's geographic (e.g., the American Western frontier) and economic location (e.g., rural Southern poverty) deeply affects religious belief.[3] In turn, like-minded believers driven by societal forces can unite and divide along predictable socio-economic loyalties. Though he generally eschewed "intellectual history," which focused more on ideas than concrete realities, he was among the 20th century's greatest purveyors of the ideal of New Testament Christianity in the present day. This was the mythic return to the source of Biblical faith for living and teaching New Testament Christianity.[4] Unlike other historians, especially of the Baby Boomer generation in the late twentieth century, who saw the importance of the primitivist story but did not adhere to it in their personal faith, the older Harrell modeled an expert accommodation of both the idealistic primitivist and the pragmatic Biblicist. He was the historian who believed in the truth of ancient Christianity and applied it practically in the forms of congregational worship and

---

3. The impact of the confinement of space and economy on religious faith are early emphases in Harrell's career. See: David Edwin Harrell, Jr., "The Fervent Frontier: Religion in the Trans-Appalachian West, 1790-1820," *Watauga Review* 1 (Fall, 1962), 28-36; "The Agrarian Myth and the Disciples of Christ in the Nineteenth Century," *Agricultural History* 41 (April, 1967), 181-192; "Religion: Symptom and Source of Change in Appalachia," in Emmett M. Essin, ed., *Appalachia: Family Traditions in Transition* (Johnson City: East Tennessee State University Research Advisory Council, 1975), 43-50.

4. The term "myth" admits two primary meanings: 1) a societal metanarrative or culturally important story that shapes peoples' lives, and 2) a tale that did not happen or isn't otherwise true. In the former sense, the primitivist ideal is a cultural script that is mythic in its influence on shaping community belief and practice, even as it truly gets back to what happened historically with Jesus and the early church. For an introduction to a myth-critical approach to Biblical interpretation and historical study, see "Chapter 1: Prison-Escape and Myth-Criticism" in John B. Weaver, *Plots of Epiphany: Prison-Escape in Acts of the Apostles*, Beihefte zur Zeitschrift für die neutestamentliche Wissenshaft und die Kunde der älteren Kirche 131 (Berlin: Walter de Gruyter, 2004), 1-27.

the practices of everyday Christian life.[5]

As a true believer, Harrell prescribed his religious commitments within the congregational (also known as "non-institutional") churches of Christ as the way to live faithfully.[6]

---

5 . Contrast the restorationist pragmatism of Harrell to the historiography on primitivism by historian, and Baby Boomer, Richard Hughes, who recognized the metanarratives of the churches of Christ perhaps better than any other 20th Century historian. See for example his focus on the "illusions" of restorationism in *Illusions of Innocence: Protestant Primitivism in America*, 1630-1875 (Chicago: University of Chicago, 1988) and Hughes' discernment of the "apocalyptic worldview" in the American Restoration Movement in *Reviving the Ancient Faith: The Story of Churches of Christ in America* (Grand Rapids: Eerdmans, 1988). Hughes (and others of his generation) went on to an academic career among religious movements other than the Churches of Christ, describing, but not prescribing the primitivist vision; see for example Richard Hughes, *Myths America Lives By: White Supremacy and the Stories That Give Us Meaning* (Champaign, Ill.: University of Illinois Press, 2018).

6. Throughout this book the adjective "congregational" is used to replace the more traditional description "non-institutional" for those churches that supported the complete congregational autonomy of the local church and, when presented with alternatives, opposed the use of church funds to support human businesses to extend or replace a church's work in evangelism, edification, or benevolence, e.g., missionary societies, colleges, orphan homes, retirement homes, and media companies. The term "congregational" is meant to express that which churches affirm in this stance: that the discernment and work of the local church should be done by the local congregation and not through parachurch or other multi-church sponsored initiatives coordinated by other churches. As with the related term "anti," the "non-institutional" moniker is a pejorative, negative designation that was used to brand those churches which viewed themselves as upholding the Biblical pattern for the church's work. Because these churches tend to deemphasize the broader collective or network of Churches of Christ as relatively unimportant to the faith and practice of the individual Christian and local church, I adopt a standard approach of designating these congregational churches with a lower case "c," in contrast to those churches that are historically more accepting of a denominational understanding of their churches as instances of the "Churches of Christ" group/network (though there is not unanimity on this point among these churches). This latter group are those affirming of the use of parachurch businesses. These "Churches of Christ" are supportive of the use of

Standing squarely in the historic mainstream of the Churches of Christ, these congregations opposed the modernizing tendencies of "institutional Churches of Christ" in the face of the hostile and seemingly inexorable forces working against them. Harrell repeatedly observed that the deeper countercultural nature of the congregational churches of Christ was misunderstood and mischaracterized by mainstream histories of the movement. Harrell regularly pointed out this disconnect in public forums. In a review of Richard Hughes' book on the history of the Churches of Christ, *Reviving the Ancient Faith*, Ed Harrell distinguishes between the non-institutionalism of some preachers like Roy Cogdill and Yater Tant and that of other preachers like Sewell Hall, Robert Turner, and even Ed Harrell:

> Hughes presents the anti-institutional critique pretty much from the vantage point of Roy Cogdill and Yater Tant, highlighting their conviction that the mainstream had abandoned its commitment to legalistic sectarianism. Had Hughes focused on my anti-institutional writings, or those of Robert Turner or Sewell Hall, he would have discovered that the basic issue at stake was a desire to retain an apocalyptic vision. Like the Churches of Christ in general, the noninstitutional movement was driven by sectarian legalism and by cultural separatism or, more often, by people who accepted some mix of both assumptions.[7]

---

institutions to expedite the work of the local congregation and are conventionally known as "institutional Churches of Christ." This designation is maintained here as not inherently negative. The designation "congregational" is here historically unrelated to the "Congregationalist" denomination prominent in the United States during the 17th and 18th centuries as the inheritors of the English Puritan tradition, though both traditions are theologically similar in their commitment to a congregational polity (as opposed to an episcopal, presbyterian, or some other less formal connectional model for the organization and identification of churches). The congregational churches of Christ have no denominational hierarchy or headquarters.

7. David Edwin Harrell, "Rethinking the History of Churches of Christ:

However, despite his life-long claims of countercultural Christian faith, Harrell did not claim to escape the forces of history upon human belief. His spiritual journey was one of more self-consciously acknowledging his cultural context and self-consciously claiming to position himself in firm relation to the fixed point of Jesus Christ as revealed in the Bible. Harrell's prescription for contemporary Christians was thus to restore New Testament Christianity in the present day. The bridge between the apostolic faith and contemporary saving faith was a religious perspective that he and others would term "Biblical primitivism"—a quest to return present-day Christianity to the "primitive" faith, that is, its earliest form as expressed in the New Testament. For Harrell, this meant a Christian spirituality of lifelong effort to live according to the Biblical constitution for Christian belief and practice, especially the congregational organization of the New Testament churches.

For many readers, this primitivist prescription for Christianity will likely seem naïve, nonsensical, and perhaps even offensive. Does not history itself show that we cannot reach back behind our inherited traditions and outside our historical context to recover

---

Responses to Richard Hughes" *Restoration Quarterly,* Vol. 38.1 (1996), 8, last modified February 25, 2005, http://www.acu.edu/sponsored/restoration_ quarterly/archives/1990s/Vol_038_no_1_contents/fosteretal.html. On the vitality of the congregational, non-institutional churches as authentic representatives of the historic emphases of the Stone-Campbell Movement, see Richard T. Hughes and James L Gorman, *Reviving the Ancient Faith: The Story of Churches of Christ in America*, 3rd ed (Grand Rapids: Eerdmans, 2024), 186-87. Gorman provides more nuance, but again errs on the side of emphasizing the legalistic and sectarian impulses of the non-institutional churches of Christ. To the contrary, it is precisely the apocalyptic and non-denominational (which might lead to unity among different churches) that is the driving force for the Biblicism of the congregational churches of Christ. As this book might demonstrate, there is an underlying spirituality of pilgrimage, of social alienation and cultural sojourn that is at the beating heart of the often-acerbic rhetoric of the congregational churches of Christ.

David Edwin Harrell Jr., Eminent Scholar in the Humanities at Auburn University, in 1991 writing the 20th century section of a major new college textbook on American history, *Unto a Good Land.* **(source: Auburn University, Profiles in Research).**

some repristinated form of New Testament Christianity? Are not the New Testament documents themselves the products of historical forces that were socially conditioned and so theologically diverse? Do not past restorationist movements show that the result of such efforts only further division and discord among Christians? Is this not an antiquarian and deeply backward approach to describing and living the upward and forward call of the Christian gospel to know God personally and relevantly in a constantly changing world? To be sure, these are valid and prevalent questions, and Harrell attempted to address them in his lifetime. But despite the difficult questions and answers, he remained an undaunted Biblical primitivist. To explain the background and formulations of Harrell's answers will take the course of this book to elaborate. But it is helpful to signal the direction of his prescription for a Christian's life by beginning where Harrell's historical scholarship would conclude near the end of his life—with a massive, 1,328-page textbook on the history of the United States, co-written and edited with a cadre of leading church historians.[8]

The textbook on the history of the United States, entitled *Unto a Good Land*, is not a work promoting Christian primitivism or restorationism. Far from it, the Disciples of Christ and Churches of Christ, which are two of the primary groups resulting from Harrell's own religious tradition in the "American Restoration Movement" (the "Stone-Campbell Movement"), are barely mentioned in the volume. The eponymous, foundational figures of this movement, Alexander Campbell and Barton Stone, are never mentioned by name. *Unto a Good Land* is not, therefore, a dogmatic theological work, but rather was written by church historians of diverse or no religious backgrounds, with Harrell organizing them in a project of expansive and objective history. It is a textbook that places an unusual emphasis on religion as a central and defining element of United States history. With this religious frame and without focusing on it or seeking to make this case, the book demonstrates the meaning and significance of "Biblical primitivism" as a Christian response to the Bible in the history of the United States. What emerges in reading the mammoth textbook is the cyclical recurrence of what is perhaps the most powerful meta-narrative or society-shaping story of human history: the recovery and intentional recurrence of the most ancient and original form of Christianity, i.e., Biblical primitivism or apostolic faith. A few summary paragraphs here about this primitivist theme in Harrell's textbook will both illuminate the historical background to the restorationist ideal that

---

8. David Edwin Harrell Jr., Edwin S. Gaustad, John B. Boles, Sally Foreman Griffith, Randall M. Miller, and Randall B. Woods, *Unto a Good Land: A History of the American People* (Grand Rapids: Eerdmans, 2005).

motivated Harrell's scholarship and perhaps explain some of why he came to say that the primitivist ideal steered his soul in a lifelong journey towards God.

In *Unto a Good Land*, Harrell and his coauthors describe how the history of the American people in many ways begins with the 16th century story of the Protestant Reformation in Europe, including the leading figures of Martin Luther (1483-1546) and John Calvin (1509-1564), who argued that Protestantism was not a new heresy, but rather "a return to the New Testament and would therefore be perceived as 'new' only by those to whom the gospel of Jesus Christ was new."[9] This restoration ideal in Europe initiated reformatory movements leading to the transatlantic migrations of religious dissidents, including the well-known Mayflower pilgrims, to the New World. Similar primitivist impulses again motivated the so-called "Puritan Awakening" following the Armada Crisis of 1580-1588, when the queen of England and her navy destroyed the Spanish "Armada" and established England as a global power. As part of the Puritan revolution in England, spiritual revolutionists sought to move the country further towards Protestantism, and Puritans "separated from the Church of England to fashion a fellowship of their own with the New Testament as their only guide."[10] Reforming Puritans like John Winthrop immigrated to New England motivated by the restorationist conviction that "a true church came only from a redeemed heart, from a faithful obedience to the New Testament standard of becoming a new creature in Christ."[11] This Puritan intention to "recreate, as

---

9. Harrell, *Unto a Good Land*, 8. On primitivism in the Reformation era, see also Theodore Dwight Bozeman, "Biblical Primitivism: An Approach to New England Puritanism," in *The American Quest for the Primitive Church*, ed Richard T. Hughes (Urbana: University of Chicago Press, 1988), 19-32, 22.

10. Ibid., 51.

11. Ibid., 53. On primitivism in the Puritan era, see also Theodore Dwight

best they could, the New Testament" recurred in the revivalist reasoning of Jonathan Edwards during the First Great Awakening of the 1730s and 1740s in which religious emotions were defended both through recourse to the New Testament and "common sense."[12] The rationalism of this American primitivism, influenced by the Enlightenment in Europe, found an extreme expression in the "Jefferson Bible" of the Revolutionary War era, which, for all its redaction of the original text, nevertheless expressed the primitivist's impulse to remove priestly and scholastic accretions and to "have all persons return 'to the plain and unsophisticated precepts of Christ.'"[13]

The next major revival in the United States began in the early 19th century with the preaching of Charles G. Finney, whose opposition to Calvinism began with a "systematic reading of the Bible" and led to a millenarian appeal to transform society through the perfect example of Jesus in Scripture."[14] This "Second Great Awakening" peaked in the 1830s and 1840s with the formation of restoration movements as diverse as the Disciples of Christ and the Mormons, with religious leaders raising different questions about how Christians should return to the primitive church.[15] In sometimes surprising ways, Primitive Baptists, Churches of Christ and other restorationist movements arising during the Second Great Awakening opposed alliances of church and state that limited individual religious freedom, such as their opposition to the so

---

Bozeman, *To Live Ancient Lives: The Primitivist Dimension in Puritanism* (Chapel Hill: University of North Carolina Press, 1988).

12. Ibid., 57, 121.

13. Ibid., 256.

14. Ibid., 312-314.

15. Ibid., 334-35. On primitivism in Mormonism, see Jan Shipps, "The Reality of the Restoration and the Restoration Ideal in the Mormon Tradition," in *The American Quest for the Primitive Church*, ed Richard T. Hughes (Urbana: University of Chicago Press, 1988), 181-195.

called "Sabbatarian movement" in the 1820s, which attempted to form a Christian political party to keep post offices closed on Sundays.[16]

The 19th century's "democratization of Christianity" empowered Christian laity to read and follow the Scriptures according to individual conscience in ways that were manifested again later in the century in missionary awakenings that made appeals to Jesus' example of addressing the social problems of urbanized America, e.g., Charles Sheldon's *In His Steps* (1896) and Walter Rauschenbusch's "Social Gospel."[17] Different from such modern attempts to rescue the original core truths of Christianity, conservative revivalists like Billy Sunday and fundamentalists like J. Gresham Machen launched rearguard actions to "defend historic evangelical theology."[18] The return to Scripture as a basis of Christian action was similarly seen in millennialist speculations during this "third great awakening" to oppose progressive Christianity "based on Biblical predictions of an imminent return of Christ to establish an earthly kingdom."[19] In contrast to the mainstream Protestant churches (such as the Episcopalians, Presbyterians, Disciples of Christ, and Methodists), which formed the Federal Council of Churches of Christ in America in 1908, and all of which declined in numerical strength over the course of the 20th century, a growing number of rural and relatively poor movements—such as the Church of God and the Churches of Christ—emphasized a return

---

16. Ibid., 402. On primitivism in the Stone-Campbell Movement, see Richard T. Hughes and Leonard C. Allen, "Illusions of Innocence: Protestant Primitivism in America, 1630-1875" (1988), *ACU Brown Library Monograph Series*, https://digitalcommons.acu.edu/acu_library_books/21, 153-187.

17. Ibid., 650-52, 781. On the "democratizing," populist ideals of the Second Great Awakening, see Nathan O. Hatch, *The Democratization of American Christianity* (New Haven: Yale, 1989).

18. Ibid., 780-782.

19. Ibid., 782.

to the Bible and provided "alternative religious havens for the most alienated Americans." The fastest growing of these revivalist groups—the Pentecostal churches—was launched at Azusa Street in California in 1901 as a fiercely anti-modern movement with a restorationist appeal to recover the miraculous spiritual gifts of the New Testament, especially speaking in tongues, as manifested on the day of Pentecost in the Biblical book of Acts.[20] Such primitivist movements continued to grow globally in the subsequent century leading to religious revivals in the "Fourth Great Awakening" among the so-called Baby Boomers in the 1960s and 70s, including the Tulsa Pentecostal evangelist Oral Roberts and the charismatic evangelical Pat Robertson, both of whom called for a return to Biblical values while utilizing the new mass medium of television.[21] In these ways, documented in Harrell's textbook, primitivist (restorationist) ideas were among the American ideals that made "religion a partner in American democracy." As Harrell and his co-authors conclude: "All nations and people profess a commitment to acting correctly, but few share the enduring American legacy of appeal to religious language and belief."[22]

In this way, dotting the path of American history like so many mountain peaks of idealistic upsurge, the broad-based revivals of Christianity in North America were evidence for what Harrell identifies as "the most vital single assumption underlying the

---

20. Ibid., 770. On primitivism in the Pentecostal movement, see Edith L. Blumhofer, *Restoring the Faith: The Assemblies of God, Pentecostalism, and American Culture* (Champaign, IL: University of Illinois Press, 1993); cf. Grant Wacker, "Playing for Keeps: The Primitivist Impulse in Early Pentecostalism" in *The American Quest for the Primitive Church*, ed Richard T. Hughes (Urbana: University of Chicago Press, 1988), 196-219.

21. Ibid., 1076.

22. Ibid., 1216. On the Baby Boomer awakening as a "fourth great awakening," see William McLoughlin, *Revivals, Awakenings, and Reform* (Chicago: University of Chicago Press, 1980).

development of American Protestantism."[23] This assumption is the "restoration ideal," that Christians should seek the restoration of Jesus's principles and the church's purity as found in the New Testament.

To be sure, the outworking of this ideal is varied in history. As even the above brief trot through American religious history suggests, revivalists as varied as the Puritans, Baptists, Mormons, and Pentecostals all have the peculiar primitivist mindset, but often with very different results. Despite their similarities, these different pursuits for a simpler Christianity were not simplistic, but were multifaceted and sophisticated, raising different theological questions to be answered by the Biblical text arising from different religious traditions and from within different cultural circumstances, e.g., Northern, Southern, urban, rural, immigrant, and indigenous. The complexity of church history is a theme of Harrell's scholarship, and he often observes how historians oversimplify religious history, thinking too often in "bipolar" ways about the history of American Christianity.[24] The history of primitivist and other Christian groups is not simply the story of fundamentalist/evangelicals and liberal/mainline Protestants (to say nothing of Roman Catholics), but a more "untidy" assortment of many denominations and sects (i.e., antiestablishment and exclusivist religious groups).[25] Harrell's more sophisticated, complex account of religious groups, particularly

---

23. David Edwin Harrell, Jr, "Epilogue," in *The American Quest for the Primitive Church*, ed Richard T. Hughes (Urbana: University of Chicago Press, 1988), 239. On the "five spiritual awakenings" in American History see William Strauss and Neil Howe, *Generations: The History of America's Future, 1584 to 2069* (New York: Harper Perennial, 1991), 93-94.

24. David Edwin Harrell, Jr, "Bipolar Protestantism: The Straight and Narrow Ways," in *Re-forming the Center: American Protestantism, 1900 to the Present*, ed. Douglas Jacobsen and William Vance Trollinger, Jr., (Grand Rapids: Eerdmans, 1998), 15-30.

25. Ibid., 29.

conservative Protestants in the American South, proves to be part of a 20th century revolution in the way many historians view the "lived religion" of their fellow Americans. This "view from the pews" generally came to eschew simplistic characterizations of religious groups. As Harrell and his fellow historians observe, the Churches of Christ in the United States exemplify the need for nuance in historical description. Formed of multiple subgroups, increasingly varied in the ways they read the Bible as the 20th century unfolded, these relatively conservative churches were neither "fundamentalist" nor "evangelical," and many insiders would recoil even at the title of "Protestant," to say nothing of the often-opposed claim that they were another Christian "denomination."[26] Thus, for all it gained in analytical nuance, the professional study of American Christianity during Harrell's tenure would increasingly undermine attempts to synthesize the stories of American churches into interpretive models of explanation and overarching stories of coherent identity and development.[27] The fragmentation of the historiography of American

---

26. For the relationship to Fundamentalism, see David Edwin Harrell, Jr., "Fundamentalism Again," *Vanguard* 5 (August 1, 1979): 241, 254. On the relationship to the broad category of "Evangelicalism," see the two volumes by William R. Baker, ed., *Evangelicalism & The Stone-Campbell Movement* (Abilene: ACU Press, 2006). For a statement of opposition of Churches of Christ to identification with Protestantism, see Robert E. Hooper, Jim Turner, and Willard Collins, *The People Person* (Nashville: 20th Century Christian, 1986), 116, 118. For recent opposition to associating churches of Christ with denominations, see the February 2023 issue of *Truth Magazine*, including the introductory article by Mark Mayberry, "The Changing Face of Denominationalism," *Truth Magazine* 67.2 (February 2023): 4-5. For a classic differentiation between the Separatists and Restorers who would flow into Churches of Christ and the Protestants who maintained clerical authority, see James Walter Shepherd, *The Church, the Falling Away, and the Restoration* (Nashville: *Gospel Advocate*, 1929), 148.

27. For expression of this viewpoint see the conclusion of Douglas Jacobsen and William Vance Trollinger: "Any new interpretive approaches will need to take into account certain postmodern insights. One of these insights is that scholars must be extremely wary of meta-narratives, or grand explanatory theories."

religion to better appreciate the marginalized movements was a legacy of David Edwin Harrell, Jr., the historian.

It is therefore ironic that the single-minded consistency of his own religious commitments is the lasting memory of Harrell the Christian believer.[28] As we will see, Harrell changed during his life's journey, but the beating heart of the primitivist is obedience to the Bible, and Harrell's passionate commitment to studying, preaching, and following the Word of God was the throughline that connected the different phases of his life, from teenage rascal in South Georgia to aged missionary in South India. This abiding loyalty to the Scriptures would also forge a lasting link to the largely poor and rural communities of conservative Christians among whom he grew up and to whom he would remain connected even as educational attainments, economic affluence, and geographic mobility pulled many of his fellow scholars, church leaders, and not a few "ordinary" Christian believers away from their legalistic and sectarian roots in the most conservative churches of Christ. His persistence in primitivism made him, by his own admission, a "period piece," an exemplar of a Christian idealism that had rich Biblical precedent and historical pedigree, but who was increasingly alien in the secularized academy and pluralistic Christianity of late 20th and early 21st century America.[29]

Douglas Jacobsen and William Vance Trollinger, Jr. eds., *Re-forming the Center: American Protestantism, 1900 to the Present*, ed. (Grand Rapids: Eerdmans, 1998), 471.

28. Harrell's attention to a great variety of religious traditions, especially marginalized sects, is treated repeatedly in his *Festschrift* volume, Waldrep and Billingsley, *Recovering the Margins*. The enduring legacy of his religious faith is treated at length in his memorial service after his death in 2021. This included the testimony of fellow preacher, Paul Earnhart: "[Ed] was absolutely the humblest person who was at ease with the lowliest and, because he was a Christian before he was a historian, that was his passion," Ed Harrell Memorial "Ed Harrell Online Memorial Service- March 20, 2021," YouTube Video, 2:06, March 30, 2021, https://www.youtube.com/watch?app=desktop&v=cXJXDvpzLM4.

29. On being a "period piece in a Disciples of Christ movement grown

His religious peculiarity would lead some of his fellow scholars to view and term his lectures and essays as "primary documents" for the history of Christian primitivism, even as he was widely recognized as among the most objective and expansive experts on the topic, whose writings constituted the most authoritative "secondary literature" on topics as diverse as American racial history, Pentecostalism, and the global growth of Christianity.[30] What emerges from the close reading of his work on these various religious movements is a paradigm shift in the way many historians, including the present author, came to view the development of Churches of Christ in North America, which would, in turn, deeply impact Harrell's own prescriptions for Biblical interpretation and Christian fellowship among congregational churches of Christ.

For readers, such as myself, committed to a faith similar (though certainly not identical) to Harrell's from among the congregational churches of Christ, the following story may serve to deepen wells of belief, for example: belief in the absolute authority of the New Testament; the importance of Christian family and congregational community to spreading the gospel; the need for a humble heart and a free and reasonable mind; the Biblical pattern of adult immersion for saving faith; the New Testament allowance for only a cappella (non-instrumental) singing in worship; and a long walk of contrite loyalty to Jesus in order to realize both saving faith and church unity. Perhaps more controversial and offensive is the religious conviction that, as Harrell once stated it, "one of the persistent marks of apostate religion is a shift in emphasis from the spiritual to

---

increasingly uncomfortable with the intellectual, social, and psychological pitfalls of restoring New Testament Christianity," see Harrell, "Epilogue," in *The American Quest for the Primitive Church*, ed Richard T. Hughes (Urbana: University of Chicago Press, 1988), 244.

30. On Harrell's works as primary texts for the study of primitivism, see the foreword to Harrell, "Epilogue," 239.

the work of social reform."[31] But for another type of reader, who is unconvinced or unconcerned about such convictions, the story of Ed Harrell's spiritual life may provide something else: a re-digging of the wells *for* true belief. This is because this biography is as much about *how* Harrell believed as *what* he believed. Readers may find in Harrell's combination of zeal and humility, of conviction and compassion, a way forward to recovering a faith that is deeper than the market-driven, experience-oriented, and all-to-often Biblically illiterate expressions of Christian faith in our early 21st century. Or perhaps as was the case for Harrell in his ground-breaking biography of the Pentecostal leader Oral Roberts, you may find that you do not accept his theology but find in him a "sincere and honorable man."[32] You might find that his story sparks an admiration and curiosity that leads you deeper into your own pursuit of true belief. Harrell's own faith was a "sojourn," as he acknowledged, and his life was in many ways an accommodating and compassionate invitation to others to join him in the spiritual odyssey of learning Jesus through commitment to His and His apostles' teachings in the New Testament.[33]

---

31. David Edwin Harrell, Jr., "The People of God—Their Attitude Toward the Social Order," *Vanguard* 5 (September 1, 1979): 327.

32. David Edwin Harrell, Jr., *Oral Roberts: An American Life* (San Francisco: Harper & Row, 1985), ix-x.

33. Harrell, "Epilogue," 245.

CHAPTER TWO

Prodigal

"I think I understand in a very human way what it means to "learn" obedience. I idolized my father when I was a lad growing up, but I disobeyed him many times. After many years of suffering hard knocks, disappointments, and failures, more and more I came to listen submissively to his instructions. By the time I was a young adult launching out on my own, I pretty unwaveringly took his advice and followed his instructions, even when I did not like the consequences. After I learned obedience, I often "experienced" it. I often was frustrated by the personal sacrifices and inconveniences that accompanied obedience, but those experiences served me well throughout my life."[1]

---

1. David Edwin Harrell, Jr., "The Price of Sin: 'By His Wounds Ye Are Healed,'" in *Of First Importance: He Died and Was Buried—Studies in the Crucifixion of Jesus*. Florida College Annual Lectures Book. (Temple Terrace, FL:

In God's providence, even the prodigal may become a prodigy, and so it was with David Edwin ("Ed") Harrell, Jr. Formed by his youthful misdirection and his father's attempts at redirection, Harrell grew to provide renowned scholarly and spiritual direction to generations of scholars, students, and adherents to the Christian faith around the world. Harrell's early years of moral indiscretion and spiritual transformation were shaped by a family and church culture that emphasized both parental responsibility and childhood/teenage accountability for growing into a more mature Christian faith on the way to adulthood. The youthful mistakes taught lessons that would shape him in later years. "I have messed up that decision [to be Christian] in countless specific ways in my life," he would later reflect. "What monumental and tough decisions youth forces upon us. I view with immense sympathy the inward struggle of a young person wrestling with such awesome choices."[2] His own struggles and ultimate choice to be a faithful Christian would shape not only Harrell's personal religious commitments and teaching career, but also his fundamental disposition toward differences and disagreements among Christians. Such difficulties were matters requiring a willingness to change (as in the institutional debates of the 1950s) and to extend compassionate support to young students (as he did throughout his teaching career), but also patient listening and guidance of Christians who disagreed with him on key points of Christian doctrine (as in his advocacy for longsuffering for Christian disagreements regarding divorce and remarriage). It was

---

Florida College Press, 2012). Kindle Edition location 202 of 4361. Harrell would go on in this lecture to relate the story of how his father directed that he and his friend, Harold Dowdy, replace the rotten sill beneath a rental house. After lifting the house and replacing the sill in obedience to his father, Harrell observed to his friend: "Harold, I'll bet I am the only repairman in Jacksonville replacing rotten sills under houses who has a Ph.D."

2. David Edwin Harrell, Jr., "It Might Have Been," *Vanguard* 6 (February 1, 1980): 40.

a longsuffering in guiding the misguided that he first observed as a youth in his father and mother. So it is that youthful indiscretions and corrections can shape future discretion.

Born February 22, 1930, in Jacksonville, Florida, the son of Dr. David Edwin and Mildred Lee Harrell, Ed Harrell Jr. was an only son with two sisters, Marilyn H. Hardage and Elinor Edwina. Likely descended from the Harrells who first came to the United States in the late 1600s, these ancestors settled in Virginia and migrated into North Carolina, and then Georgia around 1820.[3] Not all the family enjoyed privilege, however, as Harrell's paternal grandfather was a sharecropper from Coffee County, Georgia. But his father's graduation from the Medical College of Georgia led to the family's ascent to respectability and modest wealth that would position Harrell between two worlds: one of the impoverished South and the other of upper-middle class Jacksonville, Florida. Though born among the rural underclass, Doc Harrell (1896-1976), as Ed's father was called, purchased a significant amount of farmland in South Georgia by the time Ed was a teenager, including the family farm in Alma, Georgia, and over his lifetime expanded his holding of rentals and other businesses.[4]

Though his family was known for their generosity, young Ed developed a reputation in his teenage years as somewhat of a rebel. He became an adult as a member of the so-called "Silent Generation." Going through adolescence during the years of WWII, he benefitted from the protected childhood that was

---

3. Edward Jerome Harrell, *History of The Harrell Family* (Unpublished manuscript, n.d.). This genealogical analysis was sent to D.E. Harrell Jr by Edward Jerome Harrell in 1982, with the conviction that it reflects their shared lineage, though no direct connection is evidenced.

4. A brief biography was written over a decade after his death by Harold Dowdy, "Dr. David Edwin Harrell, Sr." *Christianity Magazine* 7.2 (February 1990): 49.

Dr. David Edwin and Mildred Lee Harrell Sr., with Ed and Deedee's children, Millie, Eddie and Elizabeth Harrell, and with daughter Marilyn Hardage's children, Jenny, Robert, Priscilla and David Hardage (1963).

characteristic of his generation.[5] During the war, his home city of Jacksonville flourished into a large city and the Harrell family lived in a "large and lovely" home on St. John's Avenue. But Harrell was not so domesticated. A friend of Ed's sisters during the 1940s recalls that Ed was a "fighter"; she recalled: "Ed was a little bit wild and a leader of his group."[6] These snapshots of Ed's

---

5. On the protected childhood of the "silent generation" and the accompanying characteristics of their generational profile, see William Strauss and Neil Howe, *The Fourth Turning: What the Cycles of History Tell Us About America's Next Rendezvous with Destiny* (New York: Crown, 1997), 162-165.

6. Pokey Lyerley, in discussion with the author, November 24, 2020. Jean (Pokey) Lyerly, born in 1926 on the eve of the Depression, one the friends of Ed's sister Marilyn. Marilyn and Pokey were of the same age and attended Elementary, Junior High School, and Lee High School in Jacksonville, arriving in 1936 and graduating in 1944, going to Chevy Chase Women's College. She recalled that in those days Jacksonville was already a big city with cars on the street, and recalled the Harrell family in a "lovely, gracious house" on St. John's Avenue in Jacksonville. In addition to her recollection of Ed, Pokey recalls that her friend, Marilyn, was "special."

youthful rebelliousness became more expansive during his high school years.

Doc Harrell's early efforts to shape his son might be seen as indication of Ed's mischievous personality. It seems to have been by his father's design that Ed inhabited a transitional space between town and country, between his increasingly affluent family in Jacksonville, which had grown to a major Southern city by the end of WWII, and the rural origins of his family in South Georgia. On the one hand, he was a city-dweller and member of a professional family, living in the growing city of Jacksonville during the school year. As a fifteen-year-old, he was there in 1945 when the headline of the local newspaper read "Germany Surrenders Unconditionally!" and the population of Jacksonville had topped 200,000.[7] On the other hand, while his sisters spent summer vacation at the beach, Ed was sent each summer during his teenage years to work on the family farm with the sharecroppers and other workers, both black and white. "The underclass was part of my experience," Ed remarked in later years. And, in a seemingly intentional way, these hardscrabble experiences shaped Ed, like they had his father and his father before him.[8] It was a tension between poverty and wealth, simplicity and sophistication, that shaped and, in many ways, characterized his life. "I think that my career as a historian," Ed observed, "was shaped largely by the insights I gained before I was twenty years old."[9] As with summers on the farm, many of

---

7. "Germany Surrenders Unconditionally," *Jacksonville Journal* 58.202, May 7, 1945; Florida Dept. of Agriculture and Mayo, Nathan, 1876-1960, "The seventh census of the state of Florida, 1945: Taken in accordance with the provisions of chapter 22515 Laws of Florida, Act of Legislature of 1945," (1946), Florida Heritage, 79, https://stars.library.ucf.edu/floridaheritage/79.

8. David Edwin Harrell, Jr., in discussion with the author, May 20, 2019.

9. David Edwin Harrell, Jr., "Recovering the Underside of Southern Religion," Pages 39-52 in *Autobiographical Reflections on Southern Religious History*, edited by John B. Boles (Athens, GA: University of Georgia Press, 2001), 39.

these insights would come through the direction, and sometimes the intervention, of Ed's Father, Doc Harrell.

Baptized at age twelve, Ed joined his family as a member of the Riverside Park church of Christ in Jacksonville. Though he remained a life-long member of a church of Christ somewhere in the world, Ed also recounts attending the Pentecostal tent revivals among both Caucasian and African Americans in the rural South during the 1940s. As a fifteen-year-old, Harrell began preaching in small churches of Christ across the area, but this path among churches of Christ was not inherited. His parents had been nominally associated with Methodists and Free Will Baptists, and his conversion was a family affair, driven by the evangelistic zeal of the women of the Harrell clan. His aunt Dassey was a member of the Riverside Park church and had invited Ed's oldest sister Marilyn to a Bible study taught by the preacher, Gilbert Shaffer. After Marilyn was baptized, she persisted in inviting her mother, Mildred Lee, who eventually went "in order to shut her up."[10] Ed's mother's and his other sister Elinor's conversions led to Ed's own confession of faith and then also to his father's.

Doc Harrell was, by all accounts, a devout man for the rest of his life. He used his community status and modest wealth as a physician to spread and strengthen the Christian faith to those around him, funding the construction of over twenty church buildings in Florida and South Georgia during his lifetime. Those who knew him often observed how Doc Harrell's efforts in the community extended across racial lines, regularly preaching in both white and black churches of Christ. Friends of the family recalled that Doc Harrell had a large contingent of African American clientele who benefitted from his medical services.[11]

---

10. David Edwin Harrell, Jr., in discussion with the author, May 20, 2019.

11. Pokey Lyerley, in discussion with the author, November 24, 2020.

Doc Harrell's efforts to form and reform his son through sweaty summers and special schooling would intensify in and after high school. After a time at John Gorey Jr. High School, Ed went to Lee High School in Jacksonville, where his "adolescent rebellion" earned him an expulsion.[12] By those who knew him, "mischievous" is the word often used to describe Ed. The principal told his mother that he was respectful when they called him in for discipline, but it didn't do any good in the classroom and schoolyard. Because Ed "behaved badly," Mrs. Harrell begged her husband to send him to a reform school, along with a family friend, where he might learn better behavior.[13] So it was in the summer of 1947, in an effort to reform his son, that Doc Harrell sent Ed and a close family friend, Richard Hardage, to attend a small private Christian high school at Abilene Christian College, which was founded by members of the churches of Christ in 1906. The West Texas school newspaper, *Periscope*, reported the athletic prowess of "Big Ed" Harrell, who was also the class president and "the prized possession" of a certain Shirley Dean. The tall center from Florida was also among the best players on his championship basketball team, the ACC Panthers, routinely leading the team in scoring, including twenty-one of the team's forty-six points in a 1947 win against Big Country foe, Eula High School.[14]

Harrell's trip to Abilene would be the first of many formative encounters with the growing educational institutions among the churches of Christ and other branches of the American Restoration Movement.

Following WWII and the funding for college education from the GI Bill, these churches and their affiliated colleges entered

---

12. David Edwin Harrell, Jr., in discussion with the author, May 20, 2019.

13. Deedee Harrell, in discussion with the author, November 16, 2020.

14. Nancy Montgomery, "Who's Who, Abilene Christian High School," *The Periscope*, November 1, 1946.

two generations of rapid expansion. Reflecting on this growth at ACC and other such institutions, longtime preacher Paul Earnhart recalled that he arrived at Abilene Christian College the year after Ed graduated from high school there. "When I came along at Abilene in 1949 there was an evangelistic fervor that was palpable, Earnhart recalled. "My main partner there was Everett Ferguson, who was only sixteen years old when he enrolled in the college and would go on to Harvard and become an academic. He came out of it uncorrupted. He and I had a relationship through the years."[15] Earnhart's terse recollections relate both the promise and peril of the rapid rise of academic scholars among churches of Christ over the next generation.

Given the unremarkable results of Ed's high school career and the directionless zigzag of the next few years, his classmates might be excused for not predicting the world-class scholar he became. "One of my greatest boasts is that I made it out of high school without ever reading a book," Harrell jokingly recalled.[16] He boasted that he would have been voted by his classmates as "the most likely not to succeed."[17] Despite his parents' best efforts, Ed remained unfocused after high school. An aborted attempt to attend junior college and play basketball at Southern Georgia resulted in Cs and Ds. The situation only became worse in 1948 after his redirection back to Abilene Christian College yielded worse grades. After quitting college, Ed worked for two years at his father's Ford dealership in Alma, Georgia, where he regularly played cards and participated in the accompanying carousing: "I

---

15. Paul Earnhart, in discussion with the author, May 28, 2021.

16. David Edwin Harrell, Jr., *"How My Mind Has Changed/Stayed the Same,"* *Christian Scholar's Conference,* 1991. *"Ed Harrell July 1991 CSC" Audiotape, Box 31, Tape 69, David Edwin Harrell, Jr. Papers, 1923-2017. Center for Restoration Studies MS #467. Abilene Christian University Special Collections and Archives, Brown Library.*

17. Harrell, *"How My Mind Has Changed,"* 1991 Audiotape.

partied, played poker, dated a robust Bacon County lass who was Miss Georgia in 1950, and preached," Harrell would later recall.[18]

"When the Korean War came along," Ed recalled, "it was either get serious or go to Korea. My dad engineered an appointment for me in the Naval Academy, and we were all astonished that I was able to pass the test."[19] The threat of Ed being drafted into the Korean War had led his father to petition the local congressman to grant admittance to the Naval Academy at Annapolis, Maryland. Preparation for the Academy's entrance exam took the twenty-year-old Harrell to Marion Military Institute in Alabama. His Marion record reflects that Ed got more serious. His improved grades included an "A" in history and marks of "good conduct." The gossip column in the school's newspaper did, however, cryptically muse over his extracurricular activities. "Where did all of Ed Harrell's money go to in B'ham the other weekend?"[20]

Naval Cadet Ed Harrell, 1951.

As he later admitted, everyone was surprised when Ed passed the exam in 1951 and entered the Naval Academy. Ed had preached in local congregations during his teen years, and he continued to

---

18. David Edwin Harrell, Jr., "Recovering the Underside of Southern Religion," Pages 39-52 in *Autobiographical Reflections on Southern Religious History*, edited by John B. Boles (Athens, GA: University of Georgia Press, 2001), 40.

19. Ibid.

20. Marion Military Institute student newspaper (1951). David Edwin Harrell, Jr. Papers, 1923-2017. Center for Restoration Studies MS #467. Abilene Christian University Special Collections and Archives, Brown Library.

serve local congregations in the Annapolis area, in part due to the guidance of his father. This parental provision is evident in a letter written on Doc Harrell's behalf by D. Ellis Walker, preacher at the Riverside Park Church of Christ in Jacksonville to Elvis Huffard, the preacher at the Baltimore Church of Christ near the Annapolis Naval Academy. Walker knew that the Baltimore church was endeavoring to establish a congregation in Annapolis, Maryland, and he petitioned the Baltimore preacher to reach out to the young midshipman Ed Harrell to be of service to the new congregation. He wrote, "There is a fine young man, Edwin Harrell, in the Naval Academy who would be glad to work with the group. He can preach, lead the singing, lead in prayer, and teach a class. We are very anxious for someone to contact him ... His father, Dr. D. E. Harrell, and I would appreciate it very much if you will make an effort to reach this young man."[21] Ed later reflected that his father's efforts had good effect, saying "after Naval Academy I decided that I wanted to preach." His good friend, Harold Dowdy, reflected years later that Harrell's decision to preach was the long-sought outcome of Doc Harrell's prayers and other provisions during the years of his son's dalliance with the world.[22]

Despite the young Harrell's apparent progress in Maryland, his father was concerned that the worldly influences of the Naval Academy would overcome his son and persuaded him to resign during his junior year. He intended to go into the ministry and enroll in David Lipscomb College, which was founded in Nashville, Tennessee in 1891 by members of churches of Christ. Now twenty-three years old, Ed enrolled and finished his B.A. at Lipscomb

---

21. Letter from D. Ellis Walker to Elvis Huffard, dated October 26, 1951. David Edwin Harrell, Jr. Papers, 1923-2017. Center for Restoration Studies MS #467. Abilene Christian University Special Collections and Archives, Brown Library.

22. Harold Dowdy, "Dr. David Edwin Harrell, Sr." 49.

College in 1953-54, where he excelled on the debate team, made the Dean's List, and was awarded the Greek Medal.[23]

His sudden academic improvement at Lipscomb came through encounters with two people who reoriented him to the direction that he would take for the rest of his personal and professional life: his future wife, Adelia "Deedee" Francis Roberts and an academic mentor who would set him on his life's work, Professor Howard White. "Two of the best things that ever happened to me is that I met Deedee, and that Howard White convinced me to be a historian,"[24] Ed remarked years later.

For all his parents' and professors' influences, it was Deedee who was most responsible for the settling and newfound focus of Ed's life in Nashville in 1953-54. Born in Bowling Green and baptized at age thirteen, Deedee was raised by and among Christians in local churches of Christ in Kentucky and Alabama before coming to

Lipscomb College in 1952. Ed and Deedee met during her sophomore year and were married on September 6, 1955, at the Presbyterian Church in Russellville,

Drs. David Edwin Harrell Sr. and Jr., with (grand)daughter Millie (1960).

---

23. "Winner of the Prater Greek Medal" Lipscomb New Bureau Release, Nashville Tennessee, June 10, 1954. "I certainly enjoyed seeing you," Letter from Miss Jamie Ussery to Dr. D. E. Harrell, June 10, 1954. David Edwin Harrell, Jr. Papers, 1923-2017. Center for Restoration Studies MS #467. Abilene Christian University Special Collections and Archives, Brown Library.

24. Harrell, *"How My Mind Has Changed,"* 1991 Audiotape.

Kentucky. "Both his sisters and his mother tried to convince me that he was a bad marriage risk," Deedee once recalled.[25] But their love endured for a lifetime, and over the next sixty-five years (1955-2021) she was his constant companion and colleague. While she supported him, Deedee provided an invaluable check on her husband's ego, as Harold Dowdy reportedly once observed: "Deedee is not at all impressed with Dr. David Edwin Harrell Jr."[26] Together they had six children while they lived in nine different locations across the US: John Stephen (b. April 24, 1956 in Nashville, Tennessee—d. April 25, 1956); Mildred Susan (b. April 28, 1958 in Nashville, Tennessee); David Edwin III (b. November 25, 1959 in Deland, Florida); Elinor Elizabeth (b. Sept 30, 1961 in Johnson City, Tennessee); Marilyn Lee (b. Dec 21, 1965 in Johnson City, Tennessee); and Harold Robert (b. June 8, 1967 in Norman, Oklahoma—d. July 15, 2016).

In addition to the stabilizing influence of Deedee, much of Harrell's subsequent success is attributable to the academic direction initiated by history professor Howard White, who went on to an illustrious career as president of Pepperdine University. Under White's guidance, Harrell turned to the study of history and applied for the M.A. program at Vanderbilt University in 1954. Enrolling initially on probationary status due to his mixed undergraduate record, Harrell hit his academic stride by turning his attention to the historical study of his own religious tradition, particularly the social history of the Disciples of Christ. This emphasis was facilitated both by the presence of the Disciples of Christ Historical Society near the Vanderbilt campus and especially by the influence of his graduate program director, Professor Henry Lee Swint. Swint's work reflected the rise of the academic field of sociology as an interpretive lens for the study of human community and history,

25. Deedee Harrell, in discussion with the author, November 16, 2020.
26. Steve and Bette Wolfgang, in discussion with the author, May 28, 2021.

including Christian communities. Rooted in the thought of German sociologists Max Weber and Ernst Troeltsch, and applied most directly to churches by American scholar H. Richard Niebuhr (1894-1962), Swint and a cadre of his doctoral students applied a form of history that emphasized economic and regional sources of historical developments and particularly divisions within communities and their institutions. The focus of this historiographical tradition at Vanderbilt, moreover, was Christianity in the Southern United States. Harrell's subsequent emphasis on social teachings and social sources of development among the Disciples of Christ was, therefore, part of a cottage industry of such studies by Vanderbilt graduates in the late 1950s and early 1960s, focusing variously on Methodists, Cumberland Presbyterians, Southern Baptists, and Southern White Protestantism. Enrolling in the doctoral program in 1958 under Swint's tutelage, Harrell went on to graduate with his PhD from Vanderbilt in 1962 with a string of academic promotions of increasing prestige that followed for the next forty years.

For those who knew the thirty-two-year-old Ed Harrell best, his path from a prodigal teenager to a prodigious scholar was mainly due to the loving guidance and intervention of his father, Doc Harrell. From the summer assignments on the farm and two emergency enrollments in Abilene schools, to avoidance of the war through admission to the Naval Academy and the eventual redirection to Lipscomb College, Doc Harrell steered his son through the hazards of youthful exuberance and a hostile world ready to take advantage. "In many ways, the key to David Edwin Harrell Jr. was David Edwin Harrell Sr.," observed longtime friend and colleague Steve Wolfgang. "What other kid gets kicked out of two high schools? If he didn't have David Edwin Harrell Sr. pulling strings for him, then his life might well be over, leaving a disaster."[27] Harrell's gratitude for his father's stewardship of his most impressionable years was

---

27. Ed Harrell, "Waiting," *Christianity Magazine* 3.4 (April 1986): 32.

never far from his mind and manifested itself in his attention to his own children and hundreds of students and other young Christians during his lifetime. The importance of his father's parenting was also apparent to the other most significant person in Ed Harrell's life, his wife Deedee. "His dad," she observed, "had tremendous influence on him and was his staunchest supporter."[28] "I treasure all of the things that my dad did for me that went unnoticed at the time," Harrell reflected. "He directed me and formed me ... Long after his death, he still guides me and helps me. His presence is real and powerful."[29]

28. Deedee Harrell, in discussion with the author, November 16, 2020.

29. Harrell, David Edwin, "Rear View," *Christianity Magazine*, 10.5 (June 1993): 32.

CHAPTER THREE

Prophet

"Finally, I am a Disciple.
To say so is not to define a
man very tightly, nor is it my
personal stamp of approval
on what one reads here.
But in the midst of it all, I
believe there is a heroic tale
of determined men. To any
who perceive it, I commend
that story."[1]

Bigger is not always better, and much of Harrell's early life as a graduate student and young scholar was given to studying and discerning how to engage the growth of his own religious tradition.[2]

---

1. David Edwin Harrell, Jr., "Preface" in *Sources of Division in the Disciples of Christ, 1865-1900, A Social History of the Disciples of Christ*, Volume 2, reprinted edition (Tuscaloosa: University of Alabama Press, 2003), xv. The volume was originally published in 1973 by the Disciples of Christ Historical Society.

2. As classically understood by historians, the years of 1943 to 1960, the Baby Boomer generation, focused on the development of large public institutions. The correspondence between the bigger size of the military-industrial and religious institutions during these years is explored by Benjamin E. Zeller, "American Postwar 'Big Religion': Reconceptualizing Twentieth-Century American Religion Using Big Science as a Model," *Church History* 80.2 (June 2011): 321-351. For application of this theory to non-institutional (congregational) churches of Christ and their mission work in the Philippines in the 20th century, and the

His scholarly critique and personal rejection of the mainstream growth of the Churches of Christ in the twentieth century would prove prophetic both in predicting future developments and confronting troubling realities among increasingly affluent Christians and churches.

Given Ed Harrell's religious background in the American Restoration Movement and his professional entry into the school of social-scientific historiography, it was somewhat predictable that his master's thesis and eventual 1962 doctoral dissertation, entitled "A Social History of the Disciples of Christ, 1800-1866," had the focus and methodology they did. However, all innovators draw from the resources laid at their disposal by others, and part of the significance of Harrell's doctoral dissertation was applying a relatively new methodological lens that recognized and vividly described patterns of historical development among the Disciples of Christ, especially surrounding the era during and after the Civil War, 1861-65. Historians today uniformly recognize that Harrell's social history revolutionized the study of the American Restoration Movement by demonstrating that the Disciples of Christ in the 19th century were keenly interested in the social issues of their day. Harrell's work further showed that these socio-economic problems—and especially those related to slavery, segregation, and the regional conflicts that sparked the Civil War—were underlying causes of the religious division that resulted in the division between the Disciples of Christ and Churches of Christ.

Prior to Harrell's dissertation, *Quest for a Christian America: A Social History of the Disciples of Christ*, most book-length treatments of the history of the American Restoration Movement

---

related critique of "big religion," see Brady Kal Cox, "Postwar Churches of Christ Mission Work: The Philippines as a Case Study" (2018), Digital Commons @ ACU, *Electronic Theses and Dissertations*, Paper 78, https://digitalcommons.acu. edu/etd/78.

had been written either by members of the Disciples of Christ, after their early 20th century division from the Churches of Christ, or from the viewpoint of the Independent Christian Churches, after their separation from the Disciples of Christ in the 1950s. As such, these prior histories gave little treatment to the Churches of Christ.[3] Up until the 1950s, the primary history of the movement written by a member of the Churches of Christ was Earl Irvin West's four-volume, *The Search for the Ancient Order*, which was encyclopedic in its treatment of church leaders and doctrines (e.g., missionary society, instrumental music, and premillennialism), but offered little interpretation of the underlying social reasons for the development of the movement's theological commitments.[4] Beyond the doctrinal focus, West's history (though not millennial theologically) unfolded in a unilinear historiographical direction,

---

3. An important precursor to Harrell's work among historians from the Disciples of Christ was Winfred E. Garrison, *Religion Follows the Frontier* (New York: Harper & Brothers, 1931), which draws from an interpretive school of history emphasizing the American frontier and other societal sectionalism as keys to understanding the origins of the Disciples of Christ.

4. Earl Irvin West, *The Search for the Ancient Order: A History of the Restoration Movement*, 4 Volumes (Indianapolis: Religious Book Service, 1949-1974). In his dissertation (*Quest for a Christian America*, 4), Harrell cites four "most general useful accounts of Disciples history." He observes that "two of these works are by liberal Disciples historians; the third is by a Church of Christ minister; while the last is by an independent Disciple." The four histories are those by Winfred E Garrison and DeGroot, Tucker and McAllister, Earl Irvin West, and James D. Murch. More recently, the following histories provide new understandings about the cultural alienation political stance, preaching, and leadership rhetoric of the movement, especially among churches of Christ: Richard Hughes and Jamie Gorman, *Reviving the Ancient Faith: The Story of the Churches of Christ in American, 3rd Edition* (Grand Rapids: Eerdmans, 2024); Michael W. Casey, *Saddlebags, City Streets, and Cyberspace: A History of Preaching in the Churches of Christ* (Abilene: ACU Press, 1995); Douglas Foster, *Will the Cycle be Unbroken?* (Abilene: ACU Press, 1994); and Robert E. Hooper, *A Distinct People: A History of the Churches of Christ in the Twentieth Century* (West Monroe: Louisiana: Howard Publishing, 1993).

ever upwards, acknowledging divisions, but presenting the history of the Churches of Christ as always progressing in number and acreage of influence: the church would "grow," "extend," "outnumber," and be "progressive."[5] Harrell's achievement, therefore, was to provide a detailed account of the origins and development of the American Restoration Movement, while meticulously documenting economic and geographic differences that gave rise to different conclusions about what it meant to restore New Testament Christianity.

One of Harrell's distinctive scholarly emphases was that religious divisions and controversies are not merely doctrinal. Nearly everything written about the Disciples and the Churches of Christ, including Earl West's multivolume work, was all written from the perspective of doctrinal positions, though institutional positions and growth are the focus of the fourth and final volume. Harrell's early work connected religious thought, economic status, and sectional prejudices and showed that social position was a driver of theological disposition. "He was accused of being deterministic, but Ed never thought that was the whole story," observed Steve Wolfgang. "He doesn't neglect the theological or the doctrinal aspects of it, but he does put your nose right in the evidence that these people understood that there were social forces at play in these controversies."[6]

Harrell's conclusions in his dissertation were undergirded by meticulous investigation and citation of archives in the Disciples of Christ Historical Society in Nashville, Tennessee. Created in large part through the curation of Claude Spencer, whom Harrell befriended and often praised in subsequent accounts of his early work, the library of the Historical Society was fertile ground for Harrell's painstaking research, which produced enough material for a second volume, *The Social Sources of Division in the Disciples*

---

5. West, *Search for the Ancient Order*, II. 462, III. 403, IV. 398.
6. Steve Wolfgang, in discussion with the author, May 28, 2021.

of Christ, published in 1973, seven years after the first volume and eleven years after the Vanderbilt dissertation was completed. None of the second volume appears in Harrell's original dissertation, though much of the research was done by 1961.[7] Deedee Harrell recalls her husband's methodology for research: "He worked from paper materials and also from microfilm. He would go and decide what he wanted for the dissertation, write down his notes, and I would follow and type the notes he made from the books, journals, and microfilm. We worked for two years this way."[8] The results of this work were both voluminous and punctilious. The typist of his dissertation, Lillian Swingley, whom Harrell acknowledges in the preface, bemoaned the complexity and duration of the task. She warned Harrell that it might not be done in time: "I don't believe that I can get yours finished for your degree in January since it is so long."[9]

In addition to the resources of the Disciples of Christ Historical Society, Harrell's research drew from the personal library of B. C. Goodpasture, who from 1939 to 1977 served as the editor of the *Gospel Advocate*. Along with the *Firm Foundation*, this was one of the most influential periodicals among the Churches of Christ for most of the late 19th through the mid-20th centuries. Harrell had become close friends with Goodpasture's youngest son, Cliett, during their undergraduate years at Lipscomb, and B.C. Goodpasture and his wife, Emily, had become like family to Ed and Deedee. Goodpasture's personal library of American Restoration

---

7. David Edwin Harrell, Jr., *Sources of Division in the Disciples of Christ, 1865-1900, A Social History of the Disciples of Christ*, Volume 2 (Nashville: Disciples of Christ Historical Society, 1973).

8. Deedee Harrell, in discussion with the author, November 16, 2020.

9. Card from Lillian Swingley to Mr. Ed Harrell, October 27, 1961. David Edwin Harrell, Jr. Papers, 1923-2017. Center for Restoration Studies MS #467, Abilene Christian University Special Collections and Archives, Brown Library. Abilene Christian University, Abilene, TX.

Movement materials was legendary, reportedly drawing materials on standing order from used bookstores as far away as New York City.[10] During his dissertation research, Harrell worked in the extensive library, which was stored in the building behind the Goodpasture's house. During lunch B.C. and his family would join Deedee and Ed for sandwiches.[11]

In a 1981 lecture on the life of B.C. Goodpasture, Harrell recollects that during the late-1950s he had "personal conversations" with Goodpasture about the pressing issues and difference among members of Churches of Christ in their day.[12] These were disagreements over Biblical teachings regarding the work of the church that later became known as "the institutional issues." At the core of the debate was the question of whether the New Testament authorized a local church to support institutions including colleges, missionary societies, national radio programs, and charitable organizations like homes for the elderly and orphanages. The "institutional" perspective, which came to be espoused by the *Gospel Advocate* and other "mainline" publications, argued that such larger and usually cooperative efforts among churches were authorized "expedients," in other words, that were necessary—even if additions to the local church—to fully accomplish the Great Commission and the benevolent responsibilities the Lord and his apostles had given the Church. What came to be known as the "non-institutional" or, more positively, the "congregational" church of Christ teaching was that the Biblical pattern for church work limited it to what could be directly overseen by the local congregation, and that cooperative church support of educational,

---

10. Steve Wolfgang, in discussion with the author, July 1, 2021.

11. Deedee Harrell, in discussion with the author, November 16, 2020.

12. David Edwin Harrell, Jr., "B.C. Goodpasture: Leader of Institutional Thought," in Melvin D. Curry, ed., *They Being Dead Yet Speak*, Florida College Lectures (Temple Terrace: Florida College, 1981), 245.

evangelistic, and charitable institutions was both an innovation away from the Biblical model and an accommodation to worldly influences that would ultimately undermine the restoration plea and the faithfulness of such churches of Christ. B.C. Goodpasture was at the center of this debate during the late 1950s and used his editorship of a publication with over 20,000 subscribers to manage communications and actions about the issues.

Questions about church cooperation and parachurch organizations were known and debated by Alexander Campbell, who first opposed missionary societies but changed his perspective, in part due to the growing recognition and influence of the Disciples of Christ among American Protestants in the mid-nineteenth century. As the debate over institutionalism intensified in the years after WWII, the congregational perspective was championed by brotherhood papers such as the *Gospel Guardian* and the *Preceptor*, the latter of which was edited by James R. Cope, the president of Florida Christian College in Tampa, Florida. Florida College, due in part to its refusal to accept church funds, soon became branded as an "anti" Christian college and to this day exists as the solitary college or university primarily serving Christians coming from congregational churches of Christ.

Ed Harrell's years at Vanderbilt were intellectually and spiritually formative, both in the path of his scholarship and in the track of his Christian conscience regarding institutional issues. Not only did he talk with B.C. Goodpasture, but he read the non-institutional periodicals, the *Gospel Guardian* and the *Preceptor*, and, to use his own words, these "changed my views."[13]

> I was raised in an environment of institutionalism. All the churches I preached at early on were institutional. Lipscomb College tried to hire me. Brother B. C. Goodpasture was

---

13. Harrell, "B. C. Goodpasture," 252.

my best mentor. I would have long discussions with him because I was preaching at a country church and some of those younger guys had been listening to some "anti" preaching. They would bring something up. I could fake them out in answering them, but I knew I hadn't really answered them. So, I talked to Goodpasture about it. And what finally convinced me was that he was not answering their questions. He would tell me what a rascal [the non-institutional preacher] Yater Tant was. But I was confronted with the question of whether these people were really answering the Biblical question.[14]

The studied nature of the transition in Harrell's perspective is evident in a written exchange between Harrell and Earl H. West, dean of the newly formed Central Christian College (later Oklahoma Christian University). The context for this exchange was Harrell's search for his first full-time academic post. After passing the oral exams for his doctorate, Harrell wrote multiple letters to colleges and universities in the southern United States seeking a job. While preaching at the Kingston Springs church of Christ, twenty-five miles southwest of Nashville, he eventually secured part-time and then full-time positions as an assistant and then an associate professor of history at East Tennessee State University (1961-66). In the years following the publication of his dissertation, he accepted appointments as associate professor of history at the University of Oklahoma (1966-67) and the University of Georgia (1967-70).

Harrell's first job offers, however, came from colleges associated with Churches of Christ.[15] In mid-1957, he received a job offer from

---

14. David Edwin Harrell, Jr., "Talk to Grandkids," digital audio recording, July 2012, 37:00-39:00. Recording in possession of author.

15. Personal correspondence from late 1957 indicates that Harrell explored a job at Florida Christian College (FCC), in part because it was his family's desire that he stay in Florida. In addition to Florida College, Harrell sought positions

David Lipscomb College. During the interview process he met with the college president, Athens Clay Pullias, and vice-president, Willard Collins, and came close to accepting the offer.[16] But when he read the contract, he found it included a clause stating that all instructors must agree to uphold the religious views of the Board of Directors of Lipscomb College. Knowing the "institutional" stance of the college regarding church support of colleges and other parachurch organizations, Harrell refused the offer.

Harrell reflected on his decision in responding to a subsequent job offer in October 1957 from Central Christian College in Bartlesville, Oklahoma. In describing his decision to Dean Earle H. West, Harrell explained that even if he concluded that the Lipscomb Board members were wrong in their view of institutionalism, he would not have opposed their positions openly. But he would not be restricted from privately expressing his opinions, especially if he became convinced that their beliefs were in error. This "long and useless process" at Lipscomb had alerted Harrell to the perils of his seeking employment in Christian colleges during the height of the controversy over institutionalism. His candid response to Dean West's invitation to apply for a job at Central Christian reveals his mindset:

> One other matter which I am sure would be pertinent is my position on the so-called 'current issues' in the church. I would almost say that I am without a 'position.' With the rush of studies, I have hardly had time to adequately study the problems involved. I do believe they deserve study. I do not believe that any man is entitled to uphold either position when he does not know why he is doing it. This I have and will steadfastly refuse to do. While I do not consider myself

---

at Tampa University, St. Petersburg Junior College, and the University of South Florida.

16. Deedee Harrell, in discussion with the author, November 16, 2020.

a radical 'anti,' intent on breaking up all the achievements of the church, neither am I ready to defend, as scriptural, a good many things current in the church. Until I have had occasion to study the matter thoroughly, I would defend neither side. Until this time, I could offer opinions. Some of these opinions would be "anti." For instance, although I have not studied the basic principle involved to its conclusion, it does not appear to me that it is scriptural for congregations to contribute from their funds to a college. You may not be interested in all this, and I say it only to be fair to you and the college, or perhaps to tell you before someone else did ... I hope to be able within the couple of years to be able to study these questions satisfactorily and come to my own conclusions. Until then I suppose the above is a fair representation of how I feel.[17]

The conscientious caution of the note is apparent, and one senses the unease of a young scholar. Harrell was aware of the gravity of the issues, yet he was circumspect about the possible outcomes. On the one hand, he acted to avoid the danger of being hired into a party line at Lipscomb contrary to the trajectory of his conscience. On the other hand, he distanced himself from the hazard of a precipitous and potentially destructive rush to judgment about "the principle" of institutionalism, not yet knowing its outcome either in his own mind or in the minds of those around him. A sympathetic response from the college dean shows that others shared Harrell's perspective in riding the wave of the institutional controversy in 1957. Affirming his interest in Harrell coming to lead Central Christian College's History Department, Earle West stated his own convictions in the context of a school divided by the issues:

17. Letter from D. E. Harrell Jr. to Earle H. West, December 20, 1957, David Edwin Harrell, Jr. Papers, 1923-2017. Center for Restoration Studies MS #467. Abilene Christian University Special Collections and Archives, Brown Library.

With regard to current issues in the church, I believe we would have little difficulty. First, let me say without any disparagement to any other school that we have an atmosphere of freedom here. There is no 'Board policy' or 'Presidential policy' which teachers must agree to uphold. My personal convictions are opposed to (1) churches contributing to colleges, (2) church cooperation of the type represented by *Herald of Truth*, and (3) the sponsoring type of mission work. Central Christian College does not accept contributions from churches. On the other two points, the President and I do not agree. Wherever I have preached, I have tried to do a constructive work rather than a destructive work, and it is this general attitude that we would expect in any staff member—a positive, constructive attitude accompanied by a reasonable, intelligent approach to all problems. I am sure I state correctly the intention of us all when I say that we expect to retain a conservative outlook on problems.[18]

Earle West's nuanced position reflects the fluidity of the institutional debate at mid-century. The relative openness of the discussion is evidenced by the fact that Harrell copied his note to Dean West, sending it also to Howard White, the head of the history department at Lipscomb College, where Harrell had recently declined an offer of employment. In reply to this note, Howard White, a Lipscomb history professor and Harrell's mentor, acknowledges the disagreements that exist and the need for prayerful study of the issues:

---

18. Letter from Earle H. West to D. E. Harrell Jr. and Howard White, January 1958, David Edwin Harrell, Jr. Papers, 1923-2017. Center for Restoration Studies MS #467. Abilene Christian University Special Collections and Archives, Brown Library.

Your letter to Dean West seems to explain your position very well. Although I differ with you in certain points of view, I have great respect for your integrity and sincerity and your right to hold your convictions. I do hope and pray that after much prayer and study you will be able to arrive at a solution to all of these problems that will be completely scriptural and pleasing to God, and of course, that is a wish I have for all of us.[19]

Among the influences on Ed Harrell's thinking about the institutional issues these years were church leaders that he and his father had come to trust. These included leaders of Florida Christian College in Tampa, Florida, where James R. Cope was president and Clinton Hamilton was dean in the late 1950s. These men were often on the road to preach or to conduct college business and would stop in Nashville for conversation with Harrell. "They would talk to Ed for hours about the issues," recalls Deedee Harrell.[20] Another significant influence on Harrell during these years was Harold Glenn Dowdy (1925-2015). After serving in the 100th infantry in France and Germany during WWII, attending Florida College and graduating from the University of Florida with a bachelor's degree in education, Dowdy began preaching in High Springs, Florida, and continued as an evangelist throughout the United States while also working as a bricklayer until his death in 2015. Dowdy was thirty-three years old in 1958 when he met Ed Harrell during Ed's gospel meeting in Jessup, Georgia.[21] "Doc

19. Letter from Howard White to D. E. Harrell Jr., January 1958, David Edwin Harrell, Jr. Papers, 1923-2017. Center for Restoration Studies MS #467. Abilene Christian University Special Collections and Archives, Brown Library.

20. Deedee Harrell, in discussion with the author, November 16, 2020.

21. Deedee Harrell, in discussion with the author, November 16, 2020. "Gospel meeting" is a conventional designation among churches of Christ for a multi-day series of sermons and/or Bible classes on topics meant to attract both

Harrell wanted Ed to meet my dad, no matter what happened," noted Dowdy's daughter.[22] Ed recalled that Doc Harrell was the driving force behind the introduction: "[My father] was determined that we should meet—mostly, I think, for my benefit. My father told me that in Harold he had met 'the Apostle Paul' in South Georgia."[23] The influence was reciprocal. In a brief autobiographical statement, Dowdy acknowledged that "the folks who had a lot of influence in my life were Bob Owen, Lloyd Copeland, James Cope, Homer Hailey, Doc Harrell and Ed Harrell ...".[24] Looking back on his relationship with Dowdy, Harrell acknowledged that they were friends as close as brothers: "I am probably one of a few men who could tell Harold that he was wrong and that he needed to make a change and escape with my life. And he was one of a few men who could correct my interpretation of scripture and get a serious hearing .... I found in him the model of a young evangelist ...".[25] Others recognized the long-term influence of Dowdy on Harrell: "Dowdy had a poorer background and Ed idolized him. Harold was such a strong personal worker in evangelism and built several church buildings. Ed inculcated this into himself, and his going into India as an evangelist and church builder later in his life was an outgrowth of that mindset about Dowdy."[26] In this way, the influence of preachers like Cope, Hamilton, and Dowdy mixed with his dissertation research and subsequent study of "the issues" to produce a young historian who by 1960 knew where he stood in

---

regular church members and visitors for purposes of evangelism and edification.

22. Lynn Warren and Glenn Dowdy, in discussion with the author, December 28, 2020.

23. David Edwin Harrell, Jr., "Eulogy for Harold Glenn Dowdy," August 3, 2015, David Edwin Harrell, Jr. Papers, 1923-2017, Center for Restoration Studies MS #467, Abilene Christian University Special Collections and Archives, Brown Library, Abilene Christian University, Abilene, TX.

24. Harold Dowdy, *Shooting Creek Parables* (Connie Lewis Hill, 2018), 123.

25. Ibid.

26. Brent Lewis, in discussion with the author, February 26, 2021.

the doctrinal debate about institutionalism and who would focus on evangelism not only in the United States but also around the world.

Looking back on this life thirty years later, Harrell cited the late 1950s as a moment of conversion in his life and "drastic spiritual change" away from loyalty to a "Church of Christ" denomination. Rather, he began to identify with individual churches that had no parachurch institutions or this-worldly identification larger than the local congregation.

> As almost everyone knows I came to identify with the anti-institutional churches of Christ. I wasn't born there. At Lipscomb my best friend was Cliett Goodpasture. I had moved in that [non-institutional] direction for a variety of reasons.[27]

Casting his lot with the congregational churches of Christ meant that he had come to "follow a more independent quest for New Testament Christianity," and a "principle of restoration" that was singularly loyal to Jesus Christ. He would describe it as an exclusive commitment to "come as close as possible to the Christianity of the New Testament, to speak only as 'the oracles of God' (1 Peter 4:11)."[28]

This choice to break from the institutional tendencies of Goodpasture and other friends and potential employers was a choice that would shape the remainder of his life, from his eschewing of employment at colleges and universities related to Churches of Christ to his cultivation of an "outsider" position both concerning collegiate profession and church pulpit. In the celebratory volume published after his retirement from full-time teaching, Harrell is

---

27. Harrell, *"How My Mind Has Changed,"* 1991 Audiotape.
28. Harrell, "Rear Views: How My Mind Has Changed," *Christianity Magazine* 8.10 (October 1991): 32.

repeatedly identified as an "outsider" by his colleagues, both within and without the Churches of Christ.[29] Cautious of being yet another "Church of Christ historian," in the sense of a denominational scholar, he resisted some of the most dominant descriptions and conventional explanations among other historians from within the Churches of Christ. For example, Harrell resisted the view that the Restoration Movement was primarily a "unity movement," as well as the growing use of the title "Stone-Campbell Movement." Harrell preferred the term "The American Restoration Movement" and saw Biblical restorationism as predominant over related efforts for Christian unity in the movement. His professional employment was entirely in public state universities, and he served primarily as a self-described "lay preacher" among churches of Christ, an itinerant role that would lead him to hundreds of gospel meetings—weeklong series of evening sermons meant to evangelize the unconverted, and, increasingly during his lifetime, to encourage the saints. As a result, Harrell was never known for occupying a local pulpit as a matter of professional identity, though he served as the primary preacher in several locations, most notably in Deland (1959-61) and South Jacksonville, Florida (1999-2010), where he also served as an elder from 2000-2012.

Harrell's move away from institutional Churches of Christ was, therefore, a decision borne of contemporary discussion and debate in the late 1950s. But Harrell's casting his lot with "non-institutional" churches was also borne of his historical study of the American Restoration Movement. He saw in

---

29. Wayne Flynt, "David Edwin Harrell Jr.: Restoration Activist, Christian Globalist, Social Historian, Rigorous Mentor," in *Recovering the Margins of American Religious History*, edited by B. Dwain Waldrep & Scott Billingsley (Tuscaloosa: University of Alabama Press, 2010), x, vii-xii: "Like his deeply felt (and carefully cultivated) image of himself as a loner, an outsider, a scholar beyond the magic circle of the social, religious, political, and intellectual consensus, he was drawn to people whose story mirrored his own."

this history reason to oppose a denominational support for "parachurch" institutions and the growing "social gospel" impulse among mainline, institutional Churches of Christ. This convergence of historical study and personal conviction is seen, for example, in the conclusion to his 1962 Vanderbilt dissertation on the social history of the Disciples of Christ in the 19th century. Harrell observed that the wedge driving the movement apart was not concern for the social problems that are meticulously chronicled in his dissertation—poverty, slavery, war, divorce, and other cultural ills. Harrell described various personalities and publications among the Disciples sharing a mission to restore the ancient order, while simultaneously seeking to address the spiritual and social problems of the day as individual Christians. The source of separation among these "prophets" and "people's preachers" was, Harrell observed, the introduction and expansion of religious businesses supported by intra-church activism to address social ills. The push for institutional solutions to societal problems was planted in regional differences of North and South, and exacerbated by the Civil War, but it grew from different views of how to reform the nation. In his concluding taxonomy of the tripartite division of the movement over institutional activism, Harrell identifies three approaches—conservative, moderate, and progressive—to the relationship between Christian action and social humanitarianism:

> Some, probably most during the early years, insisted that the only religious duty of the Christian was to convert sinners— social improvements would follow. A middle group believed that the Christian was obligated to actively participate in organized social reform, but only in his capacity as a compassionate Christian individual. By the 1850's, however, a growing group within the movement became committed to a philosophy of active church participation in social

regeneration. The social salvation of society was a Christian end in itself—spiritual benefits would follow.[30]

The division among Disciples of Christ, in other words, was caused by the different approaches to church and parachurch social action in the world. In this way, Harrell's social history of the Disciples exposed not only the sectional and economic sources of the schism, but also the doctrinal root of contention that grew from social sources. This doctrine was the teaching that the church should be an active social agent and political force in the world. In opposition to this progressive perspective and growth of institutions, Harrell observed, there was the "legalistic concept of a church limited to spiritual functions" and "that social evils would be solved only by conversion of individuals."[31] This is an insight from the mid-19th century history of the Disciples of Christ that would prove prophetic for the divisions fomenting among Churches of Christ in the mid-20th century.

His invitation to speak at the 1960 lectureship at Florida Christian College in Temple Terrace, Florida was the first public presentation of Harrell's prophetic history. Delivered on March 23 in Sutton Hall on the Florida College campus, Harrell's evening lecture on "The Social Gospel" addressed the doctrinal source of division among the Disciples of Christ that his dissertation had so meticulously documented.[32] He posed the question: "Is the primary

---

30. David Edwin Harrell, Jr., *Quest for a Christian America 1800-1865: A Social History of the Disciples of Christ,* Volume 1, reprinted edition (Tuscaloosa: University of Alabama Press, 2003), 223.

31. Ibid., 224.

32. David Edwin Harrell, Jr., "The Social Gospel," *Florida Christian College Lectures, March 23, 1960. Box 24,, David Edwin Harrell, Jr. Papers, 1923-2017. Center for Restoration Studies MS #467. Abilene Christian University Special Collections and Archives, Brown Library.* The lecture was subsequently printed in some of the religious periodicals among congregational churches of Christ, e.g., Ed Harrell, "The Social Gospel," *Gospel Guardian*, 12.15 (August 18, 1960),

goal of the church the salvation of men's souls or the far-reaching improvement of society?" Beyond historical analysis, the lecture was polemical in nature, an opening salvo in what would be his lifelong opposition to institutionalism in the Churches of Christ.

"The room was filled with preachers from around the country that night," recalled Bob Owen, who at the time served as Vice-President and Dean of Students at Florida College. Much of what Harrell shared that night was new to the Christians in the audience. "It was revolutionary," recalls long-time preacher, Brent Lewis, who was a student at Florida College the year of Harrell's lecture. "He was giving an aspect of what happened in the church within a broader context that nobody else among the brethren knew of."[33] The first half of his lecture was vintage Harrell, explaining the rise of social justice concerns of Christians amid the rapid industrialization of the nation, with all its related problems. His analysis concluded that it was not only theological liberals who thought social concerns should have primacy in the church. Concern for the improvement of the broader society through the church's social action was observable among both liberal and conservative Christians in the nation's past. This vulnerability of even conservative churches of Christ to the allure of the Social Gospel was a point Harrell had recently raised in response to a 1959 article by preacher J. W. Roberts in the *Gospel Advocate*. Roberts provided an amateurish summary of the history of the "Social Gospel" as a product of liberal, modern theology. Roberts argued that such was not the goal of contemporary social activities among Churches of Christ, including the operation of orphan homes or congregational meals in the building. "In reality," Roberts observed, "there is too little concern for social emphasis

---

225; cf. *The Preceptor*, Vol. 9.8 (June 1960): 115, 132, 141; *The Preceptor*, Vol. 9.9 (July 1960): 4; *Torch*, 23.3 (March 1988): 7-10; *Torch*, 23.4 (April 1988): 7-10.
33. Brent Lewis, in discussion with the author, February 26, 2021.

among conservative groups of all kinds."[34] Harrell responded to Roberts on the pages of the *Gospel Guardian* in what he later described as a "perhaps unkind" article on the meaning of the "Social Gospel" theology.[35] Harrell argued that Roberts had misrepresented the idea of the "Social Gospel" and had misused his scholarly authority among the brotherhood by representing the Social Gospel as only occurring in connection to liberal theology. The best historical scholarship, Harrell argued, clearly showed that the Social Gospel was connected also to conservative religious groups like Holiness groups, Cumberland Presbyterians, and Southern Baptists. Most importantly, the result was "a softening of the spiritual emphasis in conservative theologies."[36]

With this exchange with Roberts as a backdrop, the remainder of Harrell's 1960 lecture became more prescriptive by advancing three claims about the relation of contemporary churches to the Social Gospel. First, Harrell describes the Biblical distinction between, 1) individual attitudes and actions and, 2) the local church's duties. Harrell observed that Scripture requires the church to have a "spiritual focus," citing John 18:36, "my kingdom is not of this world." Harrell argued that the local church is not intended to cope with social injustices in the kingdom of men. Unlike that done by individual Christians, benevolence by the local church in the New Testament is only for the physical care of the saints, and even this has primarily, if not entirely, a spiritual purpose. Here Harrell's prescription for the church's spiritual work conforms to the most conservative type of social activism from the 19th century as described in the conclusion of his dissertation.

---

34. J.W. Roberts, "What is the Social Gospel?" *Gospel Advocate* 101.27 (July 2, 1959): 419-420.

35. David Edwin Harrell, Jr., "Thoughts on Dishonesty," *Gospel Guardian* 11.20 (September 24, 1959): 312-314.

36. Ibid., 313.

Second, Harrell moved into what might be termed "prophetic history." He made predictions about the church's future based on his interpretation of Scripture and his observation of patterns of past church development and division. This is a genre of discourse—drawing predictions and prescriptions from past Christian history—which he returned to repeatedly in his writings. Harrell predicted the continuing growth of social emphasis in American Christianity, and, notably, he specifically delineated examples of how the social gospel was already perverting Churches of Christ in their support of "educational institutions ... kitchens and gymnasiums, old folks homes, orphan homes, and hospitals."[37] Harrell argued that the divisions these issues fostered were primarily a matter of Christians' attitudes toward the Word of God. The division that was yet to be manifested, he concludes, *has already happened* in the hearts and minds of those involved.

This assertion that the church was moving toward social "ploys" and away from a confidence in the gospel's sufficiency to convert the world led Harrell to a third point: the cyclical nature of church history. The digression that he described on a small scale in the 20th century is part of a history of eventual "perversion" that happens "again and again" among God's people, extending back to Biblical times. Harrell interpreted the institutional divisions among churches of Christ as coinciding with the cycle of establishment, exile, and restoration that replays in different ways throughout the Biblical narrative. It is a Biblical pattern that he observed throughout 2,000 years of church history, an ongoing succession of seasons of faithfulness, apostasy, and restoration. Harrell saw this as cyclical history with contemporary

---

37. Harrell, "The Social Gospel: A lecture delivered by Ed Harrell March 23, 1960, at the Florida College lecture program, Tampa Florida," 5, David Edwin Harrell, Jr. Papers, 1923-2017, Center for Restoration Studies MS #467, Abilene Christian University Special Collections and Archives, Brown Library, Abilene Christian University, Abilene, TX.

repetitions in the 20th century. His historical analysis of past divisions of the Disciples of Christ in the 19th century continues into a prophetic critique and prediction of contemporary divisions among churches of Christ.

After Harrell delivered the lecture on the Social Gospel, the Vice-President of Florida College, Bob Owen, requested a copy and mimeographed it immediately for distribution to everyone there. "I handed out copies before the lectures were over," Owen recalled. "It triggered Ed being asked to speak at a lot of places and was the beginning of him being a brotherhood figure."[38] Ed Harrell's father, Doc Harrell, was on the Board at Florida College and present at the lecture. "Both parents were very excited," Deedee Harrell recalled. "This was the boy who behaved so badly and had been sent to the farm every summer to pick tobacco and live with the farmhands."[39]

There is one brief reference to the "denominational Church of Christ" in Harrell's 1960 FCC lecture. It might be easily overlooked but it became a concept of thematic importance to his subsequent scholarship and preaching. In his brief, initial mention of this idea, Harrell observed that a denominational church might "still be creedally conservative in its theology, but pronouncedly liberal in its attitude toward Scripture."[40] Here Harrell for the first time distinguishes between the direction of the sectarian congregational churches and the increasingly denominational institutional or mainline Church of Christ. This "sect-to-denomination" distinction was a repeated focus of his research and writing. He identified the debate over institutionalism in the 1950s as the most important division in the twentieth century, and, in this regard, Harrell went farther than his predecessors in making the case for the significance of this rupture between institutional and congregational churches.

---

38. Bob Owen, in discussion with the author, June 25, 2021.

39. Deedee Harrell, in discussion with the author, November 16, 2020.

40. Harrell, "The Social Gospel," 3.

Stepping back and commenting decades later, Harrell observed that the key issue in the institutional debate was "the proper relationship between local churches and educational and benevolent institutions."[41] This included longstanding debates over church funding for missionary societies, colleges, and orphan homes. The debates over the latter two institutions had become more focused and bitter after WWII as churches of Christ experienced unprecedented growth and affluence. Debates advanced by preachers and editors of the day were not always consistent but were increasingly acrimonious. The leading preachers and editors were Foy Wallace, Jr., James R. Cope, N. B. Hardeman, G. C. Brewer, and B. C. Goodpasture. Their minds diverged on "the issues," and so would the Christians and churches who listened to what sometimes amounted to raucous brawling in the brotherhood papers. In his later history of the division, Harrell emphasized two themes: 1) the differences in approach to disagreement, and 2) the underlying issue. First, he observed the distinction between leaders and papers, such as *The Christian Leader*, that were more irenic than polemical, a distinction representing the difference between "the builders" and "the fighters." This was a difference between a "more open, tolerant, and grace-oriented" approach and a "rational, propositional and relatively closed" approach."[42] In addition, beneath the different doctrinal positions and communication styles, Harrell discerned different attitudes towards whether the churches should desire respectability in the eyes of the world and whether restoration's open-ended search for the New Testament pattern should be sustained or foreshortened. This question of the motivation for the churches was a more basic, underlying source of division than was the debate over methods of church work.

41. David Edwin Harrell, *The Churches of Christ in the 20th Century* (Tuscaloosa: The University of Alabama Press, 2000), 73.

42. Harrell, *The Churches of Christ in the 20th Century*, 112.

The classic example of this divergence in the 1950s among churches of Christ was the so-called "Italian Episode," a polarizing event that helped consummate the institutional division of the 1950s. After a group of missionaries from churches of Christ had rocks thrown at them in Rome, and many members of the churches of Christ in America had expressed outrage, Cled Wallace, a writer for the upstart, non-institutional paper, *The Gospel Guardian*, wrote an article on "The Rock Fight," mocking the churches' denominational pride and outrage over the event.[43] The article was an expression of the concern over a diminishing separation from the broader culture among the institutional churches. This was one event in a series of volleys between brotherhood papers that lined up on either side of the issue, including *The Preceptor*, edited by Florida Christian College president James R. Cope, which served primarily non-institutional Christians.[44] The increasingly

---

43. Cled E. Wallace, "What the New Testament Teaches," *Gospel Guardian* 1.48 (April 13, 1950): 1. A later, but related opposition to overseas evangelism in Italy elicits a principled critique from Homer Hailey, expressing concern over the persecution, but caution in emphasizing "mass movements" and "spectacular" reactions that move beyond what the individual or the local congregation can do, see Homer Hailey, "Italy and Incense," *The Preceptor* 2.12 (October 1953): 2. The nascent growth of the churches at this time in the United States is illustrated by a report in the *Gospel Guardian* from 1949 that the Ozark Mountains area of the state of Arkansas was an area where "the gospel was hardly known," and where "we know only one man who lives there who's a member of the church." Cf., Cled E. Wallace, "Getting Me Straightened Out," *Gospel Guardian* 1.42: 1; Fanning Yater Tant, "Editorial: Not Alone—We Hope," *Gospel Guardian* 1.49 (April 20, 1950): 2; Earl West, "Learning a Lesson from History—No. 2," *Gospel Guardian* 1.41 (February 23, 1950): 4. Cf. W.K. Pendleton, Millennial Harbinger (1866): 494. See the treatment of these events by one of Ed Harrell's graduate students, John C. Hardin, "Rock Fights, Quarantines, and Confessionals: B. C. Goodpasture, the *Gospel Advocate*, and Keeping Order in Churches of Christ," in *Recovering the Margins of American Religious History*, edited by B. Dwain Waldrep & Scott Billingsley (Tuscaloosa: University of Alabama Press, 2010), 60-83.

44. Harrell, *The Churches of Christ in the 20th Century*, 123.

acrimonious attacks continued between the different positions and personalities. Although mediating positions were sought, such as J. D. Thomas' book *We Be Brethren* and a proposal by editors of the *Firm Foundation* that orphan homes be put under the oversight of local congregations, a decisive rupture occurred with B. C. Goodpasture's approval of an idea advanced in the *Gospel Advocate* that the "antis" (a pejorative designation of the non-institutional perspective) be "quarantined." Lines were formed and preachers were increasingly pressured to profess their allegiance or "confess" when they had changed their position, which most often was to the institutional side.[45]

Through the 1950s and early 1960s, institutional churches pressed the growth of parachurch efforts like funding of the Manhattan Church of Christ and the *Herald of Truth*, a national broadcast receiving funding from churches from across the country under oversight of the Highland Church of Christ in Abilene, Texas. As Harrell described it, the institutional churches increasingly fell in line with broader evangelicalism as "boosters" of church respectability and "settlers" within the broader society and political arena, whereas the congregational churches maintained the traditional "sojourner" mentality of the early Restoration Movement.[46]

It was within this divisive context that Harrell delivered the "Social Gospel" lecture at Florida College in 1960, and soon thereafter wrote and distributed a pamphlet that would often be republished by brotherhood periodicals and broadly distributed up to the present day. Titled *The Emergence of the "Church of*

---

45. Ibid., 131-140, Cf. Steve Wolfgang, "History and Background of the Institutional Controversy (3)," *Guardian of Truth* 33.9 (May 4, 1989): 272-275, online at https://www.truthmagazine.com/history-and-background-of-the-institutional-controversy-3.

46. Harrell, *The Churches of Christ in the 20th Century*, 166.

Christ" Denomination,[47] the pamphlet was the first time Harrell "stated openly" his sociological interpretation of the Restoration Movement geared towards an "insider," Christian audience.[48] What is most notable is this pamphlet's connection of academic study of the sect-to-denomination process, and the "moral" of its process for believers in churches of Christ. Harrell draws a direct line between his scholarly study of religious sects in the South (namely, "the sectional and sociological dimensions of nineteenth century divisions") and the emerging schism among churches of Christ in the 20th century. This is aimed at both the large segment of the most progressive churches ("led by *Mission Magazine* and *Christian Chronicle* and the liberal educational institutions") moving toward an institutional denominationalism, as well as the more gradual slide of middle-of-the-road churches ("followed by the editor of the *Firm Foundation*") into an "institutionalized sect—partially accepting denominational standards and partially clinging to the conservative plea of the past."[49]

In the pamphlet, Harrell concludes that there is a "non-institutional," conservative group among churches of Christ that is most successful among the poorer economic groups within the church. This group most resists the move toward denominationalism. This group is also the most "fanatical" and "eccentric" because "most of the people who are deeply and

---

47. David Edwin Harrell, *Emergence of the "Church of Christ" Denomination* (Lakeland: Harwell/Lewis Publishing Company, 2005, 1962).

This writing has been reprinted with permission in the appendices of this book. All future references to this material will refer to the reprint within this book.

48. As the author observes in the preface to its 2005 reprinting, his sociological interpretation of the restoration movement and its three-way division had "proven to be prophetically correct," and was developed before his identification with the non-institutional wing of the movement (Harrell, *Emergence*, 1).

49. Harrell, *Emergence*, Appendix 1, 301.

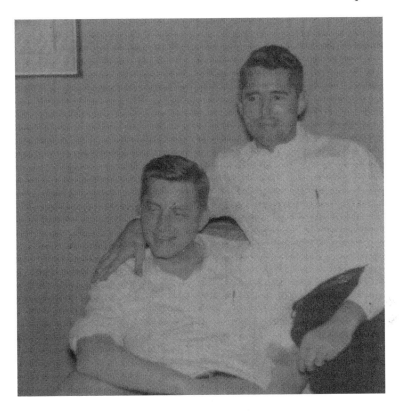

Ed Harrell with brother-in-law, Robert Hardage (c. 1965).

intensely concerned about their religion are conservatives. On the other hand, the liberal point of view attracts the contented and the complacent."[50] Reflecting on the importance of the pamphlet, historian Steve Wolfgang observes, "It was an in-your-face response to the cultured genteel among the Churches of Christ, the people in Nashville, who talked about not being a denomination but were surely as much a denomination as the Southern Baptists."[51]

What thus emerges in the tract is the identification of three wings of the movement—a three-way division in the churches of

---

50. Harrell, *Emergence*, Appendix 1, 300.

51. Steve Wolfgang, in discussion with the author, May 28, 2021.

Christ which Harrell affirmed as "prophetically correct" nearly a half-century later:

> The years from 1950 to 2005 have seen churches of Christ divided into three wings that are separated by both doctrinal and sociological tensions. In my writings, I have labeled these three wings of the movement "Non-Institutional churches of Christ," "Institutional Churches of Christ," and "Progressive Churches of Christ." The predictions and descriptions in "The Emergence of the 'Church of Christ' Denomination" deserve a continued hearing at the beginning of the 21st century.[52]

This idea of the recurring three-way division within the Restoration Movement was one of Harrell's key scholarly contributions. Nearly everyone before that time had described the Disciples division as a two-way division between instrument and non-instrument. Harrell had clearly demonstrated that it was a three-way division that produced the Disciples and the Churches of Christ, but then later split off the Disciples between the Disciples and the ultra-liberals, producing the Independent Christian Churches. Under Harrell's lens, this three-way division repeated among 20th century Churches of Christ, producing "antis" and "liberals," with the liberals splitting into two groups: the more moderate and the more progressive.

Up until 1961, one might be excused for thinking of Harrell as a "one-trick pony." He was a scholar of the Disciples of Christ's social history who could apply such sociological categories for an insider criticism or exhortation to churches of Christ. The actual breadth of his study and interests, however, became apparent in his letters to potential employers in his early career. Writing in 1964 to Joseph Parks at the University of Georgia, Harrell remarked that his interests were not as narrow as his dissertation might suggest, "Actually, my

---

52. Harrell, *Emergence*, 287.

interest is in 'western religion' and its sectional characteristics. As soon as I finish my work with the Disciples, I plan to investigate a number of similar frontier sects."[53] Indeed, the full breadth of his doctoral experience was on display in a letter three years earlier to the University of Tennessee in applying for a position in their Western Civilization department, "Medieval and modern European were my two areas of non-American concentration in my doctoral program ... I have been a teaching fellow in the Vanderbilt Western Civilization program for about three and a half years."[54] This self-promoting description of his breadth of intellectual interest and insight was more than a rhetorical ploy to get a job, as his subsequent career demonstrates.

More than only a historian of the Disciples of Christ, the breadth of Harrell's reflection on the religious and philosophical background of Western culture was on full display during the second lecture he gave at Florida Christian College on March 7, 1961.[55] The theme of the lectureship that year was "Ancient Faith and Modern Thought," and Harrell's lecture was on "The Faith vs. Intellectualism." His lecture begins with a sweeping review of European intellectual history since the Renaissance and addresses "the meaning of life." Portraying the options as set upon a battleground, he depicts one side as "intellectualism," defined as "the doctrine that knowledge is derived from pure reason." From the science of the Renaissance and

53. Letter from David E. Harrell, Jr. to Dr. Joseph H. Parks, dated November 17, 1964. David Edwin Harrell, Jr. Papers, 1923-2017, Center for Restoration Studies MS #467, Abilene Christian University Special Collections and Archives.

54. Letter from David E. Harrell, Jr. to Dr. J. Wesley Hoffman, dated May 12, 1961. David Edwin Harrell, Jr. Papers, 1923-2017, Center for Restoration Studies MS #467. Abilene Christian University Special Collections and Archives, Brown Library, Abilene Christian University, Abilene, TX.

55. The lecture was reprinted in church newsletters, including Spring and Blaine church of Christ, St. Louis, MO, "The Defender," 3.18 (March 26, 1961): 1-3. Grover Stevens and Ferrell Jenkins were evangelists at the Spring and Blaine congregation at the time.

Enlightenment to the religious responses of atheism, deism, and liberal religion, Harrell surveyed four hundred years of attempts to explain life's meaning. All such attempts based on "pure reason" are shown to crumble in the 20th century under the influence of Einstein and Freud, who show that scientists do not have all the answers. This fact is evident because of the relativism of the natural sciences (Einstein) and the irrationality of human natures (Freud). The moral vacuum that resulted in the mid-20th century was the basis for Harrell's critique of the "new faith" that had evolved in the United States.[56]

This new faith is a compromise between intellectualism and faith—a compromise that lacks courage and commitment. "American religion is a fat religion in a fat society for fat people with fat heads," Harrell quips. He contrasts this flabby mediocrity to the lean and hungry look of Biblical faith—that of Paul, Stephen, and Elijah on Mount Carmel (1 Kings 18:21) who are representative of those Christians who truly believe and truly reason and truly listen to God in their individual lives and in their churches.[57]

The intellectualism of modern religionists is therefore a "pseudo-intellectualism" which compromises both intellect and faith by denying the need for unwavering faith and irrevocable commitment to the will of God. The challenge today then, Harrell observed, is that of converting people to faith and then to *the* faith.

Harrell proceeds to situate the religious divisions of his day onto the battlefield of faith vs. intellectualism. The controversy

---

56. David Edwin Harrell, Jr., "The Faith versus Intellectualism," 1961 Florida College Lectures, (manuscript copy), 1-7. Reprinted as "The Faith Versus Intellectualism - (I)," *Gospel Guardian* 13.1 (May 4, 1961): 1,12. Available online at https://www.wordsfitlyspoken.insearchoftruth.org/gospel_guardian/v13/v13n1p1,12.html; and, "The Faith Versus Intellectualism - (II)," *Gospel Guardian* 13.2 (May 11, 1961): 1, 12.

57. Ibid., 7.

over the contemporary institutional "issues" among churches of Christ is, Harrell observed, about the deeper issue of whether one is determined to do the will of God or whether one is determined to have an "intelligent faith," in the sense of one devoted to human will and preference instead of the divine. Harrell then returned to his militant imagery in crescendo:

> I would not have the battleline stand still. Let us reclaim our brethren to the simplicity and meekness which rests in faith. But if they will not be reclaimed, if the spirit of presumptuous pseudo-rationalism is within them irrevocable, then I resolve to push them, and castigate them until the issues become not church-supported benevolent societies, and missionary societies, and educational institutions, and hospitals, but the Lord's Supper, and baptism, and the divinity of Jesus Christ—until the issues become the faith versus intellectualism. I would that they be consistent.[58]

Seen through these words, the institutional issues of his day are part of a deeper issue of reliance on the Word of God that Harrell saw as relevant not only to questions of institutionalism but also to other distinctive doctrines of churches of Christ and even more broadly to teachings about the deity of Jesus. The portrait of a "new faith" that is pseudo-intellectual and quasi-faithful is the picture Harrell paints of the institutional brethren of his day, and the solution he prescribed is twofold. On one hand, he distinguished education from intellectualism, and argued that Christians should pursue education, but be cautious about the "subtleties and guiles of the university professor." Education is fine, but it is not needed. What is needed is preaching of the undiluted word and prayer for "the faith and courage of a prophet."[59]

---

58. David Edwin Harrell, Jr., "The Faith versus Intellectualism," 10-11.
59. David Edwin Harrell, Jr., "The Faith versus Intellectualism," 12.

This call for prophetic faith in the church was initially directed only at members of the churches of Christ, and especially those among the congregational churches of Christ. However, five years later, Harrell's theme of prophetic faith would spill over into the broader American Restoration Movement. In 1966, the second-annual Forrest F. Reed lectures were hosted by the Disciples of Christ Historical Society (DCHS) on its 25th anniversary. The DCHS had invited three scholars from the three streams of the American Restoration Movement. Each speaker was to address "the contribution of his group to the Church universal and the current status of the group's relationship to the Church."[60]

As the invited representative from the Churches of Christ, Harrell joined Dr. Robert O. Fife from Milligan College (representative of the Christian Churches/Churches of Christ), and Dr. Ronald E. Osborn from Union Theological Seminary in Manila, Philippines (representative of the Disciples of Christ). The lecture occurred November 7-8, 1966.

Harrell's explanation of the contribution of the Churches of Christ both to the universal church and to the modern age unfolded in three parts. First, he disclosed his own character as a Christian and how his mindset was representative of the character of the contemporary Churches of Christ. Second, he demonstrated the correspondence of his kind of faith to the historic Disciples of Christ. And third, he addressed the relevance of the Churches of Christ and their faith to the present world, and particularly the way this faith addresses the psychological needs of modern believers. After connecting this psychology to the social status of believers who would accept his type of faith, Harrell concluded by stating the relationship among the three

---

60. Letter from Howard E. Short to David Edwin Harrell, Jr, dated October 25, 1965, David Edwin Harrell, Jr. Papers, 1923-2017, Center for Restoration Studies MS #467, Abilene Christian University Special Collections and Archives.

streams of the American Restoration Movement. The conclusion ran counter to the ecumenical hopes expressed by his two fellow-speakers in the Reed Lectures.

The lecture is a forceful exposition of what Harrell, in time, designated as the "primitivist commitment."[61] Beginning his address with a quote he repeated often during his career, Harrell cites Elmer T. Clark's book, *The Small Sects in America*. Clark asserts that it is "a peculiar type of mind which is convinced that God is interested in whether his worshipers sing with or without instrumental accompaniment."[62] Harrell admits that this is the case, but also retorts: "I thought it was 'a peculiar type of mind' which thinks it is 'a peculiar type of mind' which is convinced that instrumental music is sinful." This observation introduces a theme that ran throughout the lecture, namely that one's posture towards Christian convictions is fundamentally a psychological stance–a "type of mind"–and that all mindsets have their peculiar origins in history, society, and individual experience. The critic's mindset, in other words, is itself peculiar, reflecting a particular "psychology" regarding the Christian religion. Harrell then compared his own mindset to those who differed from him.

---

61. Edwin David Harrell, Jr. "A Primitivist Life: Embracing Objective Truth and Biblical Primitivism," [unpublished manuscript], 1, David Edwin Harrell, Jr. Papers, 1923-2017, Center for Restoration Studies MS #467. Abilene Christian University Special Collections and Archives, Brown Library, Abilene Christian University, Abilene, TX.

62. Edwin David Harrell, Jr. "Peculiar People: A Rationale for Conservative Christian Disciples," in Robert O. Fife, David Edwin Harrell, and Ronald E. Osborn, *Disciples and the Church Universal* (Nashville: Disciples of Christ Historical Society, 1967), 34. Cf. Elmer T. Clark, *The Small Sects in America* (Nashville: Abingdon Pr., 1965), 16. This book also figured prominently in Harrell's dissertation.

This writing has been reprinted with permission in the appendices of this book. All future references to this material will refer to the reprint within this book. This reference is found on page 307.

Harrell first established who he is. He is a "legalistic fanatic" and "a Biblical literalist," with a "harsh posture" aiming for the restoration of the ancient order of things–from baptism, to Lord's Supper, to biological qualifications for elderships, and "distinctions between individual and congregational activities, and hundreds of similar questions seemingly technical in nature ...".[63] His "fanaticism" is, however, committed to religious toleration and to defending everyone's right to their own convictions and their expression. But, Harrell observed, he is nevertheless zealous in believing that hell awaits the sinner who is wrong in not believing or in not obeying the literal truth in the Scriptures. From this doctrinal stance follows Harrell's answer to the first question assigned to him regarding the relation of his group to the Church Universal: "From my theological point of view, the group to which I belong *is* the church universal."[64]

In making this sweeping claim about "the church universal," i.e., the entirety of God's people around the world and in heaven—a claim that was undoubtedly shocking to many in attendance that day in 1966—Harrell was asserting that the church of Christ which he represented is the one true Church, God's "peculiar people" (the title of his lecture), who by their obedient faith to God's Word and through the grace Christ provides, can witness both to their identity as those saved by God and their concern for the souls of those who do not follow the literal, simple truths of Christ's law as revealed in the New Testament.

Aware of the contrast of his viewpoint to those around him, Harrell hastened to detail the diversity and differences among those groups stemming from the American Restoration Movement. He was not representing a "churches of Christ platform." He is different, he acknowledged, from the element within the churches of Christ

---

63. Ibid.
64. Ibid., 308.

who are "very liberal and ecumenical-minded," and from those liberal preachers and those "more sophisticated members" who are choosing to stay within the church and to influence it from within.[65] These "timid liberals" among the Disciples of Christ, he observed, have more in common with the cooperative Disciples spirit than the conservative Disciple faith he espoused. Then in a brief and focused review of the history of Christianity in America, he reports that this narrow, legalistic faith was characteristic not only of many of the 19th Century Disciples of Christ, but of many more souls, like the 17th and 18th Century English and American Puritans, who lived as "legalistic fanatics" with a "harsh theology," and an "authoritarian faith" because it met the needs of their souls in harsh times. Simple truths from their literal reading of Scripture provided the "spiritual needs" of courage, certainty, and comfort. Among the early Disciples of Christ, Harrell continued, this plea to restore the ancient order of things became blunted by a related emphasis on the union of all Christians. Because of an Enlightenment belief in the ability of all people to recognize and agree to the self-evident facts of Scripture, this desire for unity led to a millennial confidence that the restoration principle would yield "ultimate union" among all Christians. "In short," Harrell summarized, "the early leaders of the Disciples were more than legalists. They were optimistic legalists."[66] As the Disciples of Christ went through the trauma of the Civil War and its fracturing of their movement, the second generation lost their optimism, and either 1) continued to emptily mouth the dual slogans of restoration and union, or 2) they "gravitated to the emphasis that suited their needs."[67]

---

65. Ibid. Harrell here references the book, *Voices of Concern*, as indicative of the growing liberal concern within the churches of Christ. Cf. Robert Meyers, *Voices of Concern; Critical Studies in Church of Christism* (Mission Messenger, 1966).

66. Ibid.

67. Ibid., 310.

It is hard to overstate the extent to which Harrell emphasized the psychological roots of faith in the third and final section of his lecture. After laying the groundwork for this emphasis in the preceding historical review, he turned to a question that was not evidently assigned to him, but which he addressed as a central concern: "What is the pertinence of restoration legalism in modern society?" The overarching answer is that it meets the psychological needs of some people in coming to terms with life in the modern world. To explain this claim, Harrell turned to the concept of "double truth" as espoused by the 18th century philosopher, Francis Bacon. Bacon's ideas about the empirical origins of knowledge and humans' shared ability to understand and assent to these natural truths had formed an ideological framework for the restorationist appeal to the self-evident truths of the New Testament as a basis for Christian unity. Harrell observed that Bacon distinguished between the truth of philosophy and the truth of theology. The former is discerned by scientific discovery and invention and is concerned with practical mastery over the forces of nature. The latter was the reserve of divine revelation and what could be known, not by human reason, but by knowledge and application of Scripture. The two truths, Bacon observed, must be kept separate. Harrell agreed.[68]

Looking back again at the early history of the Disciples of Christ, Harrell concluded that they understood that one could disagree about the social but not the religious. There could be compromise about the secular, but not the sacred. This separation between

---

68. Ibid. Cf. Bertrand Russell, *The History of Western Philosophy* (New York: Simon and Schuster, 1945), 542: "But while [Bacon] thought that reason could show the existence of God, he regarded everything else in theology as known only by revelation. Indeed, he held that the triumph of faith is greatest when to the unaided reason a dogma appears most absurd. Philosophy, however, should depend only upon reason. He was thus an advocate of the doctrine of "double truth," that of reason and that of revelation."

reason and revelation in the mind of the believer Harrell calls a "schizoid view of truth."[69] It is noteworthy that in his rough draft of the lecture, Harrell originally designated this a "bifurcated view of truth."[70] The psychologizing thrust of his lecture is evident in the redaction. This emphasis is important to his overarching point: acceptance of a "double standard of truth" is mental assent to the reality that reason does not hold the answer to all questions and neither does revelation.

These claims about the nature of truth led to a personal claim in which Harrell, perhaps for the first time, elaborated for a broader audience his view of the social gospel movement: "I am utterly repelled by the rallying of God to the support of worldly causes. God has been on the side of every social issue I have ever studied ... I distrust the man who has a plan from God for every social ill. I trust my reason more."[71] In contrast to this dismissal of appeals to revelation for societal improvement, Harrell confessed a need for an "absolutist God with heavenly truths." This is an acceptance of his own limitations and fallibility which the Danish Christian philosopher, Soren Kierkegaard, would call "a blind leap" of faith, and Sigmund Freud would call "a delusion," insofar as it was mental submission to divine degree for the sake of consolation and happiness. Harrell agreed with these characterizations, though not with the claim that his view is false or misguided. He argued that the "legalist fanatic" mindset he espoused is a psychological response to the world that is shared by people with the same religious needs. "The Churches of Christ is a gathering of certain psychological

---

69. Harrell, "Peculiar People," 311.

70. Harrell, "Peculiar People," [Manuscript Copy], David Edwin Harrell, Jr. Papers, 1923-2017, Center for Restoration Studies MS #467. Abilene Christian University Special Collections and Archives, Brown Library, Abilene Christian University, Abilene, TX.

71. Harrell, "Peculiar People," 312.

types, as is every other religious communion."[72] Through a series of observations about both medieval Christians and the Puritans, Harrell concluded that the psychological type of the Churches of Christ is that of "humility." People of this type humble themselves to receive the higher truths only accessible through faith and revelation, and which must be received, like salvation, as a gift from God.[73]

With this turn to psychological traits shared by members of his group, Harrell bridged psychology and sociology. He characterized the social origins of the "cult of humility" as conditions of poverty, sorrow, and hardship (in contrast to economic stability and comfort which breed religious complacency). In this way, the legalistic fanaticism of the churches of Christ arises not only from psychological fervency and religious intensity, but also from the marginalized social condition of being "economically dispossessed."[74]

In conclusion, Harrell reasserted that the Churches of Christ offer a religious expression that meets the needs of some people—a certain type of believer. He acknowledges that everyone will not have these inclinations and he understands the differences. Harrell observed the Christian evangelist's role is "to find those who are of a mind to share his mind ... My religious quest is to find those who would be 'peculiar people.'"[75] This faith and the "traditional legalism of the Churches of Christ" has nothing in common with the modern liberal and is closer to "a Primitivist Baptist, or a Seventh-Day Adventist, or a medieval Roman Catholic" than to a liberal Disciple. Because he understands the mindset of the liberal Disciple, he concludes that, as it relates to his own mindset, "reconciliation is inconceivable."[76]

---

72. Ibid., 313.

73. In his historical parallels and use of the concept of "cult of humility," Harrell draws from Ralph Barton Perry, *Puritanism and Democracy* (New York: Vanguard Press, 1944), 85.

74. Harrell, "Peculiar People," 313.

75. Ibid., 314.

76. Ibid.

In his conclusion to the Reed Lecture, Harrell drew a final contrast between divine and human truths. Here, again, we see the distinction drawn between the higher truth of God's gospel and the lower truth of human society and its suppositions about God.

> As an immortal soul, my deepest hope is the attainment of salvation through literal obedience to the Word of God. As a mortal man, I believe the greatest achievement in life is the gaining of an understanding of oneself and of those who differ from you. I do not believe that we shall ever reach accord in things spiritual, but if we could attain the lower good of understanding why, the insight would serve us well in our struggle with this life.[77]

---

77. Ibid. In addition to the formal publication by the Disciples of Christ Historical Society, the entire lecture was subsequently published two and half years later by the *Gospel Guardian* 20.34 (January 2, 1969). The title of the lecture is changed to "I Am a Biblical Literalist," and the issue includes an approving article by the editor, Fanning Yater Tant, as well as a critical review of Harrell's lecture by Dr. G. E. Owen, Executive Chairman of the Disciples of Christ United Missionary Society, Division of General Departments. Owen's review originally appeared in the Disciples' periodical *Discipliana* [George Earle Owen, "Disciples and the Universal Church—A Review," *Discipliana* 27.3 (October, 1967): 50-53] along with reviews of the other two Reed Lecture speakers. Owen's critique is notable for its incredulity over Harrell's "literal approach to the Bible" given his presumed "exposure to the historical research approach and to Biblical scholarship" (50). The next issue of *Discipliana* included Harrell's rejoinder to the review [David Edwin Harrell, Jr., "Disciples and the Church Universal—A Postscript," *Discipliana* 27.4 (January 1968): 75-76], and is also published in the same 1969 issue of *The Gospel Guardian* along with his original lecture. Harrell addresses Owen's critiques in order, and his response is notable as the first time Harrell uses the phrase "world view" to distinguish faith perspectives and rationalities, viz., Owen's search for Christian unity among denominations versus Harrell's research into the Christian past, which "shows the futility of the modern ecumenical movement" (75). Harrell's rejoinder also briefly mentions his belief that the Bible sustains his view that people's religious needs are individual and that "diversity is the natural religious condition" (Ibid). He elaborated the Biblical basis for this belief in his subsequent writings.

This "lower good" of studying his own religious tradition and other diverse faiths was the professorial part of Ed Harrell's life that was best known in the public sphere.

CHAPTER FOUR
Professor

> "I was astonished to learn that I was 'a devout Pentecostal.' I confess to sometimes speaking tongue in cheek, but I assure NEWSWEEK that I have never spoken in tongues."[1]

What did Harrell mean by this "lower good of understanding that can serve us well in this life?" One reasonable answer was his historical scholarship as a university professor over the next forty years. He focused on the study of religion in the American South, and especially marginalized Christian groups. The vocabulary he used to describe these groups became stock in his trade: "rednecks," "underbelly," "plain-folk," "non-conformists," "minorities," "sectarians," "fanatics," "on the fringe." What these sects had in common was their lower-class status, their zealously held commitment to the Bible and counter-cultural beliefs, and the derision they often experienced from mainline Christianity and

---

1. David Edwin Harrell, Jr., "Letter to Editor, Newsweek, 444 Madison Avenue, New York, NY. 10022," Typewritten letter dated July 13, 1987. David Edwin Harrell, Jr. Papers, 1923-2017, Center for Restoration Studies MS #467. Abilene Christian University Special Collections and Archives, Brown Library, Abilene Christian University, Abilene, TX. The letter was written in response to a July 13, 1987, *Newsweek* article by Kenneth L. Woodward and Frank Gibney, Jr., who misidentified Harrell as a Pentecostal following his authorship of a biography on Oral Roberts.

the broader culture. The two most prominent of these sectarian groups in the twentieth century were the Churches of Christ and the various churches spawned by the healing and charismatic revivals of the early and mid-twentieth century. At a personal level, Harrell had experienced the double sting of being both a member of Churches of Christ, which in the mid-twentieth century were seeking and increasingly attaining respectability in the broader society, and the "anti's"–the congregational churches of Christ. With their principled congregationalism and counter-cultural focus on independent evangelism and "saints-only benevolence," the congregational churches were self-consciously bucking the broader mid-century religious movement towards more respectable status among Protestant denominations, such as the Lutherans, Episcopalians, Presbyterians, Southern Baptists, and Methodists.

Harrell's subsequent historical focus on the "Southern Religion" of the 19th and 20th centuries was, therefore, a natural successor to his earlier inquiry of his own religious movement and its "backwoods" and "other side of the tracks" reality and reputation. As fellow historian of the Churches of Christ, Richard Hughes, once observed, "... Harrell's work on the Churches of Christ has informed and shaped everything he has done over the course of a long career, including his study of Pentecostalism, evangelicalism, and southern sectarian movements."[2] But more than an apologetic historiography for his own faith, Harrell's focus on sectarian, Southern churches was borne of his own experience and insight that he and his fellow Christians in the congregational churches of Christ were not alone in being dismissed by cultured and mainline Christian despisers. Here his experiences as a youth

---

2 Richard T. Hughes, "David Edwin Harrell, Jr. and the History of the Stone-Campbell Tradition," in *Recovering the Margins of American Religious History*, edited by B. Dwain Waldrep & Scott Billingsley (Tuscaloosa: University of Alabama Press, 2010), 24.

played a part in shaping his scholarly sensibilities. His childhood years in northern Florida and southern Georgia had opened his eyes to an entire substratum of religion in the South that was most often unseen or ignored by scholars.

> I saw the marginal groups as a boy, and I knew there was a whole lot there beyond the Episcopalians. Oral Roberts came for a crusade when I was seventeen years old and set up a great big tent. Thousands of people poured into the tent and I went to see what it was about. My fellow students would ask me: "What are you doing?" But my experience was that my friend went to an Episcopal church with twenty people. Here was Oral Roberts with hundreds of people every night.[3]

What Ed saw as a boy and explored as a maturing historian was the societal dissonance between the respected denominations and the popular sects of both his day and the previous century. His colleagues in the historical guild would look back and recognize this emphasis throughout his career, and appropriately observe that Ed had set about the task of "recovering" both awareness and understanding of the peculiar people and leaders that had formed Christian groups like the Assemblies of God, Church of the Nazarene, Free Will Baptists, Pentecostal Fire Baptized Holiness Churches, Emmanuel Holiness Church, the Church of God of Prophecy, Cumberland Presbyterians, Primitive Baptists, New Testament Holiness, Church of God of the Mountain Assembly, Inc., and the churches of Christ.

---

3. David Edwin Harrell, Jr., in discussion with the author, May 20, 2019. For parallel accounts of Harrell's teenage encounter with Oral Roberts see David Edwin Harrell, Jr., "Recovering the Underside of Southern Religion," in *Autobiographical Reflections on Southern Religious History*, edited by John B. Boles (Athens: University of Georgia Press, 2001), 47, 39-52; and David Edwin Harrell, Jr. *Oral Roberts: An American Life* (San Francisco: Harper & Row, 1985), ix.

Varying in size, teaching, and regional origin, what all these sectarian groups shared in their origin was: 1) lack of monetary wealth; 2) a surplus of conviction about Biblical truth and community; 3) a derision by other more established Christian groups; and 4) a general disregard by most historians of American Christianity. That these religious sects were the object of Harrell's scholarship is well known and is his legacy in the academic guild of church historians. What is less recognized, and important to understanding the motivations and outcomes of Harrell's work, is that his historical "recovery" of these sectarian movements was not merely scholarly curiosity, or denominational apologetics, but an intellectual and spiritual quest to understand the "true believer," especially the psychology of leaders in sects that were closest to Harrell's own conservative, restorationist viewpoint. This scholarly journey manifests itself in what was widely regarded as evenhanded, fair-minded scholarship, but it also exhibits consistent attention to three questions that occupy the course of his career and impact the global influence that he would have among churches of Christ:

What do believers seek to restore about New Testament Christianity?

What is the difference in the responsibilities of these restorationist believers as individuals and as congregations, respectively?

How do these individuals, especially the leaders, seek to advance the gospel of Jesus Christ in the world?

In addressing these questions, Harrell describes the primitivist purpose, the congregational constraints, and the missionary methods of Christian sectarian movements. These are three leitmotifs that run through Harrell's work on religious sects in the South, both as interpretive lenses and as pragmatic conclusions to his histories. These notes of emphasis are then picked up, recombined, and played as significant parts in the Christian editorial and evangelistic work that form another facet of Harrell's life that run parallel to his work as a university professor.

Harrell's academic work was shaped by the fact that he taught as a history professor in mostly flagship state universities of the southeastern United States. Following his aborted attempts for employment at Lipscomb College and Central Christian College, he was offered and accepted a teaching position at East Tennessee State University (ETSU) beginning in 1961. He continued at ETSU until 1966 after earning tenure in 1964. He departed for the University of Oklahoma in the fall of 1966 and then for the University of Georgia in 1967, where he stayed for three years. His annual salary at ETSU was $10,080 ($104,000 in 2024 dollars, adjusted for inflation), which raised to $13,000 at UGA in 1967-68.[4]

---

4. Dossett, Burgin, "Confirmation of 1966-67 employment," Series 1.B.2, David Edwin Harrell, Jr. Papers, 1923-2017, Center for Restoration Studies MS #467, Abilene Christian University Special Collections and Archives. Davison, Fred, "Notice of Appointment for the Academic Year." 1.D.1. His salary at UAB would rise to $38,300 in 1978. "Letter from Virginia Hamilton to Ed Harrell," I.F.6. In 1995 his salary at Auburn was $97,239 (~$190,000 in 2024, adjusted for inflation) plus benefits. (I.G.12). These salary figures show the upper middle-class status that Harrell's academic posts afforded him, and his increasing affluence over the course of his career, which mirrored many post WWII professionals of the "Silent Generation," and bespeaks the challenge of maintaining conservative religious conviction and a personal focus on a heavenly home after this life. As Harrell often observed, upward mobility and affluence often undermined a Biblical Christian faith that deemphasizes social respectability and this-worldly contentment. This was increasingly a challenge in congregational churches of Christ in the twentieth century. The question of whether this counter-cultural stance among these churches will endure in an era of rising educational and financial levels among members is a question underlying this biography of Harrell and the churches in which he preached.

Now in his early thirties at ETSU, Harrell quickly became one of the students' favorite professors, renowned for his stylish clothing and his sarcastic wit. His theatrics in the classroom included reports of playing a banjo at the front of the lecture hall to illustrate the merging of American folk and religious tunes. A student at ETSU in 1962-63, Gary Kulhanjian,

1962 Vanderbilt PhD graduate, Dr. David Edwin Harrell, Jr.

recalled that he was inspired by Harrell's knowledge and learning. Harrell's example led the nineteen-year-old student to pursue his own fifty-two-year-long career in teaching history at the secondary and collegiate levels.

> I had told him that he was my favorite professor at East Tennessee State University. His classes were always filled, and his lectures were exciting ... he would walk into class with notes but hardly referred to them while teaching and lecturing. His charisma was boundless. We talked about his lectures everywhere on campus. My favorite story was when he received his Ph.D. and walked into class with a happy and surprised look. The students had purchased a watermelon for the celebration and had a red crepe paper

"red carpet" for him to walk on from his office to the classroom.[5]

For the first ten years after graduate school, Harrell continued to publish articles based on his dissertation research on such topics as slavery, pacifism, taxation, and sectional divisions among the Disciples of Christ and Churches of Christ.[6] The first volume of his dissertation on the social history of the Disciples of Christ was published by the Disciples of Christ Historical Society in 1966 and that fall ETSU offered him the position of Dean of the Graduate School. Harrell declined and would often in his later years recall how he usually eschewed administrative posts during his career, seeking to focus on his teaching, research, and writing. Though he wanted to teach at the University of Georgia, "because Daddy had gone to school there," he accepted a job offer in 1966 from the University of Oklahoma to teach in their History Department.[7] After

---

5. Email from Gary Kulhanjian to Adelia Harrell, August 8, 2021. Copy in possession of the author.

6. Scholarly articles related to his dissertation included, David Edwin Harrell, Jr., "The Disciples of Christ and Social Force in Tennessee, 1865-1900," *The East Tennessee Historical Society's Publications*, 38 (1966): 30-47; "Sin and Sectionalism: A Case Study of Morality in the Nineteenth Century South," *Mississippi Quarterly*, 19 (Fall, 1966): 157-170; "The Sectional Origins of the Churches of Christ," *Journal of Southern History*, 30 (August, 1964): 261-277; "The Disciples of Christ and the Single Tax Movement," *Encounter* 26 (Winter, 1964): 261- 277; "The Fervent Frontier: Religion in the Trans-Appalachian West, 1790-1820," *Watauga Review* 1 (Fall, 1962): 28-36; "Disciples of Christ Pacifism in Nineteenth Century Tennessee," *Tennessee Historical Quarterly* 21 (September, 1962): 263-274; "Brothers Go to War," *World Call* 43 (October, 1961): 6-15; "The Sectional Pattern: The Divisive Impact of Slavery on the Disciples of Christ," *Discipliana* 31 (March, 1961): 26-28; "The Agrarian Myth and the Disciples of Christ in the Nineteenth Century," *Agricultural History* 41 (April, 1967): 181-192; "The Significance of Social Force in Disciples History," *Integrity* IX (October, 1977) 67-73; "From Consent to Dissent: The Emergence of the Churches of Christ in America," *Restoration Quarterly* 29 (Second Quarter, 1976): 98-111.

7. David Edwin Harrell, Jr., in discussion with the author, May 20, 2019.

only one year in Oklahoma (when he delivered the aforementioned Reed Lecture at the Disciples of Christ Historical Society), he received an offer from the University of Georgia, where he would teach for three years until 1970, and published two biographical essays on religious reformers, Pardee Butler and James Shannon.[8] "It was raucous at Georgia," Harrell recalled. Deep fissures emerged in the History department over leadership and disregard of the preferences of a majority of the faculty, including Harrell.[9] The department had grown rapidly due to an influx of funding. There were seven new faculty, and the old and new groups clashed. "Soon after I arrived, fifteen faculty members left, and each went on to soon write a book. Fifteen books out the door."[10] These circumstances and another offer from a flagship state school, the University of Alabama at Birmingham, positioned him in 1970 to accept a full professorship as chair of the History Department. He would later step down from the chair role in order to pursue more fully research, publication and teaching.[11] With the exception of one year as a Senior Fulbright Lecturer in India (1976-77) and five years at the University of Arkansas, as a visiting professor (1980-81) and as a distinguished professor of history (1981-85), Harrell would spend the next twenty years of his career in successively senior roles at the University of Alabama, departing there in 1990 as a University Scholar in History. In 1989, Harrell applied for a Breeden Eminent Scholar position at Auburn. This "super-endowed

---

8. David Edwin Harrell, Jr., "James Shannon," *Missouri Historical Review*, 63 (January, 1969): 135-170. "Pardee Butler: Kansas Crusader" *Kansas Historical Quarterly*, 34 (Winter, 1968).

9. Harrell, David Edwin, Jr., "Letter to Carl Vipperman, January 5, 1972," Series I.F.1, David Edwin Harrell, Jr. Papers, 1923-2017, Center for Restoration Studies MS #467, Abilene Christian University Special Collections and Archives.

10. David Edwin Harrell, Jr., in discussion with the author, May 20, 2019.

11. Harrell, David Edwin, Jr., "Letter to George E Passey," I.F.3 Series, David Edwin Harrell, Jr. Papers, 1923-2017, Center for Restoration Studies MS #467, Abilene Christian University Special Collections and Archives.

chair," as Harrell termed it, was funded by Auburn alum Daniel F. Breeden and provided funding for seven distinguished faculty positions at the university. In his application for the Eminent Scholar role, Harrell cited two reasons for his application: 1) the ability to impact doctoral students in the active field of American religious history; and 2) his arrival at Auburn alongside his good friend Wayne Flynt in the same department "would make Auburn the most visible program in the country for the study of Southern religion."[12] The search committee agreed. The public announcement of his appointment in the Auburn newsletter quoted the dean of the college to this effect: "Dr. Harrell will join with Dr. Wayne Flynt on our History faculty to bring Auburn University international recognition in the field of Southern religious history."[13] He left the University of Alabama in 1990 to become the Daniel F. Breeden Eminent Scholar in the Humanities at Auburn University, where he served until his retirement in 2005, with the notable exception of a two-year Distinguished Fulbright Grant that brought him to India to direct the American Studies Research Centre in Hyderabad. During the years at Auburn, his travel and research was supported by a $20,000 annual research budget, and a $4,400 operating budget.[14] In his final years at Auburn, Harrell taught three courses per fall semester and would go on leave in the spring semesters.[15]

---

12. David Edwin Harrell Jr., "Letter to the Breeden Scholar Search Committee, August 3, 1989," Series I.G.2, David Edwin Harrell, Jr. Papers, 1923-2017, Center for Restoration Studies MS #467, Abilene Christian University Special Collections and Archives.

13. "UAB Historian Harrell Named Breeden Scholar," *AU Report* 23.13 (April 19, 1990), 1.

14. Wicky Henkels, "Letter to March Pitzer, January 6, 2000," Series 2.G.12, I.F.3 Series, David Edwin Harrell, Jr. Papers, 1923-2017, Center for Restoration Studies MS #467, Abilene Christian University Special Collections and Archives.

15. The courses he taught in the fall included Survey of US History since 1887, American Religious History, and Contemporary History. Auburn University, "Americanists Course Rotation," Series II.G.12, David Edwin Harrell, Jr. Papers,

Contexts for creativity are important, and these sites of scholarship afforded Harrell a degree of independence from religious orthodoxy in denominational schools and access to resources for scholarly conference, research, and writing that were important to his productivity. His research crisscrossed religious lines of allegiance and increasingly depended on national and international travel. His university posts enabled not only comparative understanding of marginal, understudied religious groups across the world, but also provided for a unique respectability and availability as a traveling preacher among churches of Christ in the US and India for over half a century.

Harrell's move to Alabama in 1970 at the age of 40 led to his emergence as a historian of sectarian Christian groups in the American South. The previous year, in July 1969, fellow preacher and historian Steve Wolfgang first met Ed. "He was young, sandy-haired, and rugged," recalls Wolfgang. "He was driving around the South that summer attending a lot of Pentecostal camp meetings ... I was enthralled."[16]

These summer trips marked Harrell's transition into a study of relatively unknown Pentecostal groups in the South. This work had begun back in 1969-70 with trips to nine denominational libraries across the country, focused on "the attitude of radical Southern sets toward the Negro since 1945."[17] This was research for his first major monograph following the publication of the first volume of his dissertation research, which had included a chapter on the 19th century Disciples of Christ and their attitudes about race and

1923-2017, Center for Restoration Studies MS #467, Abilene Christian University Special Collections and Archives.

16. Steve and Bette Wolfgang, in discussion with the author, May 28, 2021.

17. David Edwin Harrell, Jr., "Description of Research Plans to Dean McWhorter, March 25, 1969," Series I.D.1, David Edwin Harrell, Jr. Papers, 1923-2017, Center for Restoration Studies MS #467, Abilene Christian University Special Collections and Archives.

slavery. The book, *White Sects and Black Men in the Recent South*, was published in 1971 by Vanderbilt Press. Harrell originally wanted to entitle the book "Redneck Religion," but was dissuaded by the publisher, who suggested the chosen title. The title would cause Harrell trouble on the speaking circuit. He would repeatedly have to clarify that the second word of the title was spelled S-E-C-T-S. The potential for confusion with the similar sounding word, "sex," was on full display in his phone call to his mother during which he shared news of the book's publication. After hearing the title of the book, she misunderstood the word in question and proclaimed in dismay: "What do you know about that?"[18] Hilarity ensued.

The book, which was nominated for a Pulitzer Prize, is an analysis of the racial views and actions of sectarian churches in the South, which he termed "radical cult-type religion."[19] In the book, Harrell turns to analysis of racial views he engages with contemporary scholarly analyses of the socio-economic stratification of the United States and the Southern states.[20] Harrell seeks to demonstrate that attitudes toward racial differences between blacks and whites were less segregationist among the poorer, more sectarian religious groups than among the mainline middle-class churches. This latter, more affluent group identified less with African Americans of the day because of their differing socio-economic status. The book concludes that sects, because they draw frequently from the lowest, most dispossessed classes, often display the least racial prejudice in their leadership and community life. This observation was counter-intuitive to uninformed readers, who likely expected a more racist

---

18. Deedee Harrell, in discussion with the author, November 16, 2020.

19. David Edwin Harrell, Jr., *White Sects and Black Men in the Recent South* (Nashville: Vanderbilt, 1971), 12.

20. Harrell, *White Sects and Black Men*, 115. Among the contemporary works that Harrell utilizes is W. Lloyd Warner, *Social Class in America: A Manual of Procedure for the Measurement of Social Status* (New York: Harper & Row, 1960).

view among "backwood," "redneck" religion in the South. Harrell knew better than to presume this.

> I was conscious from childhood of levels of Christians, including blacks and whites. I knew this because I stayed on the farm so much. I knew groups had distinctive places, for example, Blacks were welcomed as Christians but in different ways. My work on *White Sects and Black Men* showed how mainline churches would try to defend themselves by saying they had blacks, but they were not visible. In reality, there was a "third world" of black churches in the American South that often connected to poor, white churches.[21]

This insight is a classic example of Harrell upending conventional understandings of the lower-class religious groups. In this vein, he showed that some in the churches of Christ fit neatly into the pattern of complex, but counterintuitive inclusion of African Americans.[22]

In its attention to the sectarian churches, *White Sects and Black Men* presages the next twenty years of Harrell's academic focus on the charismatic movement and faith healers. Reporting to the university administration in 1973, Harrell detailed over three years of two dozen trips gathering materials for his work on faith healing in the US since 1945.[23] The book also focused

---

21 David Edwin Harrell, Jr., in discussion with the author, May 20, 2019.

22. The book and its identification of churches of Christ as a "sect" garnered criticism from across the theological spectrum of churches of Christ and editors among them, e.g., Cecil Willis, ""White Sects and Black Men," *Truth Magazine* 16.16 (February 24, 1972): 3-5: "But I am a member of the Church of Christ, and I do object to the Lord's church being represented as just another 'sect.'" Negative reviews of the book also occurred in the *Firm Foundation*.

23. David Edwin Harrell Jr., "Three-year research report, March 13, 1973," Series I.F.3, David Edwin Harrell, Jr. Papers, 1923-2017, Center for Restoration Studies MS #467, Abilene Christian University Special Collections and Archives.

on religious doctrines, ideas that Harrell had described in his dissertation and that he would develop more polemically in his teachings among churches of Christ, including identification of sectarian doctrines spanning across different Christian groups. Most notable is the teaching that "the church, as opposed to an individual, cannot become adequately involved in social reform."[24] Viewed as a "doctrine of separation from the world," this concept is cited not only from among writers of *The Christian Chronicle* and *Firm Foundation* ("mainstream" publications among Churches of Christ), but also from other sectarian publications like *Pentecostal Evangel* (Assemblies of God) and *Pentecostal Holiness Advocate* (Pentecostal Holiness Church).[25] Sometimes termed "saints only benevolence," this is a teaching that local congregations should, based on Scriptural precedent, avoid proactive efforts to improve their secular environment or to solve broader societal problems either directly or through cooperation in parachurch organizations. Though often individual Christians would engage in broader charitable activities beyond the local church, Harrell observes in these poorer and largely rural sects a Biblically based and pragmatically oriented focus on support for their own Christian family, with a congregational focus for benevolence.[26]

As Harrell did regularly in his writing, the final paragraphs of *White Sects and Black Men* provide a predictive, even prophetic expression. Foreshadowing his 2005 textbook on the role of religion in the history of the United States, Harrell concludes: "the student who would understand Southern society must study religion, the Southern religionist who would understand his church must understand Southern society."[27] The understanding of society

---

24. Harrell, *White Sects and Black Men*, 71.
25. Ibid., 48.
26. Ibid., 94-95.
27. Ibid., 134.

Ed and Deedee Harrell with children, Millie, Eddie, Elizabeth, Lee and Robert Harrell (Jan 1975, after first stay at the Institute for Ecumenical and Cultural Research in Collegeville Minnesota).

in *White Sects and Black Men* that gave insight into religion was that racial segregation (or lack thereof) among Christians was not primarily the result of a denomination's formal teaching about society, but rather of the economic class of churches and the corresponding religious psychology of the members. If one is to understand the social consciousness of the modern Southerner, Harrell concludes, then "it is not through self-righteousness and bombast, but by careful analysis of class interests and the psychology of the common man."[28] Though he does not say so explicitly here, Harrell leaves little doubt that this is a salvo launched at the liberal religionists of his time who viewed improvement of racial and other social standing as a religious mission to the

---

28. Ibid., 134.

masses and not an already lived reality among local congregations of the poor, who might be better learned from than taught. In making this point, Harrell repeatedly emphasizes the "otherworldliness" of the sectarian groups and their emphasis on the salvation of souls over the amelioration of society in general. These doctrinal points, of course, aligned with Harrell's own viewpoint as well as that of the congregational churches of Christ, which is one of the marginalized sects under analysis in his book. But these understandings of otherworldly soteriology and congregationalist polity and social ethic are achieved by Harrell, not through dogmatic assertion, but through historical classification and sociological analysis of sectarian religion.

It is noteworthy that the book's study of religious cults emphasizes Oral Roberts as the most well-known and successful of post-World War II faith healers.[29] Roberts not only impresses in the book as an example of a moderate, and relatively inclusive perspective on race relations in the mid-20th century, but also as an embodiment of the other-worldly focus of lower-class Southern sects and cults. Harrell observed, "When faced with the theoretical ethical problem of racial injustice, Roberts has consistently reacted with typical sectarian otherworldliness ... 'I don't dabble in politics—I just preach the Gospel and win souls.'"[30]

This biographical treatment of charismatics among the "white sects" is prelude to the next major monograph written during Harrell's first decade at the University of Alabama: *All Things are Possible: The Healing & Charismatic Revivals in Modern America*.[31] Notably published by Indiana University Press, a major

---

29. Ibid., 33ff.

30. Ibid., 102.

31. David Edwin Harrell, Jr., *All Things are Possible: The Healing & Charismatic Revivals in Modern America* (Bloomington: Indiana University Press, 1975).

university publishing house, the book established Harrell is among the foremost experts on the history of the independent, often schismatic Protestant sectarian groups comprising the Pentecostal revivals that flourished and morphed throughout the early and mid-20th century. These revivals occurred first in the United States, predominantly in the American South, and then around the world to an extent that is now widely recognized by scholars as of epochal significance. Harrell researched and completed the book during a sabbatical stay as a Research Fellow at the Institute for Ecumenical and Cultural Research in Collegeville, Minnesota in 1974. His family went with him to the ecumenical institute–a longstanding writing retreat for scholars—and it was a time for growth for the whole family, as he shared to the director of the Institute in his research report:

> I want to say one final word about the personal ecumenical impact of the Institute for Ecumenical and Cultural Research. No member of my family had ever attended a Catholic mass before coming to Minnesota. I was the only member of the family who had ever spoken to a priest, a nun, or a monk, and my experience had been limited indeed. Our visit opened a whole new world to us, as I expect exposure to me opened a new world for some people in Collegeville. If an ecumenical spirit begins with understanding–and I believe it does–our visit at the Institute was an important episode in our lives.[32]

All Things are Possible was heralded both for its evenhanded cataloging and comparison of Pentecostal movements that had

---

32. Harrell, Jr., David Edwin, "Research Report, 1975," series I.F.4, David Edwin Harrell, Jr. Papers, 1923-2017, Center for Restoration Studies MS #467, Abilene Christian University Special Collections and Archives.

theretofore not received much scholarly attention, and for the sympathetic retelling of the lives of Pentecostal leaders like Jack Coe, A.A. Allen, William Branham, and, most notably, Oral Roberts. The biographical format of much of the history was not lost on its reviewers. In *New York Times Book Review*, Harvey Cox observed that the biographical way that Harrell had chosen to tell the story "makes for lively reading."[33] Reflecting in the late 1980s on what would become his life-long penchant for the genre, Harrell observed how writing biography intrigued him:

> I think it is a genre that particularly fits my writing style. The thing that most fascinates me about biography, however, is how certain lives seem to encapsulate a culture, clarifying the emotions and subjective mind of the masses. It is those cultural nuances (captured best, it seems to me, in narrative descriptions) that most interest me. At the same time, I remain a historian at heart and all my writing is based on exhaustive research. I would be uncomfortable telling stories that were not well grounded in fact.[34]

When *All Things are Possible* was published it attracted attention and admirers because of its factual reporting of the beliefs and practices of faith healers. The book described their deeply held and often self-sacrificing religious convictions about the power of the Holy Spirit to speak directly and miraculously act in the lives of believers. Also appreciated by reviewers of the book was the author's description of the internal debates and doubts about the reality and

---

33. Harvey Cox, "All Things Are Possible," *New York Times Book Review* (February 22, 1976): 2. The quote is printed as a blurb advertisement on the back cover of the 1975 paperback edition of *All Things Are Possible*.

34. David Edwin Harrell, Jr., "Proposal for a Biography of Ian Paisley, [1987]," series I.N.2, David Edwin Harrell, Jr. Papers, 1923-2017, Center for Restoration Studies MS #467, Abilene Christian University Special Collections and Archives.

rectitude of the faith healers' claims, as well as the external critiques from medical doctors and non-charismatic Christian groups, both mainline and marginal. As he repeatedly observes in the book, leaders among the churches of Christ were among the most vocal opponents to the Pentecostal claims of miraculous gifts of the Holy Spirit in the post-apostolic age.[35] Though not identifying his own religious identity specifically, Harrell acknowledges his own demurral from the theological claims of the healing and charismatic religious movements that he aims to treat objectively:

> As it happens, I do not share the religious presuppositions
> of the charismatic revivalists, but in my many conversations
> with them, I have insisted that my own religious views are, if
> I do my job properly, irrelevant to the telling of the story.[36]

In addition to illuminating the origins, trajectories, and chief characters of the Pentecostal movement from 1947 to 1974, Harrell advanced a historical interpretation of development of the various independent healing revivals. He distinguished two phases of the revival: the "healing revival" and the "charismatic revival." For the first phase, Harrell portrays a diverse movement of independent revivalists focused primarily on the miraculous gift of healing the sick. During the first decade of the movement, the charismatic personas and presumed miraculous gifts of these evangelists were "the spark" that set off the claims of religious healing of thousands of believers with enough faith to receive the Holy Spirit's power. But by the mid-1950s the ecstatic enthusiasm and ecumenical unity among a fragmented movement began to wane.[37] Opposition by medical professionals, the press, and even the Internal Revenue Service placed increased pressure on a movement already viewed

---

35. Harrell, *All Things are Possible*, 62, 100, 230.
36. Ibid., ix.
37. Ibid., 95-96.

by the broader culture and other Christian groups as outside the boundaries of respectable religion. The growing authority and coordination of the General Presbytery of the Assemblies of God exhibited the classic trajectory of the "sect-to-denomination" framework popularized by Max Weber, Ernst Troeltsch, and Reinhold Niebuhr. It is a sociological evolution utilized by Harrell as a historiographical lens for understanding the development of small, but growing radical and subaltern groups into larger, more accommodating, and increasingly mainstream denominations, such as the Assemblies of God.

In his analysis, Harrell notes that the early Pentecostals appealed to a Biblical theology of miraculous healing rooted in Biblical passages, as well as the example of the miraculous gifts of early Christians and the reception of the baptism of the Holy Spirit in Acts.[38] While these restorationist impulses remained in the second phase of the revivals, they were increasing softened and accommodated broader cultural and denominational goals towards institutionalization and cultural acceptance, including the Assembly of God's enforcement of rules about religious services and the financial dealings of the church's ministers.[39] The charismatic movement was accepted into some mainline Protestant denominations—most notably Oral Roberts' move into the United Methodist Church—and into Roman Catholicism as a revitalizing, but tightly controlled accommodation. Harrell depicts how the Pentecostal movement shifted increasingly towards the "prosperity gospel" with revivalists supplanting the emphasis on miraculous healing with a turn toward the promise of financial prosperity for followers who would give money to the charismatic ministries.[40]

---

38. Ibid., 84-85. Biblical proof-texts for the Pentecostals included Hebrews 13:8; John 14:12; 15:7; James 4:10; 5:15.

39. Ibid., 231.

40. Ibid., 229.

The increasing appeal of the movement to the middle class also meant a greater emphasis on the "psychosomatic" impact of the Spirit's healing and coordination with the benefits of medical sciences and educational institutions—symbolized most powerfully by the formation of Oral Roberts University, with its education of the whole person (body, mind and spirit).[41]

Harrell emphasizes the impact of denominational and broader cultural influences on the individual healing ministries that had been more independently but still effectively coordinated in the earlier phase of the movement:

> By the 1970's the charismatic revival had gone through cultural evolution much like other historical religious movements. The independent ministries, once the spearhead of a simple revival with a powerful appeal to simple people, eventually adapted their styles to needs of vastly different social groups. What was once a homogeneous revival became a heterogeneous movement, united only by a few doctrinal themes and a common heritage.[42]

In this way, Harrell describes a sectarian, restorationist movement that began from the individual authority of prophetic figures among local congregations of the poor and dispossessed, with an emphasis on the New Testament promise of the Holy Spirit's power for individual believers, and with an outreach that progressed "on the sawdust trail" (an image of the walkway leading to the front where the healings occurred) of tent meetings and direct financial support of independent ministries. Through detailing the broader social forces set upon the Pentecostal movement, Harrell shows how the revivalists began with a primitivist appeal to New Testament spiritual gifts and Biblical passages that connected these

41. Ibid., 154.
42. Ibid., 232.

miracles to physical health, as in 3 John 2: "Beloved, I wish above all things that thou mayest prosper and be in health, even as thy soul prospereth."[43] Harrell further shows how the early individual and spiritual authority of the local revivalist and the independence of the local ministry were domesticated by both new and longstanding denominational identities that moved them towards social respectability, large-scale growth through missions and new media, and increasing emphasis on the social needs of the broader society, as opposed to the spiritual and bodily needs of the individual believer. The now standard interpretive themes of Harrell's scholarship are now here in play, both illuminating marginalized religious movements and providing sociological understanding as to why the historical changes and diverging theological paths occur.

Stepping back to look at the broader trajectory of Harrell's academic career, the decade of the 1970s at the University of Alabama was one of intensive research and engagement in scholarly associations. Almost every year he applied for and received research grants from the University of Alabama or the Institute for Ecumenical and Cultural Research in Collegeville, Minnesota, where he and the family retreated for his writing. His engagement in national scholarly societies increased during these years, with growing involvement as a chairman in the Southern Historical Association, which was the leading scholarly organization on the topic of history in the American South and was Harrell's primary academic society for the next twenty years. In this vein, he served as a national consultant for the Center for the Study of Southern Culture at the University of Mississippi and ascended to the Executive Council of the Southern Historical Association in 1980, where he would serve in different capacities throughout the next decade, including as Chair of the Program Committee in 1987.

---

43. Ibid., 229.

These collaborations were formative for Harrell's identity as a historian of the American South. The effect of these associations in the academic guild was twofold. First, it established him as a pioneer in the relatively new academic discipline of Southern religious history. As his colleague and fellow historian Charles Reagan Wilson later wrote: "David Edwin Harrell Jr. is one of the founding fathers in the study of religion in the American South."[44] Second, the scholarly community around Southern Religions that Harrell helped to lead placed his academic interests in marginal sectarian movements at the heart of conferences and publications that were produced by these academic conferences and other associations. His steering role in the scholarly conversation in the 1970s was on full display in his creation of the Hugo L. Black Symposium at the University of Alabama in 1978. His colleague, Virginia Hamilton, had written a book about Hugo Black, who was an Alabama state senator and long-time associate U.S. Supreme Court justice. Hamilton and Harrell arranged a conference about him in Birmingham. The conference was high profile with William Martin, Martin Marty and other well-known historians.[45] The publication in 1981 of the papers presented at the conference was edited by Harrell and entitled *Varieties of Southern Evangelicalism*. It marks a high point in his leadership of the association of historians of Southern religion.

In his introduction to the book, Harrell acknowledges the differences among the Southern Evangelicals that are the focus of the collected presentations. These are distinctions between mainstream denominations and the smaller sects, between inclusive and more

---

44. Charles Reagan Wilson, "David Edwin Harrell Jr. and the Broadening of Southern Religious Studies," in *Recovering the Margins of American Religious History*, edited by B. Dwain Waldrep & Scott Billingsley (Tuscaloosa: University of Alabama Press, 2010), 33.

45. Deedee Harrell, in discussion with the author, November 16, 2020.

exclusive styles of religious leadership, and between empathetic and ecstatic religious expression—from heart-warming songs of Christian piety to nerve-wracking handling of snakes. But Harrell leaves his most recognizable stamp on the book in his summary of the distinctiveness of Southern religious experience, which is found in the degree to which it expresses certain theological beliefs:

> Southern Evangelicals have been more individualistic, less confident in social reform, more literal in their views of the Bible, more moved by personal religious experience; southern religion has been more given to sectarianism in the twentieth century—or so it is argued in this book. More obvious, the South has been the most solidly evangelical section of the country .... The Bible Belt was a well-entrenched stereotype by the early twentieth century, and it was one with clear substance to it.[46]

This overview of Southern Evangelical religion also summarizes the themes of Harrell's own scholarly interests and emphases, notwithstanding the fact that the identification of the Churches of Christ as an "evangelical" movement has been much debated. The book's argument for the prominence of sectarians in the South is seen primarily in Harrell's contribution, entitled "The South: Seedbed of Sectarianism," which explores what Harrell terms "another layer of religion" beneath the media-grabbing Fundamentalists (like Jerry Falwell) and the mainline denominations, like the Southern Baptists.

Harrell's essay depicts two religious viewpoints. First are the upwardly mobile, middle-class denominations. And second are the more virulent, narrow Christians who fragment off from of these mainline groups with an exclusionary stance towards the

---

46. David Edwin Harrell, Jr, "Introduction," in David Edwin Harrell, Jr., ed. *Varieties of Southern Evangelicalism* (Macon: Mercer University Press, 1981), 2.

mainstream churches, and "who doubt the eternal salvation of their most devout neighbors."[47]

Under Harrell's reading, these "sectarian" groups, most prominently the Churches of Christ and the Assemblies of God, are separated from established religion by the social stresses of the Civil War, migration, new technology, and poverty. They then consolidate around the realities of their lower class status, which has the effect of making them less racist and more supportive as individuals and independent congregations of the poor working class that constitutes their underclass culture and church membership.

The evangelical upshot of this sectarian spirit is a sectarian gospel that dismisses this-worldly social reform and political action and heralds other-worldly salvation. Harrell put it this way:

> The heart of the sectarian gospel ... was a three-pronged message which gave spiritual meaning to poverty, offered an otherworldly escape, and held out a slim hope for miraculous relief from suffering.[48]

This escapist theology offered hope in this world for a better life in the world to come. It offered meaning for a bleak existence by accepting poverty and suffering as a permanent, but purposeful existence. As Harrell notes in conclusion, the upward mobility of members of these sects, particularly in the Churches of Christ and Assemblies of God, was making them less effective in the United States; the richest harvest of the gospel to the poor was increasingly found overseas in places like Puerto Rico, the Philippines, and Latin America. It is an observation about the global migration and growth of religious sects that would prove prescient for Harrell's own

---

47. David Edwin Harrell, Jr, "The South: Seedbed of Sectarianism," Pages 45-57 in David Edwin Harrell, Jr., ed. *Varieties of Southern Evangelicalism* (Macon: Mercer University Press, 1981), 46.

48. Ibid., 54.

future work in India and the growth of Christianity in the Global South more broadly.[49]

Now in his fifties in the early 1980s, Dr. Edwin David Harrell, Jr., the historian of religion in the American South, was in full professional bloom. The full scope of his expertise in the field and his sharpened definition of the interpretive themes identified earlier are on display in an essay presented three years after his "Seedbed of Sectarianism" essay at the Hugo Black Conference in 1979. Here again in the context of an academic conference, this time on the "Varieties of Southern Religious Experience," Harrell combines the depth of his knowledge of the 19th century origins of revivalism with his more recent development of the social origins of Pentecostalism. The result is an essay on "The Evolution of Plain-Folk Religion in the South" that surveys the drive towards societal respectability among Protestant denominations in the 19th and early 20th centuries, and the ways these elevations of wealth, educational achievement, and institutional formation of missionary societies produced a backlash among lower class Christians, particularly in the South. Examples include the formation of the Cumberland Presbyterians, Primitive Baptists, Baptist Landmarkism, the Disciples of Christ, and the various sects arising out of the Holiness movement in the late 19th century, including the Church of the Nazarene. All these relatively conservative groups, though formed in different contexts, were commonly shaped in response to the liberal tendencies and denominational apparatus of the Baptists and Methodists in the early and mid-19th century. These conservative Protestant groups, together with the related

---

49. On the growth of global Christianity see Philip Jenkins, *The Next Christendom: The Coming of Global Christianity* (London: Oxford, 2011). For the relevance of this shift to a North American context, see John B. Weaver, "Theological Libraries and The Next Christendom: Connecting North American Theological Education to Uses of the Book in the Global South," *Theological Librarianship* 1.2 (Winter 2008): 38-48.

"antimission movement" and the subsequent rise of Pentecostal churches in the early 20th century, form what Harrell terms "plain-peoples churches." Many adherents of this plain-folk religion preach a "Biblical-primitivist belief that all church-related organizations were unscriptural" and reassert "emphasis on the independence of the local congregation."[50] As one would expect, Harrell details how some of these churches, particularly the Cumberland Presbyterians and the Disciples of Christ, "evolve" into the denomination structures and middle-class social concerns that they had originally opposed. Fragments of these newly formed denominations break off and repeat the cycle of plain folks' primitivist reading of the Bible, with its congregationalism, evangelistic concern for spiritual salvation, as opposed to broadscale societal amelioration. They provide, instead, a local concern for the physical well-being of church members.

Many of these analytical categories were now well-worn historical lenses in the Harrell repertoire, but two new interpretive moves will emerge and recur in his work in both academic and church-oriented contexts. First, the nomenclature of "plain people" and "primitivist" belief makes their first appearances as descriptions of the sectarian, lower-class movements that Harrell studied since graduate school. Second, to the fullest extent that he would explore in his scholarly works, Harrell describes the congregational benevolence of plain-people, primitive churches. The social significance of the religious communities of the plain people is often overlooked by mainstream Christians, Harrell observes, because they are "misled by the simplistic theologies of the sects, their disinterest in politics and social reform, their opposition to organized social Christianity, and their intense individualism

---

50. David Edwin Harrell, Jr. "The Evolution of Plain-Folk Religion in the South, 1835-1920," in *Varieties of Southern Religious Experience* (Baton Rouge: Louisiana State University Press, 1988), 28-30.

...".[51] In contrast to these misperceptions, primitive Baptist group and churches of Christ, among others, are seen to exhibit care both for the poor and vulnerable of their own communities in feeding and clothing widows and orphans, and in their own "individualistic and limited way" extending their concern to others in the neighborhood.[52] The simple churches of plain folk are seen, therefore, as focused as a group on benevolence for the saints in the local congregation, and also as doing good to others more broadly as individuals as need and provision allow.

Underlying these and other writings about the religious history of the South is Harrell's repeated emphasis on these movements' origins in poverty and how this produces a distinctive, sectarian social ethic and theology. Religion among the poor promotes a literal reading of the Bible, a focus on earthly suffering and heavenly reward, and a localized focus on the social condition of the local congregation, with individualized concern for charitable action in the broader world. On the one hand, this is a simple approach necessitated by simple conditions. In this way, primitivism is a product of circumstance. On the other hand, Harrell's history seeks to correct academic and mainline misunderstandings of simple-folk religion. Namely, he shows that, though it is different than middle-class, institutionalized religion, "the churches of the poor succeeded because they insisted on being religious in their own way, in their own places, and with their own preachers."[53] There is then both a reclaiming of awareness of the "margins" of the Christian religion in the South, and also a prophetic call to action to reengage these marginalized sects, though this call to action always comes most directly through the past voices of historical sources that Harrell quotes.

---

51. Ibid., 44.
52. Ibid., 45.
53. Ibid., 46.

During the 1980s, Harrell launched two research and writing endeavors that would garner him the most national notoriety during this career: book-length biographies of Oral Roberts and Pat Robertson. These books continued Harrell's work in Southern evangelicalism and Pentecostalism, and reopened a biographical approach to religious history that would characterize much of his work for the rest of his life. Harrell had written several article-length biographies of religious figures, extending back to his earliest days in graduate school. More recently he had focused on multiple biographical accounts of Pentecostal revivalists in *All Things Are Possible*. But the Oral Roberts and Pat Robertson projects were his first book-length biographies and Harrell threw himself into them with aplomb. He relocated to the University of Arkansas to study Oral Roberts nearer to the Pentecostal leader's home and university in Tulsa, Oklahoma. With the assistance of his long-time friend, Willard Gatewood (history professor and later chancellor at the University of Arkansas in Fayetteville), Harrell first arrived in Arkansas as a visiting professor in 1980, and was appointed a distinguished professor of history from 1981-1985.[54]

A retrospective reading of Harrell's work in the 1970s on the healing and charismatic revivals of the mid-twentieth century makes it unsurprising that he pursued a biography about Oral Roberts. Roberts, who was the leading Pentecostal leader of his generation,

---

54. Harrell spent a full quarter in 1980 at the University of Arkansas as a Visiting Professor of Regional Studies, and was granted a leave of absence from the University of Alabama without pay. David Edwin Harrell, Jr., "Letter to Virginia Hamilton, May 16, 1980," I.F.6, David Edwin Harrell, Jr. Papers, 1923-2017, Center for Restoration Studies MS #467, Abilene Christian University Special Collections and Archives. When Harrell left UAB to serve as a Distinguished Professor of History at the University of Arkansas, Fayetteville, his assignment was 12 semester hours per calendar year and an expense account of $2,500. Timothy Donovon, "Letter to David E. Harrell, February 4, 1981," Series I.F.10, David Edwin Harrell, Jr. Papers, 1923-2017, Center for Restoration Studies MS #467, Abilene Christian University Special Collections and Archives.

was generally ignored by the scholarly community. Harrell notes that no "serious and objective book had been written about him," and that the most celebrated textbook survey of contemporary American religions barely mentioned him.[55]

Harrell worked five years on the Oral Roberts biography, until its publication in 1985. Writing in 1983 to his department chair at UAB, Harrell reports spending three months in Tulsa and being the first ever allowed into the Oral Roberts archives. Harrell reported on his preparation for beginning writing later that year:

> Oral is very bright, and he understands exactly what I am doing. In one of our conversations, while I was asking his help in lining up interviews with Billy Graham and other hard-to-get types, he said, 'I want you to be sure to interview all of my enemies, too.' I assured him that he didn't need to worry about that, but I was delighted to know that he wants a genuinely reputable book. Won't really know until he sees it, and I have gathered some penetrating criticisms of him, but if he likes it ....[56]

The publication of the Oral Roberts book by Indiana University Press in 1985 (and subsequently the paperback edition through Harper & Row in 1987), for which he received a $10,000 advance and did a national book tour, showed that Harrell could work effectively with a large trade house publisher.[57]

---

55. David Edwin Harrell, Jr., *Oral Roberts: An American Life* (San Francisco: Harper & Row, 1985), viii.

56. David Edwin Harrell, Jr., "Letter to Virginia Hamilton, 22 February 1983," Series I.F.9, David Edwin Harrell, Jr. Papers, 1923-2017, Center for Restoration Studies MS #467, Abilene Christian University Special Collections and Archives.

57. Roy M. Carlisle, "Letter to Patricia Newforth about Harrell project on Oral Roberts, December 10, 1985," series I.N.28, David Edwin Harrell, Jr. Papers, 1923-2017, Center for Restoration Studies MS #467, Abilene Christian University

Now an established author, his 1987 contract with Harper & Row Publishers for the Pat Robertson biography was the most lucrative of his career, with an advance of $40,000. The book explored why and how Pat Robertson emerged as an important religious and political figure. It was written for a more widespread audience than Harrell's previous works, with fewer footnotes. Exploring Robertson's personal and political roots up to 1959 (when he reportedly spoke in tongues), Harrell explores the political career of Robertson's father and the sources of his theology as a Southern Baptist. Harrell shows how Robertson's background made him an anomalous Charismatic leader, and how his Charismatic identity led to tensions among fundamentalist Christians and national voters. Of special note to Harrell is Robertson's use of technology, especially the rise of the Christian Broadcasting Network (CBN) television network, as one key to Robertson's rise from the grassroots level as a serious presidential candidate.

In addition to his research and writing as a professor, Harrell also taught regularly at the graduate level during the latter half of his career, including a seminar on American Religious History that usually included approximately 15 students. Harrell was known for his insightful and entertaining classroom lectures and his accessible style. "We loved him," recalled one of his former graduate students. "He walked around in sweatpants and swinging an imaginary golf club most of the time. He had a real easy-going nature about him, but you knew that come test time, you better be prepared."[58] In his peer evaluation of Ed's teaching late in his career at Auburn in 2001, fellow historian Bill Trimble reported that "in general, I was much impressed with what I saw." In addition to observing Harrell's proper pace, engagement, and humor, Trimble made special note of how Harrell's travel and worldwide experience enriched the

---

Special Collections and Archives.

58. Scott Billingsley, in discussion with the author, July 19, 2021.

class: "His personal knowledge of the area and contacts with people there provided an immediacy to the subject and helped keep the students' interest."[59]

The travel schedule that enriched his teaching also prevented Harrell from having as many doctoral students as other Auburn professors, such as Wayne Flynt. During the 1990s he would routinely teach three classes per year during one semester, with the other semester off for travel. Even during the teaching semester, Harrell would fly into Auburn on Monday, teach Tuesday through Thursday, and would be gone again by Friday to research or make a presentation elsewhere.[60] Despite this itinerant existence, Harrell managed to mentor a small cadre of doctoral students, including John Hardin, B. Dwain Waldrep, and Robert Vejnar. His final doctoral student, Scott Billingsley, had applied to Auburn to study the American Restoration Movement under Harrell's direction at the advice of historian Doug Foster, himself a renowned historian among the Churches of Christ. "As a mentor, [Harrell] was one of the most gracious and generous people I have ever met, but he was not a touchy-feely person. He was a cerebral guy. I had to get his schedule, get in, and talk about the most important things first. When I would see him start to swivel around in his chair to his computer, that was my signal to get out of there."[61]

In support of their dissertation research, Harrell introduced his graduate students to scholars and historical figures they needed to know. For example, Harrell flew out to Dallas with Scott Billingsley to assist him with interviews in Dallas and Tulsa in 2001

---

59. Bill Trimble, "Report on Visit to Ed Harrell, HIST 3670 Contemporary History, October 9, 2001," series I.G.21, David Edwin Harrell, Jr. Papers, 1923-2017, Center for Restoration Studies MS #467, Abilene Christian University Special Collections and Archives.

60. Scott Billingsley, in discussion with the author, July 19, 2021.

61. Scott Billingsley, in discussion with the author, July 19, 2021.

for Billingsley's dissertation research. Harrell taught his students to go in with a tape recorder and start-talking about what you wanted to know in a conversational type of interview. He had also written several letters recommending Billingsley to procure needed documents and interviews, including letters to Kenneth Copeland, Ken Hagin Jr, and Oral Roberts University. "I could not have done that work without Ed," Billingsley observed.[62]

Looking back on this trajectory of historical research and writing in the late 20th century, Harrell's colleagues in the academic guild of American church historians would write in the early 21st century about an "authorial heartbeat" running through his study of American religious history.[63] Retrospective descriptions of his scholarly work often observed his consistent effort to understand the religious faith of individuals on their own terms and to describe them objectively, even as he acted with consistent commitment to his own Christian beliefs.[64] In 2012, for example, the Duke historian Grant Wacker reflected on Ed's work as a model of "evenhandedness" and "objectivity," which narrated both the good and bad about people through a systematic and exhaustive reading

---

62. Scott Billingsley, in discussion with the author, July 19, 2021.

63. James R. Goff, "Elijah's Never-Failing Cruse of Oil: David Harrell and the Historiography of American's Pentecostals," in *Recovering the Margins of American Religious History*, 14. It is noteworthy that these commentators on his career later in his life included a veritable "Who's who" of church historians during Harrell's lifetime: from the oft-cited dean of church history at the University of Chicago, Martin Marty, to the Methodist historian, Grant Wacker, at Duke University, to other founding figures in the discipline of Southern religious history: Wayne Flynt, Samuel Hill, Charles Reagan Wilson, and James Goff (a Pentecostal historian, who was Harrell's first doctoral student), and Richard T. Hughes (the author of a widely utilized history of the Churches of Christ).

64. This absence of prejudicial polemic in Harrell's academic histories is affirmed broadly, including by Samuel S. Hill, David Edwin Harrell Jr. American Religious Historian," in *Recovering the Margins of American Religious History*, 12-13.

and an unbiased retelling of the primary sources. Harrell did this, Wacker observed, to tell the truth about how they saw themselves.[65] The term most used to describe this historical approach to religious voices was "fairness." It was an evidentiary, self-conscious approach to writing history that was both principled and pragmatic for Harrell. "Good historians understand that history is selective and not totally objective," he once observed, "but this is different from saying that [history] is just constructs of the imagination. A historian's story is based on evidence and logic."[66]

Harrell's evenhanded fairness in writing about those who differed from his own beliefs had manifested itself early on in his dissertation and in early essays and initial articles on the Disciples of Christ. Historian Richard Hughes recalled using Harrell's dissertation both as a graduate student and as a reading in his history courses while teaching. He would ask his students what they thought was the religious background of the author of the book on the social dynamics of the Restoration Movement in the 19th century. Given Harrell's objective focus on the social activism among many in the most progressive wing of the Restoration Movement, the students presumed that he was a liberal-minded member of the Disciples of Christ and were shocked to learn that he was a member of the most conservative group among the churches of Christ. Hughes reports that fellow students in his own graduate school program had jumped to the same conclusion.[67] The story

---

65. Grant Wacker, "Preface," in *Recovering the Margins of American Religious History*, xiv.

66. Harrell, David Edwin, Jr., "Homer Hailey's Personal Journey of Faith - Part 3," audio recording, February 20, 2001; (https://texashistory.unt.edu/ark:/67531/metapth792899/m1/, 28:00-28:11: accessed August 26, 2024), University of North Texas Libraries, The Portal to Texas History, https://texashistory.unt.edu; crediting Abilene Christian University Library.

67. Richard T. Hughes, "David Edwin Harrell, Jr. and the History of the Stone-Campbell Tradition," in *Recovering the Margins of American Religious*

illustrates the degree to which Harrell wrote without apparent bias about religious viewpoints different than his own. "When I first read his work," observed one of Harrell's former graduate students, "I was certain that he was a Disciple, that he was as far on the left side of the spectrum as you can get in our movement. And shortly before I went down to Auburn one of my friends, who was a mentor at Lipscomb, mentioned that Ed is an 'anti.' Sure enough."[68] Similarly, Harrell recalled once being told by a surprised student that he heard Harrell was an "anti." He responded: "You don't know the half of it: I'm an anti-anti."[69] Such accounts illustrate his reputation as one with a balanced approach to retelling history by relating different sides of the story as comprehensively as possible. It was an objective approach to historiography that he passed on to his students.

Scholarly reviews of his books on American religion in the 1970s and 1980s often highlighted his success in treating his subjects seriously and fairly. This objectivity was especially appreciated in the Pentecostal circles that became a focus of his scholarship during the middle-portion of his academic career.[70] The Pentecostal historian, James Goff, reports that among Harrell's major contributions was that "he dealt with Pentecostals fairly, accepting that they were genuine in their convictions ... He validated that Pentecostals and the theology they espoused could be studied objectively, with a healthy

---

History, edited by B. Dwain Waldrep & Scott Billingsley (Tuscaloosa: University of Alabama Press, 2010), 24-25.

68. Scott Billingsley, in discussion with the author, July 19, 2021.

69. David Edwin Harrell, Jr., in discussion with the author, May 20, 2019.

70. Some of these reviews are cited approvingly by Charles Regan Wilson in "Broadening of Southern Religious Studies," 36-37. Cf. the multiple citations of book reviews praising Harrell's fairness and evenhandedness assembled by James R. Goff Jr, "Elijah's Never-Failing Cruse of Oil: David Harrell and the Historiography of American's Pentecostals," in Recovering the Margins of American Religious History, 20-22.

degree of skepticism moderated by a degree of admiration for their tenacity and considerable list of accomplishments."[71] Some of his fellow believers among the churches of Christ would sometimes view it differently. To some Christians, like long-time preacher Paul Earnhart, Harrell's accommodation of different theological perspectives in his history was at first troubling. "I had an issue with his biography of the Tulsa miracle worker, Oral Roberts, when he said he thought he was an 'honest man,'" recalled Earnhart. "I finally came to grips with that when I realized that he was saying that he was not a hypocrite, but that he had a background that would have led to these sorts of visionary things." Earnhart had come to respect that Harrell was a fair-minded historian, but also that his fellow scholars knew Harrell's convictions: "There was no question about his own convictions; all his academic compatriots knew what they were, and they respected him."[72]

Indeed, fellow historians often observed the contrast between Harrell's historical objectivity and his personal religious commitment. In their reflections on his work they both praised him as "fair" and "generous," but also recognized him as "conservative," "not incapable of stiff-necked confrontations," "loves a good fight," "a pugilistic spirit," "no ecumenist," and "a lifelong member of the so-called anti-institutional wing of the Churches (or churches) of Christ."[73] In her concluding observations on Harrell's "very civil convictions," the historian Beth Barton Schweiger describes the "balance," "juxtaposition," and "tension" between his "starkly exclusionist view" that "a literal reading of the Bible is necessary

---

71. James R. Goff Jr., "Elijah's Never-Failing Cruse of Oil," 18.

72. Paul Earnhart, in discussion with the author, May 28, 2021.

73. Wayne Flynt, "Foreward," in *Recovering the Margins of American Religious History*, edited by B. Dwain Waldrep & Scott Billingsley, vii, xi; Grant Wacker, "Preface," in *Recovering the Margins of American Religious History*, xv; James R. Goff, Jr., "Elijah's Never-Failing Cruse of Oil," in *Recovering the Margins of American Religious History*, 22.

to salvation" and his "openness to and interest in those who disagree with him."[74] The purpose of this tension, she concludes, is "understanding, which holds out the prospect of peace, or at least, of somehow dulling human strife." In making this point about the irenic intention of Harrell's tolerant and generous historiography, Schweiger quotes from the concluding reflection in his 1966 Reed Lecture about the purpose of historical understanding: "I do not believe that we shall ever reach accord in things spiritual, but if we could attain the lower good of understanding why [humans come to different views of God], the insight would serve us well in our struggle with this life." The bracketed portion of this last sentence is inserted by Schweiger as an explanation that Harrell's historical "understanding" serves to recognize differences and live in peace with those who differ from us. And Harrell was, in fact, "civil" about his and different religious beliefs. He observes in his Reed Lecture that his theological point of view "does not imply that I would restrict anyone's right to believe as he pleases ...." And, indeed, much of his later work overseas as a Fulbright scholar was focused on interreligious dialogue and civil coexistence amidst religious differences. Further, this irenic spirit is seen during his deep involvement with debates in the 1990's among members of the congregational churches of Christ over the bounds of Christian unity, and to what extent and by what means Christians can maintain fellowship with those with whom they disagree on matters of core Christian doctrine. Both in scholarly and ecclesial contexts, therefore, Harrell's writings clarified the differences between religious beliefs, while also seeking to provide clear indication of how these different beliefs corresponded to the teachings of the Bible. His readers sensed, and sometimes chafed at, the tension between his compassionate explication of these differences in

---

74. Beth Barton Schweiger, "Conclusion: The Very Civil Convictions of Ed Harrell," in *Recovering the Margins of American Religious History*, 103.

historical Christian beliefs and his own conscientious conviction that one of these beliefs was true, corresponding to the Biblical reality. Harrell gives voice to this tension between Christian unity and conscience in one of his class lectures on the Restoration Movement:

> I'll tell you about Christian unity. All of us live with some dissonance. Somebody that thinks they don't has just got their head in the mud. But the question of how much dissonance I can tolerate is an issue of conscience. And any time you take a step toward Christian unity, you take a step away from conscience in some matter of conviction. So what everybody has to do is to decide how much can I compromise my own conviction in order to have relationships with other people ... It's a question that by and large implicates only what local church I can associate with.[75]

The churches with which he associated and whom he supported in preaching, writing, and funding missionaries were the congregational churches of Christ.

---

75. David Edwin Harrell, Jr., "Homer Hailey's Personal Journey of Faith—Part 3." Lecture delivered February 20, 2001, ACU Summit Lecture Series audio recording, February 20, 2001, (https://texashistory.unt.edu/ark:/67531/metapth792899/m1/, 52:00-53:00, accessed August 26, 2024, University of North Texas Libraries, The Portal to Texas History, https://texashistory.unt.edu; crediting Abilene Christian University Library.

Polemicist

"As long as brethren honor those who have no credentials but a knowledge of the word of God ... who are unafraid to speak their mind, who care preeminently that the truth prevails, who have no fear of open confrontation— that long, and just that long, can they feel secure about themselves. When the time comes that the churches honor respectable managers (and surely it will come again, though, I think, not in my lifetime) it will be time for every Christian to look in the mirror."[1]

In 1953, a 14-year-old Bill Calton and his family, including brother Gary and sister Sharon, were worshiping with their parents, George and Clytie Calton, at the Second Street church of Christ in Portales in east central New Mexico. Known for cattle ranches and peanut-

---

1. David Edwin Harrell, Jr., "B.C. Goodpasture: Leader of Institutional Thought," in Melvin D. Curry, ed., *They Being Dead Yet Speak*, Florida College Lectures (Temple Terrace: Florida College, 1981), 252-53.

processing, the small city of Portales was already home to two buildings with the name "Church of Christ" over the door.[2]

A local dairyman had given land to the other church in town, Pine Street (aka 4th Street) Church of Christ, which had built on the donated land a building to care for orphaned children. Bill's father, a preacher, and other members of the Second Street church had objected to the way the orphanage was being run outside the oversight of the local congregation, and the disagreement had grown to the point that the elders of the Second Street church announced that they were withdrawing fellowship from seven members of their church who disagreed about the ways the local church should work through institutions like orphanages and colleges.

That day of separation impacted Bill's father George, a preacher, his mother Clytie and seven other grown Christians including three Bible teachers. Including their children, around 30 people were told not to return to their home congregation. That evening, the elders posted two off-duty policemen at the door to bar reentry. Following their expulsion, those who were disfellowshipped immediately rented a room from the local American Legion for the 40-50 people that the new congregation would start with. They then set out to build a new church building. "I remember helping to mix the cement," Bill recalls.

Their building completed around 1955, the congregational church of Christ in Portales grew and appointed elders and hired a full-time preacher. To the present day, Bill and his sister Sharon worship with their family at the Portales Valley Church, which still

---

2. Bill Calton, in discussion with the author, November 12, 2023. An earlier, unpublished version of this chapter was presented at the 2024 Florida College Lectureship (Temple Terrace, FL) as, John B. Weaver, "David Edwin Harrell Jr. and Journalism Among Congregational Churches of Christ," February 6, 2024, YouTube video, last accessed September 9, 2024, https://www.youtube.com/watch?v=s2XDGJfj7Dw.

includes multiple members who remember the traumatic events surrounding the original split in 1953.[3]

The traumatic events of the 1950s were undoubtedly complex and multidirectional, felt by different sides of the division over institutionalism. We should dismiss both triumphalist accounts of the institutional division, and one-sided accounts of victimization. But the pain and sacrifice caused by the rupture over doctrinal difference fell especially hard on the Christians who could not in good conscience support congregational support for institutions outside the churches or networks of churches larger than the local church. The nature of the division was such that the money and property were most often retained by those supporting institutional outreach by local congregations. Preachers lost their jobs and were prevented from finding other jobs, Christian families lost their previous fellowships, and Christians across the country were displaced from meeting houses. In some cases they were actively harassed and reportedly slandered because of their conscientious concern for maintaining the New Testament example of congregational autonomy and the Biblical command to speak and act as the oracles of God. At the same time, these Christians were accused of unconcern and inaction in evangelism and benevolence. These charges came from Christians who supported congregational support of colleges, orphan homes, missionary societies, national radio broadcasts, and other businesses supported by one or more churches without direct oversight by a local eldership. The trauma was both a physical and social exile as well as a spiritual shaming. Despite widespread individual and congregational support of evangelistic efforts, adoption of orphans, and other benevolence, the charges against congregational churches of Christ that they were unlovingly dogmatic continue to the present day. These are charges of shallow callousness towards those in need, despite deep

---

3. Bill Calton, in discussion with the author, November 12, 2023.

conviction of conscience about the Scriptural pattern for Christian service.

As the preceding chapters suggest, the entry for David Edwin Harrell Jr. in *Who's Who in America* lists his many scholarly accomplishments and accolades as a dean of the academic study of American history, and especially the religion of the Southern United States in the 19th and 20th centuries.[4] Multiple honorary university appointments, governmental and academic career awards, and celebratory books—*Festschrifts*—written by adoring colleagues and students point to his recognition and honor in universities, politics, and even popular media. However, not generally recognized in these popular accolades was Harrell's personal adherence to and expression of a marginalized form of Christianity in the American religious scene: the congregational churches of Christ or "antis"—a choice term among dissenters among the institutional Churches of Christ. Throughout the time Dr. Harrell was a professor in increasingly distinguished positions, he was also an active contributor and polemicist within the religious periodicals that proliferated among this countercultural fellowship in the late 20th century.

The first twenty years of his writing for periodicals, from 1963 to 1983, was an eclectic mix of contributions to various journals, but most of his writing was done for *Vanguard Magazine*, started by evangelist editor Yater Tant in 1975.[5] Throughout these decades,

---

4. See for example the entry for Harrell in *Who's who in America*, 1990-1991 (Wilmette: Marquis Who's Who, 1990), 1397.

5. E.g., David Edwin Harrell, Jr., "The Emergence of the Church of Christ Denomination," 1962. (The essay was tract was reprinted repeatedly as a tract or article, for example in *Gospel Guardian* 18.40, 41, 42 [February 16, 23 and March 2, 1967); Cf. "Some Practical Observations on the Middle of the Road," *Gospel Guardian* 20 (September 5, 1968): 273-278; "Emergence of the Church of Christ Denomination Update," *Vanguard* 5.2 (January 25, 1979): 1, 14-15. The tract was published in 2005 by Harwell/Lewis publishing company (Lakeland, FL). With permission, it is included in the appendices of this book.

Ed Harrell in a picture used for a line-drawing portrait that depicted him in many of his *Vanguard* articles during the 1970's.

Harrell exhibits an awareness both of historical developments among churches of Christ that were unfolding around him and of his own participation in and contribution to that movement. His consciousness of the movement's development is seen, for example, in the repeated reprinting in *Vanguard* and other papers of his seminal 1962 essay on "The Emergence of the Church of Christ Denomination," with its critique of the upward mobility of progressive elements within the American Restoration Movement.[6] In his 1979 "retrospective elaboration" of the essay, Harrell affirms the correctness of his historical thesis concerning the three-way division of the Restoration movement between Disciples of Christ (Christian Church), Christian Churches, and Churches of Christ (a cappella). Harrell's famous observation that the Churches of Christ were, in turn, dividing into three sociologically and ideologically distinct groups, comes with the caveat that the most conservative group, the congregational churches of Christ, should not come to view itself as a denomination: "So, let's remember that what we begin with," Harrell concludes, "and what we are left with after denominational groups appear, is the undenominational church of Jesus Christ—no group."[7] In this way, Harrell seeks to retain the original non-institutional, non-denominational, "sectarian" identity for the most conservative elements of the churches of Christ. For some observers, this hardline approach in *Vanguard* was distinctive in Harrell's journalistic history. "If you go back and read Ed in the Uno/Duo and other things he wrote in the 77th Street Bulletin and in *Vanguard Magazine*, there's a sharp edge to Ed Harrell that is not present in *Christianity Magazine*," observed historian Steve Wolfgang. "It's almost like what was said of Alexander Campbell that after he got to be 'Mr. *Millennial Harbinger*' and College President; it somehow changed him."[8]

Whatever his later positions, Harrell's dogmatic conclusion in *Vanguard Magazine*—that the Lord's churches should and can be undenominational and congregational—is repeated in other Harrell articles during the 1970s and is characteristic of other religious

---

6. As seen in the previous note, the essay is reprinted across multiple months of *Vanguard Magazine* in both 1978-79 and 1983.

7. David Edwin Harrell, Jr., "Emergence of the Church of Christ Denomination Update," *Vanguard* 5.2 (January 25, 1979): 283.

8. Steve Wolfgang, in discussion with the author, October 17, 2022

journalism during this era. For example, Harrell writes that, in contrast to the Reformed Churches and other denominations which focus on self-serving institutions, Christians should seek simply to be Christians and relate only to a church of Christ, "not an American Christian, or an anti-Christian or a restoration Christian."[9] Though not a "restoration Christian," Harrell acknowledged that his call for unity and obedience based on the "one constitution which God has provided in his word" stemmed from the American Restoration Movement and particularly the 1809 "Declaration and Address" written by Thomas Campbell.[10] This return to unity based upon primitive Christianity stood in contrast, Harrell observed, to the mid-twentieth century "Evangelical" movement, which, like the earlier "Fundamentalist" movement, was inclusive of a broad spectrum of conservative Christian groups formed out of a desire for cultural power and social respectability, rather than Biblical truth.[11] Harrell's scholarship also contributed to his theological critique of the Pentecostal/Charismatic movement, of which he was one of the chief historians. Here again, his critique is comparative, observing that a Christian Charismatic would deny the truth of a Muslim's speaking in tongues such as observed in the Indonesian island of Java. But this same Charismatic would assert the genuineness of his or her own experience of speaking in tongues, which, as Harrell argues, is contrary to the New Testament's teaching about such miraculous gifts of the Holy Spirit, that they would end with the completion of revelation (1 Corinthians 13:8).[12] Closer to home, Harrell's call

---

9. David Edwin Harrell, Jr., "The American Dutch Reformed Chinese," *Vanguard* 5 (March 22, 1979): 121.

10. David Edwin Harrell, Jr., "Disciples Motto," *Vanguard* 5 (June 1, 1979): 106.

11. David Edwin Harrell, Jr., "Fundamentalism Again," *Vanguard* 5 (August 1, 1979): 241, 254.

12. David Edwin Harrell, Jr., "Javanese Tongue Speaking," *Vanguard* 7 (Feb 1, 1981): 40.

for Biblical unity opposed the methods of the Disciples of Christ as described by critics of their denominational businesses in the early 20th century. The growth of institutions such as the missionary society or (drawing in a more recent example among institutional Churches of Christ) the Herald of Truth ultimately supported more administrators than they did missionaries: "God's methods bring glory to God and Man's methods bring glory to man."[13] In addition to criticizing church support for worldly institutions, Harrell quotes long-time preacher F. D. Srygley to support the simplicity of church buildings. The extravagance of church buildings beyond the basic size and needs of the local congregation was evidence of "a human rather than a spiritual value system."[14] This "on the march" mentality of the progressive Churches of Christ was the target of Harrell's parody on more than one occasion during the 1970s, contrasting the simple gospel proclaimed in local churches with regular baptisms to the large new programs of worldly wisdom that were, in fact, leading to declining membership. The question to such "on the march" Christians is "where are you going?"[15]

This is a polemical approach to writing in religious periodicals that is meant to distinguish congregational churches from institutional Churches and to draw historical parallels between this theological division in the mid-20th century and the prior divisions of Churches of Christ from Disciples of Christ in the late 19th and early 20th centuries. It is a confrontational approach that is especially prominent in the 1950s-1980s and that continues to the present day.[16]

---

13. David Edwin Harrell, Jr., "Wrong Attitudes Beget Wrong Practices," *Vanguard* 6 (August 1, 1980): 173.

14. David Edwin Harrell, Jr., "The Church and Human Pride," *Vanguard* 6 (Sept 1, 1980): 335.

15. David Edwin Harrell, Jr., "On the March," *Vanguard* 7 (March 1, 1981): 63.

16. See, for example, Mark Mayberry, "Editorial: Progressive Perverseness,"

When Harrell began writing for *Vanguard Magazine* in 1975, the periodical was one of at least five new papers started in 1975-76. This brought the total number of subscribed papers among the congregational churches of Christ to at least thirteen, based on the observation of one contemporary survey.[17] Stepping back with a broader sweep of history, we can identify at least 36 periodicals that were initiated among congregational churches of Christ and available for subscription in the second half of the twentieth century, including one that is still active in the present day: *Truth Magazine*.[18] Of course, the Restoration Movement included many periodicals

---

Truth Magazine 68.2 (February, 2024): 3-13. Mayberry harkens back to the division between the Disciples of Christ and the Churches of Christ as evidence of a tendency towards liberalism and digression in the church: "Over time, the leftward drift of progressive mindset becomes ever more pronounced. The sundering of the restoration movement in the nineteenth century initially resulted in a division between the Christian Church (on the left) and Churches of Christ (on the right) ... The sundering the restoration movement in the twentieth century initially resulted in a division among the institutional churches of Christ (on the left) and non-institutional churches of Christ (on the right)" (6). This analysis reflects the influence of Harrell's historical conclusions regarding the sources and outcomes of division in the American Restoration Movement.

17. Jeffry Kingry, "Know When to Drop a Subscription," *Sentry Magazine* 1.1 (January 31, 1974): 3-4. See the contemporaneous survey of new journals by Cecil Willis, "New Papers Galore" *Truth Magazine* 18.6 (December 12, 1974): 82-87. Online at: https://www.truthmagazine.com/new-papers-galore. Last accessed July 24, 2024.

18. Roger Shouse, "Brotherhood Papers," *Christianity Magazine* (January 1993): 9. Cf. Roger Shouse, *A History of Publications Among Brethren in the Churches of Christ* (Greenwood, IN: Roger L. Shouse, 1991), 35. These three dozen magazines are part of a much larger tradition of journalism among churches of Christ. One survey of periodicals by members of the churches of Christ reported that there have been 571 papers published since the beginning of the American Restoration Movement, with 89 still being published among churches of Christ of all types in 1993, including the oldest paper that was still being published and associated with brethren in the Churches of Christ: *Gospel Advocate*, first published in 1855. In the present day, even the *Gospel Advocate* has ceased publication, at least for a time.

prior to the 1950s and the headwaters of the non-institutional journalism in the American Restoration Movement goes all the way back to what is widely recognized as the first religious newspaper in the United States, and perhaps the first in the world. *The Herald of Gospel Liberty* was published by Elias Smith on September 1, 1808, with a primitivist appeal to Christians to return to obedience to the Scriptures and liberation from human religious traditions and denominational organizations.[19]

This primitivist appeal for congregational and undenominational Christianity is broadly attested in journalism among Churches of Christ in the late 1940s through the mid-1980s and beyond. The first sustained journalistic turn towards a critique

---

19. Elias Smith, *The Herald of Gospel Liberty* 1.1 (September 1, 1808): 1-4, available online at https://digitalshowcase.oru.edu/hsbooks/3 Last accessed January 5, 2024. Aware that his efforts at a religious newspaper were the first of its kind, Smith writes weekly from Portsmouth, New Hampshire, on the efforts at religious liberty in his day. By "religious liberty," Smith explains, he means those efforts to overcome the interference of authorities, institutions, and their laws in the religious beliefs and practices of individuals. Smith reports on various revivalist efforts to overcome institutional structures for Christian faith, including ordinations outside traditional clerical authorities and the 1804 dissolution of denominational organization by the "Last Will and Testament of the Springfield Presbytery," which eliminated church government beyond the local congregation. The document was famously signed by Barton W. Stone whose fellowship with the primitivist group known simply as the Christians would merge with the associates of Alexander Campbell on January 1, 1832, and form the core group of what became known as the American Restoration Movement, or Stone-Campbell Movement. Most noteworthy in *The Herald of Gospel Liberty* are the themes of spiritual submission to God's Word, religious "simplicity" in adhering to the pattern of the New Testament, and opposition to church authorities and government larger than the local congregation. These themes recur in subsequent restorationist periodicals, including Alexander Campbell's early journalism in the *Christian Baptist* (1823-30), and in the late 19th and early- to mid-20th centuries in the movement's most long-standing journals, the *Gospel Advocate* and the *Firm Foundation*, both of which aired different views over the institutional issues into the mid-20th century.

of institutionalism in church work is seen in the early writing of Foy E. Wallace and his brother Cled E. Wallace in the 1930s, beginning with the first *Gospel Guardian* in 1935.[20] In his introduction to the periodical, Wallace announces his intent that the mission and policy of the periodical is "controversial—doctrinal to the core." He also affirms the need to review and reaffirm the restoration plea and "remove preachers [who] are becoming mere pastors, presidents of Ministerial Associations, stage performers and star actors at worldly clubs." This concern over denominational traditions and institutions is extended to the Christian colleges of his day—"Schools have been tempted to abandon their original purpose to vie with the standards of worldly schools."[21] These early Wallace articles against growing support for colleges, homes, and societies bring to the surface three emphases that became thematic to congregational churches of Christ and the journalism that represents them in the twentieth century:

1) A critique of the institutions that divert the churches from their mission and the restoration plea.

2) A warning against preachers and teachers promoting denominational and institutional beliefs.

3) A call for Christians to empty themselves of religious traditions and worldly standards in service to Christ.

The first emphasis regarding churches using institutions to do

---

20. Foy E. Wallace, Jr., "The Gospel Guardian," *Gospel Guardian* 1 (October 1935): 1-2. Wallace announced that the journal's "special attention will be given to some doctrinal errors, including premillennialism." This includes over 75 articles on the topic, many of them authored by Foy E. Wallace, Jr., in the two years of the journal's publication. Other prominent themes include critiques of Baptist doctrine and other denominationalism. Cf. Terry J. Gardner, *The Original Gospel Guardian (1935-1936) and The Bible Banner (1938-1949) Indexed by Author and Subject Complied by Terry J. Gardner with A Biographical Sketch of the Life of Cled E. Wallace* (Indianapolis, Indiana: Terry Gardner, 1994), 15.

21. Ibid.

their work is evident in many of the articles in the first two years of *Gospel Guardian* in the 1930s. The articles by O. C. Lambert are illustrative of this theme, opposing congregations who appoint a board of regents over orphanages or put the orphanage under the eldership. Lambert concludes: "When the New Testament churches contributed to the support of Paul or the relief of the distressed, they did so as individual congregations. They had no get-together meetings, no interlocking committees nor any other machinery tying the congregations together."[22] Opposition to institutional support of evangelism, edification, and benevolence is repeatedly evident in the 1930s.[23]

The same theme is evident in Wallace's journal publication, the *Bible Banner*, which from 1938-40 was "devoted to the defense of the Church against all errors and innovations." In his opening editorial, Wallace opposes the "doctrinal softness" pervading the churches, especially the "institutionalism" seen in the affiliation of the colleges and churches: "The current campaign to put Abilene Christian College in the budget of churches in Texas is one example of it. When it is said that 'the church that does not put the college in its budget does not have the right to a preacher'—that is college domination."[24] This focus on institutionalism was continued in

---

22. C. O. Lambert, "The Problem of Organized Cooperation," *Gospel Guardian* 2.3 (Mar-Apr 1936): 32.

23 Similarly, in the March/April edition from 1926, C. A. Norred writes negatively towards using the local congregation for "public material benevolence" to care for the sick and poor: "The individual therefore who would employ the church in the field of public benevolences undertakes a work for which there is no inspired example and for which there exists no divinely approved machinery." See C. A. Norred, "A Home\ily on Benevolences," *Gospel Guardian* 2.3 (Mar/Apr 1936): 39. See also the opposition to colleges supported by businesses, churches and association with regional accrediting agencies, John T. Lewis, "Bible Colleges as I See Them," *Gospel Guardian* 2.4 (May 1936): 4.

24. Foy E. Wallace, Jr., "Editorial," *Bible Banner* (July 1938): 2-3. On ACC President G. C. Brewer's statements in 1930 supporting church financial

Foy Wallace, Jr's 1950 publication of *Torch* magazine. Here Wallace begins the publication by denying that the churches should fund the colleges because it ignores the nature and mission of the church.[25]

Following this early journalism in the first half of the 20th century, the *Gospel Guardian* was restarted in 1949 with the purpose of combating institutionalism and human organizations that promoted a program larger than the individual local congregation.[26] Launched now by Foy E .Wallace and Fanning Yater Tant, the periodical was overtly "combative" in orientation, including repeated appeals to the remnant of God's people, and often focused upon the difference between the churches of Christ and the Christian Church as related to the Biblical pattern.[27] In 1949, the publication was already promoting Florida Christian College, including a letter written by the college's new president Jim Cope to Fanning Yater Tant affirming that the college would not accept contributions from churches, even as it maintained an amicable relationship to other schools and brethren with whom the faculty disagreed on matters of opinion.[28] The debate was still alive in 1949 concerning whether or not churches should fund colleges, as is noted in a news piece regarding the planned Central Christian College at Bartlesville, Oklahoma, founded by L.R. Wilson, president of the school and former president of Florida College.[29] At that time the bylaws of

---

support of colleges, see W. W. Otey, "From the Written Record—Brother Brewer's Memory," *Gospel Guardian* 5.34 (January 7, 1954): 11.

25. Foy E. Wallace, "Compendium of Issues," *Torch* 1.1. (July 1950): 5.4-22.

26. Foy E. Wallace, "The Issues Before Us," *Gospel Guardian* 1.1. (May 5, 1949): 3.

27. E.g., Thomas Allen Robertson, "The Christian Church—How They Got That Way," *Gospel Guardian* 1.1. (May 5, 1949): 5.

28. Fanning Yater Tant, "Jim Cope and Florida Christian College," *Gospel Guardian* 1.5 (June 2, 1949): 2.

29. Fanning Yater Tant, "The Overflow: The Bartlesville School." *Gospel Guardian* 1.21 (September 29, 1949): 8.

the articles of the Oklahoma college prohibited contributions from churches. It was a policy on non-acceptance of church funds that was reportedly adopted by Abilene Christian College for a time, and reportedly opposed by Freed-Hardeman College.[30]

The next major non-institutional periodical was the *Preceptor*. Launched by members of the faculty of Florida Christian College in 1951, the *Preceptor* was announced as an effort to encourage Christians and to be an aid to evangelism of non-Christians.[31] As

---

30. Fanning Yater Tant, "The Overflow: New Policy for Abilene Christian College?" *Gospel Guardian* 1.28 (November 17, 1949): 1. The complexity of the institutional issue is illustrated later in 1949 by articles by G. K. Wallace and Homer Hailey on the topic of orphans' homes. These were viewed as acceptable if run by local elderships, even if under the oversight of a separate board of directors. As one reader perceptively inquired, "If giving to an orphan home thus operated would not constitute a 'super-structure' over and above the local congregation, why would giving to a Christian college, similarly set up and operated, constitute a 'super-structure' and tend toward destroying the autonomy of the local church?" G.K. Wallace, "Orphan Homes," *Gospel Guardian* 1.28 (November 17, 1949): 1; Homer Hailey, "Dependent Children," *Gospel Guardian* 1.28 (November 17, 1949): 5. This later article had been previously published and was disavowed by Hailey in later years. Cf. N.B. Hardeman, "Spending the Lord's Money," *Gospel Advocate* 92 (May 29, 1947): 372, and "The Banner Boys Become Enraged," *Firm Foundation* 64:43 (October 28, 1947): 1; Foy E. Wallace, Jr., *Bible Banner* (September, 1947): 16; The argument advanced by N.B. Hardeman that the orphanage and the college "stand or fall together" was later presented by Batsell Barrett Baxter, *Questions and Issues of the Day in the Light of the Scriptures* (Nashville, 1963), and reviewed by James R. Cope, *Where Is the Scripture?* (Temple Terrace, FL), 1964; and James P. Needham, *A Review of Batsell Barrett Baxter's Tract: "May the Church Scripturally Support a College?"* (Orlando, FL: Truth Magazine Bookstore [reprint], 1970). Another supporter of church support of colleges is J.D. Thomas, *We Be Brethren: A Study in Biblical Interpretation* (Abilene: Biblical Research Press, 1958), 186-194. On this history, see especially Steve Wolfgang, "Speech Delivered at the Nashville Meeting: History and Background of the Institutional Controversy (1)," *Guardian of Truth* 33.7, (April 6, 1989): 208-211.

31. Launched by members of the faculty of Florida College in 1951, *The*

in the *Gospel Guardian*, the *Preceptor* advanced the comparison of institutional churches of Christ to the Disciples of Christ and their "foreign-to-the-New-Testament-pattern" of support for church cooperation and human institutions. The "digression" in the "liberalism" and "modernism" of the "liberal wing of the Disciples of Christ Denomination" was still a relatively recent historical experience for mid-20th century writers, and there were apparent similarities to the secularization of church functions among progressive Churches of Christ supporting church organizations larger than the local church.[32] For the next 60 years under different editors, until its dissolution in 2011, the pages of the *Preceptor* would emphasize the undenominational and noninstitutional nature of the church.

This same thematic opposition to denominationalism and institutionalism is seen in subsequent periodicals, from *Truth Magazine* (begun in 1956) to another popular publication, *Searching the Scriptures* (started in 1960).[33] The continuity of this doctrinal polemic is perhaps best illustrated by the periodical,

---

Preceptor was announced as a desire to "balance positive and negative" in its writings. The journal was an effort to avoid the doctrinal wranglings and personal attacks that had become prominent in some journals and would continue to appear as a primary mode of journalism for the next fifty years. See James R. Cope, "The Preceptor," *The Preceptor* 1.1 (November 1951): 2-3.

32. Ibid., "The Church and Community Agencies," *The Preceptor* 1.5 (March 1952): 5. Cf. G. K. Wallace, 'The Difference Between the Christian Church and the Church of Christ II," *The Preceptor* 2.1 (November 1952): 8.

33. In his description of periodicals among congregational churches of Christ in 1989, Steve Wolfgang reports the subscription levels: "The largest of these are the monthlies *Christianity* and *Searching the Scriptures* with about 6500 and 5500 subscribers, respectively. *Guardian of Truth* (the result of the 1981 merger of the *Gospel Guardian* and *Truth Magazine*) is issued twice monthly, has about 4500 subscribers," Steve Wolfgang, "History and Background of the Institutional Controversy (3)," *Guardian of Truth* 33.9 (May 4, 1989): 272-275. Online at: https://www.truthmagazine.com/archives/volume33/GOT033130.html#N_4_. Last accessed on February 3, 2024.

Torch, which was among the first journals of the noninstitutional movement. In 1950, Foy E. Wallace Jr. launched *Torch*, freeing himself of primary editorial work for *Gospel Guardian* and *Bible Banner*. In *Torch*, Wallace explicitly sought to hold and pass the torch of sound teaching following the death of his father and the aging of a generation of leaders, such as R. L. Whiteside and A. G. Freed, especially as relates to the issues of the day, and specifically regarding church funding of colleges and missionary organizations. Wallace observes with dismay the direction that the more "liberal" and "progressives" are going, in a way nearly as harmful as the more reactionary groups that he had fought in previous years:

> It is a pity that after we have made the fight against the cranks, anti-class, anti-literature, anti-college and anti-everything, that liberalists and extremists are now running away with things, disarm us, and all but make us wish we had not made the fight against the hobbyists, for between the two their cranky notions are less harmful. I am not anti-Sunday school (when it is a Bible class on Sunday); nor anti-literature (when it is the right kind); nor anti-college (when it is not made a church school); nor anti-missionary (when the New Testament way is observed)—but I am anti what is going on.[34]

Though Wallace soon departed as editor, *Torch* continued for nearly 40 years. The periodical was published by J. P. Needham from 1970-1986, during which time its subscription was built to about 2,000.[35] In its final issue, with a circulation of around 740, before a reboot as the magazine *Gospel Truths* in December 1989 under editor J.T. Smith, a three-page expose of institutionalism by David Bonner quotes from Foy Wallace Jr. in 1931 and other early

---

34. Foy E. Wallace, Jr., "Comment," *Torch* 1.1 (July 1950): 29.

35. See J. T. Smith's history of *Torch* on the back page of the final issue of *Torch* 24.12 (December 1989) under the title of "Finis."

twentieth century preachers taking sides during the institutional division that "took place from about 1952-1956." Bonner connects these issues to the "New Hermeneutic" approach to cultural interpretation of the Bible at ACU in 1989, which, among other things, allowed women worship leaders.[36] Also present throughout the issue is the militant spirituality that rejects unbiblical practices and ideas, but that also stands firm in opposition to the new hermeneutical approaches.

Reflecting on these new methods of interpretation, historian John Mark Hicks attributed the search for a new hermeneutic to the controversy over institutionalism.

> The hermeneutic essentially imploded under the weight of the institutional controversy. It appeared to many that the noninstitutional advocates were rigorously and as consistently as possible applying the hermeneutic but their [mainstream] own Biblical-theological instincts could not agree with some of the noninstitutional conclusions (e.g., refusal to use money from the church treasury to help the unbelieving poor). The hermeneutic led to another division which disillusioned some and emboldened them to seek a different hermeneutical path.[37]

---

36. David Bonner, "Biggest Departure Now!!" *Torch* 24.12 (December 1989): 5-7.

37. John Mark Hicks, "Stone-Campbell Hermeneutics VI—Appreciation and Critique," Personal Blog, June 1, 2008. Online at http://johnmarkhicks. wordpress.com/2008/06/01/stone-campbell-hermeneutics-vi-appreciation-and-critique/. Cited by Gardner Hall, "Sewell Hall: A Combination of Convictions and Forbearance," Unpublished Manuscript, 118. At the 1990 "Dallas Meeting," Harrell would observe that the main difference between the institutional and congregational churches was that the former was loyal to the denominational idea of the Churches of Christ and the latter was loyal to the restorationist hermeneutic of the Bible. "The Dallas Meeting | 1990 | Uniting Institutional & Non-Institutional Churches of Christ | Day 1," YouTube video, Last accessed September 9, 2024, https://www.youtube.com/watch?v=pcOTk15eGaA.

This emphasis on the New Testament pattern and doctrinal polemic is also seen in *Sentry Magazine*, which began in 1974, a generation after the explosion of the controversy over institutionalism in the early 1950s. The editor, Floyd Chappelear, sought to justify the creation of yet another periodical among congregational churches of Christ. He gives three reasons. First, the "old guard" of preachers who fought the battles over institutionalism were aging out and dying off, observes Chappelear regretfully. Second, the trajectory of "brotherhood papers," beginning with *Gospel Guardian* in 1949 and *Truth Magazine* in 1956 did not exhaust the ability and interest of capable writers in the fellowship of conservative churches of Christ, nor do any of these other papers provide the perspective of Christians in the northeastern United States. (*Sentry Magazine* was published in Fairfax, Virginia.) And third, *Sentry* focused on individual Christians, especially their spiritual lives, and not only preachers. It did not seek "to be part of any political structure which may arise to regulate the brotherhood." This was part of a broader thematic emphasis on the humility of Christians to "not think too big" about their faith.[38]

Chappelear's introductory essay and many subsequent articles in *Sentry Magazine* illustrate several journalistic themes that point to theological priorities among congregational churches of Christ in the mid to late-20th century. There is emphasis on Biblical patterns for church work and a repeated distinction between individual and collective responsibility for benevolence. Articles in *Sentry Magazine* also often express the non-institutional arguments

---

38. Floyd Chappelear, "Editorial," *Sentry Magazine* 1.1 (January 31, 1974): 3-4. See for example the focus on the virtue of humility like Jesus ["Humility," *Sentry Magazine* 1.2 (July 31, 1975): 11], and spiritual submission to God's word by Kenneth Frazier, "As the Oracles of God," *Sentry Magazine* 1.7 (July 31, 1975): 6. The magazine's focus on Christian abnegation (denial of self and service to others) comes primarily through pervasive attention to Christian families and their various Biblical roles (spouse, parent, children).

and invoke allied preachers and periodicals arising from the 1950s fight with the "heresy" of institutionalism.[39]

In addition to this tradition of polemical journalism against church businesses, there was a second theme in Harrell's articles from *Vanguard* in the 1970s that is echoed in the broader context of brotherhood periodicals during the surrounding decades: a critique of institutional preachers and a related caution about upward mobility among younger preachers in the congregational churches. This was a theme of what we might call pastoral admonition, or supervisory warning about changes in theological attitudes caused by sociological shifts among the population of the congregational churches of Christ in the United States. This cautionary note is an expected motif after the "biggism" and "on the march" mentality of institutional churches of Christ in the 1940s and 1950s. The focus on worldly growth and glory among institutional churches is broadly recognized as part a broader national attitude after WWII that leveraged newfound social and economic affluence in pursuit of numerical growth and cultural acceptance.[40] In this vein, Harrell notes in 1979 that the "conservative churches" among churches of Christ were also subject to an "evolution" and "major sociological dividing."[41] While he does not describe the likely outcome of this

---

39. Floyd Chappelear and other *Sentry* writers repeatedly affirm congregational principles in the writing and funding of *Sentry Magazine*, e.g., "Editorial" *Sentry Magazine* 1.7 (July 31, 1975): 2-3: "We do not believe that individuals or churches should funnel funds through a congregation of the Lord to underwrite the expenses of a subscription journal." The existence of Florida College is a regular source of discussion and concern, e.g., Jeffrey Kingry: "Is Florida College a Seminary?" *Sentry Magazine* 1.9-10 (Sep-Oct 1975): 5-8; Floyd Chappelear, "Florida College, another view," *Sentry Magazine* 1.9-10 (Sep-Oct 1975): 10-12.

40. See Brady Kai Cox, "Postwar Churches of Christ Mission Work," https://digitalcommons.acu.edu/etd/78.

41. David Edwin Harrell," Emergence of the Church of Christ Denomination Update," *Vanguard* 5.2 (January 25, 1979): 14.

division among conservatives, he does specify that the relative affluence of conservative preachers is a potential source of digression and his specific concern: "The youngest generation worries me (am I really getting old?)," Harrell reflects. "I find it hard to get used to preachers who are well-educated, well-fed, and well-paid. And I know that they ought to be all of those things."[42] Not only is this pastoral caution a theme of other articles by Harrell, but it also reflects a more broadly expressed concern among periodicals like *Vanguard*.[43]

The concern, at its root, is that money and power corrupt loyalty to God and submission to God's Word when push comes to shove, and that straightforward obedience to the Bible conflicts with ecumenical and societal standards of acceptability. It is a concern for young preachers seen early in the *Gospel Guardian*, for example, in 1949 in the articles of young Leslie Diestelkamp, who argued against gospel preachers wanting high degrees in the world.[44] Similarly, this pastoral warning against worldly influence is seen in the early issues of the *Preceptor Magazine*, in the articles by Homer Hailey, then the Bible Chair at Florida College. For example, writing on the topic of "The Silver Thermometer," Hailey observes that pursuing monetary contributions and numerical membership are not the true thermometer of the temperature of the spiritual body. The reality is that, like the church of Smyrna in Revelation 2:9, the physically poor are often the truly rich, and Hailey takes aim at many Churches of Christ "on the march" in his day with the observation that "extravagant buildings and impressive contributions, elaborate programs and glorified reports could

---

42. Ibid., 15.

43. E.g., "I sometimes hear young men saying the same things that I think need saying—but our thoughts lead us to act in different ways," David Edwin Harrell, Jr., "Love it or Leave it," *Vanguard* 3.21 (November 11, 1977): 10.

44. Leslie Diestelkamp, "Flee From It," *Gospel Guardian* 1.21 (September 29, 1949): 3.

denote ability to promote, and not necessarily true devotion."[45] This cautionary note against seeking "bigness" for its own sake is a recurring motif that is more directly aimed at church leaders in other periodicals over the next twenty years. Articles in the early years of the *Preceptor* also caution against obsessive and worldly emphasis on higher education—including several gospel preachers who took graduate work at the University of Chicago and other liberal institutions. The danger is a spiritual one: that "material progress and approval by worldly men" are held as the highest good of existence and as our spiritual goals.[46] Of specific concern in educational attainments is the disposition of younger preachers in losing a sense of the distinctiveness of the church from the denominations, as well as the distinctiveness of preaching and Bible study in the Restoration Movement, where the silence of Scripture is respected and the positive instructions of Scripture are well studied and known.[47] This concern for the disposition of younger preachers is thematic in the next twenty years of journalism.

For example, in the 1980s, in a telling expose of a younger preacher's criticism of the "bad attitudes" with which both sides debated the "institutional issues" in the 1950s-60s, the editor of *Torch Magazine* and Florida College faculty member, James P. Needham, defends himself and others from a previous generation. Needham argues that younger preachers ought not to approach the institutional issues from an emotional or prejudicial standpoint, but from a Scriptural one. Needham goes on to recount the traumatic reactions he experienced at the hands of his opponents:

---

45. Homer Hailey, "The Silver Thermometer," *The Preceptor* 1.2 (December 1951): 8-9.

46. Homer Hailey, "Attitudes," *The Preceptor* 1.8 (June 1952): 10.

47. James R. Cope, "The Problem of Institutionalism (No.1)," *The Preceptor* 2.6 (April 1953): 4-5. Cf. the emphasis on spiritual sentiment and doctrinal position in James R. Cope, "The Problem of Institutionalism (No.6)," *The Preceptor* 2.10 (August 1953): 8-9.

physical assault, verbal abuse, lies, threats, gunshots, lawsuits, and harassment of his family. Needham's experience "in the foxhole" causes him to call for greater appreciation of the sacrifices of the past, and to question whether younger preachers are more interested in a good church and salary than working where they can do the best. "We are also wondering what will happen in the future when momentous issues arise that have to be met with courage, solid Bible knowledge, and a spirit that says, 'I'll never give up or give in.'"[48]

Other examples of this concern over future generations of preachers could be multiplied. Repeatedly, journalists in *Truth Magazine* turn attention to the inner disposition of their primary audience—preachers among congregational churches of Christ. The oft-repeated question is whether they are willing to make the personal sacrifices of sacred tradition and status achievement that it takes to be truth-tellers, e.g., "Shall the church of the Lord follow the pathway of least resistance?" Johnny Ramsey asks. "In our desire to become big, respected, and powerful shall we forget that the head of the church, Jesus Christ, demands doctrinal soundness?"[49]

The same concern over upwardly mobile preachers is evident in the first issues of one of the longest running periodicals among congregational churches of Christ, *Searching the Scriptures*, a periodical begun in 1960 by H. E. Philips and James P. Miller. Articles in the early years of *Searching the Scriptures* battled against what is presented as a mid-20th century digression from the historic opposition to extra-congregational institutions among Churches of Christ. Many preachers who once were "anti's" are no longer such, observes the editors, not because of a change in Scripture,

---

48. J. P Needham, "Don't Criticize me until You've Walked a Mile in My Shoes," *Torch* 24.12 (December 1989): 8-10.

49. E.g., Johnny Ramsey, "Plain Preaching," *Truth Magazine* 1.9 (June 1956): 16-17.

but because of a change in their attitude toward Scripture and the world.[50] What is the cause of the institutional digression and heresy? Multiple articles in the first years of *Searching the Scriptures* make the case that the problem is human power and social pride, the desire to be respected and to grow big. Articles on the worldliness of institutional Churches of Christ run parallel to articles on the need for Christian humility and willingness to change past perspectives and curb personal preferences for the sake of obedience to the pattern of God's word.[51]

This leads to a third and final theme in the religious periodicals of this era: a call for Christians to empty themselves of religious traditions and worldly standards in service to Christ. What is remarkable about the doctrinal polemics and pastoral admonitions of this era is the oft overlooked encouragement to grow in relationship with God. Stated differently, the negative doctrinal slant of the "non-institutional" movement—its "anti" opposition to worldly organization and influence—is often restated in positive spiritual terms in the journalism among congregational churches of Christ in the 1950s onward. Although this constructive spirituality is neglected in past historical works about the Restoration Movement, the presence of a positive concept of God, the Bible, and Christian life among congregational churches of Christ has often been asserted among sympathetic authors.[52] This positive

---

50. James P. Miller, "Changing with the Times," *Searching the Scriptures* 1.7 (July 1960): 4

51. H. E. Phillips, "Editorial," *Searching the Scriptures* 11.10 (Oct 1961), 2; F. F. Locke, "Do Justly, Love Mercy, Walk Humbly," *Searching the Scriptures* 11.6 (June 1961): 7-8.

52. Most notably Homer Hailey, Gardner Hall, and Steve Wolfgang. E.g., "In truth, although logic and doctrine played an important role, division came not just because brethren disagreed (which they did) or because some people misbehaved (which also occurred). They divided because they had divergent concepts of God, the Bible, the church, how to live as a Christian, and a host

spirituality is also discernible in the primary sources from the past seventy-five years of religious periodicals among congregational churches of Christ, including the early journalistic writings of Ed Harrell, which provide an important corrective to dominant cultural narratives about the congregational churches of Christ as a primarily oppositional and subversive movement. What emerges from study of the primary sources is a view of these churches and leaders as advocates and stewards for a heavenly-oriented and Christ-centered spirituality. It is an otherworldly, countercultural mindset that is in service to this world, and is consistent with the original "apocalyptic" motivations of much of the early American Restoration movement, as has been argued by Richard Hughes and Jamie Gorman in their recently updated history of the Churches of Christ in America.[53]

Ed Harrell's journalism during the 1960s and 70s repeatedly describes the spirit he hoped would inhabit both gospel preachers and other Christians of the day. These are moments of what might be called pastoral encouragement. They are called to have to a humble heart and submissive mindset towards God. Amid cultural revolution in the US, Harrell's articles regularly express concern for the spirituality of Christians, especially shifting attitudes towards marriage, divorce, and child-rearing within an increasingly selfish society. He observed the need for Christians to be in the world but not of it.[54] This included an attitude toward the social order

---

of other things", Steve Wolfgang, "History and Background of the Institutional Controversy (4)," *Guardian of Truth* 33.2 (January 19, 1989): 49-51.

53. Richard T. Hughes, James L Gorman, *Reviving the Ancient Faith: The Story of Churches of Christ in America*, 3rd Edition (Grand Rapids: Eerdmans, 2024), 3-4.

54. David Edwin Harrell, Jr., "Something Permanent," *Vanguard* 5 (March 8, 1979): 193; "Fashions Change—Morals Don't," *Vanguard* 6 (November 1, 1980): 356.

that recognizes inequalities and injustice in society but is resigned to their existence. This spiritual resignation to social injustice is balanced, however, in true Christian spirituality (John 18:36) by fervent concern and work for "the eternal salvation of the honest souls."[55] Harrell wrote how this "unembarrassed fresh faith in the gospel of Christ" was exemplified for him in Christians he visited on his travels throughout the US. One couple had hung tract racks in their living room to influence guests. Another Christian couple held two Bible studies a week outside of the regular classes of the church. Harrell recognized that many would think these behaviors "crazy," but he pointed to them as models of zealous evangelism at the heart of truly Biblical spirituality.[56] Harrell's articles consistently guard against an evangelism deriving from spiritual pride or triumphalism of purpose, with repeated and often personal confessions of the sin, shame, and hurt that every Christian feels in their journey towards heaven, with confidence not in their own righteous works, but in continual repentance and confession towards the God whose grace saves. "Lord," Harrell prays in one of his articles, "may my unworthy past give me a greater desire to honor thee in purity and holiness."[57]

Given his global travels and broad scholarship, Harrell viewed this Biblical spirituality within a broader comparative frame and often shared this perspective with his readers. Once comparing it to Buddhist spirituality, his prescription for Christian disposition and action shared a similar focus on "self-control and selflessness." But unlike the Buddhist resignation and contemplation which is an end-in-itself, the Christian's regiment is focused on a life after this one, that is, a life committed to Christ with a view to salvation, both

---

55. David Edwin Harrell, Jr., "The People of God—Their Attitude Toward the Social Order," *Vanguard* 5 (September 1, 1979): 327.

56. David Edwin Harrell, Jr., "David and Susan and Orville and Debbie," *Vanguard* 5 (November 1, 1979): 339.

57. David Edwin Harrell, Jr., "Pain of Sin," *Vanguard* 6 (June 1, 1980): 137.

our own and those we lead to Christ: "resurrection compels us," he concludes.[58]

Sometimes Harrell expresses this encouragement nostalgically, as in his 1979 article on the emergence of "the Church of Christ Denomination." Here Harrell reflects wistfully on the generation of preachers that fought the battles over institutionalism in the 1950s. "How I loved those lean and hungry preachers who lost their jobs in the 1950s and 1960s," Harrell recalls. "Those were exhilarating times, times that did indeed try men's souls. Churches [today] are becoming filled with bright young people who say all the right things but leave me wondering."[59] The self-sacrifice and self-emptying pertained to both the physical livelihood of having enough to eat because of job loss, and a spiritual abnegation and self-denial that preferred God's will over one's own tradition and penchants.

What emerges in Harrell's description of the old-style preachers of his day echoes his Reed Lecture designation of a psychological type of "humility" among Churches of Christ and is indicative of a more broadly held spirituality that is positively cultivated among other journalists among congregational churches of Christ from the late 1950s into the 1980s, but especially in the spiritual awakening led by Baby Boomers in the 1960s and 1970s. In this era, both secular "hippie" culture and Christian youth culture emphasized "soul over science" and "meaning over things" in contrast to the civic-minded institutionalism and "big-society" triumphalism of the GI generation in the late 1940s and 1950s.[60] This humility among

58. David Edwin Harrell, Jr., "Eightfold Path of Buddhism," *Vanguard* 6 (March 1, 1980): 54.

59. David Edwin Harrell," Emergence of the Church of Christ Denomination Update," *Vanguard* 5.2 (January 25, 1979): 38-39. Concerns over the loss of older leaders and the counsel needed by younger preachers is voiced by Floyd Chappelear, "Editorial" *Sentry Magazine* 1.3 (March 31, 1975): 2-3.

60. On the "consciousness revolution of the 1960s and 70s," see William

congregational churches of Christ is accurately described as a spirituality insofar as it is a prescribed relation to God and especially God's Son and His humble service in the self-emptying incarnation of deity. As is broadly recognized in the history of Christianity, the Greek term for Jesus' self-emptying incarnation in Philippians 2:7 is "*kenosis.*"

> ...though he was in the form of God, [he] did not count equality with God a thing to be grasped but emptied (*ekenōsen* from the verb *kenoō*) himself, by taking the form of a servant, being born in the likeness of men. (Philippians 2:6–7)

To purposely empty oneself of already held or attainable power and to adopt a lower status that purposefully serves God and other people is a "kenotic spirituality." And so, what emerges in the 1960s and the 1970s is a kenotic spirituality that views the sacrifice and self-denial of congregational Christians and churches through the intentional humiliation and self-emptying service of Jesus. As Jesus emptied himself in obedience, so Christians should empty themselves of pretentions to power.

Evidence of this kenotic spirituality is seen in the early years of the *Gospel Guardian*, including Cled E. Wallace's 1949 article entitled, "Tricks of Pride," in which he argues for the need for humility among Christians. To overcome the institutionalism of their day, Wallace explains Christians must divest themselves of human traditions and personal pride and empty themselves of human conceits in the interest of the restoration plea to return to the New

---

Strauss and Neil Howe, *The Fourth Turning* (New York: Three Rivers, 1997), 171-200. Seen upon the broader palette of the cyclical progression of American generations, the institutional debates of the late 1950s and 60s can be seen as a turn in generational perspective from the outward to the inward, from community to the individual, and from civic to prophetic.

Testament pattern.[61] This Christian spirituality is also evidenced in the multi-article series of J. Herman Campbell, who wrote in the *Gospel Guardian* about the development of modernism among churches in the early 1950s especially the tendency to promote "an excessive use of committees and intra-church organizations to get work done that should be handled by the local congregational organization."[62] The need to empty oneself of prior conceptions and conceits is also repeated in articles about self-denial by Elbridge B. Lynn, who observed that Jesus' instruction to deny oneself should be extended not only to personal piety, but also to congregational practice of local assembly and worship, including the manner of observing the Lord's supper.[63] This theme of self-denial and self-emptying is also highlighted by well-known preacher W. W. Otey in the first issue of the *Gospel Guardian* in 1950. Otey argues that those of high mental capacity, as well as great wealth, should empty themselves of their position and possessions in service to others.[64]

A similar spirituality of frugality and abnegation towards worldly and financial power is seen throughout early articles in the *Preceptor*. During its early years of publication, the *Preceptor* alternates between didactic articles making a variety of doctrinal arguments, especially against institutionalism, and other devotional articles describing the character of Christian heart and spirit that believes and teaches these positions. For example, articles on congregational independence, non-institutional evangelism, and benevolence are often adjacent to articles on the "spirituality"

---

61. Cled E. Wallace, "Tricks of Pride," *Gospel Guardian* 1.13 (August 4, 1949): 1.

62. J. Herman Campbell, "When Unity Ceases—No. 3," *Gospel Guardian* 1.21 (September 29, 1949): 5.

63. Eldridge B. Linn, "Let Him Deny Himself," *Gospel Guardian* 1.34 (January 5, 1950): 3.

64. W. W. Otey, "What Will You Leave?" *Gospel Guardian* 1.37 (January 26, 1950): 1.

of Jesus and the simplicity, humility, and self-abasement that characterized his person and ministry.[65] Chief Editor, James R. Cope, captured the connection between the congregational doctrine and Christ-like abnegation and self-emptying in an early editorial on "Consistency and Character," arguing that Christians should not be afraid or ashamed when they change their perspective on the institutional issues, as long as the result is greater accord with the spirit of Christ and truth of Scripture. Cope calls his readers to be willing to root their Christian conviction in a revised understanding of Scripture, despite possible loss of popularity or influence. This conscientious self-denial was, Cope observed, characteristic of many in the American Restoration Movement.

> One of the fundamental reasons why the Restoration Movement commended itself to the sober thinkers of the times and progressed as it did was the disposition of its leaders to surrender former views in the light of newly found truths. Once they were convinced of error, they gladly gave it up and espoused the truth learned. True enough they had their verbal battles, but many of the fundamental principles upon which the church stood in Apostolic days and at the present came to be taught and practiced by the Restorers as these principles were forged into unmistakable clarity in the fires of controversy. Disciples today have gone too far too fast if either they surrender these eternal principles found or forsake the attitude of mind and heart which characterized the search for them.[66]

---

65. Bond Stocks, "Why Christ was Persecuted," *The Preceptor* 13.2 (December 1951): 12-13; Harris J. Dark, "Congregational Independence," *The Preceptor* 1.2 (December 1951): 22-23; See also the combination of non-institutional doctrine and selfless spirituality in James R. Cope, "Majorities and Manners," *The Preceptor* 1.4 (February 1952): 4-5. Cf. Bill Humble, "Restoration and Reaction," *The Preceptor* 2.10 (August 1953): 6-7.

66. James R. Cope, "Consistency and Character," *The Preceptor* 1.2 (December 1951): 4.

Cope here articulates a spirituality of self-surrender in the early Restoration movement, which he implies is continued in the congregationalism of the non-institutional churches in the 1950s. Like the earlier restorers, Christians of his day should have a principled spirit of self-denial and submission to God's truth—an apostolic disposition of emptying one's mind and heart of former concepts and conceits in search of and service to God's truth. This self-emptying, which is akin to Jesus' self-emptying of his divine power (*kenosis*) in his incarnation (Philippians 2) to become a man in service to others, is the theological and spiritual basis for Cope's and other restorers' emphases on Biblical authority and the Scriptural pattern. It is a similar emphasis on spiritual humility and surrender that recurs in Ed Harrell's journalism throughout the 1960s and 70s.

This positive spirituality of Christlikeness is perhaps best seen throughout the early years of *Truth Magazine*, which was begun in 1956 in Aurora, Illinois, to combat modernism, but also premillennialism, and "immorality" more generally.[67] *Truth* is one of a very few number of journals begun in the 1950's to survive to the present day and is noteworthy for its early emphasis on the spirit and heart Christians should exhibit in the world, especially brotherly love that is free from bitterness in pursuit of the restoration of New Testament Christianity.[68] In addition to predictable articles on church cooperation and congregational autonomy, the magazine also provided extended attention to Christian spiritual life and discipline.[69] In addition to the inaugural article of the magazine, which was focused on love for God and neighbor, subsequent issues

---

67. Ron Halbrook, "Gospel Preaching, Gospel Preachers, Gospel Papers: The Heritage of Truth Magazine," *Truth Magazine* 50.13 (July 2006): 12-16.

68. Bryan Vinson, Jr. "Is There a Need for 'Truth'?" *Truth Magazine* 1.2 (November 1956): 2.

69. H. Leo Boles, "Voices from the Past: Church Cooperation," *Truth Magazine* 1.3 (December 1956): 8-9; Ray Ferris, "What is 'Autonomy'?" *Truth Magazine* 1.5 (February 1957): 6-7, 19.

featured articles on the nature of the Christian heart, particularly the preacher's need to "exemplify Christianity in life and word."[70]

This spirituality of self-emptying and purposeful abnegation in the Church is directly connected by early *Truth* writers to contemporary controversies over the question of institutionalism and the call for the "quarantining" of congregational preachers by B. C. Goodpasture on the pages of the *Gospel Advocate*.[71] Through this lens, the question of the "quarantine" of the "anti's" is whether or not Christians will conform their convictions in the institutional debate to the viewpoints of powerful, institutional brethren who had publicly threatened those of differing viewpoint. According to the *Truth Magazine* authors, the important question was "would not such 'logic' [of the institutional perspective] demand that the same type of agreement be expressed on all the issues before the brethren ... [e.g.] marriage, divorce, and remarriage, position on the war question, [and] position on the Paul's teaching concerning women being covered in 1 Cor. 11, and [the] position of the various controversies over the qualifications of elders."[72] Written in the midst both of a national culture war and a brotherhood contest over how churches should support their work—via a network of churches or strictly congregationally—the *Truth* articles reflect a focus on a Christian spirituality that is willing to sacrifice personal status and societal acclaim in exchange for a faithfulness to God's Word and a focus on the truly Biblical outcomes of the local Church's work, as measured by adherence to the New Testament pattern and not the preferences of powerful brethren or broader societal acclaim.

This spirituality is seen also in an early article on attitudes

---

70. Ollie Duffield, Jr. "The Outlet of the Heart," *Truth Magazine* 1.6 (March 1957): 14-15.

71. Bryan Vinson Jr., "I recommend ...," *Truth Magazine* 1.11 (August 1957): 2, 13.

72. Ibid., 13.

toward issues of the day by the well-known preacher and author, Robert Turner. Turner makes clear that the key issue in addressing institutionalism is whether one knows God's way, is willing to be humble in acknowledging it, and is willing to obey it even when it means self-correction or self-denial. "Our first step in settling the current church problems," Turner writes, "is to settle ourselves."[73] Similarly, the example of Jesus humbling himself in Philippians 2:8 is held up as a model of obedience to God's word that comes from kenotic self-emptying: "May we ever look unto Jesus," observes one writer, "and in humility obey his Word."[74] This focus on the self-emptying (*kenotic*) and humble service of preachers and local congregations would be a motif of early issues of *Truth Magazine*. It is seen in a cautionary note sounded by preacher and historian, Earl Kimbrough, in 1958. Warning against an overly zealous approach to purity in church work and worship, Kimbrough evokes the kenotic imagination of his readers in calling them to self-emptying and humility in their thinking about worship and how it should genuinely engage the heart and not just the mind set on orthodoxy:

> Let us not become so filled with worldly pride and conceit and so desirous of worldly applause that we forget to whom and for what purpose our worship is rendered. Let us not in our zeal for order and perfection in carrying out the acts of worship lose the heart in the shuffle.[75]

A similar kenotic spirituality of self-emptying of prior traditions and desire to power is seen in the first issue of another brotherhood

73. Robert F. Turner, "Attitudes Toward Current Issues," *Truth Magazine* 1.9, (June 1957): 2, 17-18, Accessible online at https://www.truthmagazine.com/archives/volume1/TM001078.htm. Last accessed January 5, 2024.

74. Bill Echols, "Humility," *Truth Magazine* 2.2 (May 1958): 20-21, 23.

75. Earl Kimbrough, "Landmarks of the Lord's Church (No. 3)" *Truth Magazine* 2.10 (July 1958): 21-23.

paper, the *Bible Standard*, which began in November 1972. The opening issue includes facing pages focused on spiritual self-denial, on the one hand, and avoidance of the "purposes and structures of denominationalism" on the other.[76] This paralleling of spiritual renewal and doctrinal restoration is seen also in the writings of a regular *Bible Standard* author, Dee Bowman, who was the writer of the journal's first article and whose writings tended to subversively bend and redirect the traditional themes of journalism among congregational churches of Christ in order to prompt reflection.[77] Bowman's articles emphasize the need for spiritual insight and self-awareness in relation to the "battle against institutionalism, innovationism, and hyper-organizationalism." Specifically, in their "abiding by the teaching of Christ (2 John 9)," Bowman advises that against spiritual pride that emphasizes the church over God's word, that does not respect the silence of Scriptures, and that goes "too far" in opposing church support for evangelistic and educational organizations so that they "become guilty of doing nothing at all."[78]

Dee Bowman's efforts to provide a balanced and positive approach to the institutional debates are seen in his willingness to criticize those in his own camp and identify proactive steps

---

76. The Church vs Denominationalism," *The Bible Standard* 1.2 (November 20, 1972): 17. The same juxtaposition of themes is seen repeatedly, including Donald R. Givens, "Putting Self in God's Place," *The Bible Standard* 1.5 (January 5, 1973): 52 and David Smitherman, "The Work of the Local Church?" *The Bible Standard* 1.5 (January 5, 1973): 53. Cf. R. L. (Bob) Craig, "Everyone is Right?" *The Bible Standard* 1.6 (January 20, 1972): 61-62, 66; Kent Ellis, "A Generation that Knew Not" *The Bible Standard* 1.4 (December 20, 1972): 39-4.

77. Dee Bowman, "What it Means to Love God," *The Bible Standard* 1.1 (November 5, 1972): 1-2; Dee Bowman, "Going too far (The Other Way)," *The Bible Standard* 1.5 (January 5, 1973): 57-58; Dee Bowman, "Wrong Tendencies and Broadway's Out-of-the-church Religion" *The Bible Standard* 1.12 (April 20, 1973): 138-40.

78. Dee Bowman, "Going Too Far (The Other Way)," 58.

that congregations should take in lieu of institutional support, including active scheduling of Bible classes at the church building or in the local neighborhood throughout the week, direct funding of domestic and foreign missionaries, and congregational training of preachers. This self-conscious and positive approach to the non-institutional movement among churches of Christ would find a ready ally in the compassionate conservatism of Ed Harrell, who approached Bowman in the early 1980s about starting a new periodical, *Christianity Magazine*.

CHAPTER SIX

Preacher

> "The preacher of that golden age
> was a farmer ... He was useful,
> popular, and tenderly loved. As a
> rule, he was kindhearted, deeply
> pious, and always hospitable
> even to a fault ... in his artless but
> often eloquent style he pointed
> them to the time when they
> should all meet in the Saviour's
> presence ...".[1]

Writing in his daily journal in 1981, Dee Bowman recalls preaching
with Ed Harrell at the Fairview Lectureship in Garden Grove,
California.

> Ed Harrell was the outstanding speaker at the lecture. His
> message was clear, concise, lucid. His usual "down home"
> manner was again his outstanding trait, except for his
> obvious brilliance, which coalesces with his philosophical

---

1. Moses Lard, "Pioneer Preaching in the West," *Apostolic Times* 3 (February
1872): 346; quoted by David Edwin Harrell, Jr., "The Agrarian Myth and the
Disciples of Christ in the Nineteenth Century," *Agricultural History* 41 (April
1967): 184; also quoted by Michael W. Casey, *Saddlebags, City Streets and
Cyberspace: A History of Preaching in the Churches of Christ* (Abilene: ACU
Press, 1995), 43.

humor to form a unique and very exciting combination. He is in my opinion the best preacher going right now.[2]

This was high praise, indeed, coming from Bowman, who taught a course on Homiletics at Florida College as a visiting professor, and was himself widely recognized as one of the most gifted preachers of his generation. By this time in the 1980s, Harrell's reputation as an effective preacher had developed over the years since he gave up full-time preaching in Deland, Florida in 1961. He had not enjoyed the grind of preaching for a local congregation but had moved into academic pursuits with the encouragement of his good friend Harold Dowdy. For the remainder of his life, both in the United States and abroad, especially in India, Harrell preached regularly for "gospel meetings," for newly planted congregations (such as in Athens, Georgia), or churches without located preachers, with the notable exception of 1999-2010, when he served as the primary preacher for the South Jacksonville church of Christ.

While Harrell was in Birmingham at the University of Alabama in the 1970s, he often held weeklong meetings every weekday afternoon Monday through Friday. During one such week, after he had taught at UAB in the morning, Harrell drove to a small country church outside of Athens, Alabama, without any payment for his expenses or services. The sacrificial nature of the endeavor and Harrell's commitment to preaching during his academic career was long remembered by Sewell Hall, who at the time was preaching in nearby Athens, Alabama. "His sincerity made a deep impression on me," recalled Hall.[3]

An important context for Hall's appreciation of Harrell's sacrificial service in preaching is the increasing professionalization

---

2. Dee Bowman personal journal entry, dated Jan 22, 1981, shared with the author.

3. Sewell Hall, in discussion with the author, May 25, 2021.

and "pastoralization" of preaching and evangelism during the late 20th century, especially among the institutional Churches of Christ. An example of the professionalization of the preacher's role is the importance given to the preacher's titles among some of these churches. Harrell and others like Sewell Hall would often bemoan invitations to "brotherhood campaigns" which proclaimed in bold print the degrees and worldly accomplishments of the featured speakers. As an example of this mindset, the following classified appeared in the May 1995 issue of the *Gospel Advocate*.

> **MINISTER WANTED**: The Lake Jackson Church of Christ is soliciting resumes and applications for a new ministry position. **Primary Responsibility**: The design and implementation of the education ministry, including but not limited to, "cradle to grave" curriculum development, ongoing teacher training and recruitment and "brother keeper" (member tracking and care) functions within the adult Bible Classes. Secondary Responsibility: The design and implementation of the involvement ministry, including but not limited to, working with our deacons to coordinate and maximize the use of members' gifts and talents in service of the Master. We hope a person who is educated and/or distinguished will be able to join our works of service.[4]

Such a situated, credentialed, and "pastoral" role stood in stark contrast to the preaching role of Harrell as an itinerant evangelist who went where he was called. Harrell's personal calendars from the 1950s through the 1990s reflect a nearly weekly occurrence of travel for preaching. Members of the congregations where he and his family worshiped in the 1970s (e.g., the 77th Street Church of Christ in Birmingham) recalled that he was rarely there due to

---

4. "Minister Wanted" Advertisement, *Gospel Advocate*, 137.5 (May 1995): 60; cited in Gardner Hall, "Sewell Hall: A Combination of Convictions and Forbearance," Unpublished Manuscript, 108.

his schedule in gospel meetings and as a "supply preacher" for congregations in need.[5] By the early 1970s, Harrell's standard list of five gospel meeting sermons included a lesson on "The Social Gospel," "The Limits of Fellowship," and "What the Church Needs Now," the last of which was a treatment of the "restoration principle."[6] During the 1970s, he preached two series widely: one on "current doctrinal issues" including the topics above, as well as a lesson on "emotionalism and the Holy Spirit" (addressing the errors of Pentecostalism). The second series, on "problems of the young," also including lessons on "standing for the truth" and "the problem of morality."[7] In the 1980s and 1990s Harrell continued to focus on these same themes: the problem of worldly living, the interpretative principles of restorationism, and the problem of fellowship in undenominational Christianity.[8] Following the publication of his historical biography on Homer Hailey and the Churches of Christ in 20th Century, Harrell often preached meetings on the "Restoration Principle" and the "Restoration Movement," which by 2006 had shifted to a greater focus on "primitivist" hermeneutics and history, with "lessons from the past" on apostolic authority, as well as now classic sermons on sources of division in the Restoration Movement,

---

5. Bill Hall, in discussion with the author, July 5, 2021.

6. These are among the sermon topics proposed by Harrell in his correspondence with preachers and elders arranging meetings. "Letter from Ed Harrell to Brother Graves, November 1972;" "Letter to Paul Andrews, November 1, 1972; "Letter from Ed Harrell to Dale, August 21, 1972;" and "Letter from Ed Harrell to James R. Cope, September 12, 1972," series 2.A.10, David Edwin Harrell, Jr. Papers, 1923-2017, Center for Restoration Studies MS #467, Abilene Christian University Special Collections and Archives.

7. "Letter from Ed Harrell to Gene Holder, July 25, 1973," Series 2.A.11, David Edwin Harrell, Jr. Papers, 1923-2017, Center for Restoration Studies MS #467, Abilene Christian University Special Collections and Archives.

8. "Letter from Ed Harrell to Tommy and Wicky Poarch, March 3, 2001," Series 2.A.38, David Edwin Harrell, Jr. Papers, 1923-2017, Center for Restoration Studies MS #467, Abilene Christian University Special Collections and Archives, B rown Library, Abilene Christian University, Abilene, TX.

as well as an increasing focus on congregationalism as the Biblical form of church organization. Another frequent series of lessons in his final years focused on "Ancient Wisdom for Modern Times," with lessons on the meaning of life from Ecclesiastes, Psalms 8, Job, Proverbs 30, and an often heralded lesson on becoming a "complete person" from Colossians 3.[9] By 2008, a core set of these lessons on Biblical interpretation and church history came to be known as Ed's "Thinking Inside the Box" lessons, accompanied by a similarly titled pamphlet.[10]

Throughout these decades of presenting lesson series, the distinctiveness of Harrell's peaching came through not only in their content—most often centered on practical lessons from the Bible and church history—but also Harrell's emotional appeal and his authoritative status in relationship to his audience. His emotional impact came primarily through his brevity, humor, and nonchalance. Harrell's sermons would often come quickly to the point and, though he was famous for illustrative stories from his life, he did not often go long in time. Harrell would poke fun at other preachers' long-windedness, including the well-known evangelist, Paul Earnhart. "Never have I been known for my brevity," admitted Earnhart. "And [Harrell] once made the comment to me that he could have made three sermons out of my sermon. I remember Ed said it with a grin on his face."[11]

The efficiency and relative brevity of his focus was balanced by witty humor and a casual presence in the pulpit that rendered his preaching almost conversational in style. "I felt like in many

---

9. "Letter from Ed Harrell to Berry Kercheville, August 24, 2006," Series 2.A.44, David Edwin Harrell, Jr. Papers, 1923-2017, Center for Restoration Studies MS #467, Abilene Christian University Special Collections and Archives.

10. Letter from Paul Cook to Ed Harrell, September 25, 2008," Series 2.A.47, David Edwin Harrell, Jr. Papers, 1923-2017, Center for Restoration Studies MS #467, Abilene Christian University Special Collections and Archives.

11. Paul Earnhart, in discussion with the author, June 28, 2021.

ways he conversed with his audience, but he could make his point," Earnhart observed.[12] His humor often took the form of personal anecdotes to introduce his lesson by establishing connection with the audience or to illustrate the Biblical point he was making. This wit was on display in Florence, Alabama, when Harrell began one of his sermons, following younger preacher, Jeff May, in the lectureship: "Every time I hear a young man like Jeff preach," Harrell quipped, "it just surprises me that these young guys can preach like that. I hear them say so many good things that I get to thinking: 'I wonder where they heard me say that.'"[13]

Most famous was Harrell's dry humor from the pulpit, and especially his witty repartee with Dee Bowman, with whom he would repeatedly join forces at the annual Fairview Lectureship in Garden Grove, California. They both were invited to participate in the lectureship together by the preacher at the Fairview Church of Christ, Brent Lewis. Lewis had been the preacher at Studebaker Road in California from 1970 to 1975 and moved to the Fairview Congregation in Garden Grove, California in 1975, where Floyd Thompson had preached previously for 25 years. Brent Lewis suggested to the congregation that they have a lectureship program and reached out to Dee Bowman, suggesting that they also invite Ed Harrell to come and speak. Within a couple of years, in 1978, it was arranged, and Bowman and Harrell would return to the Fairview lectureships four more times in subsequent years, preaching throughout California during their time there in adjoining weeks.[14] "The congregation was enamored with both of those fellows," Brent Lewis recalled. Both men were experienced preachers and excellent

---

12. Paul Earnhart, in discussion with the author, June 28, 2021.

13. David Edwin Harrell, Jr., "Tape recording of sermon on Intellectualism from College View Church of Christ Lectures," Series 3.31.76, David Edwin Harrell, Jr. Papers, 1923-2017, Center for Restoration Studies MS #467, Abilene Christian University Special Collections and Archives.

14. Brent Lewis, in discussion with the author, February 26, 2021.

communicators of the Word, but part of their appeal was undoubtedly their shared sense of humor. One evening of the lectureship, for example, a well-dressed Dee Bowman introduced his sermon with a quip about the other preacher: "Ladies and Gentleman, I've got it figured out. If I had Ed's mind and my suits, there is no telling what I could do." The ensuing laughter challenged Harrell, who, not to be outdone, began his subsequent sermon with the rejoinder: "If Dee had my mind, he wouldn't want his suits."[15]

Ed Harrell preaching in his distinctive sartorial style, eyeglasses in hand.

Adding to the emotional effect of his humor, Harrell's casual presence in the pulpit was impactful, especially upon his fellow preachers. Ed's preaching style, as he once said, "couldn't be more relaxed without going to sleep."[16] He would slouch in the pulpit and lean on the edge of the podium, often removing his glasses and running his fingers through his hair as he leaned into his southern drawl and rhetorical pauses to emphasize certain points, often beginning with the phrase, "Now I will tell you that ...". The effect on the audience was both memorable and endearing, and other

---

15. Dee Bowman, in discussion with the author, July 25, 2021.

16. David Edwin Harrell, Jr., in discussion with the author, May 20, 2019.

preachers would later admit to imitating his mannerisms out of admiration. "He was such a big influence on me that Bette [my wife] kind of had to beat me off of subconsciously mimicking Ed's style," observed Steve Wolfgang.[17] Others were not immune: "I once said [in a gospel meeting with Harrell] that his preaching style was so infectious that at times it made me want to brush the hair out of my face," recalled Paul Earnhart. "He would not let that stand. So, the next service he came with his hair slicked down with some kind of greasy solution. That was his answer."[18] Similarly, one time after Ed had preached a meeting, Sewell Hall caught himself taking his glasses off three times while preaching. "I thought to myself, 'Glasses, get back on where you belong!' I hadn't intended to do that!"[19]

The succinct content and emotional impact of Harrell's preaching contributed to the perception of him as an evangelist for the common folk, a populist preacher who simplified things so that everyone could understand. His regular preaching companion, Dee Bowman, often observed the simplifying tendency in Harrell's preaching: "he was an absolute genius at taking a profound passage of Scripture and making it take a lap into your life. He was an expert at application."[20] Harrell himself also observed this tendency in his own preaching, in contrast to the more expansive and eloquent style of Bowman: "I have kind of been noted in my academic career as someone who took very complicated things and simplified them, and I think there is a certain amount of truth to that. And what Dee does is that Dee takes very simple things and elaborates and builds them out and makes them flourish."[21]

17. Steve Wolfgang, in discussion with the author, May 28, 2021.

18. Coulter Wickerham and David Holder, "*Christianity Magazine Part 13*," YouTube video, 8:23, 10 Feb. 2009, https://www.youtube.com/watch?v=ZwaYTtDOjxk.

19. Sewell Hall, in discussion with the author, May 25, 2021.

20. Brent Lewis, in discussion with the author, February 26, 2021.

21. David Edwin Harrell, Jr., "Taped Sermon on Nehemiah 8, From Lessons

This public perception of Harrell as a simple preacher was often seen in comments about how his folksy preaching persona belied his scholarly sophistication and intellectual complexity. Like the Apostle Paul noted in 1 Corinthians 9, he sought to become "all things to all people." Harrell likewise accommodated himself to his audiences in a self-effacing way. He did not "talk down" to the uneducated, but addressed them with a self-deprecating humor, straightforward clarity and genuine respect that cultivated understanding and affinity. A long-time friend to the Harrells, Bette Wolfgang, recalled a Christian lady in St. Louis who heard Ed preach and commented, "He is educated, but you can't tell it."[22]

This non-conformity to established biases against the educated elite was central to Harrell's pulpit persona. He was educated, but he used his insights and skills to underscore both rural sensibilities and conservative orthodoxy in the churches. This was undoubtedly a pleasant surprise to many who heard him. Christians in conservative churches of Christ often warned against the dangers of a college education leading young people away from the Christian faith. In this light, Harrell's doctorate in church history from Vanderbilt might be taken as nearly rock-solid evidence of his current or impending apostasy. The extent to which Harrell deflected this critique in his years of preaching is therefore remarkable. Expression of how this worked is seen in an account by Sewell Hall of a visit to the congregation in Athens, Georgia, started by Ed and Deedee Harrell. When he arrived to preach in Athens, a visitor from the local institutional Church of Christ complained to Sewell, "that [institutional] church is run by a bunch of PhDs." Harrell overhead the comment and responded sarcastically with his

---

from Restoration History, Kirkland WA May 13-14, 2005," Series 3.31.76, David Edwin Harrell, Jr. Papers, 1923-2017. Center for Restoration Studies MS #467. Abilene Christian University Special Collections and Archives.

22. Bette Wolfgang, in discussion with the author, May 28, 2021.

country drawl, "yeah, those PhDs, you really have to watch them!" It occurred to Sewell that if the visitor ever learned that Ed had his PhD, he would be totally embarrassed. Sewell conscientiously spoke up and said, pointing towards Harrell, "Yeah, this guy has his PhD!" The man responded, "Yes, but it looks to me like he's got something to say."[23]

The rhetorical effectiveness of Harrell's preaching, therefore, resulted from the age-old combination of engaging content, emotional appeal, and his own persuasive character that could speak authoritatively yet authentically to the spiritual needs of Christians coming from lower to middle-class rural and suburban backgrounds. Members of churches of Christ, especially congregational churches in the latter half of the 20th century, were made up of people from the margins of society both economically and culturally, with predominantly agrarian backgrounds. Harrell's special ability was to bridge the gap between these primarily rural and conservative Christians and an increasingly affluent, urban, and educated society in the United States. It was an upward mobility that impacted many families in congregational churches of Christ during the late 20th century. Harrell's straightforward Biblical preaching emphasized that the way to navigate this journey was with simple obedience to Scripture amid growing affluence and higher education.

Harrell's preaching also focused on the need for restoration of the New Testament order. As previously mentioned, the "Restoration Movement" or the "Restoration Principle" was a regular theme of Harrell's preaching throughout his life, serving as a focusing lens for instruction about both church work (e.g., group evangelism and non-institutionalism) and personal ethical instruction (e.g., love of strangers and charitable use of money).[24] This is evident in

---

23. Sewell Hall, in discussion with the author, May 25, 2021.

24. The Restoration theme is seen in a variety of Harrell's archived sermons, e.g., Series 3.31.43, "The Original Church" and "The Original Worship," Ed

a few concluding lines from a Harrell sermon on Nehemiah chapter 8, which traces the stages of the rebuilding of Jerusalem, from Zerubbabel to Ezra and Nehemiah.

> "I've been talking to you about this concept of going back and being New Testament Christians, and in a very simple and uncomplicated way that means that you go back and read the Bible, and on every issue that God tells us that He's concerned about our conduct we just go do what it says. I would suggest to you that this is a story that is repeated over and over in the Scriptures. Most of the stories in the Bible are about a confrontation between someone and God. Our lives are about our confrontation with God. We either end up being obedient or disobedient."[25]

With such words Harrell seeks repentance toward God and not respect for the preacher. The fact that, even among congregational churches of Christ, preachers could focus too much on their own status and education made Harrell's integrity in the pulpit appreciated by many of his peers. Reflecting on Harrell's preaching style, Sewell Hall hoped for its lasting impact:

> I wish the simplicity of Ed's preaching had had more influence. It was a blessing for people to realize that the gospel was for the common man. Ed excelled at that. He

---

Harrell, 20 July 1986; Series 3.31.52, "Responsibility to Spread the Original Gospel;" and "Responsibility to Live the Original Gospel," Ed Harrell, 23 July 1986; Series 3.31.58, "The New Testament Church" and "The Catholic Experience," Ed Harrell, 6-7 November 1987, David Edwin Harrell, Jr. Papers, 1923-2017, Center for Restoration Studies MS #467, Abilene Christian University Special Collections and Archives.

25. Harrell, David Edwin Jr. "Taped Sermon on Nehemiah 8, Lessons from Restoration History," Kirkland, WA, May 13-14, 2005," Series 3.31.76, David Edwin Harrell, Jr. Papers, 1923-2017, Center for Restoration Studies MS #467, Abilene Christian University Special Collections and Archives.

didn't impress people with his education. He tried not to. The simplicity of his lessons was what was appreciated.[26]

Whatever the impact of his preaching, his contemporaries saw that his preaching style arose from his background and training. The ability to synthesize complex ideas into short and simple lessons was recognized and respected as a product of his career in academic research and writing. In both writing history and preaching the gospel, he routinely analyzed and distilled large amounts of data to teach those with only a passing knowledge of his topic. "Though his academic world was different than preaching, Ed had the same skill in preaching," observed Paul Earnhart. "He could quickly with ease analyze a subject and preach on it in the simplest way."[27] His preaching from stories and in colloquial terms for the common person was, furthermore, rooted in his upbringing in southern Georgia. In reflecting on his scholarly work, Harrell recognized how his upbringing affected his work as a historian, from his focus on churches of Christ to his attention to Southern religion, including black and Pentecostal churches. Even down to his final major work—a textbook on American history that thematically presented religious elements of history—Harrell self-consciously sought to represent the Christians of his youth. These were those people who were, in his words, "the devout, churchgoing, God-fearing southerners who had populated my childhood—and my adult life."[28]

This background in the Bible-belt of the American South among marginalized primitivist Christians seems to have shaped his preaching to a style geared toward congregational churches of

---

26. Sewell Hall, in discussion with the author, May 25, 2021.

27. Paul Earnhart, in discussion with the author, May 28, 2021.

28. David Edwin Harrell, Jr., "Recovering the Underside of Southern Religion," 50.

Christ. As Steve Wolfgang observes: "[Harrell] brought things down to the common person ... He saw a lot of farming and he never lost that understanding of the average person. He wrote in the way he preached: succinct and impactful. He would see things in a different way and state it in a folksy way."[29] Harrell's experience led him to preach sermons deeply informed by the lessons of past church history yet also conversant with academic Biblical criticism. He was deeply Biblicist in his assertion of the authority of Scripture while being populist in his concern for holding his audience's attention with stories, humor, and driving home points with aphorisms. Harrell's concern for his audience's response to his preaching is evidenced in the account by Brent Lewis of one of the first Fairview Lectures, when Harrell moved back into the audience of 700 people to see how they responded to Dee Bowman's preaching.[30]

Harrell's preaching circuit not only allowed him to see the churches, but it allowed them to see him. Many of the most insightful observations about his daily habits come from preachers and other Christians who observed him during preaching and meetings, living in his house or with him visiting them. For example, the local preacher in Birmingham in the 1970s saw how Harrell at 10:30 am would go to Ollie's Barbecue every day to order two barbecue sandwiches, dosing them with barbecue sauce "until it was running in the plate." When he would get halfway through the second sandwich the waitress would bring him a piece of coconut cream pie. The restaurant workers affectionately termed it the "professor's special." "They knew him, and they knew exactly what he wanted," recalled Bill Hall. "He went at that hour because that's when they baked the pie, and he knew they would come straight out of the oven. Anytime I needed to talk to Ed about anything, I knew that I would be welcome to come down to the barbecue place and talk

29. Steve Wolfgang, in discussion with the author, May 28, 2021.
30. Brent Lewis, in discussion with the author, February 26, 2021.

to him. Then he would spend a lot of afternoons out on the golf course. That was his daily practice. The next day he would get up at 4-4:30 am."[31] Harrell's daily schedule—rising by 3-4 am and in bed to sleep by 7-8 pm—was a feature of his life that left an impression on those who stayed with him and with whom he stayed during gospel meetings. His disciplined life of slow but steady productivity set aside time for daily and high-quality attention to creative endeavors of research and writing books in the early morning before most people were awake. It was an unusual daily schedule that was most often revealed to those hosts and guests who encountered Harrell at bedtime. It left a lasting impression. Paul Earnhart recalled preaching a meeting in Birmingham at a small church. Ed and Deedee had invited him to stay with them, and Ed was nowhere to be seen when Paul arrived in the early evening. "He never did show up," Paul recalled. "I asked Deedee where Ed was. She replied that he was already in bed. She said he was early to bed because he's getting up at four in the morning. That was his way."[32] When they learned of his sleep schedule, visitors would often ask him what he told his children about going to be so early. To which he quipped, "I tell them 'Goodnight!'"[33]

In addition to the rigor of his sleeping and work schedule, Ed knew how to relax and enjoy the company of others, especially in golf. He was a devoted golfer and was infamous for traveling to a gospel meeting prepared for the links the next day. Dee Bowman recalled that during their first lectureship together at the Garden Grove Church in 1978, Harrell pulled out his golf clubs from his luggage and his preaching suit was wrapped around the clubs.[34] From his high school days as a basketball center, to his adult years

31. Bill Hall, in discussion with the author, June 5, 2021.
32. Paul Earnhart, in discussion with the author, May 28, 2021.
33. David Edwin Harrell, Jr., in discussion with the author, May 20, 2019.
34. Dee Bowman, in discussion with the author, July 25, 2021.

playing tennis and golf, Harrell was an avid sportsman. Dee Bowman reported that Ed had called him before the Fairview Lectures that he should bring his tennis rackets and golf clubs. "Ed beat me like a drum," said Bowman. After they played, Harrell offered his concluding reflection. "Dee, I'll tell you what's wrong in a sentence. You ain't any good."[35] Despite Harrell's competitive drive, Bowman loved him: "He was one of the best friends I ever had."[36]

What emerges from accounts of the preacher Ed Harrell is the image of a man suspended between two worlds: he taught a simple gospel in primarily rural churches while at the same time living an urbane lifestyle in a sophisticated academic career. He spoke authentically as a "farmer preacher," but was also a "professional minister" as defined by the norms of modern America: upwardly mobile, highly educated, and culturally elite, with the club memberships to prove it.[37] The tension is exemplified in an often-told story from Ed's preaching trip to a small congregation in rural east Tennessee. He was driving his new Mercedes Benz, which he paid for with the publisher's advance for his Pat Robinson biography. A local farmer approached him and asked him: "what kind of car is that?" Embarrassedly, Harrell mumbled the name of the luxury car maker under his breath, "Merraahs Beens." The farmer reflected for a moment and responded, "I bet it gets good gas mileage." Harrell heaved a sigh of relief, sensing he was still acceptable.[38] It was an example of a connection to the farmer and other common folk in his preaching efforts that he would work to maintain all his life, partly through his publication of *Christianity Magazine.*

---

35. Dee Bowman personal journal entry, dated January 22, 1981, shared with the author.

36. Dee Bowman, in discussion with the author, July 25, 2021.

37. On the contrast between the farmer preacher and professional preacher in the early American Restoration Movement, see Michael Casey, *Saddlebags*, 43-44.

38. Sewell Hall, in discussion with the author, May 25, 2021.

CHAPTER SEVEN

Publisher

"We don't have bishops; we have
editors."[1]

Given the congregational organization of the churches of Christ,
institutions such as colleges and publishing businesses have had
an especially strong influence in shaping the opinions of Christians
who join in disparate local assemblies. This fact is evidenced by
the oft-observed power of the "editor bishops," such as Alexander
Campbell, David Lipscomb, G. H. P. Showalter, Foy Wallace, Jr, and
B.C. Goodpasture. Though limited in actual subscriptions, the
influence of these periodicals was augmented by the repetition
of their content from pulpits and across informal networks of
communication among congregations. The printed periodical was
an influential form of technology in the 19th and 20th centuries,
amplifying the views of editors and small groups of authors for
influencing churches. In his study of 20th century Christianity
and especially the Pentecostal movement, Harrell was among the
first to write about the importance of mass media to the spread
of charismatic theology.[2] This was in addition to the printed

---

1. This is a commonplace saying among Disciples of Christ and Churches of
Christ going back to the 19th century, reflecting the authority of the *Millennial
Harbinger*, the *Gospel Advocate*, and many other serial publications and their
editorial leadership among the congregations and Christians in the American
Restoration Movement.

2. See his emphasis on the growth of new media communications within the

periodicals in the American Restoration Movement that formed the backbone of Harrell's own historical study of 19th and 20th century Christianity. Harrell therefore especially recognized the importance of the serial publications to the propagation and maintenance of the Christian faith.[3]

Unlike institutional Churches of Christ, the congregational churches of Christ did not broadly utilize the mass media appeal of radio and TV beyond local channels. This utilization of digital technology beyond the local context changed and increased with the advent of the Internet. In the final stages of what has been termed the "Gutenberg Parenthesis," in which print media held sway only temporarily as the primary means of communication among Christian communities after the introduction of the printing press in the 15th century and before the advent of online media in the 1990's, the congregational churches of Christ would find a leading print communication through the efforts of Ed Harrell and his fellow editors of the *Christianity Magazine*.[4] This cultural moment in the twilight of print-dominated media is evidenced by

---

Pentecostal Movement, e.g., "Oral Roberts: Religious Media Pioneer," in Leonard Sweet, ed., *Communication and Change in American Religious History* (Grand Rapids: Eerdmans, 1994), 320-334; "Pentecost at Prime Time," *Christian History*, 15.1 (January, 1996): 52-54; "Healers and Televangelists After World War 11," in Vinson Synan, ed., *The Century of the Holy Spirit* (Nashville: Thomas Nelson, 2001), 325-348. In addition, Harrell himself participated in over ten major TV network interviews (ABC, CBS, NBC, NPR ...) and over 20 radio network interviews, in addition to scores of local TV, radio, and newspaper interviews.

3. See his extensive research in the primary documents of 19th Century periodicals in the American Restoration Movement in David Edwin Harrell, Jr., *Quest for a Christian America*, 229-231.

4. On the "Gutenberg Parenthesis" and the impact of the digital revolution on Christian faith and community, see John B. Weaver, "The Bible in Digital Culture," in *Oxford Handbook of the Bible in America* (New York: Oxford University Press, 2017), 149-162; and John B. Weaver, "Transforming Practice: American Bible Reading in Digital Culture," in *The Bible in American Life*, edited by Philip Goff, et. al (New York: Oxford University Press, 2017), 249-255.

the fact that there is not a single reference to the World Wide Web in the sixteen years of the publication which ran from January 1984 to December of 1999. The first issue was prior to the Internet, and the last issue didn't refer to it.[5]

The idea for *Christianity Magazine* was entirely Harrell's at the start. It stemmed from the Fairview Lectures, where Harrell had suggested to Dee Bowman the idea of a magazine that would be readable for a broader audience.[6] The idea was Harrell's though it was not unique to him. In many ways, the previously begun *20th Century Christian* was of the same ilk. Originally begun without regard to the institutional issues and recommended by voices such as Jim Cope, *20th Century Christian* became a paper representing institutional Churches of Christ, promoting such human businesses as Pepperdine University and *Herald of Truth*, among other organizations larger than the local congregation. This association of a popularizing positive magazine with the institutional churches would prove influential to some people's perception of *Christianity Magazine*.

On the way to the airport after the second annual Fairview Lectures with Dee Bowman, Harrell proposed a periodical "for the people in the pews and not just the preacher."[7] In their initial discussion, several features of the paper were identified, including multiple editors (Harrell had wanted Dee Bowman to edit it alone, but he declined) and a one page limit for articles. They met in Dallas shortly thereafter with Brent Lewis, recruiting him for layout and graphics, and then with Paul Earnhart and Sewell Hall,

---

5. Harrell similarly observes the pre-Internet content and context of the magazine. Coulter Wickerham and David Holder, "Intro Part 1," YouTube video, February 10, 2009, https://www.youtube.com/watch?v=R-dL2GdZhIk&t=62s.

6. Coulter Wickerham and David Holder, "Intro Part 1," YouTube video, 7:16, February 10, 2009, https://www.youtube.com/watch?v=R-dL2GdZhIk&t=62s.

7. Ibid.

popular preachers who were amenable to the idea of the paper and potentially willing to edit issues.[8] In his daily journal entry, Dee Bowman reflected on the seminal meeting with Harrell and Lewis about the new magazine:

> I'm at 35,000 feet heading back to Houston after an all-day meeting regarding the new paper. It will be called *Christianity Magazine*, a 32-page monthly, to be published in Lubbock, Texas with the business affairs to be handled in Jacksonville, Florida. Ed Harrell, Brent Lewis, Paul Earnhart, and possibly Sewell Hall will be the sharers of the editorial responsibilities. The paper will have its beginning January next, and the first edition will be 12,000 copies. We hope to have somewhere near 5,000 subscribers before the initial drive is concluded.[9]

The willingness of all the editors to be involved in the magazine was not immediate. Not only was Sewell Hall hesitant, but Paul Earnhart was also slow to accept the role of editor. "They contacted me and wanted to know if I would write two articles a month," recalls Earnhart. "I hesitated to make that commitment. I hadn't been doing a lot of writing, but Dee and Ed had heard me preach." Earnhart eventually did sign on full-time, as did Sewell Hall, but both were essentially added to the list of editors without their full permission. "When the first edition came out, they listed me as an editor without me saying so," Sewell Hall wryly recalls. "They knew good and well they did that to me."[10] Sewell proceeded to be an editor and continued writing articles most often focused on evangelism both in the US and around the world. The editors had two articles to write each month, and to edit a themed issue on a rotating basis. By their

---

8. Brent Lewis, in discussion with the author, February 26, 2021.

9. Dee Bowman personal journal entry, dated July 19, 1983, shared with the author.

10. Sewell Hall, in discussion with the author, May 25, 2021.

own admission, the experience shaped them as writers. The one-page articles were about 750 words. It was a practice that promoted conciseness and attention to deadlines. This was because, as Harrell would observe, "getting a paper out on time goes together with subscriptions."[11]

For most of its existence, the subscription list of the magazine stayed around 4,000-5,000 subscribers. Harrell's brother-in-law and sister, Bob and Marilyn Hardage, along with preacher Harold Dowdy, worked tirelessly in taking care of the business side of the subscription list. "It was a real work of love on their part," observed Brent Lewis.[12] The editors also took on this loving work and became like an extended family. Every July 4th the editors and their families would meet for a week in Jacksonville, worshiping and preaching a meeting with the South Jacksonville (now Parental Road) church of Christ in the evenings and dicussing the magazine during the days. "Those of us with any ability played golf," Harrell observed laughingly. "Others did other things."

Every year there was the question of whether they would continue the magazine. Though it would continue for seventeen years, the editors never intended to pass on the magazine to their children or other family members. "The first decision we made each year when we met in Jacksonville," observed Dee Bowman, "was whether or not we would continue the paper for another year ... The five editors were the ones who would begin the paper and end the paper."[13] When they finally concluded the magazine in 1999, it was because they felt it had accomplished its purpose.[14] In

---

11. Coulter Wickerham and David Holder, "Intro Part 4," YouTube video, 9:17, February 10, 2009, https://www.youtube.com/watch?v=7xpdXiqu3kA.

12. Coulter Wickerham and David Holder, "Intro Part 2," YouTube video, 7:58, February 10, 2009, https://youtu.be/LG64Zi8zUVY.

13. Ibid.

14. Dee Bowman, in discussion with the author, July 25, 2021.

Ed and Deedee Harrell with Brent and Joy Lewis, Dee and Norma Bowman, and Robert "Bobby" Hardage.

reflecting on this purpose, Sewell Hall observed that the magazine was interested in supporting the common Christian. "I found that in a lot of places I went that the preacher didn't take the paper but members of the congregation did and would mention articles that had been written ... That was the original plan, and we were glad it did that."[15]

All the editors were united in thinking how publishing a Christian magazine could be done peaceably and with less polemic among Christians than had been the case with many past religious periodicals, while at the same time maintaining their commitment to the authority of the Bible. As Paul Earnhart expressed it:

> We didn't always agree but we were all committed to taking the New Testament documents and building on that alone, and to do that without a party spirit. I went through the

15. Coulter Wickerham and David Holder, "Intro Part 1," YouTube video, 7:16, February 10, 2009, https://www.youtube.com/watch?v=R-dL2GdZhIk&t=62s.

institutional controversy, and the problem that I had was the personalities. Robert Turner helped me a great deal because he always addressed the subject Biblically and never personally. I think that was something of the concept of the magazine—that we should get something done that the average Christian could read with profit. It was not a preacher magazine, though it was not averse to controversy, but did not want to be known for that, and certainly not personal conflict.[16]

The tone for this approach was set in the magazine's first issue featuring a front-page article by Dee Bowman entitled "Positive Christianity." The article's first line stated that "sin is inherently negative, and forgiveness is inherently positive." The rest of the article built on that line, acknowledging the need for some negativity, but planning for the magazine to focus on the positive. There were critiques of this approach from other Christians, including from the editors and writers of *Truth Magazine* and *Searching the Scriptures*, which were widely read periodicals among congregational churches of Christ. Editors Mike Willis (*Truth Magazine*) and Connie Adams (*Searching the Scriptures*) and others criticized the positive approach. They perceived *Christianity Magazine* as soft-pedaling issues. "Dee's first article was criticized by other papers," Brent Lewis recalled. "There came to be an 'anti-everything,' ultraconservative mindset that did not like the approach we took in the magazine. We got labeled by brethren as being soft."[17]

One reason for the criticism was that this was not the first time a periodical had promoted a "positive" approach. In a previous generation, the magazine *20th Century Christian* began with an appeal to the average Christian and the believer in the pew as opposed to a preacher's journal. In fact, *20th Century Christian*

---

16. Paul Earnhart, in discussion with the author, May 28, 2021.
17. Brent Lewis, in discussion with the author, February 26, 2021.

had been a model for the work in *Christianity Magazine*. "There was a need for something that you could give to anyone and feel comfortable about it. It really served what the *20th Century Christian* did," acknowledged Sewell Hall. "For me, even when I was a subscriber to the *Gospel Advocate*, I would not encourage a weak Christian or non-Christian to subscribe to the *Gospel Advocate*. I would encourage them to take the *20th Century Christian*."[18] This similarity to the *20th Century Christian* was a concern among those who criticized Bowman's opening article on "positive Christianity" and the populist trajectory of the magazine.[19] "We were very uncomfortable at the way that *Christianity Magazine* was birthed," observed *Truth Magazine* writer, Ron Halbrook. "The *20th Century Christian* magazine was focused positively and initially endorsed by Jim Cope in one of the early issues, but it wasn't long before the institutional issues started popping up and that paper immediately went that direction [i.e., toward support of institutions]."[20] Editor Mike Willis and others had seen the trajectory of positively oriented periodicals during the institutional division and other debates over the "new hermeneutic."[21] History had shown that periodicals with a positive emphasis avoided publishing disagreements over Biblical doctrine that were sometimes negative in tone, but often helpful to Christian understanding of and adherence to the truth. This potentially problematic direction seemed substantiated by the policy of *Christianity Magazine* to not publish reader responses and not to announce any brotherhood debates. In the minds of those looking to maintain adherence to New Testament

---

18. Sewell Hall, in discussion with the author, May 25, 2021.

19. For critique of the trajectory of *20th Century Christian* and comparison to the positive approach of *Christianity Magazine*, see Ron Halbrook, *Trends Pointing Toward a New Apostasy* (Athens, AL: Truth Publications, 2017), 44-47.

20. Ron Halbrook, in discussion with the author, October 17, 2022.

21. Mike Willis, in discussion with the author, October 17, 2022.

Christianity, these editorial policies raised concerns about the direction of the magazine.

These concerns were variously expressed in brotherhood periodicals during the 1980s and 1990s, especially in *Truth Magazine*, where writers were reportedly accused of "turning off a whole generation of younger preachers" because of the "hard preaching" being done.[22] To this was contrasted the "smooth words" of *Christianity Magazine*, with its focus on the positive, and appeal for a "popular style of writing."[23] Different audiences and authors resulted in different publication styles. In his historical review of the history of *Truth Magazine*, one of its writers concluded that, "it can be seen that *Truth Magazine* represents the militant spirit of New Testament Christianity in upholding the truth of the gospel and in opposing every departure from it ... In short, *Truth Magazine* is a gospel paper used by gospel preachers."[24]

The concern that *Christianity Magazine* might compromise Biblical truth for the sake of "Christian unity" and other "positive" initiatives was shared by the editors of *Christianity Magazine*.

---

22. Tom M. Roberts, "Speaking Smooth Things About ... Romans 14 and Fellowship," *Truth Magazine* 42 (1998), https://www.truthmagazine.com/speaking-smooth-things-about-romans-14-and-fellowship.

23. Ibid. Cf. Keith M. Greer, "Quarreling Brethren: Discouragement to a Young Preacher," *Truth Magazine*, 41.3 (Dec. 4, 1997): 21-22.

24. Ron Halbrook, "Gospel Preaching, Gospel Preachers, Gospel Papers: The Heritage of the Guardian of Truth" in the *Guardian of Truth* 39.14 (July 20, 1995): 433-436. First published in 1956 under the oversight of Leslie Diestelkamp in the Chicagoland area and designed to combat modernism, its attention shifted under Roy Cogdill and then Cecil Willis to opposing institutionalism and the "grace/unity" movement in the 1960s-1980s. After merging with *The Gospel Guardian* (1949-80)—itself edited by such preachers as Yater Tant and Roy Cogdill and focused on defense of non-institutionalism and other issues related to the Biblical pattern—the magazine was changed in name to *Guardian of Truth* (December 1980) and then back to *Truth Magazine* (1998) after merging with *Searching the Scriptures* in 1992.

Sewell Hall was, for example, concerned that the magazine should not shy away from potentially divisive topics, but that it should address every contemporary controversial issue. To this end, in the 1990s, Hall reviewed the past issues of the magazine and found that premillennialism was the only controversial topic that had not been covered. Hall made sure that it was covered in the next issue he edited.[25]

Despite addressing debatable topics in *Christianity Magazine*, some readers could still observe the difference in content between the articles in the *Preceptor,* the *Gospel Guardian*, *Searching Scripture*, *Truth Magazine*, and those articles published in *Christianity Magazine*. It was a shift like what was seen in *20th Century Christian*, which was not necessarily a move toward sinful content, but potentially a resistance to fighting error and exposing false doctrine.[26] Upon this view, *Christianity Magazine* moved toward the kind of preaching that characterized *20th Century Christian*. Reflecting upon this broader trajectory, *Truth Magazine* editor Mike Willis observed that "by the 1980s the debaters had become about the least respected brothers among us."[27]

Theological controversy and division are at once deeply personal and impersonal. Disagreements and debates take on names that define them, but they are ultimately about ideas and movements that defy personal identification. In this way, the early concern over the "positive" nature of Christianity and subsequent debates over Christian fellowship took a personal toll, but were not personal, at least in the eyes of those who questioned *Christianity Magazine*. For his part, Dee Bowman took the brunt of the criticism in the early years. In his personal journals, he would make a point

---

25. Coulter Wickerham and David Holder, "Intro Part 4," YouTube video, 9:17, February 10, 2009, https://www.youtube.com/watch?v=7xpdXiqu3kA.

26. Cf. Ron Halbrook, *Trends Pointing Toward a New Apostasy*, 46.

27. Mike Willis, in discussion with the author, October 17, 2022.

of naming those who he felt had wronged him in their public criticism of the magazine. Bowman would pray for them specifically, finding catharsis in seeking to love those who had treated him as an enemy.[28] For those questioning the motives of *Christianity Magazine*, the critique was not personal but rather a question of the direction of their efforts as related to Biblical truth. Reflecting on the disagreement years later, editor Brent Lewis observed that he felt "most of the fellows who were so hard about 'positive Christianity' came to feel that they had overreacted. People who would hardly speak to me then are now very kind and cordial."[29]

Whatever the personal cost of the publication to the editors, there were financial costs that were borne primarily by Harrell and his family. The paper was funded by a charitable foundation that Harrell's father had founded and left him to manage. By all accounts, this seed money was critical in starting the paper. The editors mailed 15,000 copies of the first issue and began with about 6,500 subscriptions.[30] However, the paper never did break-even financially. "The success of *Christianity Magazine* was made possible by the Harrell Foundation money," observed Steve Wolfgang. "The sad trajectory of every paper in the Restoration Movement is that you can't run a paper solely on subscriptions. You must have either a bookstore or a college using their general funds to underwrite it or have something like foundation money."[31]

Despite Harrell's backing, the magazine faced financial challenges, as was indicated by Harrell's letter to the other editors in 1990. Harrell notes that the rising costs and declining circulation had led him to the conclusion that "our financial situation was more

28. Dee Bowman, in discussion with the author, July 25, 2021.

29. Brent Lewis, in discussion with the author, February 26, 2021.

30. Coulter Wickerham and David Holder, "Intro Part 2," YouTube video, 7:58, February 10, 2009, https://www.youtube.com/watch?v=LG64Zi8zUVY.

31. Steve Wolfgang, in discussion with the author, May 28, 2021.

grim than we thought." The sources of this decline, he opined, was due in part to the increasing resistance that the magazine had received in the past eighteen months due to the controversy over Homer Hailey.[32] Though the magazine would continue for another nine years after the Hailey issue, until publication was discontinued in 1999 and the subscription list given to *Focus* magazine, the articles related to the "Hailey controversy" would remain one of the most enduring and oft-cited contributions of the magazine both to the spiritual journey of Ed Harrell, as well as the broader history of congregational churches of Christ in the United States.

---

32. Harrell, David Edwin Harrell, Jr., "Letter to the Christianity Magazine Editors, October 30, 1990," Series 2.F.8, David Edwin Harrell, Jr. Papers, 1923-2017, Center for Restoration Studies MS #467, Abilene Christian University Special Collections and Archives.

CHAPTER EIGHT

Peacemaker

> "In the forty-five years that I have been preaching the gospel, I can never remember a time when different interpretations on marriage and divorce were not a matter of debate among brethren and soul-searching decision-making at the congregational level."[1]

The third major biography that Harrell wrote was about Homer Hailey. Published in 2000, the work was a hybrid—both a biography of Hailey, who had been one of the most influential figures in the congregational churches in the second half of the 20th century, and a history of the churches of Christ in the 20th century. This "innovative biography," as one of Harrell's historian colleagues called it, provided a retrospective look at a Christian figure who represented Harrell's father's generation of Christians. Hailey was born in 1903, twenty-seven years older than Harrell Jr., born in 1930, and seven years younger than Ed Harrell's father, David Edwin Harrell Sr., who was born in 1896.

---

1. David Edwin Harrell, Jr., "Divorce and Fellowship," 1. Discussion Presentation at the 1991 Florida College Lectureship, 12-13, Series II.G.38, David Edwin Harrell, Jr. Papers, 1923-2017. Center for Restoration Studies MS #467, Abilene Christian University Special Collections and Archives.

In the Hailey biography, Harrell surveyed the most formative moments among Churches of Christ in the 20th century and included some events in which Harrell himself had played a role. As he notes in his preface to the work, "I have been a spokesman in the debates that have taken place."[2] The hybrid genre of the book, Harrell's final monograph, is a synthesis of Harrell's past emphases on the history of Christian movements and the lives of Christian leaders in the 20th Century. It was "a dual book, two books in one."[3]

Harrell frames his narrative of Hailey's life within the historical development of Churches of Christ from 1920 to 1999. From the beginning of the 20th century, this history was one of varying degrees of unity and division over doctrinal differences. When significant divisions did occur, Harrell asserts, it was not so much over doctrines, as it was the fundamental assent to the restorationist hermeneutic. Harrell emphasizes the role of the powerful "editor bishops" within the Churches of Christ, and how the religious periodicals aligned themselves with one faction or the other on the major issues of the day.[4] Men such as Foy Wallace Jr. and B. C. Goodpasture utilized their leadership of the periodical papers to torch or ban those they believed caused division.[5] In the first half of the 20th century, divisions were limited because of general allegiance to a restorationist hermeneutic that sought in the New Testament a pattern for individual and congregational life. Early leaders were faithful to this primitivist

---

2. David Edwin Harrell, *The Churches of Christ in the 20th Century* (Tuscaloosa: The University of Alabama Press, 2000), xv.

3. Harrell, David Edwin, Jr., "Homer Hailey's Personal Journey of Faith - Part 1," audio recording, February 20, 2001; (https://texashistory.unt.edu/ark:/67531/metapth791513/: accessed August 27, 2024), University of North Texas Libraries, The Portal to Texas History, https://texashistory.unt.edu; crediting Abilene Christian University Library.

4. Harrell, *The Churches of Christ in the 20th Century*, 6.

5. Ibid., 50.

vision, and Homer Hailey chose to attend Abilene Christian University because it identified with such a conservative approach.[6] This contrasted with schools like Texas Christian University, a Disciples of Christ school, which by the 1930s had jettisoned the rationalism and Biblical primitivism that had characterized the theology of the Disciples of Christ in the previous century.[7]

Unity and Disunity

Focusing on the controversies among mainstream Churches of Christ between 1920 and 1950, the Hailey biography spotlights the growth of doctrinal fissures within the rapidly growing Churches of Christ between the world wars and especially after WWII. These churches had remained relatively united because they were committed to restoring New Testament Christianity. The main ingredients of this unifying primitivist principle were: 1) a common-sense reading of the New Testament; and 2) a conviction that they were the faithful remnant of God amid a world that was not their home.[8] Other qualities that held them together were a shared commitment to freedom of thought and expression, which was often unruly but that pursued a shared goal within the "wild democracy" of the Churches of Christ. This shared purpose held the churches together, Harrell observes, although their populist confidence was tested by differences in belief and practice, from the use of a single or multiple cups during the Lord's Supper, to the convening of Bible classes and youth meetings, to teachings about whether a Christian needed to separate from his or her spouse at the point of becoming a Christian because of an unscriptural divorce in their background. This final issue, often termed "Marriage, Divorce, and Remarriage" (or "MDR") was a recurring issue in the history

---

6. Ibid., 7-9.
7. Ibid., 34.
8. Ibid., 42.

of the churches of Christ (as well as other Christian groups) that grew in prominence and divisiveness during and after the cultural upheavals (and rapid rise in divorce rates) in American society during the 1960s and 1970s. Underlying these potentially divisive issues was the question of fellowship: to what extent can I worship with someone with whom I disagree on matters of Biblical teaching. What is essential and what is trivial?[9] As Harrell describes it,

> Of course, defining triviality was the essence of an inherent fellowship dilemma in the churches of Christ. One person's triviality was another's test of loyalty to New Testament authority. No clear New Testament teaching was trivial to a restorer. Thus, the only test was whether a matter was clearly established by the Scriptures or merely a misguided opinion.[10]

This question of fellowship amid disagreement is a motif recurring throughout the Hailey biography and is most often addressed by Harrell with an analysis of what various preachers taught about it. David Lipscomb, a 19th century leader among Churches of Christ, argued for patient teaching of those with whom

---

9. Another background and context for the disagreements over MDR was the "Grace-Unity Movement" among institutional Churches of Christ, peaking in the 1970s and attracting several preachers from among the congregational churches of Christ (e.g., Ed Fudge). Sparked by the ecumenical and culturally accommodative writings of preachers Carl Ketcherside and Leroy Garrett, the movement emphasized the power of God's grace over doctrinal disagreements, so that true Christian unity was possible even among those Christians with a diversity of views on core doctrinal matters, e.g., the necessity of baptism, the deity of Christ, and the reality of eternal hell. Some opponents of Harrell's views on Christian fellowship would describe him as falling prey to the heresy of "unity in diversity," which misapplied God's grace as an excuse for continuing in sinful belief and practice. This was a charge that Harrell flatly and consistently denied, emphasizing the important of obedience to the doctrine of Christ as revealed in the New Testament in order to receive the saving grace of God.

10. Ibid., 45.

one differed. Foy Wallace, Jr., a leading figure of the 20th century, identified and sought to eradicate what were regarded as deviant teachings arguing for Christian pacifism and premillennialism.[11] Though the suppression of these doctrines was divisive, Harrell argues like historian Richard Hughes before him, both sides in these debates had an "apocalyptic" or otherworldly mindset that maintained a core set of attitudes despite doctrinal differences. Harrell clarifies that this distinctive and unifying mindset in the mid-20th century is best described as the worldview of "sojourners" or a "peculiar people" who experience and express alienation and separatism from the culture and have a low estimation of human ability to improve it.[12]

When his *History of the Churches of Christ in the 20th Century* turns to focus on the congregational churches of Christ, Harrell highlights the fact that Homer Hailey was a lifelong pacifist.[13] No one "issue" defined Homer Hailey, but like most people he held minority viewpoints that distinguished him from others, and that he would share when asked, but did not actively promote. This pacificist perspective was a belief shared by Hailey and Harrell. In his early adulthood, Harrell took a separatist viewpoint regarding the relationship of Christians to the government, both declining requests to run for public office during his time at ETSU and also refusing to vote.[14] Harrell mentioned this latter fact in a 1975 academic conference—that he had voted only once in his life in 1964 against presidential candidate Barry Goldwater—and it so scandalized his fellow historian Sidney E. Mead that Mead subsequently wrote a letter of concern to the conference organizer.[15] The pacificist

---

11. Ibid., 50-57.

12. Ibid., 71-73. This is a mindset of otherworldly alterity that Harrell elsewhere in the book (pp. 167-69) associates with simplicity of life and doctrine.

13. Harrell, *The Churches of Christ in the 20th Century*, 278.

14. Deedee Harrell, in discussion with the author, November 16, 2020.

15. Richard T. Hughes, "David Edwin Harrell, Jr. and the History of the Stone-

perspective was noteworthy in Harrell's thinking as an example of a matter of Christian faith about which Christians disagree but find it still possible to fellowship with believers of a different persuasion. This, along with disagreements over women's wearing of a head-covering during worship and the indwelling of the Holy Spirit are evidence, Harrell observed, of an expansive understanding of the nature of Christian fellowship among churches of Christ that maintains a unified commitment in pursuit of Biblical truth while allowing for diversity of faithful perspectives on matters of truth.

In his biography of Hailey, Harrell details much of the debate over the topic of "Marriage, Divorce, and Remarriage" that was sparked by Hailey's teaching on the topic and the subsequent reactions to it. Harrell sets Hailey within a trajectory of other well-known preachers who had diverse perspectives on the topic of divorce and remarriage, including Harding University professor James D. Bales and *Gospel Guardian* editor James W. Adams.[16] The

---

Campbell Tradition," in *Recovering the Margins of American Religious History*, edited by B. Dwain Waldrep & Scott Billingsley (Tuscaloosa, Al: University of Alabama Press, 2010), 24-32, 26.

16. Harrell, *The Churches of Christ in the 20th Century*, 341-346. The position of James Adams and responses to him by Connie Adams and others evidence that the debate over MDR and fellowship occurred in different eras in a repeated, cyclical way. James W. Adams, "False Conclusions from Just Principles," *Gospel Guardian* (June 1, 1976): 220-221; "Johnny-Come-Lately-Sommerites," *Gospel Guardian* (February 1, 1978): 52-53; James W. Adams, "Speak for Yourself John," *Gospel Guardian* (January, 15, 1978), 28-29; James W. Adams, "Every Way of Man is Right In His Own Eyes," *Gospel Guardian* 30.10 (May 15, 1978): 220-221; James W. Adams, "Splendid Murder," *The Apostolic Messenger* (July 1989): 3. Cf. James D. Bales, *Not Under Bondage* (Searcy: J.D. Bales, 1979). See the summary of and responses to Bales' work in Dennis G Allen and Gary Fisher, eds., *Is It Lawful? A Comprehensive Study of Divorce* (Auburn, MI: Allan and Fisher, 1989): 219-227, 269-285. As is seen in throughout Allen and Fisher's book, Bales is one of several preachers and/or professors (e.g., Lloyd Moyer, Olan Hicks, Glen Lovelady, Jack Freeman, Pat Harrell, E. C. Fuqua, Jim Puterbaugh, and Jerry Bassett) who taught what were considered by some

most controversial aspect of Hailey's belief and teaching is that non-Christians who were divorced and remarried prior to becoming Christians were not under the new covenant that Jesus initiated and that made the marriage sinful. Therefore, they could remarry before becoming Christians and remain married after they became Christians. Hailey's views on Marriage, Divorce, and Remarriage were not unknown. For example, in February 1988 he preached a sermon in California presenting his interpretation of the issue:

> Now when God says, "I will remember them no more ... I will blot them out," I can't understand our brethren who want to bring up certain things that a person did back yonder before he obeyed the gospel and now then want to charge that against him now.[17]

In March of that same year, 1988, Hailey presented his views about divorce and remarriage at the church in Belen, New Mexico, allowing the session to be recorded. The church then shared the videos with Ron Halbrook, a preacher at the church of Christ in West

---

Christians to be falsely permissive interpretations of Biblical passages related to divorce and remarriage during the 1960s through 1990s. Set within this context, Harrell's defense of Hailey was seen by some as perpetuating a heretical stream of worldly teaching in churches about Biblical marriage. For a description of this "apostate movement" and simultaneous defense against attacks by others (e.g., J.T. Smith) with more restrictive understandings of Matt 19, see Jeff Belknap, "Ron Halbrook's Letter to J. T. Smith in 1993," last updated January 26, 2006, last Accessed November 17, 2024, https://www.mentaldivorce.com/mdrstudies/RonHalbrooksLetterToJTSmithIn1993Examined.htm.

17. Homer Hailey, "Sermon at El Cajon, CA, Feb 25. 1988—A.M. Session," Series 2.D.1, David Edwin Harrell, Jr. Papers, 1923-2017, Center for Restoration Studies MS #467, Abilene Christian University Special Collections and Archives. Harrell would observe privately that he thought Hailey's views on MDR resulted from his lifelong zeal for evangelism, given that his accommodative view was more conducive to divorced couples being converted out of a worldly background (David Edwin Harrell, "Talk to Grandkids." Digital audio recording. July 2012. Recording in possession of author).

Columbia, Texas, seeking his opposing view. In a subsequent letter to Hailey, after his invited trip to Belen to share his views, Halbrook expressed his respect for Hailey and his effort not to personalize the discussion. At the same time, he states his confusion and concern over Hailey's position on the issue, both cautioning about the impact that Hailey's viewpoint could have among Christians and also urging Hailey to consider a number of points that Halbrook delineates in his letter, including the questions of whether non-Christians are amenable to the law of Christ (Halbrooks affirms they are, contrary to Hailey), and of whether 1 Corinthians 7:15 teaches that a Christian deserted by a non-Christian spouse is free to remarry (Halbrooks affirmed he or she is not, contrary to Hailey). Halbrook concludes his letter with hope of continuing fellowship: "May God bless us as we continue to keep doors of communication and study open with one another to a view that we might be united upon his word."[18] In his response to Halbrook, Hailey states his regret over their differing views, but affirms that he was comfortable with the view he holds, and regardless of the influence he might have on others, he "seek[s] only the favor of God ... I have never sought to conceal my views but have always expressed myself when asked."[19] What comes through in this and other parts of Hailey's response is a strong sense of personal responsibility for study of God's Word on the issue and conscientious conclusions on that basis.

Strains in a Common Mind

In the summer of 1988, the editor of *Torch* J.T. Smith wrote

---

18. Ron Halbrook, "Letter to Homer Hailey, April 15, 1988," Box 28, David Edwin Harrell Jr. Papers 1923-2017, Center for Restoration Studies MS #467, Abilene Christian University Special Collections and Archives.

19. Homer Hailey, "Letter to Ron Halbrook, May 4, 1988," Box 28, David Edwin Harrell Jr. Papers 1923-2017, Center for Restoration Studies MS #467, Abilene Christian University Special Collections and Archives, Brown Library. Abilene Christian University, Abilene, TX.

a series of articles critiquing Hailey's position and describing him as a false teacher.[20] In response, Harrell wrote a defense of Hailey in the fall of that same year in an article entitled, "Homer Hailey: False Teacher?" The article was an exception to *Christianity Magazine's* standard policies, both in taking up a controversial topic with a "personal exchange" and stretching the length of the article beyond the normal length, from one page to four. Harrell would decades later acknowledge that this mention of the Hailey controversy was his "single transgression" changing the paper away from its primary purpose and intention.[21] In addition to pointing out the difficulty and historical diversity of viewpoints around the issue of "Marriage, Divorce and Remarriage" (MDR), Harrell argued that the title of "false teacher" leveled at Hailey was not appropriate insofar as his motivations were not evil, but came from a place of honest difference over committed interpretation of Scripture and its application to Christian life.[22] In the article, Harrell signals a number of themes that he would address in *Christianity Magazine* throughout the following year in a series of sixteen articles on the "bounds of Christian fellowship."[23]

Harrell's historical treatment of the events that unfolded from 1988 through 1990 in his biography of Hailey provides an insightful, if largely (and uncharacteristically) one-sided account of the debate over the issue of "Marriage, Divorce, and Remarriage"

---

20. J. T. Smith, "Did I Misrepresent Homer Hailey," *Torch* 23.8 (August 1988): 2-8; J. T. Smith, "Homer Hailey's Teaching on Divorce and Remarriage," *Torch* 23.6 (June 1988) 21-22; J. T. Smith, "Brethren Do Strange Things," *Torch* 23.5 (May 1988): 7.

21. Coulter Wickerham and David Holder, "Intro Part 1," YouTube video, 7:16, February 10, 2009, https://www.youtube.com/watch?v=R-dL2GdZhIk&t=62s.

22. David Edwin Harrell Jr., "Homer Hailey: False Teacher?" *Christianity Magazine* 5.11 (November 1988): 326.

23. The first of the sixteen articles was "The Bounds of Christian Unity (1)" *Christianity Magazine* 6.2 (February 1989): 38. An article in the series appeared in every issue until the final one in Christianity Magazine 7.5 (May 1990): 134.

and the effects of the Hailey controversy that continued through the next decade. This includes Harrell's own analysis of the debate over Hailey's position as an expression of two divergent tendencies within the American Restoration Movement: 1) a drive to define truth so as to be certain about the facts of Scripture, defining what God requires of His people; versus 2) a drive to unify believers so as to pursue restoration through ongoing efforts to explore what the Bible teaches about God's will and how we can best restore this. Harrell depicts this as "strains in a common mind" and as a tension between truth as a proposition and truth as a pursuit. Those more judgmental of Hailey's position were in the former camp defining true propositions, versus those, like Harrell, who disagreed with Hailey's teaching on divorce and marriage, but maintained fellowship because they both were pursuing truth with a Biblical process and goal. Echoing the criteria for Christian fellowship that he delineates in his sixteen-part series on the topic in *Christianity Magazine*, Harrell explains in the Hailey biography that he maintained fellowship with Hailey because Hailey was neither divisive nor dishonest, but rather had a reputation as a moral man with the obediently submissive mind of Jesus. Furthermore, Hailey taught what Harrell considered to be error, but error taught in good conscience on matters that were less than fully clear in Scripture.[24] In the Hailey biography, the contrast between the two tendencies in the Restoration Movement is exemplified in the persons of Mike Willis and Ron Halbrook, on the one hand, and Ed Harrell and Robert Turner on the other.[25] For Willis and Halbrook, the heresy of Hailey's view was "clear-cut" and there was need for "concrete definition of the boundaries of fellowship" and "rigid doctrinal boundaries."[26] For Harrell and Turner, the approach

---

24. Harrell, *The Churches of Christ in the 20th Century*, 349, 354.
25. Ibid., 361-366.
26. Ibid., 361.

was less divisive and more cohesive, with the bounds of fellowship set by a common mindset and character that can produce common doctrinal conclusions through "principled commitment."[27]

Like all theoretical constructs, Harrell's two-way distinction between propositional and process approaches to fellowship is too neat to describe the complexities of the history of congregational churches of Christ and the various voices involved in the debate over Homer Hailey's teachings. For example, the propositional mindset that sought clear lines of fellowship could also pursue personal and principled processes for coming to mutual understanding. As the previously mentioned letter from Ron Halbrook to Homer Hailey demonstrates, Halbrook was concerned for the task of coming to better understanding of Hailey's position and not simply marking him out as a false teacher.[28] In fact, the editor and writers for *Truth Magazine* had not termed Homer Hailey a "false teacher." It was the label given to Hailey by J. T. Smith that prompted Harrell's response in *Christianity Magazine*. "The *Truth Magazine* guys got hit with a lot of splatter from J. T. Smith," recalled *Truth* board member, Steve Wolfgang. "A lot of the reaction of the Hailey thing was because J. T. said Hailey was a false teacher. The *Truth Magazine* staff said relatively little compared to J. T."[29] Furthermore, the mindset that sought unity through shared principles and relationships could be rigidly propositional in defense of this perspective. An example of this was Harrell's assertion that Romans 14 addresses not only matters of "indifference" or "opinion" (e.g., whether or not to observe Christmas at home or serve in the government as a profession) but also questions of faith and truth that were

---

27. Ibid., 363.

28. See the similar sentiment in Ron Halbrook, et al., "To Set the Record Straight: Recent Studies With Homer Halley On Divorce And Remarriage," *Guardian of Truth* 32.22 (November 17, 1988): 689-91.

29. Steve Wolfgang, in discussion with the author, October 17, 2022.

matters of spiritual significance and clearly taught in Scripture. Harrell's interpretation was counter to a widely held view that Romans 14 was exclusively concerned with how Christians should address matters of religious opinion, i.e., scruples of conscience and not core matters of doctrinal truth. In opposition to this more commonplace interpretation, Harrell asserts that "the issue in Romans 14 is precisely the establishment of the right of brethren to differ in matters of 'faith.'"[30] In his book about Hailey, Harrell adduces allies in this view of Romans 14, but does not acknowledge differing views, which were both established viewpoints and forthcoming from dissenting voices before and after publishing his series of articles on the "bounds of Christian unity" in 1989-90.[31] Harrell's stance shows how his concrete definition of propositions (viz., the meaning and significance of Romans 14) was prerequisite to his mindset and approach to unity, which he saw focused on honest character and principled commitment as the true basis of Christian fellowship. The "propositional" and "principled" perspectives were thus intertwined in his position on MDR and Christian fellowship. This is further evidenced by the disagreement over his interpretation of Romans 14 among at least some of the *Christianity Magazine* editors. For his part, Sewell Hall disagreed with Harrell on Romans 14, but Hall nevertheless "agreed with him on where Ed came out on fellowship."[32] Similarly, fellow editor and preacher Paul Earnhart diverged on this point. "I didn't agree with his use of Romans 14, but I did agree with where he came out. The end results were exactly what we practiced all those years and that result had been expressed in *Christianity Magazine*."[33] Earnhart also wrote articles taking a different view of Romans 14 than that

---

30. Harrell, "The Bounds of Christian Unity (3)," *Christianity Magazine* (April 1989): 134. See more on this topic below in this chapter.

31. Harrell, *The Churches of Christ in the 20th Century*, 359-60

32. Sewell Hall, in discussion with the author, May 25, 2021.

33. Paul Earnhart, in discussion with the author, May 28, 2021

of Harrell.[34] "I took a good bit of heat on that," he recalled.[35] Thus, even more tolerant, open-ended approaches to Christian fellowship like Harrell's were rooted in firm assertion of truth and divisive Biblical interpretation that defined a process of truth-seeking fellowship.

Harrell was aware of this. He observes in his biography of Hailey that the two mindsets—propositional and principled process—are not divergent, but overlapping, with relatively different emphases. The two viewpoints are "strains in a common mind," with everyone in the movement having both perspectives but emphasizing one over the other.[36] The complexity of mindset is further seen, for example, in a more recent book by preacher Gardner Hall, *Conviction and Mercy*. Hall portrays Biblical wisdom as a merger of the two perspectives: both conviction and mercy.[37] As Hall observes, Jesus' conviction to oppose the teaching of the Pharisees and Sadducees existed in tension with his mercy for the tax collectors and sinners. Both perspectives came with a cost but were according to the divine will. With rigid and rational conviction, Jesus quickly opposed the rules of the Pharisees (e.g., refuting their shallow approach to serving God in Matthew 23) and set up strict doctrinal boundaries against the Sadducees (e.g., opposing their teaching about the

---

34. E.g., Paul Earnhart, "When Christians Disagree," Last updated April 2022. Last Accessed November 18, 2024. https://www.cedarparkchurchofchrist.org/resources/articles/2022/04/04/when-christians-disagree.

35. Paul Earnhart, in discussion with the author, May 28, 2021

36. Harrell, *The Churches of Christ in the 20th Century*, 361: "Every person in noninstitutional churches of Christ was a distinctive mix of both concepts, but some defined their religious identity more narrowly and propositionally, while others had a higher tolerance for dissent and uncertainty."

37. Gardner Hall, *Conviction vs Mercy: Merging the Two to Deal with Modern Spiritual Challenges* (Port Murray, NJ: Mount Bethel Publishing, 2013), 71-75. Those with strong conviction are, of course, not without mercy, and vice versa.

resurrection in Luke 20).[38] But Jesus also conversed with Pharisees like Nicodemus and ate with tax collectors like Zacchaeus, effecting their illumination and salvation by building on their good characters and shared priority for God's will.

Despite their different perspectives, both sides of the debate were concerned for the health of a broader brotherhood. Harrell had begun *Christianity Magazine* with a concern that the congregational churches not become unnecessarily factious. "*Christianity Magazine* fulfilled a fairly significant function in its seventeen-year period in noninstitutional churches in giving a certain cohesion to what could have become a Sommerite movement," Harrell later reflected. "[Non-institutional churches] could have become an extremely narrow base, factional movement. It has not become that. The magazine will be looked on as a centrist expression in a time that could have become quickly factionalist."[39] Similarly, Harrell's concern to defend Hailey clearly arose from a concern for Hailey's reputation among the broader brotherhood. At the same time, Harrell identified denominational concepts of unity—i.e., the idea that individual churches were somehow part of a larger church organization—as a source of confusion and dissension in setting the bounds of fellowship: "Sometimes our own speculators take on a denominational ring—will some issue 'split the church?' Or 'what will be the next thing that will divide us?' Such statements may reflect a perception that the universal church is a functioning organization. Or they may imply a creedal understanding of the bounds of Christian unity."[40] To this, his interlocutors among the editor and writers of *Truth Magazine* responded that it may *seem*

---

38. Ibid, 68-70.

39. Coulter Wickerham and David Holder, "Intro Part 13," YouTube video, 8:23, February 10, 2009, https://www.youtube.com/watch?v=ZwaYTtDOjxk.

40. David Edwin Harrell, Jr., "The Bounds of Christian Unity (2)," *Christianity Magazine* 6.3 (March 1989): 70.

that this is the case, but it was not. In a public forum at the Florida College lectures in 1990, Mike Willis acknowledged the need for clear lines of fellowship on doctrinal matters in the brotherhood.[41] But in calling for this, Willis was not seeking to create a denominational identity over which he or other writers should have some sway, but rather to witness to the Biblical truth that individual Christians and individual congregations must discern how to apply truth in their respective contexts. "I think we would view ourselves as walking in the footsteps of brother [Clinton] Hamilton, brother [Jim] Cope, Melvin [Curry], and so forth," observed Mike Willis. "They took that same stand in the institutional battle that we felt we have tried to take in our own issues that we see before us today, whether or not we see them clearly or plainly."[42]

In this way, the advocates for opposing Hailey's views on divorce and remarriage viewed their public stand on the issue as an obedient and public witness to the truth of God's Word for the good of individual Christians and congregations. No less than the debate over institutionalism, upon this view, the debate over MDR was a question of "kenotic spirituality," of emptying oneself of conceits and personal preferences in obedience and in glorifying to God. For such Christian "watchmen," it was a question of whether preachers and other Christians would follow Jesus in His self-emptying love and teaching, and simply doing what Scripture teaches. As at least one writer observed, Harrell's dogged defense of his friend Hailey was a matter of thinking of himself more highly than he should in defense of a friend.[43]

---

41. Mike Willis, "What Saith the Scriptures? Divorce and Remarriage and Fellowship," Speech Delivered at Florida College (5 February 1991).

42. Mike Willis, in discussion with the author, October 17, 2022.

43. See the quotation of a bulletin authored by Ken Leach—"A perfect example of thinking more highly of man than one ought to think is the Ed Harrell editorial"—cited by Samuel G. Dawson, "Fellowship on Marriage, Divorce, & Remarriage," page 6, last Accessed September 10, 2023, https://www.

Similarly, all sides in the debate were concerned to maintain Biblical orthodoxy. One such effort in the 1990s was an attempted delineation of "twenty-one propositions" about which Christians should be able to agree to stay in fellowship.[44] These efforts at codifying unity were, however, part of Ron Halbrook's broader concern over the signs of an "apostasy" underway among congregational churches of Christ that extended to changing Christian attitudes.[45] Harrell agreed these broader cultural concerns were warranted.[46] Halbrook viewed the MDR issue and related fellowship questions as key indicators of how Christians should engage the increasingly hostile society. What might be perceived as rigid creedalism could also be viewed as a principled stand against the processes by which Christians are allured and changed by an ungodly culture.

Evidence for the broader cultural concern over MDR came in 1993, when Ron Halbrook was invited by Olen Holderby, who had spent almost all his life preaching in California, to come and preach on the West Coast, arranging invitations to preach at seven different congregations. As he traveled, Halbrook asked members of the churches to tell him about the area in which they lived and about the churches in their area. As he reported in *Truth Magazine*, about a third of the churches (there were about 120 congregational churches of Christ in California at that time) were committed to the error on divorce and remarriage (i.e., of not requiring the separation of a couple who had married contrary to Scripture before they became Christians). About a third were committed to

---

samuelgdawson.com/uploads/1/1/5/5/115526689/fellowship_on_mdr.pdf.

44. Ron Halbrook, "Are We Doomed to Divide Over Every Difference on Divorce and Remarriage? (2)," *Guardian of Truth* 40.17 (September 5, 1996): 16-18.

45. Ron Halbrook, *Trends Pointing Toward a New Apostasy* (Bowling Green: Guardian of Truth, 2000).

46. Harrell, *The History Churches of Christ in the 20th Century*, 358.

teaching that unscriptural divorce and remarriage was a matter of Christian fellowship. And about a third could swing either way—it didn't matter.[47] "It's not just that issue [of MDR] that defined the three groups," observed Halbrook. "The people who would have accepted the divorce issue were more comfortable with Christians going to the casino, mixed swimming parties, and social drinking. The churches not accepting the divorce and remarriage issue would have been the flipside of all these other issues."[48]

Set within this broader context of shifting cultural beliefs and values in the late 20th century, the "propositional mindset" identified by Harrell is seen not only as a rigidity about the interpretation of Scripture, but also as a guard against broader societal trends seeking to accommodate sinful practices as either acceptable "diversity in unity" or misguided wrongdoing covered by God's grace.

Principle Personalities

Another important factor, not addressed by Harrell in his Hailey biography, was at the core of the debates over the MDR and bounds of fellowship in the 1980s and 1990s: personal disagreements among Christian leaders over the principles under discussion. Negative interpersonal relationships were a catalyst for public doctrinal arguments. At least one writer observed that Harrell's initial defense of Hailey seemed overly personal.[49] And

---

47. Ron Halbrook, "The Continuing Battle Over Divorce & Remarriage" *Guardian of Truth* 37.10 (May 20, 1993): 16-19.

48. Ron Halbrook, in discussion with the author, October 17, 2022.

49. Keith Greer "Romans 14—Where Are We Heading?" Last accessed September 13, 2024, https://www.knollwoodchurch.org/yr2001/h01_heading. html: "The opening article written to defend a close friend of brother Harrell—the late Homer Hailey, the center of the discussion has been wrong." Cf. Connie Adam's review of Harrell's biography of Hailey as being overly slanted towards his friends and against detractors, in "Editorial Left-overs," *Truth Magazine* 44.17

it was, in fact, a personal attack by J. T. Smith on Homer Hailey as a "false teacher" that occasioned Harrell's entry into the debate and much of the ensuing back and forth involving the question of Christian fellowship. Beyond these public attacks among preachers, more emotions existed privately beneath the surface. "There was original unease among some on the *Truth* staff because of the 'positive Christianity' approach," observed *Truth Magazine* editor Mike Willis. "This was more directed at Dee than at Ed. Ed was held in high esteem by everyone on the *Truth* staff until he wrote about Hailey in 1988 and the articles on fellowship." Throughout its history, *Christianity Magazine* was an invitation-only paper. Only authors asked to write articles were accepted for publication. In the early years of *Christianity*, Steve Wolfgang and his wife Bette were invited to write, but after the Hailey controversy they weren't. Steve Wolfgang interpreted this as due to his affiliation with the wrong crowd. Whether or not this was the case, the potential for this type of personal animus was predicted and guarded against by *Truth* editor, Mike Willis, who invited Sewell Hall, one of the *Christianity Magazine* editors, to come to the congregation where he preached in Danville, Indiana. He did this when the controversy over Hailey began to heat up in order to explore how far apart they were on the issues and interpersonally. "He stayed in my home, and we had extensive conversations," recalled Willis. "There was no bad blood."[50]

This concern for harmony would persist, but it was partly undermined by a series of public mistakes in published content. The first came from *Truth Magazine's* special article on Divorce and Remarriage in January 1990. Steve Wolfgang had written the lead article on the history of the issue and outlined some of the

---

(September 7, 2000): 3.

50. Mike Willis, in discussion with the author, October 17, 2022. Willis had reached out to Dee Bowman and Sewell Hall on more than one occasion to discuss the issues.

different positions.[51] He properly cited two quotations from Harrell's dissertation about early preachers' comments about marriage, divorce, and remarriage in the Restoration Movement. A few months later, Mike Willis picked up these historical quotations and prominently presented them in an article called "Ed Harrell on Divorce and Remarriage."[52] Harrell responded forcefully to the confusion caused by the quotation and threatened to sue.[53] His personal letter to Mike Willis and other members of the *Guardian of Truth* board of directors reported his attorney's judgment that the paper's journalism was libelous in its malicious misrepresentation and undermining of credibility (though Harrell stated he had no intention of filing suit) and expressed his belief that "my views have been misrepresented in the *Guardian of Truth*."[54] Willis later wrote a retraction apologizing for the error.

Harrell's response to Willis included mention of his willingness to meet at Florida College for a discussion of the issues. Accordingly, the two met the following year at Florida College in 1991. Each read a paper on the topics of MDR, Hailey, and the fellowship issues.[55] The dialogue was cordial, but afterwards, Clinton Hamilton, former Vice President at Florida College, went onto the stage during the

51. Steve Wolfgang, "Marriage, Divorce and Remarriage in Church History," *Guardian of Truth* 34.1 (January 4, 1990): 27, 29-3.

52. Mike Willis, "Ed Harrell on Divorce and Remarriage," *Guardian of Truth* 34.8 (April 19, 1990): 227.

53. Steve Wolfgang, in discussion with the author, October 17, 2022. Cf. Ed Harrell, "A Response by Ed Harrell," *Guardian of Truth* 34.15 (August 2, 1990): 455-456.

54. David Edwin Harrell, Jr., "Letter to Mike Willis, undated." Series 2.F.8, David Edwin Harrell, Jr. Papers, 1923-2017, Center for Restoration Studies MS #467, Abilene Christian University Special Collections and Archives.

55. The Progressive Primitivist, "Divorce & Remarriage and Fellowship Discussion | Florida College 1991 | Dr.Ed Harrell & Mike Willis," YouTube Video, Uploaded December 6, 2023, https://www.youtube.com/watch?v=x3rF_-mLM6g.

open forum and made a statement about how the young men were "trying to make a name for themselves" and goading Hailey into the position in which he found himself. Hamilton was reportedly quite upset about it. When he was finished the audience broke out in applause.[56] Others felt Hamilton's comments were inappropriate in expressing greater concern about those who replied to Hailey than about what Hailey taught. The next day, preacher and editor Connie Adams spoke to the audience, both expressing his love for Hailey, but also defending those who had the courage to speak out against the teaching of someone of his stature.[57]

Harrell wrote Hailey the month after the lectureship and reflected that his speech at Florida College "went pretty well," and that "Clinton Hamilton stole the show with his quip about you. There was a kind of pent-up release of emotion when he told the truth."[58] Responses to the exchange varied. For his part, Hailey reported hearing a recording of the discussion with Mike Willis and having great appreciation for how Harrell defended him: "Even though one differs from my view, I do not consider it to be such as to brand me a false teacher, any more than I do brand my opponents, though I believe them to be wrong with the same intensity with which they believe me to be wrong ... Please study what I have written, and then consider that the only passages they have are those in the Gospels, especially Matthew 19, and that none of these deal with the alien [sinner] ...".[59]

---

56. Steve Wolfgang, in discussion with the author, October 17, 2022.

57. Steve Wolfgang, in discussion with the author, June 8, 2024.

58. "Ed Harrell letter to Homer Hailey, February 28, 1991," Series 2.A.29, David Edwin Harrell, Jr. Papers, 1923-2017, Center for Restoration Studies MS #467, Abilene Christian University Special Collections and Archives. Additional perspectives expressed support for Harrell's presentation, e.g., "Letter from Gardner Hall to Ed Harrell, Feb 27, 1991," Series 2.A.28, David Edwin Harrell, Jr. Papers, 1923-2017. Center for Restoration Studies MS #467. Abilene Christian University Special Collections and Archives, Brown Library, Abilene Christian University, Abilene, TX.

59. "Letter from Homer Hailey to Ed Harrell, February 28, 1991," Series

Years later, Harrell's biography of Hailey would cause public tensions to boil over again when Harrell misattributed to Mike Willis a critique of Robert Turner and other preachers that had actually been made by *Faith and Facts* editor, John Welch.[60] When Steve Wolfgang asked why he had been not able to review the manuscript, Harrell said he was afraid that Wolfgang would share it with other people on the *Truth* staff, which stung Wolfgang even more. "The angriest argument I ever had with Ed took place shortly after the Hailey book was published in the empty parking lot after the Christian Scholars Conference at Pepperdine University, looking out over the Pacific Ocean," recalled Wolfgang. "I told him that he made some serious errors of fact in the Hailey biography and that I could have saved him from that." Harrell did make the change in subsequent editions of the biography, and the publisher had to reset the typeface for the whole page to make the change. Harrell never made a public acknowledgment of the error and did not publish an errata statement in the subsequent printings. These decisions seemed to some writers for *Truth Magazine* to be inconsistent with Harrell's insistence on fair treatment of his own words in previous years.[61]

Doctrinal differences often reflect and exacerbate personal disagreements, sometimes spreading to other individuals and entire congregations. "This [disagreement] was more about personalities, and I think there were some 'preacher issues,' perhaps even jealousy involved in this," observed preacher Wilson Adams.

2.A.28, David Edwin Harrell, Jr. Papers, 1923-2017, Center for Restoration Studies MS #467, Abilene Christian University Special Collections and Archives.

60. The error occurred on page 353 of the first printing of the Hailey biography. Cf. Connie Adams, "Editorial Left-overs," 3: "Mike Willis was misrepresented twice ... A later apology to Mike Willis does not undo the harm done by the copies of the book already in circulation."

61. Steve Wolfgang, in discussion with the author, May 28, 2021.

"There seemed to be a lot of mistrust."[62] The editors of *Christianity Magazine*, for example, were accused of supporting Homer Hailey's position. Editor Sewell Hall received a letter from a fellow preacher, questioning "whether the editors of *Christianity Magazine* agreed with Homer Hailey's teaching on MDR."[63] In responding to these and other questions about his beliefs (ranging from the existence of true Christians in denominations, to the duration of the days of creation), Hall observed that an unknown man had recently sent letters to his Christian contacts in England (where Hall was working) to let them know that Sewell Hall was one of the "New Apostasy preachers" who "only preach to entertain, just tell jokes, never preach against anything, don't use scriptures in their preaching, believe in evolution, error on divorce & remarriage, etc. etc." Hall suggested to the brother in England who called him about it that, if he felt he should reply, he should just say, "'This is not the Sewell Hall I have heard preach,' and let it go at that."[64]

The effects of the disagreement spread to churches and their treatment of the preachers involved. Sewell Hall recalled that Ed Harrell had been to Eastside Church in Athens two to three times and the members had liked him. Sewell invited Ed to preach again in his absence and Ed agreed. Sewell went to the elders' meeting on the day after the *Guardian of Truth* magazine contained a very critical article about Harrell. Just as soon as Sewell mentioned Harrell, one of the elders spoke up saying: "Nope, we're not having him [Ed Harrell] here." "That cancelled Ed," Sewell Hall observed. "No paper ought to have that sort of power."[65]

---

62. Wilson Adams, in discussion with the author, June 25, 2024. In the interview, Wilson Adams (son of Connie Adams) observed that he was not judging the hearts of the men involved.

63. Sewell Hall, in discussion with the author, May 25, 2021.

64. Sewell Hall, "Email to Ed Harrell and Paul Earnhart, September 4, 2002," Series 2.D.4, David Edwin Harrell, Jr. Papers, 1923-2017, Center for Restoration Studies MS #467, Abilene Christian University Special Collections and Archives.

65. Sewell Hall, in discussion with the author, May 25, 2021.

The "cancelling" of preachers who had been named, or who had named names, in doctrinal battles has a long history among churches of Christ. The effect of this was felt on both sides of the debate over Homer Hailey.

> There are churches that would have none of the [*Truth Magazine* writers] to preach meetings. In the past you could almost tell [the nature of the church] by looking in the tract rack, where they bought their tracts. The new way is to look on their website and see who they invite for gospel meetings. It is also true that there are '*Truth Magazine* churches' who would not have someone from Florida College if he was the last man standing. It's not a one-sided division, but it's clearly there, and has been for twenty to thirty years.[66]

Reflecting on the effect of the MDR and fellowship exchanges in the 1990's, editor Mike Willis observed that most of the regular writers of *Truth Magazine* had become "pariahs." "It pretty well ended my [gospel] meeting career," reflected Willis. "I think that's a fall out of what happened on this."[67] The

---

66. Steve Wolfgang, in discussion with the author, October 17, 2022. (A previous version of this book inaccurately attributed this quotation to Mike Willis.) A related concern over the partisanship of Florida College in the MDR and Fellowship debates would be voiced repeatedly. E.g., "This seems to be the road Florida College wants to take. 'We want and have many friends, and we stand with our friends.' This is the 'unity in diversity' that has been advocated and practiced for many years," O.C. Birdwell, Jr. "2001 Florida College Lectures" *Truth Magazine* 45.11 (June 7, 2001): 6; cf. Truman Smith, "Neo-Institutionalism," Last accessed August 30, 2024, https://www.knollwoodchurch.org/yr2001/l06_neo_inst.html: "Many of our brethren who have jumped on the bandwagon for such an erroneous use of Romans 14 are, in some way, associated with Florida College in Tampa, Florida. Yes, I am well aware that it is a 'cardinal sin' to say anything negative about Florida College! Sadly, to many, this school has become a 'sacred cow.'" At the end of this article, Truman Smith invokes the memory of nineteenth-century reformer Daniel Sommer in his critique of the Christian college.

67. Mike Willis, in discussion with the author, October 17, 2022.

exchange over Hailey had the effect of canceling preachers on both sides of the issue.

Despite the conflict with some writers for *Guardian of Truth*, Harrell remained optimistic about the possibility of continued conversation and fellowship. In a note to Mike Willis after their discussion at Florida College, Ed apologized for his own "intemperate language" in one of his written responses to Willis, and noted his belief that continued engagement on the issues was valuable: "I think a continued discussion of both the questions of divorce and remarriage and the grounds of fellowship are important."[68] One such discussion was prepared for in January 1999, when preacher Wilson Adams wrote to a group of ten invitees including Mike Willis, Steve Wolfgang, Weldon Warnock and Connie Adams. "They often disagreed sharply," Wilson Adams recalled, "but it helps when brethren get together to talk *with* each other, and not *at* each other."[69] The three-day conference in June of that year, sequestered in a Nashville hotel, would focus on discussion of issues pertaining to fellowship, as well as the trends and tones of the papers (especially *Guardian of Truth* and *Christianity Magazine*). After a reading of position papers on the issues, especially MDR and Romans 14, the men would sit and discuss. Wilson Adams opined that "there is no reason why ten brethren cannot sit down and reasonably discuss areas of concern in a way that reflects respect for one another and love for the Cause ... I pray and trust that something good will result."[70] The meeting was arranged to include the writers

---

68. Harrell, David Edwin Harrell, Jr., "Letter to Mike Willis, undated," Series 2.F.8, David Edwin Harrell, Jr. Papers, 1923-2017, Center for Restoration Studies MS #467, Abilene Christian University Special Collections and Archives.

69. Wilson Adams, in discussion with the author, June 25, 2024. Mike Willis had made a number of previous attempts to arrange such a meeting.

70. Adams, Wilson, "Email to editors of Christianity Magazine and Guardian of Truth, January 14, 1999," Series 2.E.1, David Edwin Harrell, Jr. Papers, 1923-2017, Center for Restoration Studies MS #467, Abilene Christian University Special Collections and Archives.

of *Christianity* on the condition that Ron Halbrook not be included in the discussion, because he had named some of the *Christianity* editors' names in his gospel meetings, typically on Thursday nights when his lesson focused on how the brotherhood was drifting. Dee Bowman especially bristled at the negative public accusations.[71] This exclusion of Halbrook from the discussion was part of a larger perceived blackballing of the long-time preacher because of his stridency on "the issues." In the preface to Halbrook's 1998 booklet on the MDR issue, Mike Willis expressed his dismay over the attacks on Halbrook: "One could get the impression from listening to the comments made about him ... that brother Halbrook is the incarnation of the Devil himself. Yet, when, one reads their material closely and checks the sources for himself, he sees that no one has answered the scriptural arguments that are made and the documented material state exactly what it is quoted as saying."[72] Despite Halbrook's absence from the gathering convened by Wilson Adams in 1999, the results were mixed.[73] While some participants recall that they departed on a more positive note than when they began, others felt that it was too little, too late, and "it didn't accomplish much of anything."[74] "I think it produced a deeper trust and appreciation for each other," concluded Wilson Adams. "It didn't help everyone the same. But there were ten men with different perspectives."[75]

---

71. Steve Wolfgang, in discussion with the author, October 17, 2022. "There would not have been a meeting if Ron came," Wilson Adams, in discussion with the author, June 20, 2024 and June 25, 2024.

72. Mike Willis, in discussion with the author, October 17, 2022. Cf. Ron Halbrook, *Understanding the Controversy Over Divorce-Remarriage, Romans 14, and Fellowship* (Bowling Green: Guardian of Truth, 1998), 3. Ron Halbrook, Trends Pointing Toward a New Apostasy (Athens, AL: Truth Publications, 2017).

73. When Ron Halbrook agreed to step aside (at the insistence of the CM editors), O.C. Birdwell (longtime *Truth Magazine* board member, writer, and bookstore manager) was asked to be the 5th person.

74 Mike Willis, in discussion with the author, October 17, 2022.

75. Wilson Adams, in discussion with the author, June 25, 2024.

The different results of the discussions resulted not only from the different individual perspectives, but also the complexity of the issues packed into the disagreement over Hailey's position and Harrell's defense of him. It is important to ask: why do Christians, after multiple efforts to reconcile their personalities and beliefs, walk away from such efforts in continued division over the issues? One explanation for the complex response is the actual complexity of the issue(s) involved in their disagreement. The debate included four overlapping problems, which were all controversial and often not clearly stated. The four problems changed over time in their focus and were easily confused in ways that engendered dissension. Though they were never delineated by Harrell in this way, the four problems can be identified as follows: 1) the clarity of Scripture in differences between the truths of "faith" and "opinion;" 2) the meaning and significance of Romans 14 in dealing with differences of faith; 3) the difference between individual and congregational fellowship, and 4) the role of preachers and editors in addressing brotherhood issues, including the identification of false teachers.[76]

1. Different Views of a Common Mind

The first and most foundational problem was the clarity of Biblical truth in matters of faith and Christian doctrine. The difficulty was first presented as the question of what constituted a false teacher. J.T. Smith had labeled Hailey a false teacher in his periodical *Gospel Truths*."[77] In subsequent years Ron Halbrook, among others, identified Hailey as teaching one of five "false theories on divorce and remarriage," namely, "that Matthew 19:9 is 'kingdom law'—it applies only to the marriages of Christians and does not apply to

---

76. I seek here to describe impartially the complexity and challenge of these "four problems" without taking sides in the debates.

77. Harrell, *The Churches of Christ in the 20th Century*, 348.

the world."[78] The implications were thought to be clear. Hailey's teaching was a "false doctrine" that accepted adulterous marriage and, if accepted, opened the door to all such theories. It was a violation of the "doctrine of Christ" (2 John 9-11) and was not a matter of personal conscience, so that "no matter how convinced or sincere he seems to be about the truth of his false doctrine, from the objective standpoint of God and His Word the man violates the doctrine of Christ and cannot be received into fellowship."[79] For his part, Hailey had felt the impact of this perspective. He knew he was "being charged as a false teacher, unfit for the fellowship of certain ones who differ from me."[80]

As we have seen, Harrell led the charge in defending of Hailey, observing that he was not a false teacher because he was sincere and not schismatic.[81] Others lined up in support of Hailey, including former Florida College president, Bob Owen. The issues would quickly become a disagreement focused on the limits of Christian fellowship involving interpretations of Romans 14 and how best to communicate these concerns with other Christians across the brotherhood. But the most divisive issue was, at its core, about the nature of Biblical truth. Harrell viewed Biblical truth as at most times obvious and to be affirmed without question. But when Christians of "like minds" disagree, Harrell acknowledged that the Bible could be less than fully clear, and this ambiguity required both more study and patient judgment of the honesty of a Christian with whom one

---

78. Ron Halbrook, *Understanding the Controversy Over Divorce-Remarriage*, 9.

79. Ron Halbrook, *Understanding the Controversy Over Divorce-Remarriage, Romans 14, and Fellowship* (Bowling Green: Guardian of Truth, 1998), 9-10, 13.

80. Homer Hailey, "Homer Hailey Speaks," *Christianity Magazine* (November 1988): 327.

81. David Edwin Harrell Jr., "Homer Hailey: False Teacher?" 326.

disagrees on certain passages and their application.[82] In his sixteen articles on the "Bounds of Christian Unity," Harrell concluded that judgment about the clarity of New Testament instruction was foundational for other questions of identifying false teachers and fellowshipping of those in error: "Our assessment about the clarity of a passage becomes the basis for all our decisions about the bounds of Christian unity."[83] In such cases, therefore, one's judgment of the truth or falsehood expressed by a like-minded Christian was connected to their moral character. If a Christian flagrantly perverts the clear teaching of Scripture or dishonestly disagrees on a matter of unclear teaching, then one should judge that Christian to be immoral and a false teacher. However, if one seems honestly to disagree over a matter of unclear teaching, then a discerning Christian may be justified in not judging that person as a "false teacher" and continued fellowship is possible. For example, for J. T. Smith to call Homer Hailey a "false teacher" seemed to contradict the fact that most everyone had long recognized Hailey as a good and honest man and had not disfellowshipped him over his stance on the MDR issues. This was presumably, Harrell implied, because people recognized that people of good conscience could disagree over MDR because of the relative lack of clarity about the specific applications of the clear Biblical doctrine that adultery is sin and that marriage is a permanently binding commitment. Many Christians in the past, Harrell observes, had not viewed this as an issue requiring disfellowshipping. Such contextual considerations do not make Hailey's teaching true, but they do call into question

---

82. David Edwin Harrell, Jr., The Bounds of Christian Unity (7)," *Christianity Magazine* (August 1989): 230.

83. David Edwin Harrell, Jr., "The Bounds of Christian Unity (16)," *Christianity Magazine* (May 1990): 134. See also how this issue is signaled in the first article: "Sometimes the judgments of God are clear and unmistakable ..." Harrell, "The Bounds of Christian Unity (1)," *Christianity Magazine* (February 1989): 38.

the charges that he was a false teacher, because he seemed to be honest in his interpretation about relatively unclear passages.

Harrell's perspective on the nature of Biblical truth appears in his writings at multiple points in his defense of Homer Hailey and especially in his 1991 discussion with Mike Willis in their public discussion at Florida College on the topic of "Divorce and Fellowship." After affirming that he and Willis both agreed that there is clear scriptural teaching and it should never be violated, Harrell observes that both men also "acknowledge that there are honest disagreements of belief among brethren because all Biblical teaching is not of equal clarity."[84] Citing different views on women's head coverings, serving in the military, as well as interpretations of Matthew 19, Harrell concludes that the judgment to entrust these views to God is an admission that "we regard the subject as sufficiently lacking in clarity to accept a brother who disagrees with us."[85] For Harrell, therefore, the judgment about "clarity" is one both about the clarity of the Scripture and clarity about the character of a Christian with whom one disagrees. The issue of the clarity of Scripture was a longstanding discussion in the history of Christian theology but it was rarely articulated in the writings of the 1990s when the debate over Hailey was most active. Harrell's writings were relatively unique in making it clear that assumptions about the clarity of Scripture often underlie personal conclusions about the bounds of fellowship. The problem, he observes, is that some Christians judge a relatively few Biblical truths to be less certainly apprehended, while all parties agree that most of the

---

84. Harrell, Jr., "Divorce and Fellowship," 9. Cf. Bob Owen, "We Differ, Can We Fellowship," PM Sermon, and Q&A Period, Concord, NC (February 19, 1995): " ...I heartily concur that there are some things that are taught in the Scripture that are more explicitly covered and that we agree on more universally than some other issues." Last Accessed August 4, 2024, https://soundteaching.org/fellowship/owen3.htm.

85. Ed Harrell, "Divorce & Fellowship," 10-11.

Bible is clear in its meaning and significance. These few unclear passages rendered some Christians more tolerant of differences in their interpretation and application. Harrell states that Christians should recognize and acknowledge that they regularly experience varying levels of clarity in their understanding of Biblical teaching. He stated this most pointedly in his written exchange with Dudley Ross Spears. Harrell observed that if every unresolved doctrinal disagreement over matters of faith led to disfellowship, then "that principle would divide and redivide every congregation in the nation."[86]

One such guard against abuse of this uncomfortable truth about the unclarity of some Biblical truths comes in Harrell's observation that the debate over MDR and fellowship was unlike the division over institutionalism in the 1950s. This difference was because those involved in the contemporary debates over MDR remained convinced that others were committed to "speaking as the oracles of God" and that they respected the intent behind one another's arguments. In the historic division over institutionalism, Harrell argued, broad-scale rupture resulted only when people developed "divergent concepts of God, the Bible, the Church, and how to live as Christians ...".[87] In this vein, half of the articles in Harrell's sixteen-article series on "The Bounds of Christiani Unity" were less about

---

86. David Edwin Harrell, Jr., "Ed Harrell's 3rd Response to Dudley Ross Spears," last accessed July 29, 2024, https://www.biblebanner.com/ga_art/rom14/eh2drs3.htm.

87. David Edwin Harrell, Jr., "Divorce and Fellowship," Discussion Presentation at the 1999 Florida College Lectureship, 12-13, Series II.G.38, David Edwin Harrell, Jr. Papers, 1923-2017. Center for Restoration Studies MS #467, Abilene Christian University Special Collections and Archives. Harrell is citing the work of Steve Wolfgang, "History and Background of the Institutional Controversy (4)," *Guardian of Truth* 33.10 (May 18, 1989): 296-297, 309-310. Cf. The Progressive Primitivist, "Divorce & Remarriage and Fellowship Discussion | Florida College 1991 | Dr. Ed Harrell & Mike Willis," Last Accessed August 4, 2024," https://www.youtube.com/watch?v=x3rF_-mLM6g.

Biblical exegesis and more concerned with lessons from church history about truth and fellowship during the American Restoration Movement. This focus on disagreements among Christians over the past two centuries was criticized by his opponents; but Harrell had focused purposefully on church history to illuminate a single point: divisions in religious movements recur not over a particular doctrinal disagreement but over different religious mindsets.[88] This historical context served to deemphasize *what* Christians disagree about and to reemphasize *why* they disagree. To illustrate his point, Harrell observes that the earliest purveyors of institutionalism among the Churches of Christ were not termed "false teachers," but that the cleavage among groups of churches (whether it be division from the Disciples of Christ or the institutional Churches of Christ) grew into differences of Christian worldviews and religious mindsets, and did not occur due to disagreements over particular doctrines (e.g., instrumental music or church-supported colleges).[89]

> I have always insisted that the division over liberalism came not because brethren discovered that they had conscientious differences, but because they concluded that some were no longer trying to follow the New Testament pattern.[90]

These mindset divergences were differences in the way believers viewed the world, the church, and, most importantly, the Bible. "Our movement basically divides in two ways over hermeneutical dissonance, when people come to the point that they are no longer reading and interpreting the Scriptures the same way, and

---

88. For the criticism of Harrell's sociological approach and historical emphasis in his sixteen articles on the bounds of Christian unity, see Mike Willis, "When Apostasy Occurs," *Guardian of Truth* 34.8 (April 19, 1990): 226, 246-248.

89. Harrell, "The Bounds of Christian Unity (16)," 134.

90. "Letter from Ed Harrell to Tom Roberts, November 24, 1990." David Edwin Harrell, Jr. Papers, 1923-2017. Center for Restoration Studies MS #467. Abilene Christian University Special Collections and Archives, Brown Library.

over generational changes in which over a period of time people no longer behave in the same way."[91] Unlike the division of the 1950s, most Christians in contemporary congregational churches of Christ agree about the authoritative truths and nonnegotiable morals taught by Scripture. These are questions of the truth of Jesus and his deity, how one becomes a Christian, the character of the Christian (e.g., that one should not be a liar or adulterer), and how the church as a community should worship and work together. As Harrell put it, "disagreement cannot be tolerated if it is the source of factiousness (Romans 14:1) [and] clear and open immorality is intolerable (1 Corinthians 5)."[92]

It is important to pause and observe the extraordinary nature of Harrell's explanation of the bounds of Christian unity in his *Christianity Magazine* articles. In making his appeal to the *experience* of disagreements among Christians in their local congregations and the *history* of divisions in the tradition of the churches of Christ, extending back over a hundred years, Harrell is bringing to bear a greater variety of sources of religious authority (namely, contemporary experience and past tradition) than were regularly invoked (at least explicitly) in determining how to overcome doctrinal differences among churches of Christ. It is important to recall that academic authorities on the topic of religious primitivism accepted it as given that primitivists were essentially and sometimes intentionally ignorant of the lessons of church history. As expressed by one of the leading church historians of the day, most primitivists were only unwittingly and unwillingly aware of "the hermeneutical circle," that is "the realization that all

---

91. Coulter Wickerham and David Holder, *"Christianity Magazine* Part 7," YouTube video, 5:23, 10 Feb. 2009, https://youtu.be/Nwu2NX61CXU?si=iWfyc6MGA4A4kJGf&t=170.

92. David Edwin Harrell, Jr., The Bounds of Christian Unity (16)," *Christianity Magazine* 7.5 (May 1990): 134.

interpreters bring something to interpretation."[93] Harrell's cultural and historical consciousness of the nature of congregational churches of Christ focused him more upon the restorationist disposition and Biblicist perspective among these churches as the key to their unity. This was more about the shared process of coming to Christian belief through obedience to the Word of God, rather than punctilious agreement about personal beliefs that were not necessarily impacting congregational unity. Harrell's broader perspective of the history of the Restoration Movement led to a more accommodating view of doctrinal differences, due both to his own personal conservatism on the issues in question (as he often pointed out, he felt he was more restrictive in Christian belief and behavior than his interlocuters), and due to his belief that honest zeal for the New Testament pattern was more important to Christian union than agreement regarding teachings that were uncommonly unclear, as evidenced by experience and history.[94]

The extraordinary nature of Harrell's argument, however, does not necessarily mean he was right. Harrell's appeal to personal experience and past church history as sources of authority in seeking understanding of disagreements of MDR gave many of his fellow Christians pause. For example, Dudley Ross Spears, Harrell's student and friend, expresses his shock over Harrell's acknowledgement that the Bible admits different interpretations and conscientious fellowship of individuals with whom one disagreed in matters of faith: "He has gone much further away from truth than anyone would have anticipated. This is not only a

---

93. Martin E. Marty, "Primitivism and Modernization: Assessing the Relationship," in *The Primitive Church in the Modern World*, edited by Richard T. Hughes, ed (Urbana: University of Illinois, 1995), 7, 1-13.

94. For examples of Harrell's claims that he was more conservative (or "more restrictive" than his interlocuter or other Christians), see Harrell, "Ed Harrell's 3rd Response" and Harrell, ""Divorce and Fellowship."

surprise, it is sad."[95] When Harrell compares differences over MDR to disagreements over the head covering and pacifism, Dudley Ross Spears questions Harrell's view of the clarity of God's revelation: "Is Ed willing to deny that God has clearly revealed His will on marriage, divorce, and remarriage?"[96] Responding to his own question, Spears asserted that just because we don't have "answers to the knotty problems that may be posed" does not mean that God has not revealed His will clearly and that, instead, people have allowed any number of factors to bring them to a misunderstanding of the truth as God revealed it. Dudley's point is threefold. First, as many others would observe, the New Testament has multiple commands that Christians should be of the same mind and that we should not have fellowship with those outside the doctrine of Christ. Second, the tradition of the Restoration Movement shows that until the late 20th century, there was near unanimity about the sin of adultery and that sexual immorality was the only exception. It is, therefore, American culture that has changed and created uncertainty about MDR. God's word has not changed. Third, people often appeal to the lack of clarity in God's Word in self-serving ways or in ways that justify a course of action already chosen by friends or family.[97]

Despite Harrell's calls and claims for a single mindset between him and his interlocutors in the Hailey affair, others were not so optimistic about their similarity in worldview and hermeneutical approach. In his reflections on the concerns over Homer Hailey's teaching on MDR, the preacher and editor Connie Adams perceived "two mindsets," "a different mindset," or at least "diverging mindsets," related to the issue.[98] The one mindset was a "soft" one on Biblical

---

95. Dudley Ross Spears, "In Response to Ed Harrell—#3," last accessed July 29, 2024, https://www.biblebanner.com/ga_art/rom14/drs2eh3.htm.

96. Dudley Ross Spears, "In Response to Ed Harrell—#2," https://www.biblebanner.com/ga_art/rom14/drs2eh2.htm.

97. Ibid.

98. Connie W. Adams, "Introduction," in Halbrook, "Understanding the

teaching. The other was a tenacious one which "continues to hold to the pattern of sound words ...".[99] The soft mindset was, Adams observed, to be seen in Ed Harrell and his fellow editors, both in their positive focus in the content of *Christianity Magazine*, and in their nonconfrontational editorial policies and accommodation of those who taught error. The opposing and more tenacious mindset opposed everything contrary to the "faith once delivered to the saints" and this mindset was willing to stand up for the faith.[100] Under this view, the mindset willing to oppose any error in remarriage was the viewpoint holding fast to Scripture. This viewpoint insisted on the clarity of the Scriptures, denying ambiguity in Jesus's teachings on marriage, divorce and remarriage: "Matthew 19:9 is just as simple as Acts 2:38."[101] For his part, Harrell in a different context would respond that the question was not whether or not one opposes sin and error, but on the basis of what principle will one decide what is unscriptural. "The question before us is this: How do Christians decide what disagreements involve such clear teachings [to which all Christians must subscribe] and what disagreements arise from an inability on the part of like-minded people to reach a common

---

Controversy," 6-7. Similarly, "A different mindset has been clearly established," Connie W. Adams, "Harsh Treatment at Florida College," *Truth Magazine* 45.11 (June 7, 2001): 8.

99. Connie Adams, "Introduction," in Halbrook, "Understanding the Controversy," 6.

100. Connie Adams, "Introduction," in Halbrook, "Understanding the Controversy," 6.

101. Donnie V. Rader, "What God Has Joined Together—Jesus on Marriage. Lecture given at Florida College (February 8, 2001)," Last updated October 31, 2008, last accessed August 4, 2024, https://www.truthmagazine.com/what-god-has-joined-together-jesus-on-marriage. This lecture and particularly its naming of names of preachers holding different positions produced a strong counterresponse during the FC Lectureship. Various accounts are collected by Mark Mayberry, "FC Lecture 2001," created October 31, 2008, last accessed August 20, 2024, https://www.truthmagazine.com/fc-lecture-2001.

belief."[102] His sixteen articles in *Christianity Magazine* on the "Bounds of Christian Unity" had attempted to answer that question by giving criteria for judging whether to maintain fellowship with another Christian: from avoidance of factiousness to being clear and honest. The underlying disagreement was not whether there was a clear pattern of Christian belief and practice in the New Testament, and whether Christians should hold to it, but whether MDR always was a part of that clear pattern. For some, the answer was "yes," the Scriptures are clear.[103] In contrast to this adamant mindset, Harrell proposed an accommodative approach by which the answer was "no" and "yes." On the one hand, Harrell thought Matthew 19 was clear, and he disagreed with Hailey, believing that Christians and non-Christians should not divorce or remarry except in cases where they are victims of fornication. But Harrell nevertheless knew honest Christians who disagreed with him on this point, and he acknowledged the implications of this experience in the lack of clarity of Scripture in such cases. He believed he should fellowship those who honestly and morally disagreed with him on questions related to marriage, divorce and remarriage.

The differences between the adamant and accommodative mindsets toward MDR underwent a significant alteration in the 1990s when some of those with the more rigid mindset came to their own disagreement over what constituted matters of Christian faith/doctrine in distinction from religious opinion/scruples. In addition to questions of different justifications for divorce besides

---

102. David Edwin Harrell, Jr., "Divorce and Fellowship," 3.

103. See, for example, several *Guardian of Truth* articles rejecting Harrell's view on the the lack of clarity in certain Scriptures, e.g., "Truth is objective, not subject to my permission, approval or agreement. The fact that something may not be clear to me does not alter its binding force nor suggest that we may have fellowship simply because we disagree or fail to understand it alike," in Tom M. Roberts, "Review of the Harrell-Willis Exchange," *Guardian of Truth* 35.14 (July 18, 1991): 432-435.

fornication (e.g., physical abuse), a central and public disagreement occurred over whether the innocent party in the divorce (the one who did not fornicate) could divorce the spouse who committed adultery, if that guilty party had already divorced him/her.[104] In such a case of the guilty spouse wrongly "racing-to-the-courthouse" (which raised questions of the role of civil government in divorce) the innocent spouse might be considered unable to remarry unless they could divorce as Jesus prescribed in Matthew 19:9. Given the presumed absence of a formal, civil government divorce document in this case, the situation was pejoratively described as "mental divorce." When some writers for *Truth Magazine* expressed an openness to this possible interpretation of Jesus's teaching in Matthew 19, others who were adamant about the meaning of Matthew 19 disagreed.[105] While some viewed it as an opinion or different judgment about the application of the Matthew 19 passage,

---

104. For defense of the right of the innocent party to divorce his/ her adulterous spouse after being divorced through a court action, see Bill Cavender, "A Response to Brother David Watts. Jr. November 14, 2004." Online at https://www.biblebanner.com/articles/mdr/bc2dw1.htm. For criticism of the position that there are more than one reason for scriptural divorce (a position attributed to Mike Willis), see Don Martin, "Mike Willis Responds!" Last accessed August 4, 2024 at https://www.bibletruths.net/Archives/BTAR348. htm. For criticism of multiple writers of *Truth Magazine*, comparing them to Ed Harrell and editors of *Christianity Magazine*, see Don Martin," Exchange started by Pat Donahue with Mike Willis," Page updated January 26, 2006 , Last Accessed August 4, 2024, https://www.mentaldivorce.com/mdrstudies/ ExchangeStartedByPatDonahueWithMikeWillis.htm.

105. Correspondence among the *Truth* writers evidenced a drawing of boundaries between, 1) those who believed the issue was a matter of conscience (Willis, Halbrook, Cavender, Haile, Warnock, Alexander), and 2) an uncompromisingly adamant mindset that viewed it as a matter of Christ's doctrine and clear Biblical truth (e.g. Rader, Watts, Jr., Belknap, J.T. Smith, Gwin). These names are mentioned and the accusations of blackballing by those who "are not in any compromising mood" by Bill Cavender, "Donnie Rader's Resignation," email dated October 03, 2005, last accessed August 4, 2024, https:// www.mentaldivorce.com/mdrstudies/DonniesResignation.htm.

others viewed the "mental divorce" position as a matter of the doctrine of Christ, a matter of faith, and therefore a false teaching to be opposed.[106] Though Halbrook and others adamantly maintained the difference between their appeal to 1) conscientious opinion and 2) the doctrine of Christ on MDR, they and others nevertheless faced the charge of false teaching (or fellowship with false teachers) that some had leveled against Hailey (and Harrell).[107] In the view of some, the internal disagreement among the *Truth Magazine* writers over MDR issues undermined the collective impact of the writers' critique of Harrell (and Hailey), as well as the longer-term influence of the periodical in the brotherhood.[108] Regardless of the external

---

106. Ron Halbrook appeals to the judgment of Mike Willis that their disagreement about the mental divorce situation is "a difference of judgment in the realm of application of the one law of divorce and remarriage and not the teaching of another law," Ron Halbrook, "False Teachers: Ron Halbrook's Rebuttal to Bob Owen," *Toward a Better Understanding*: The Burnet Meeting, last modified July 17, 2002, accessed August 4, 2024. Cf. Ron Halbrook, "Why Halbrook Fellowships Smith, Rader, and Other Faithful Men in Spite of Some Differences," Last updated November 1, 2008, available online at: https://www.truthmagazine.com/why-halbrook-fellowships-smith-rader-and-other-faithful-men-in-spite-of-some-differences. The background of this concern over further disagreement among *Truth* writers is detailed in correspondence and publications posted by Jeff Belknap at https://www.mentaldivorce.com/. For a different perspective, see Tom O'Neal's critique of those "obsessed with certain technicalities and minutiae related to divorce and remarriage" (referring to Jeff Belknap's concern over advocates of "mental divorce") in Thomas G. O'Neal, "Tom O'Neal's Letters Exposing Jeff Belknap's Binding of MDR Scruples," Last accessed August 4, 2024, https://www.biblebanner.com/articles/mdr/tgon2jb1.htm.

107. "These brethren who have so forcefully *condemned* the false doctrine which they now fellowship are the very same men who *condemned* the Romans 14 route to continued fellowship with Homer Hailey and his "adulterous" doctrine. Their earlier intolerance for error where *others* were concerned only magnifies their *own* inconsistencies," Jeff Belknap, "An Examination of Ron Halbrook's Charts," Last updated January 26, 2006, Last accessed August 30, 2024, https://www.mentaldivorce.com/mdrstudies/AnEximinationOfRonHalbrooksCharts.htm.

108. Interview with David Holder, Fort Worth, TX, July 28, 2024. The

perception, those in disagreement over the question of "mental divorce" recognized how those with a more accommodative view of Biblical truth and Christian fellowship would seize on the disagreements over doctrine to argue for a less adamant mindset.

The disagreements over the MDR issue and particularly the clarity of Scripture and its implication for identification of matters of doctrine and opinion might be viewed as conforming to the cyclical three-way division among mindsets in the American Restoration Movement. Harrell first applied this in 1962 to explain the separations of the Disciples of Christ and then the institutional Churches of Christ from the congregational churches of Christ in the late 19th and mid-20th centuries, respectively. Upon this view, the most uncompromising elements among the congregational churches of Christ, opposing any uncertainty or allowance of difference over Biblical teachings about MDR was represented by the paper *Gospel Truths*. This was most contrasted to the accommodating viewpoint represented by interpreters arguing for greater latitude in Biblical teaching about marriage, divorce and remarriage, including figures like Homer Hailey, Olan Hicks, and James Bales.[109] Within a broad middle space, along a spectrum of belief being hit from both sides,

---

undermining of the case against Hailey and the more accommodative viewpoint by the "mental divorce" debate among the more adamant mindset is observed often in the internecine correspondence, e.g., "We remember all too well the agony of the apostasy of brother Hailey," Thomas G. O'Neal, "Tom O'Neal's Letters Exposing Jeff Belknap's Binding of MDR Scruples," Last accessed August 30, 2024, https://www.biblebanner.com/articles/mdr/tgon2jb1.htm.

109. With the rise of laws permitting no-fault divorce in the United States in 1969, the incidence of divorce more than doubled between 1960 and 1980. At this same time, several Christians made the case for more accommodating views, especially regarding divorce and remarriage among non-Christians, as well as in mixed marriages involving a Christian and an unbeliever, e.g., Pat E. Harrell, *Divorce and Remarriage in the Early Church* (1967). Olan Hicks, *What the Bible Says About Marriage, Divorce and Remarriage* (1987) and James Bales, *Not Under Bondage* (1979).

was both the more accommodating *Christianity Magazine* and the more adamant *Truth Magazine*, with writers from both periodicals viewing the most uncompromising elements as "hobbyists" and the most the accommodating interpreters as "soft" in doctrine.[110]

To be sure, this historical interpretation of a three-way division over MDR among congregational churches of Christ in the late 20th century was not Harrell's viewpoint. Harrell explicitly states that the Hailey and MDR issue was not a "conservative versus liberal issue." And second, he was not willing to cede the cautionary high ground. He repeatedly states that he was more conservative than many of his interlocuters on other issues. These two premises are apparent in his discussion with Mike Willis:

> This discussion is not a liberal-conservative showdown. I yield to no one in this auditorium in my determination to follow every instruction in the word of God. I share the profound concern of all brethren about the collapse of marriage in our society. I am reasonably certain that I stand to the right of Mike Willis on most of the unsettled questions that trouble our common conscience. I oppose the use of church buildings for marriages and funerals ... I believe that the Lord's Supper should be observed only by a congregation assembled for that purpose, I oppose a local church purposely securing money in any way other than a collection on the first day of the week. All of those questions, like every matter of obedience to God's word, are important, and I would be happy to debate brother

---

110. For the views of *Truth Magazine* editor, Mike Willis, as balanced and Donnie Rader as a "hobbyist," see Bill Cavender, "Donnie Rader's Resignation." The view of *Christianity Magazine* and Harrell as "smooth" and "soft" is expressed by Tom M. Roberts, "Speaking Smooth Things About ... Romans 14 and Fellowship," *Truth Magazine* 42 (1998): https://www.truthmagazine.com/speaking-smooth-things-about-romans-14-and-fellowship.

Willis about the "liberal" views that I suspect he holds on all of them. I regard Mike Willis as a brother not because I think he is right about every question, nor because we disagree only about unimportant matters, but because I believe that we are united by the singular intent to do God's will, and to defend our actions with a "thus saith the Lord.[111]

Harrell here articulates the underlying unity of mindset that he would continue to see in the congregational churches of Christ on the MDR issue. Indeed, across the spectrum, every party repeatedly emphasized: 1) their intent to do what the Scriptures clearly taught, 2) their intent to limit their own thinking and practice and to break fellowship where this mindset was manifestly not present, and 3) their unwillingness to teach unscriptural doctrine due either to loyalty to human religious tradition or to relevance to changing cultural conditions. In this regard, from the most uncompromising to the most accommodating on the MDR issue, Harrell viewed the congregational churches as a movement of one mind that was under tension, and a primary source of tension was disagreement over the clarity of Scripture.[112]

2. The Strong and the Weak

A second problem and confusion in the debates around Hailey's view and Harrell's defense of him was the meaning and significance

---

111. Harrell, "Divorce and Fellowship," 5. See the similar rhetorical moves in his dialogue with Dudley Ross Spears, arguing against "supposedly conservative brethren" and presenting his own approach as "balanced," in David Edwin Harrell, Jr., "Ed Harrell's 3rd Response to Dudley Ross Spears." See also Harrell, *The Churches of Christ in the 20th Century*, 358.

112. See the chapter subsection on "Strains in a Common Mind," Harrell, "The Churches of Christ in the 20th Century," 360-366.

of Romans 14 and the limits of Christian unity. In Romans 14, Paul applies the Christian ethic of love to disagreements over matters of "faith" (Romans 14:1) and the maintenance of Christian fellowship in "peace" (14:19). In his defense of Hailey, Harrell appeals to Romans 14 as a Biblical basis for Christians to disagree over matters of "faith" (not just opinions or matters of indifference) while maintaining peace in fellowship.[113] This reception of individual Christians who disagree on matters of faith is done by acknowledging that each individual Christian is ultimately accountable to God and not to other Christians (Romans 14:3). As noted earlier, Harrell sets limits on this fellowship—e.g., factiousness, faith, honesty, etc.—but his core claim is that Romans 14 provides a warrant and a way for Christians to disagree on important issues of the Christian faith so that separation is not necessary.

This interpretation was not novel to Harrell. As he details at length in his Hailey biography, the editor of *Gospel Guardian*, James Adams, and other preachers, such as Marshall Patton and Melvin Curry, held similar views on Romans 14, viewing it as allowing conscientious disagreement among individual Christians on substantive issues of faith, while not interpreting the chapter to justify any accommodation of individual sin or congregational divisiveness.[114]

---

113. Romans 14 is mentioned a few times in the 16 articles on "The Bounds of Christian Unity." The chapter is mentioned once in passing in the first article, once in the fourth article (addressing factiousness), four times in the sixth article on respecting others' consciences, but mostly with specific references to eleven verses in Romans 14 in the third article, focused on his general interpretation of the chapter. He summarizes his interpretation in the final article: David Edwin Harrell, Jr., "The Bounds of Christian Unity (16)," *Christianity Magazine* 7.5 (May 1990): 134.

114. James W. Adams, "False Conclusions from Just Principles," *Gospel Guardian* (June 1, 1976): 244-45; "Speak for Yourself, John," *Gospel Guardian* (January 15, 1978): 28-29; "Johnny-Come-Lately-Sommerites," *Gospel Guardian*

Harrell's view of Romans 14 was an interpretation also shared by fellow preacher Bob Owen. In multiple sermons and conference presentations, Owen asserted that some truths might allow disagreement and continued fellowship of Christians together, if the matter of faith under question "does not compromise the other brethren, where it does not imply endorsement of error, and where it does not ... include in this the fellowshipping of fornicators, drunkards, homosexuals, thieves, etc. This principle does not deal with matters such as instrumental music in worship or congregational support of human organizations ...".[115] Similarly, in his presentations on truths about which Christians disagreed, preacher Don Patton used Romans 14 in calling for humility and patience in not being divisive towards Christians with whom we disagree on individual matters of conscience, even when these are matters of faith rooted in Christ's doctrine. "We must continue to learn," Patton encourages his audience. "We are commanded in 1 Peter 1:5 to grow in knowledge. We must be humble, knowing that we don't know it all and that we are in error about some things we'll learn about maybe next week. We must be patient and forbearing,

---

(February 1, 1978): 52-53; "Every Way of Man is Right in His Own Eyes," *Gospel Guardian* (May 15, 1978): 220-21; "While I was Musing the Fire Burned," *Gospel Guardian* (July 1978): 268-69; "Attempting to Fight the Lord's Battles," *Gospel Guardian* (September 1978): 332-22; Marshall E. Patton, "Divorce and Remarriage," *Searching the Scriptures* (January 1977): 249-51; Melvin D. Curry, Jr., "Being a Sojourner and Pilgrim in this World," *Christianity Magazine* (May 1998): 12; Harrell, *The Churches of Christ in the 20th Century*, 344-46, 362. On Curry's position on Romans 14, see Melvin Curry, "Follow after Things Which Make Peace," Truth Magazine (January 4, 1979): 28–30. Last Accessed online December 12, 2024, https://www.truthmagazine.com/archives/volume23/TM023010.html."

115. Bob Owen, "False Teaching and False Teachers," *Toward a Better Understanding*: The Burnet Meeting, last modified July 17, 2002, accessed July 27, 2024, https://web.archive.org/web/20020717114053/http://www.cedarparkchurchofchrist.org/tabu/false_owen.htm.

and we must receive one another under these circumstances."[116] But also, like Harrell, Patton emphasized the limits to such humility and patience in disagreement. There could be no compromise in matters of congregational belief and practice—matters that might lead to church division—and in cases of individual rebelliousness and obvious immorality.[117] These perspectives are indicative of a broader viewpoint among Christians that not all matters of "the doctrine of Christ" were equally knowable, and, although the vast majority of truths *were* clear, how to treat others who disagreed about such matters requires good judgment.

These precursors to his own interpretation notwithstanding, Harrell's approach was not the majority understanding of Romans 14 among congregational churches of Christ, which tended to view it as primarily addressing "opinions" or indifferent matters of scruples, and not matters of "the doctrine of Christ," i.e., core matters of faith.[118] Because this less common interpretation was understood to accommodate any and all falsehoods as long as it was

---

116. Don Patton, "Romans 14—Fellowship," Transcription of sermon preached at the Judson Road congregation in Longview, TX on April 12, 1990. Last accessed July 27, 2024. https://soundteaching.org/fellowship/patton2.htm.

117. Ibid.

118. For a more common view among congregational churches of Christ, see the statement of Kyle Pope that Romans 14 is about "matters of indifference before God," in "A Conscience without Offense toward God and Man" *Focus Online* (February 4, 2014): https://focusmagazine.org/a-conscience-without-offense-toward-god-and-man.php. Similarly, see the conclusions of Tom Roberts, "Brother Harrell has taught that he can have fellowship with brother Hailey in his teaching about adulterous marriages. That is a misuse of Romans 14," "Fellowship: Tom Roberts Rebuttal to Harry Pickup, Jr.," Toward a Better Understanding: The Burnet Meeting. Last Accessed August 8, 2024, http://www. cedarparkchurchofchrist.org/tabu/fellow_roberts_rebuttal.htm. This standard interpretation is reflected in various commentaries stemming from among Churches of Christ, e.g., Moses Lard, *Commentary on Paul's Letter to Romans* (Lexington: Transylvania, 1875), 412: [Romans 14] is pre-eminently the chapter of duties in regard to things indifferent in themselves."

held with conviction, the response and defense of the objectivity of Biblical teaching was fierce and prolonged.[119] Harrell signaled his recognition of the controversial nature of his interpretation in his concluding article, observing that "Within certain limits, God grants to Christians the right to a private conscience in matters of 'faith.' I believe that right is discussed in Romans 14. However, whether or not one accepts my exegesis of that passage, honest minds must acknowledge the reality of a past and present Christian world that tolerates contradictory Christian teachings and practices on important moral and doctrinal questions."[120]

As we have seen, most, if not all, of Harrell's fellow editors at *Christianity Magazine* disagreed with him on his interpretation of Romans 14, viewing it more along traditional lines as a question of how to resolve matters of religious opinion. But some of these editors, like Sewell Hall, agreed nonetheless with his viewpoint on Christian fellowship. In other words, Romans 14 may be about matters of "indifferent opinion" which were originally about eating of meats and special observance of days, but the balance of the New Testament teaches that Christians should receive and be patient with good and honest hearts (Luke 8:15) seeking to know the way of the Lord more accurately (Acts 18:26). The accommodation of Harrell's main point (that we should sometimes

---

119. The subjectivity and flexibility of Harrell's interpretation is fiercely equated with teaching by past heretics among Churches of Christ—e.g., W. Carl Ketcherside, Edward Fudge, and R.L. Kilpatrick—as well as earlier digressives within the American Restoration Movement. For the former see, Connie W. Adams, "The Harrell Booklet on the Bounds of Christian Unity," *Truth Magazine* 42.7 (April 2,1998): 195-196. For the broader critique, including teachings about instrumental music, premillennialism, and institutionalism, see Ron Halbrook, "Romans 14 Abused to Accommodate False Doctrine," *Guardian of Truth* 36.1 (January 2, 1992): 27-32.

120. David Edwin Harrell, Jr., "The Bounds of Christian Unity (16)," 134.

fellowship Christians who disagree with us on important matter of doctrine), despite disagreement with his exegesis of Romans 14, is an important point of agreement among the different sides in the debate over Homer Hailey that is often overlooked. Preachers on both sides of the issues argue that multiple New Testament passages, setting aside Romans 14, teach the need for openness and longsuffering towards those teaching and practicing in ways contrary to God's revealed will in Scripture. For example, in his extended exegesis of Romans 14 as a pattern for Christian disagreement on core issues of faith and doctrine, Don Patton appeals to other passages that Christians should be forbearing in matters of disagreement, e.g., Ephesians 4:2; 1 Thessalonians 5:14; Matthew 18:15-16.[121] Similarly, in his defense against a more restrictive view of Matthew 19 than his own, Ron Halbrook cites other New Testament passages on the need to receive, learn with, and patiently correct those in error, e.g., Philippians 1:10; 4:5; Hebrews 5:14; 2 Pet. 3:18.[122] Because it underscored points of shared conviction about how to get along with those in disagreement on doctrines, Harrell's use of Romans 14 served to highlight other New Testament teachings, even as it divided over interpretation of that chapter. Despite misunderstandings and divisive responses, Harrell's clear and consistent interpretation of Romans 14 as including matters of important doctrine and core Christian faith made a significant theological claim: it argued Christians could be confident of the meaning of Scripture for themselves and in some cases maintain fellowship with Christians who differ about what it means to have a true relationship with God. This freedom

---

121. Don Patton, "Exegesis of Romans 14, Preachers' Study - Grand Prairie, TX (November 10, 1994)," Last accessed October 13, 2024, https://soundteaching.org/fellowship/patton5.htm.

122. Ron Halbrook, "Are We Doomed to Divide Over Every Difference on Divorce and Remarriage? (2)" *Guardian of Truth* 40.17 (September 5, 1996): 16-18.

to accommodate significant doctrinal differences with other Christians is the most significant aspect of Harrell's interpretation of Romans 14. Though he argued for the importance of diligent and honest study of the potentially divisive issue (a teaching that his critics would point out is not present in Romans 14), the clear implication of Harrell's interpretation is that Christians might live and die in peace and mutual upbuilding (Romans 14:19) with other Christians with whom one disagreed on important matters of faith. At its root, Harrell claims, this belief that saving faith is belief that accommodates significant differences of faith in its community of believers is a matter of Biblical principle and not merely personal accommodation.

Opponents of Harrell argued that Romans 14 is not about "the faith" but only what individuals hold as a matter of conviction, and that Harrell's view was a "Trojan Horse" that would allow in every heresy under the guise of personal faith to be received and accepted.[123] In response, Harrell argued that there were clear boundaries on the important doctrines that Romans 14 would allow and that conscientious acceptance of important matters of individual faith were the rule in local communities of Christian believers and not the exception. Those opposed to Harrell's interpretation of Romans 14 were not, he avers, living their faith in the real world where Christians differ on what are matters of indifference to faith but still do not divide over them. It is a "refusal to grant that [we] live in a world where honest differences in Biblical interpretation exist." But they do, Harrell argued. When those circumstances arise "we are forced to make a judgment about the clarity of Biblical instruction, and, by extension, about the attitudes of our brethren."[124] Some of those who disagreed

---

123. Tom M. Roberts, "Romans 14: Satan's Trojan Horse for Fellowship With Error," *Guardian of Truth* 39.4 (February 16, 1995): 14-17.

124. David Edwin Harrell, Jr., "Ed Harrell's 3rd Response to Dudley Ross

with Harrell about Christian fellowship publicly acknowledged that Christians could agreeably disagree about the "application of Christian doctrine," but would not recognize that the boundary between what is "doctrine" and its "application" was itself a core matter of faith that was widely contested.[125]

Opponents of Harrell's interpretation of Romans 14 thought it undermined the authority of Christ's teaching in Matthew 19. This is the position stated by Mike Willis in his discussion with Ed Harrell at Florida College in 1991 on the topic of MDR and Christian fellowship. Regarding Romans 14, Willis argued against Harrell's argument that Hailey's teaching on MDR fit within the type of Christian belief that would allow for difference without disputation and eventual agreement. There was, Willis argued, a clear pattern of Scripture regulating marriage, divorce, and remarriage, and "men are not divided over what the Bible says, but over what the Bible does not say."[126] The sin of adultery and whether Jesus' instructions in Matthew 19 are applicable to all people, whether Christian or not, is a matter of faith and not addressed by Romans 14, but Christians could still disagree on matters of personal opinion (which Willis viewed as including women's wearing of head-coverings during worship and the question of whether Christians could justifiably participate in warfare). The fact that there are clear doctrines of

---

Spears," Last accessed August 31, 2024, https://www.biblebanner.com/ga_art/rom14/eh2drs3.htm.

125. For acknowledgement that Christians discussed "difficult points of application" of Matt 19 without dividing, see Ron Halbrook, "Are We Doomed to Divide Over Every Difference on Divorce and Remarriage? (2)" *Guardian of Truth* 40.17 (September 5, 1996): 16-18.

126. Mike Willis, "What Saith the Scriptures? Divorce and Remarriage and Fellowship," Speech Delivered at Florida College, Manuscript Copy (5 February 1991), 10. Cf. Mike Willis, "*What Saith the Scriptures? Divorce and Remarriage and Fellowship: Speech Delivered at Florida College Guardian of Truth* 25.3 (February 7, 1991): 80-88. Available online at: https://www.youtube.com/watch?v=x3rF_-mLM6g.

Christ about marriage and remarriage, Willis observes, means that there can be Christian unity on the basis of Matthew 19 and related passages, which are essential, and not matters of indifference. In this way, Willis observes, Matthew 19 and Jesus' teaching about divorce is like the Biblical teachings about the deity of Jesus and the necessity of baptism.

Harrell's defense of Hailey and his acknowledgment of honest disagreements over matters of faith and the "doctrine of Christ" and especially his basis for this in Romans 14 rendered him, in the view of some Christians, a false teacher in his own right.[127] It is difficult to overstate how controversial his perspective on Romans 14 was among some preachers within congregational churches of Christ. Some disagreed and some agreed with him. Those disagreeing with him often saw his views as dangerous. Others saw his perspective as faithful and healthy. It was a position that he would hold the rest of his life and that would exert an influence among churches of Christ. "In recent years I've noted that there are a lot more people who kind of agree with my interpretation of Romans 14," Harrell observed retrospectively.[128]

3. The One and the Many

A third problem in the debate over Hailey was the difference between individual fellowship and congregational fellowship. This distinction was an underlying and foundational consideration for

---

127. For example of one preacher who classified Harrell's teaching about Harrell and Romans 14 as "false teaching," see Don Martin, "Who is a False Teacher?" last accessed July 29, 2024, https://www.bibletruths.net/Archives/BTAR108.htm: "I overwhelmingly documented the false teaching of certain preachers within the church of Christ (Ed Harrell, Homer Hailey, etc.)."

128. Coulter Wickerham and David Holder, "Christianity Magazine Part 7," YouTube video, 5:23, 10 Feb. 2009, https://youtu.be/Nwu2NX61CXU?si=iWfyc6MGA4A4kJGf&t=170.

many of those who aligned more with the interpretation espoused by Ed Harrell regarding Biblical truth and Christian fellowship, yet its espousal was implicit or often somehow buried within the broader arguments about the Bible, faith, and the church. The key point is distinctive to the congregational organization of churches of Christ. This combination of factors in the problem—its implicitness and relative uniqueness—has contributed to misunderstanding and disunity, perhaps more than any other complicating factor in the MDR debate.

Among congregational churches of Christ in the early 21st century, the predominant view of the organization of the Church was bipartite: there is the universal church made up of individual Christians of all periods and places, and the local church made up of individuals who join themselves to a local congregation of those who confess faith in Christ.[129] Beyond this, there is only a loosely identified and configured "brotherhood" (1 Peter 2:17) and "churches" (Romans 16:16), which in the New Testament are a special concern of the apostles, whose unique mission directed them to preach the gospel to everyone, both Jews and Gentiles, across the inhabited world. Upon this view, the visible church was limited to the local church composed of Christians who are part of the universal church because of their relationship to the ascended Lord and not because of any assured relation of their church to the Lord or to any such group of churches.

The congregational organization of the churches of Christ limits the boundaries of Christian fellowship to the conscience of the individual Christian and the judgment of the local church. Lacking denominational or other institutional structure to govern Christian belief and practice, every Christian is free to decide what

---

129. A classic statement of this difference is Roy E. Cogdill, "The Called out Body," in *The New Testament Church* (Lufkin: Gospel Guardian, 1959), 2.

the Scriptures teach and which local congregation to identify with as the best reflection of the New Testament church. As a result, authors on the topic of Christian fellowship often repeated the mantra that "Christianity is individual," meaning that each person must have a relationship with Jesus Christ and must conscientiously judge the meaning of Scripture and the best community for their fellowship with others who profess to imitate Jesus and follow the teachings and examples of the apostles.[130] Viewed within this context, Harrell's repeated appeals to Romans 14 as a basis for disagreement on doctrine among Christians is an overt appeal for freedom of conscience and judgment among individual Christians. In his initial articles and explanatory essays on the bounds of Christian fellowship, Harrell repeatedly states that Romans 14 addresses the receptiveness of individual Christians towards those with whom they disagree on matters of faith and doctrine: " ... we work and worship together, leaving many matters of individual judgment in the hands of God. That behavior, uniformly practiced throughout the history of Christianity is, I believe, the issue addressed in Romans 14."[131] Similarly in his appeal to Romans 14 as a basis for Christian disagreement over doctrinal concerns, Don Patton emphasizes the individual scope of this judgment about fellowship, as does Bob Owen: "When their practice is private, when their behavior is not disruptive, when their practice does not shame the church and divide the church, we need to work for ways that we can continue together, to study together, to work together,

---

130. For an example of this emphasis on the individual nature of Christianity—"Christianity is an individual religion"—as a basis for decisions about fellowship, see Bob Owen, "Local Church and Salvation," Bible class at Concord, NC (February 19, 1995), Last accessed August 7, 2024, https://soundteaching.org/fellowship/owen2.htm.

131. David Edwin Harrell Jr., "The Bounds of Christian Unity (4)," *Christianity Magazine* 6.5 (May 1989): 6.

to pray together."[132] All these preachers thus interpret Romans 14 within the limited confines of interpersonal relationships between two believers.

Beyond the prioritization of personal conscience in service to God, Harrell's emphasis on the individual basis of Christian fellowship in Romans 14 has two primary implications for Christian faith and practice. First, Harrell's interpretation of "the bounds of Christian fellowship" presumes that Romans 14 and reception of Christians with different but faithful judgments should not be "factious." In other words, anything that would divide a local congregation because of the public and shared nature of the religious teaching is not the focus of Romans 14. Though Harrell alludes to the distinctively individual nature of Christian disagreement in Romans 14–"whatever the rights of Christians to private conscience, our disagreements cannot be allowed to create an environment that destroys our capacity to work together as Christians"–this important distinction between individual and congregational fellowship as a lens for interpreting Romans 14 is consistent in Harrell's writings. He regularly distinguishes individual conscience and congregational fellowship:

> I believe that every local church must make its own decisions about what one position (or two or three) on marriage and divorce is acceptable to that fellowship. Each Christian must decide how he or she relates to those who hold contrary views. A local church has every right to restrict its fellowship to those whose marriages conform to the restrictions of Matthew 19:3-12; I have never worshiped in a congregation that did otherwise. I believe that a Christian has the right to mark as a false teacher every person who disagrees with him about marriage and divorce.[133]

---

132. Bob Owen, "Local Congregational Fellowship," Sermon at Temple Terrace Church of Christ, Temple Terrace, FL (March 28, 1996), last accessed August 7. 2024, https://soundteaching.org/fellowship/owen4.htm

133. David Edwin Harrell, Jr., "Ed Harrell's 3rd Response to Dudley Ross

Harrell's relative lack of clarity about how these principles relate to Romans 14 may have led others with a similar interpretation of Romans 14 to elaborate on this distinction. For example, former Florida College president and long-time preacher Bob Owen repeatedly emphasized in sermons and other lectures that Romans 14 is focused on individual fellowship and that anything that might divide the church was to be decided differently within the local congregation: "You've got to keep in mind a difference between practices that are individual by nature and practices that are congregational by nature. The use of the instrument, the missionary society, the institutional question, those are questions that deal with the group practice. But a lot of other issues are individually practiced."[134] Similarly, in his well-known explanation of Romans 14 as addressing matters of individual conviction and faith, beyond opinions and scruples, Don Patton repeatedly emphasizes how this understanding of fellowship despite disagreement should not open the door to church splits and broader digressions: "The scope is much narrower in Romans 14 ... when false doctrine is being promoted, then it is no longer an individual matter and this in Romans 14 pertains only to the individual, between him and the Lord. Not like Hymenaeus and Philetus overthrowing the faith of others. When congregations are disrupted, then we are not talking about the situation in Romans 14, it would be terminated here."[135]

What Harrell, Owen, and Patton articulate is a key interpretive distinction deeply embedded in the restorationist mindset of many members of the congregational churches of Christ: the difference

---

Spears," fifth to last paragraph on page.

134. Bob Owen, "We Differ, Can We Fellowship," PM Sermon, and Q&A Period, Concord, NC (February 19, 1995), https://soundteaching.org/fellowship/owen3.htm.

135. Don Patton, "Exegesis of Romans 14," Preachers' Study - Grand Prairie, TX (November 10, 1994). Last accessed August 7, 2024, https://soundteaching.org/fellowship/patton5.htm.

between individual and corporate responsibility. Outside of interpretations of Romans 14, this appeal to individual and congregational judgment is evident in the writings of editor James W. Adams, who described the "Marriage and Divorce Question," "Carnal Warfare" and the "Artificial Covering for Women" as matters that have one thing in common: "they have to do with the practice of the individual Christian and not of a congregation as a congregation."[136] Similarly, preacher and professor Ferrell Jenkins observed the same regarding differing interpretations of the "days of creation" and the age of the earth:

> Is there a place in a congregation—and that's all that I can deal with—the congregation where I am a member? That is the only fellowship God gave me and my brethren any authority to withdraw from people, to exclude and include people. I don't have any choice in the church universal. Because everyone who obeys the gospel, the Lord takes care of that count.[137]

With reference to Romans 14, those interpreting it in pursuit of an accommodation of different beliefs among Christians (beliefs viewed as significant and not "indifferent") consistently appealed to the "individual" nature of the beliefs under consideration.[138] The

---

136. James W. Adams, "False Conclusions from Just Principles," *Gospel Guardian* (June 1, 1976): 220-221.

137. Ferrell Jenkins, "The 'Days' of Genesis 1," Puckett Auditorium, Florida College Lectures (February 8, 2000): 7-8, last accessed August 4, 2024, https://bibleworld.com/daysgen1.pdf. See the critique of Jenkins on this point, and Florida College, as expounders of a "unity in diversity" viewpoint, Don Martin, "An Exchange on Unity in Diversity," Accessed August 4. 2024, https://www.bibletruths.net/Archives/BTAR210.htm.

138. On the individual basis of fellowship decisions, see the judgment of Jesse Jenkin expresses a common judgment that fellowship over disagreed doctrines is largely a question of how much of a public issue it becomes: "If he pretty much keeps it to himself, I do not believe I have to sever fellowship. But if he presses it, I personally, do not believe I can continue to fellowship him," Jesse

effect was twofold: one, it insulated this position from charges that it opened Christians to capitulation to past heresies that had split churches (e.g., instrumental music and institutionalism). And two, it highlighted Biblical patterns for both individual and communal adjudication of doctrinal differences.[139] In his discussion with Ron Halbrook, Owen highlighted the importance of each congregation being able to determine what and how it will fellowship: "If we're going to insist that everybody treat every case exactly the same, then we're forcing ourselves into a sectarian view of the brotherhood. We're demanding that every congregation follow the same *judgment* call and if you're going to do that, we have written a creed, whether it be orally done or whether it be in writing. That kind of thinking is to me the most dangerous kind of thinking that can face us today."[140]

Opposing statements to this viewpoint distinguishing individual and collective congregational fellowship were not commonplace. But among the articulated critiques was the point that Romans 14 does not clearly address individual discussion and consensus-building on convictions of faith and core Christian doctrine. Rather, Romans 14 is about not "quarrelling" and not "passing judgment" on those who disagree with you.[141] In addition, a distinction between individual Christian and collective church fellowship is not made clearly by the Apostle Paul in Romans 14.

G. Jenkins, "Romans 14," Toward a Better Understanding: The Burnet Meeting, Last Accessed August 8, 2024, https://web.archive.org/web/20020718003231/http://www.cedarparkchurchofchrist.org/tabu/romans_jenkins.htm.

139. Bob Owen, in discussion with the author, June 25, 2021.

140. Bob Owen, "False Teachers: Bob Owen's Rebuttal to Ron Halbrook," Toward a Better Understanding: The Burnet Meeting, last modified July 17, 2002, accessed July 26, 2024, https://web.archive.org/web/20020717114053/http://www.cedarparkchurchofchrist.org/tabu/false_owen.htm.

141. Tom Roberts: "Liberty in Christ: An Analytical Exegesis of Romans 14:1 - 15:7," Last Accessed Sept 13, 2024, https://soundteaching.org/fellowship/fellowship7.htm.

Some interpreters questioned whether it was present at all in the text.[142] Beyond this, some argued for a "universal fellowship" by which individual judgments should be applied across congregations in the broader "brotherhood" in judgment of the truth or error of a teacher's doctrine: "Mutual participation may be concurrent among individuals and not only congregational."[143] Fellowship, in other words, is seen to exist outside the context of the local congregation: "..the movement to limit fellowship to local churches and individuals within the same local church is without divine authority."[144] Despite such demurrals, the distinction between individual and congregational fellowship would remain an important principle for Harrell and other interpreters seeking both adamant congregational conviction about Biblical teaching, and a more accommodative individual fellowship among those in disagreement.

---

142. Tom Roberts "Response to Don Patton," *Guardian of Truth*, 39.4 (February 16, 1995): 23-27: "Limiting Romans 14 to individual action is another fallacy."

143. Tom Roberts, "Fellowship," Toward a Better Understanding: The Burnet Meeting. Last Accessed August 8, 2024, Internet Archive, https://web.archive.org/web/20020717111339/http://www.cedarparkchurchofchrist.org/tabu/fellow_ha.htm. The argument for universal fellowship and its implications for cooperation among individuals in parachurch efforts like the Guardian of Truth organization is made in Tom Roberts, "The church is the pillar and ground of truth," in *Great Truths from Historic Controversies: Truth Magazine Annual Lectures, June 22-25, 2009*, edited by Mike Willis (Bowling Green, KY: Guardian of Truth Foundation, 2009), 2-36. That this position is taken to emphasize the ideal of the universal church over against the sufficiency of the local congregation is seen in the critique by Tim Haile, "A Review of Tom Roberts' Book: 'The Church is the Pillar and Ground of Truth' (1 Timothy 3:15)," Last accessed August 21, 2024, https://www.biblebanner.com/articles/general/roberts.htm. For a different explanation of universal fellowship distinguishing "fellowship within" (worship) vs "fellowship without" (evangelism and benevolence) see Art Ogden, "The Fellowship of Churches," *Gospel Truths Magazine* (February 1991): 13-14.

144. Don Martin, ""Is Fellowship a 'Brotherhood' Issue?" - a Review," Last Accessed August 10, 2024, https://www.bibletruths.net/Archives/BTAR116.htm.

4. Brotherhood Watch

In addition to indicating the distinction between individual and congregational fellowship, Harrell's focus on individual conscience over matters of faith in Romans 14 also indicates a fourth problem raised by the controversy over Hailey's teaching: the role of local preachers and editors in monitoring and heralding the truth and error they perceived among and across the churches of Christ. The individualistic nature of personal faith and the congregational polity of the churches of Christ were often adduced as arguments against the need for and influence of parachurch authorities, including "brotherhood watchdogs" who wrote for religious papers and (increasingly after the mid-1990s) electronic publications. Such brotherhood voices judged and warned against false teaching outside the local context. Harrell's use of Romans 14 as a warrant for fellowship of individual Christians with whom one disagrees calls into question the public broadcast of such disagreements via print periodical, digital email/blog, or online social media. This limitation is made clear by Harrell in an opening article on "The Bounds of Christian Unity" in which he distinguishes between the Biblical judgments described by the Apostle Paul and the all-too-common public tribunals among preachers of different congregations in the context of the United States in the 20th century:

> All New Testament judgments about fellowship were either individual or congregational. Anyone who imagines that he is participating in a larger scenario has constructed a denominational world. Some of the legal problems surrounding church discipline in recent years have grown out of local congregations acting as though they were components in a larger organization. Individuals and local congregations must be content to exercise the responsibilities of judgment authorized by the New Testament.[145]

---

145. David Edwin Harrell Jr., "The Bounds of Christian Unity (2),"

The specific concern over brotherhood "watchdogs" who publicly named other preachers for their false teaching was an especially volatile issue during the debate over the identification of Hailey as a false teacher. In addition to Harrell's defense of Hailey, a spark for the debate was an acerbic article authored by the usually irenic preacher, Paul Earnhart. His titular topic was "Watch Them Dogs" which, in a forceful but indirect way, expressed concern about contemporary preachers who took it upon themselves to try to police the brotherhood with published warnings about false teachers: "All of us could be usefully admonished to firmly teach the sound doctrine and live lives worthy of the gospel, but also to avoid the party spirit which carefully gathers its loyalists and looks with profound suspicion on any who do not walk with them."[146] The immediate and forceful response from different quarters was evidence of the significant and contested question of what individual evangelists/Christians should do in defense of Biblical Christianity, given the congregational bounds to fellowship among congregational churches of Christ.[147] The avoidance of partisan concepts of the church was a central concern of members of the undenominational churches of Christ, and this led to critiques of those communicating across many churches to influence their belief.[148] An example of this critique is seen in Bob Owen's 1995 sermon on Christian fellowship:

Christianity Magazine (March 1989): 70.

146. Paul Earnhart, "Watch Them Dogs" *Christianity Magazine* 13.7 (July 1996): 10.

147. Connie Adams, "Watch Which Dogs?" *Guardian of Truth* (February 6, 1997): 67-68.

148. "This is another problem with man-made orders and foundations such as the *Guardian of Truth*, they place brethren with serious and divergent views together with little if any structure and restrictions. Moreover, to some this is the real advantage of such orders, 'We are not a local church; therefore, we can do as we please'" Don Martin, "A Commendable Resignation," Last updated Thursday, January 26, 2006, last accessed August 4, 2024, https://www.mentaldivorce.com/mdrstudies/ACommendableResignation-DMartin.htm.

"It appears to me that there are some preachers who are really not just dealing with their opportunities in their places, but they've got an attitude that they've got the charge to speak to the whole brotherhood and to direct the whole brotherhood. If God wanted us organized as a brotherhood rather than local congregations God knew how to do it. He did it with the Jews 1,500 years before."[149]

The 'bishop-editor" or brotherhood "watchdog" tactics were closely related to concerns over the positions and power of religious publications. These seemed to develop party loyalty among segments of the churches of Christ. These "watchdog" tactics were a concern for some preachers insofar as they indicated a denominational and unbiblical approach to Christian unity: "I really believe that a major difference between 'us and them' (though I don't like to use that language) is the comprehension of what the New Testament church is," observed Sewell Hall about the partisanship based on periodicals. "*Truth Magazine* has a slogan, 'Subscribe to *Truth* and keep in contact.' Keep in contact with what? Are the Ethiopian churches not in contact because they don't subscribe to *Truth Magazine*?"[150] Similar to this concern over institutional loyalties, Harrell had sounded concern over human pride in conceptions and manipulations of the churches as denominational entities, especially through the officiating work of editors and formulation of unwritten creeds as tests of brotherhood orthodoxy: "We must be ever vigilant not to turn the church into an operational national organization, even

---

149. Bob Owen, "We Differ, Can We Fellowship" Concord, NC PM Sermon, and Q&A Period, February 19, 1995, last accessed August 10, 2024, https://soundteaching.org/fellowship/owen3.htm.

150. Sewell Hall, in discussion with the author, May 25, 2021. It should be noted that years later when asked about this slogan, the editor and writers of *Truth Magazine* could not recall it and did not regard it as more than indicating an intent to connect subscribers with each other.

though the alternative is to live in a relatively disorderly world of independence."[151]

Retorts to this defense of congregationalism were not frequently voiced, but when they did occur, they were focused on appeal to apostolic commands and examples of loving the brotherhood (1 Peter 2:17) or anxiety for all the churches (2 Corinthians 11:28), or a more general concern for false teaching without the intent to influence beyond the local congregation (Acts 20).

Thus in these four problematic ways, the concern over Hailey's teaching and his relationship to other Christians was a flashpoint for disagreement and debate about core issues of belief and practice within the restorationist tradition of the congregational churches of Christ. First, the question of Hailey's falsity raised contested questions about the clarity of Scripture and the appropriateness of negating Christians based on their apparently honest disagreement over unclear and contested passages of Scriptures. Second, the debate over the application of Romans 14 to the MDR issues raised important but nevertheless confusing questions over whether Christians should disagree over important matters of faith and not just indifferent scruples. Even if Harrell's interpretation of Romans 14 was dismissed, the extent of Christian patience towards heterodox teaching was debated on the basis of other New Testament passages.[152] Third, the focus on interpersonal relationships in Harrell's account of Christian fellowship distinguished it from congregational fellowship and issues that divided the broader Restoration Movement in ways that

---

151. David Edwin Harrell, Jr., "The Church and Human Pride," *Vanguard* 6 (Sept 1, 1980): 335.

152. "I believe I acted in a way that pleased the Lord [by continuing in fellowship with a brother in error]. But Romans 14 is not the proof that I did. Passages that tell us to be longsuffering and to help a brother overtaken in error, such as Ephesians 4:1-3 and Galatians 6:1, are my proof for my behavior in this matter," Jesse G. Jenkins, "Romans 14."

were unique to the congregational churches of Christ and that were contested, but usually not fully appreciated among those who disagreed. This includes a fourth and final question over how much individual preachers or papers should police the broader Christian fellowship beyond the individual relationship and the local congregation. As a result of these different complexities, confusion and disunity often resulted from the debate over Hailey and the proper response to divorce and remarriage. Despite these differences, all parties seemingly agreed that, 1) there was an authoritative New Testament pattern for individual and collective Christian action; 2) that this was a pattern (including Romans 14 or not) that taught patience towards what some judged to be false teaching; and 3) autonomy of decisions for the local congregations was the Biblical model of the church, including independence of congregational judgments about how to handle both individual consciences and brotherhood communications related to MDR. Insofar as these premises constituted a united mindset, Harrell observed, the congregational churches of Christ maintained their unity in Christ through radical, counter-cultural adherence to the apostolic writings, a common sense hermeneutic, and the New Testament pattern of congregational autonomy.

This concern over the role of brotherhood papers in policing local congregations and their beliefs was balanced by a concern for disregard of doctrinal error at the local church level. Was there to be, in other words, no information or communication beyond the local church to "build up or tear down" with words of encouragement or admonition? One of the reasons for the start of *Christianity Magazine*, for example, was to provide "Christians in the pews" with positive messages encouraging faithful living and a tool for evangelistic outreach. Harrell acknowledged this need, and observed the positive role of the brotherhood periodical in creating awareness and cohesion among Christians associated by their Biblical faith:

I believe [*Christianity Magazine*] came along in a period in which there was some danger of just a factiousness that was destructive. And it was driving many congregations into what I have called a hyper-congregationalism—a separatism, just withdrawing, saying I don't want anything to do with any paper or any other kind of association. And I felt that we were providing a more unifying kind of presentation of what we were trying to be and what we were trying to do. That served a useful purpose. It was not a purpose that was universally agreed on and consequently we received some criticism.[153]

Harrell thus viewed the editors of *Christianity Magazine* as serving a unifying function by becoming lightning rods for debate and criticism in a way that surfaced doctrinal concerns that were shared by many, even though the magazine eschewed controversy as a matter of policy.[154] Rather than militarizing disagreements into further factionalism, the editors absorbed the criticism, and the resulting record was a basis for deeper and broader understandings

---

153. Harrell, Jr, David Edwin. Interview by David Holder and Coulter Wickerham. *Christianity Magazine Part 6*, Feb. 10, 2009, https://youtu. be/6Xz94ExxSHk?si=pGHIph_WqdiXIUh8. Cf. "In the Bible they were concerned about what other people were doing in other places," Harrell, Jr, David Edwin. Interview by David Holder and Coulter Wickerham, *Christianity Magazine Part 9*, Feb. 10, 2009, https://youtu.be/6Xz94ExxSHk?si=pGHIph_WqdiXIUh8.

154. The brotherhood role of Christianity Magazine as a lightning rod for criticism was repeatedly stated in Harrell's private correspondence with the other editors, e.g.: "I believe it has been important to show that the bullying tactics of the Guardian of Truth and others do not have a strangle hold on those trying to be Christians. We would be cowards to let that kind of intimidation go without challenge. I believe it has been important to stand up to them. It might even have been good for them. But I know that there are many people around the country who are delighted that we have provided some rational response to this recent pressure." David Edwin Harrell, Jr., "Dear Brent, Dee, Paul, and Sewell," Letter dated August 15, 1990, Series 2.A.27, David Edwin Harrell, Jr. Papers, 1923-2017, Center for Restoration Studies MS #467, Abilene Christian University Special Collections and Archives.

of a shared hermeneutic and common Christian commitment across generational divides, which were two chief sources of division in the history of the Stone-Campbell movement.

Generational Peace

Harrell's role in the Hailey controversy and his subsequent biography of Hailey sought to mediate differences between Hailey and his critics, many of whom were of a younger generation. His drive for Christian consensus and processes of maintaining fellowship were pursued through application of his historical expertise and editorial/authorial skills. Writing about the "GI Generation" (born 1901-1924) figure of Hailey and with a reading audience that was mainly "Baby Boomers" (born 1943-1960), Harrell served as a bridge between two dominant generations.[155] With his focus on the social dimensions and primitivist commitments of the Restoration Movement, Harrell was in many ways more inwardly focused on the social psychology of the Restoration Movement than were the older civic-minded WWII generation, but he was also more attentive to the social cohesion of the movement than were some of the idealistic and increasingly individualistic "Baby Boomers." Among Christian Baby Boomers, this idealism could manifest itself as a rigorous dogmatism.

In ways consistent with his generational location, therefore, Harrell was focused on "process" over "result," and more seeking of consensus than certainty.[156] This is seen in his historical account of

---

155. William Strauss and Neil Howe, *Generations: The History of America's Future, 1584 to 2069* (New York: Harper Perennial, 1991), 74, 279-294.

156. Strauss and Howe, *Generations*, 282, cf. 291: "Silent [Generation] appeals for change have seldom arisen from power or fury, but rather through a self-conscious humanity and tender social conscience ... Lacking an independent voice, they have adopted the moral relativism of the skilled arbitrator, mediating the conflicts between others—and reaching out to people of all cultures."

the late twentieth-century debates among congregational churches of Christ as differences between deliberative "process" and definitive "product" or "proposition." Whether or not it is attributable to his chronological age and generational identity, Harrell in his biography of Hailey and *Christianity Magazine* articles sought to mediate between: 1) the GI Generation (born 1901-1924) figures like Homer Hailey (b. 1903), Fanning Yater Tant (b. 1908) and James W. Adams (b. 1914), who fought in the trenches of the institutional division and held more accommodating views of differences over MDR, and; 2) the Baby Boomers (b. 1943-1960), like Ron Halbrook (b. 1946) Donnie Rader (b. 1960), and Mike Willis (b. 1947) with more idealistic, creedal-like statements seeking conformity to the New Testament. Rightly or wrongly, Harrell emphasized the need for compassionate dialogue and artful compromise among brethren who disagree about Biblical teachings that he would admit are less than fully clear to some interpreters. "My exposure to the world has caused the things that I'm not sure about or I'm less sure about," Harrell observed in 1991. "It doesn't bother me to say that I'm less likely to be judgmental and I commend courteous, patient dialogue, diligent care for souls of others. Such a witness of our own faith that has a ring of integrity."[157] In this regard, Harrell was a Silent-Generation "peacemaker," seeking understanding and accord among church-building elders and younger idealists seeking doctrinal purity. Harrell sought processes of consensus and fellowship over institutions and ideals that were inherently suspicious to him, in part because of his own generational location. Harrell had seen the social and civic activism of older generations in building religious institutions to accomplish their sense of justice in the world and he was doubtful of their motivations and effectiveness. Harrell was also skeptical of the idealism of younger generations: "I don't take our intellectual life as seriously as many

---

157. Harrell, *"How My Mind Has Changed,"* 1991 Audiotape.

of us do. I'm interested and informed by it, but I will not be ruled by it," he once observed regarding the younger generation of scholars.[158] In both regards, Harrell expresses an adaptive, mediating perspective that we will see extended to the relationship between the modern and postmodern worldviews of his day. He emphasized the need for conversation and compassion between different ages of religious knowledge, seeking harmonious relations among Christians reflecting the different cultural emphases of their respective generations.

---

158. Harrell, *"How My Mind Has Changed,"* 1991 Audiotape.

CHAPTER NINE

Proselytizer

"If you cannot find clear Scriptural authority for a practice—reject that practice."[1]

Because of his concern that evangelism not feed personal pride or ambition, much of what Harrell did to spread the gospel will never be known in a public way. It is thus no surprise that the first indications of Ed Harrell's own interest in overseas evangelistic missions comes from private correspondence with Homer Hailey, which would never have seen the light of day unless it were for their archiving as part of his private correspondence. In 1957, Hailey privately wrote an American missionary in the Philippines on behalf of 27-year-old Ed Harrell, providing the first in a series of $100 per month payments from Harrell in support of the work in the Philippines, for which Harrell wanted "no publicity."[2] The letter indicates that Harrell was already financially

---

1. *David Edwin Harrell, Jr., Reviewing the Harrell—Waldron Debate* (Hyderabad: V. J. Benson, no date), 8. Cf. Harrell's repeated characterization of Jim Waldron's arguments for institutional business support of overseas missions: "it is an effort to confuse the issue of Biblical authority in order to defend one's unscriptural practices." Harrell repeated the sentence as a sort of mantra seven times across the eight pages of his review of the debate, characterizing his opponents twisting of the Scriptures to justify his unbiblical missionary methods, *Idem.*, pages 2, 3, 4, 5, 6, 7, 8.

2. Homer Hailey, "Dear Brother Brashears," Letter dated January 5, 1957. Series II.A.1, David Edwin Harrell, Jr. Papers, 1923-2017, Center for Restoration Studies MS #467, Abilene Christian University Special Collections and Archives.

supporting missionaries in Africa and other places, in addition to his own evangelism in the southern United States, where "many people have never heard of the Church of Christ."[3]

Harrell's concern to avoid prideful publicity was matched only by his emphasis on zealous engagement and adherence to Biblical models of missionary work. In addition to Harrell's own work, this combination of zeal and caution is perhaps best exemplified in the preacher, Sewell Hall, whose many articles in brotherhood publications were most often focused on the overseas evangelism that he and others were engaging.

> I think that preachers ought to be pretty much equal. It all grows out of a concern I've had for years about the dependence of so much of the work overseas on American money. There are different attitudes. There are some men who do that because they feel like it is a necessity in order to accomplish what needs to be accomplished. I really think that there are some who take some kind of pride out of the fact that these preachers are in my charge—my flock of preachers that I oversee. The Lord will judge that.[4]

Harrell's public engagement with overseas mission work began with similar cautionary notes. Christians reading the brotherhood periodicals among the churches of Christ had their first encounter with Ed Harrell outside of *Vanguard Magazine* in his writings in *Searching the Scriptures*, edited by Connie Adams, an American preacher and missionary to the Philippines. Along with fellow evangelist Tommy Poarch, Harrell cowrote a controversial critique of overseas missions to the Philippines among congregational churches of Christ. Harrell and Poarch made an international trip in 1979 spanning five continents visiting missionaries and local churches in locales as diverse as Argentina, South Africa, Australia, and the Philippines. Their experience

---

3. Ibid. This additional information occurs as a handwritten note on back of the typed page.

4. Sewell Hall, in discussion with the author, May 25, 2021.

in this last country led to a salvo of concerns and recommendations regarding the amount of financial support being sent to Filipino evangelists. They had observed American supporters paying Filipino preachers what were upper-class salaries in the Philippines, with reportedly over $1 million flowing annually, as well as other abuses such as "undercover money" deceptively solicited by preachers. Harrell recommended a multipart strategy of limiting support to a certain level ($150 per month), cutting off suspect preachers, and regularly reducing support in order to encourage self-sufficiency. Beyond the details of the monetary abuses, Harrell and Poarch recommended a more accountable method of sending missionary funds that relies on "direct relationships" with men known and trusted to distribute funds. They hoped additionally that Americans might move to the Philippines to provide such trusted sources: "What should be avoided is the 'recommending system' whereby an American or Filipino preacher is able to create a network of native preachers who empower him to receive recommendations and thereby create little more than a denominational hierarchy."[5]

Though their "reappraisal and warning" was full of praise for the work being done by evangelists in the Philippines, it was met with resistance in the same issue of *Searching the Scriptures* by the editor, Connie Adams, who had been a missionary to the Philippines and who was personally familiar with over 400 native Filipino evangelists. Adams contested the proposals of Harrell and Poarch, observing their limited stay (two weekends), the narrowness of their visit (not visiting major areas of growth), and the draconian nature of their proposed cuts to evangelist salaries (had they considered how congregational expenses were taken out of the preachers' salaries?). Adams agreed that foreign preachers should be held accountable

---

5. David Edwin Harrell Jr and Tommy Poarch, "The Philippines—A Reappraisal and A Warning," *Searching the Scriptures* 21 (June 1980): 125-128; cf. *Truth Magazine* 24.25 (June 19, 1980): 408-411.

to reasonable standards, but he questioned the reason for more American preachers to move overseas as stationed trusted agents. Were there not honest men among the more 600 native preachers to receive and make good recommendations?[6]

Harrell and Adams, in subsequent issues of the magazine, respectfully responded to each other, but affirmed their basic positions, with Harrell describing what he saw as widespread corruption in the Philippines and the need to cut off the evangelists and churches there in the next three years in order "that the Filipino Christians should learn to live without American money. The worse that could happen is that the brethren would have to live as they did before they became Christians."[7] In all of this, Harrell's primary concern was that money be removed as the basis of American work in the Philippines.

In his report about churches' overspending in the Philippines, Harrell specifically referenced the work of Wallace H. Little as a source of concern. Little was a longtime American missionary in the Philippines and in the next issue of *Searching the Scriptures* (a parallel account appeared in *Guardian of Truth* magazine), Little defended his past selection of missionaries for support and the amounts paid. In short, he observed that he had never created a "recommending system" for support of Filipino preachers, and that the levels he recommended for overseas support were appropriate to actual costs of living when all factors were considered. Harrell and Poarch's critique was not without merit, Little acknowledged, but the level of abuse and the measures proposed for addressing the problems were deeply problematic and misguided, given their limited knowledge of the complex relationships and economy in the Philippines.[8] Wallace Little concluded his response

---

6. Connie Adams, "Appraising 'A Reappraisal and Warning,'" *Searching the Scriptures* 21 (June 1980): 123-125.

7. David Edwin Harrell Jr, "The Philippines—A Warning Repeated," *Searching the Scriptures* 21 (June 1980): 209-211.

8. Wallace H. Little, "'The Philippines—A Reappraisal and a Warning'—My

by encouraging elders in American churches to visit the Filipino preachers they supported. None have done so, Little observed. "I plead again: please visit your work! The Filipino preachers would welcome such visits."[9]

In introducing the exchange between Wallace Little and Ed Harrell, the editor Connie Adams again affirmed his opposition to the critique by Ed Harrell, both due to Harrell's inexperience in the Philippines leading him to be wrong about his recommended level of support, and because there is nothing unscriptural about the support of the Filipino evangelists, even if some of the higher paid evangelists "abound" and are "full," as the Apostle Paul was at times (Philippians 4:11-12).[10]

The exchange over the Filipino preachers demonstrates both the personal concern of Harrell for sustainable and Biblical overseas mission, and also his willingness to express his judgment in the face of more experienced missionaries with public criticism. Whatever the full truth of the situation in the Philippines, Harrell's criticism was borne of his experience in India as well as the testimony of American and Filipino preachers about abuses of American support. Preachers from the Philippines wrote Harrell with approval for his comments made about preachers' support and benevolence coming from the United States. They had read his articles addressing Tommy Poarch in *Truth Magazine* and W. Little in *Searching the Scriptures*. One Filipino preacher observed that "I'm grateful because you have observed the situation and have not kept silent."[11] Other foreign evangelists acknowledged that similar problems existed elsewhere. "Ed got a lot of flak for opposing [Connie Adams] on that," observed Sewell Hall.

Reply," *Searching the Scriptures* 21 (September 1, 1980): 211-215.

9. Ibid.

10. Connie Adams, "Warnings Assessed—Again," *Searching the Scriptures* 21 (September 1, 1980): 207.

11. Simeon A. Balbag, "Letter to Brother Ed Harrell, June 10, 1981," Series 2.I.1, David Edwin Harrell, Jr. Papers, 1923-2017, Center for Restoration Studies MS #467, Abilene Christian University Special Collections and Archives.

"I'm sure that in India Ed was careful to try to avoid some of the abuses that developed. I had personally seen in Nigeria a man who went a solid year never attending services, and he never missed a preaching paycheck."[12]

The exchange over the Philippines highlights Harrell's concern both for the effectiveness of overseas funding and the model of missionary support. Like the well-known missionary Roland Allen, whose classic book on Biblical missionary methods was read and shared widely among members of congregational churches of Christ in the late 20th century, Harrell was especially interested in developing self-supportive and self-governing churches, both to exercise the spiritual responsibilities of the native Christians and to best utilize the generosity of American Christians.[13] This focus was likely borne of his past debates with preachers in the institutional churches of Christ over inefficient and unduly developed missionary societies and Bible schools. In years to come, his reputation for generous, yet efficient support of overseas missionaries would serve him well in raising funds for evangelists in India. There in India, as in the Philippines, a central concern was creating missionary endeavors of integrity, both in the appropriate level of financial support and in promoting independence among indigenous churches where possible.

The history of Ed Harrell and his evangelism in India encompasses almost a half-century of Harrell's life as a preacher, administrator, and philanthropist. His India evangelism was an important aspect of his life that was little known within the elite circle of American universities in which he moved during his career as a leading historian of religion in America in the late 20th Century. "His work in India was significant," observed fellow preacher Paul Earnhart. "He learned Telugu when he was 50 years old ... He did that so he could communicate with them.

---

12. Sewell Hall, in discussion with the author, May 25, 2021.

13. Roland Allen, *Missionary Methods: St. Paul's or Ours?* (London: R. Scott, 1912).

This is important."[14] As his commitment to learning the language suggests, the India work was a primary focus during the final quarter of Harrell's life until his death in 2021. Along with his itinerant preaching of gospel meetings throughout the US, traveling for overseas missions was a focus of the second half of Harrell's life, although he and Deedee had already privately funded missionaries beginning in the mid-1950s. Sewell Hall once observed in retrospect that "Ed probably preached in more countries than any other preacher of my acquaintance ... Someone once questioned whether he really thought of himself as a missionary. I believe that is exactly what he thought of himself."[15] India was a primary focus of conversation and collaboration between Harrell and elderships and other individual Christians among congregational churches of Christ in the US. This was done almost entirely through an informal network of personal relationships, and partly done through Harrell's frequent references to the India work in *Christianity Magazine*. As Steve Wolfgang has observed, at least 33 of Harrell's *Christianity Magazine* articles between 1984 and 1999—ten percent of his total writing in the magazine—concerned conditions in India.[16] Many of these looks at India occurred in "Rear Views," which was the title of his regular column in *Christianity Magazine*.

As a reflection of these relationships with American Christians and churches, Harrell's history in India is also the story of many congregational churches of Christ in the US during the late 20th and early 21st centuries, which, after the church divisions of the

---

14. Paul Earnhart, in discussion with the author, May 28, 2021.

15. Sewell Hall tribute to Ed Harrell, "Ed Harrell Online Memorial Service-March 20, 2021," YouTube Video, 2:06, March 30, 2021, https://www.youtube.com/watch?app=desktop&v=cXJXDvpzLM4.

16. Steve Wolfgang, "Ed Harrell as Preacher and Public Historian," Unpublished paper presented at the Christian Scholars' Conference, David Lipscomb University, Nashville, 2022. Samples include "Indian Medical Clinic," *Christianity Magazine* 11.1 (January 1994): 32; "Snake and Tiger Stories," *Christianity Magazine* 11.3 (March-April 1994): 32.

1950s, had charted a course for overseas missions different than those churches which utilized institutions for evangelism. These institutions often pooled funds from different "sponsoring" churches to send out missionaries through a directing corporation. These institutional churches would also use Bible Institutes, which often served as missionary boards for distribution of centralized funds for both training, and management–Harrell would call it "control"–of preachers in local congregations.[17]

In the years following WWII, there was an influx of preachers into India from Churches of Christ in the United States. Many of these came to build Bible schools and converted Indians mainly from denominational Christian groups like the Pentecostals, Methodists, and Baptists. During the division over institutionalism in the 1950s, many of the more progressive churches of Christ lost interest in the India work, and it primarily fell into the hands of conservative institutional churches who pooled their moneys to create networks which created missionary societies, Bible schools, orphan homes, and other institutional works.

During the 1970s and 1980s, several preachers from congregational churches of Christ in the United States began working in India, including Billy Raymer, Bernard Bolton, Gayle Towels, and Ken McDaniel. Most of these missionaries were coming to India every other year in the early 1970s.[18] During one of these trips in 1972, a 10-year-old V. J. Benson encountered Raymer and Bolton and was baptized eight years later, on July 13, 1980, after his father and mother, Judson and Grace, became Christians in 1977. Raymer invited Benson to his home congregation in Pisgah, Ohio, to view a functioning church. Returning to India, V. J. Benson continued to work in the police department full-time and

---

17. David Edwin Harrell, Jr., in discussion with author, January 17, 2017, New Delhi, India.

18. V. J. Benson, in discussion with author, January 22, 2023, Hyderabad, India.

preached the gospel part-time, including evangelism in the villages. He made another trip to the US in 1992, receiving $1,000 from American churches for preaching there for 3 months, and used $400 towards inviting men in the villages in Andhra Pradesh to teach them the gospel and encourage young men to become leaders. During this trip, he was persuaded by the American brethren to preach full-time. Benson then applied for a long-term leave from his job and started working full-time as an evangelist.

As a result of these developments, when Harrell first came to India in 1976, he observed that some congregational preachers had been in India in traditional ways of going out into villages and trying to find someone. "I thought from my experience that the results were pretty superficial," Harrell observed.[19] Harrell came to India on a Fulbright Fellowship (a US government funded program for faculty to teach and research overseas) in 1976-77 and taught for a year in the city of Allahabad. The Harrell family—his wife Deedee and the youngest four of their six children—had come with him and lived in austere housing with no running or hot water and, for a time, no refrigerator, which necessitated that they boil water and that block ice be placed in the bathtub daily, as well as other hardships. Though a cook was provided, the cooking facilities and quality of food selection was limited.[20]

Allahabad was in a strong Hindu area, and there were almost no Christians of any variety there. Harrell later recalled that he "made no headway in trying to find anyone." There was, however, a big academic center in Hyderabad, in south-central India, where Ed visited and lectured twice. While there he went out into the

19. David Edwin Harrell, Jr., in discussion with author, January 17, 2017, New Delhi, India.

20. Cf. Wolfgang, 19. For some of Ed's in-print reflections, see, "Don't Fish in the Ganges," *Vanguard* 3.18 (September 22, 1977): 419, and "This Land Is Filled With Sorrow," *Vanguard* 3.10 (March 26, 1977): 240, in which Ed acknowledges that his observations are "Admittedly the first impressions of a stranger from a culture that is filled with false optimism and rampant human egotism."

Ed and Deedee at the Taj Mahal, with children Eddie, Elizabeth, Lee and Robert Harrell (October 1976).

countryside and met a few people who were receptive to the gospel. "I thought that if I ever have the chance I could come back and try to see if something could be established here. I knew I would like to come to Hyderabad."[21]

Ed's next stay in India would occur sixteen years later. After an set of esteemed professorships at leading American state universities, leading to his appointment as Breeden Eminent Scholar of Southern History at Auburn, Ed applied for a Fulbright Scholarship and obtained leave from Auburn for a two-year program to direct the American Studies Research Centre (ASRC) in Hyderabad.

Harrell had written the dean of the department of history at the University of Allahabad, India, in 1986 after his time at the University of Arkansas and his return to Alabama. His inquiry about becoming

---

21. David Edwin Harrell, Jr., in discussion with author, January 17, 2017, New Delhi, India.

the next director of the ASRC was met with enthusiasm.[22] The public announcement in 1992 of the 1993-94 Fulbright Program in India extended a call for a recognized scholar to lecture across India and to direct the academic work of the Centre, which was one of the largest outside the United States with over 90 employees, 153,000 library items and supporting more than 225 Indian scholars and hundreds more from around the world.[23] Ed had been given his choice of locations for the Fulbright. "I put my fleece out," he later observed, and determined he would go to India if he had the chance.[24] Harrell was successful in his application and Auburn approved a two-year stay in Hyderabad. The next year Ed went to India with Deedee, as all six children were grown and out of the house.

This position of authority within the American government and India's educational system proved to be pivotal. Harrell operated within India from a position of cultural influence, working more from the top down, unlike most missionaries who operated near the bottom of formal institutional power within the government and the schools. "The main difference between India and other Christian work overseas was his access to money and also his institutional base of being the director of the largest American library outside the United States," observed historian Steve Wolfgang. "His secular work put the missionary work on a more solid foundation. He was better able to encourage the

22. C. B. Tripathi, "Letter to David E. Harrell, May 15, 1986," Series I.F.12, David Edwin Harrell, Jr. Papers, 1923-2017, Center for Restoration Studies MS #467, Abilene Christian University Special Collections and Archives.

23. "Distinguished Award in American Studies, 1993-94." Series I.J.2, David Edwin Harrell, Jr. Papers, 1923-2017, Center for Restoration Studies MS #467, Abilene Christian University Special Collections and Archives.

24. David Edwin Harrell, Jr., in discussion with author, January 17, 2017, New Delhi, India.

Indian preachers to develop."[25] Other missionaries saw Harrell's advantage similarly. "One of the differences in India is the fact that Ed was looked to as the authority. He was probably more familiar with the culture of the people than most men are," observed Sewell Hall. "There was an influence exerted over all the men who went to work there that was wholesome in keeping under control some of the excesses that has been characteristic of the other places."[26]

Despite his relatively high authority, Harrell was known in India as a man who was personally committed to his Christian discipleship during his leadership of the ASRC and was known for leading a number of his employees to Biblical belief in and baptism into Jesus Christ. "He was a man of deep faith while at the center," observed Paul Gideon, former director of programs at the American Center and director of the library there.[27] The Centre was at its peak in the early 1990's, but the fall of the Soviet Union led to the diminishment of US funds for the Centre, which was transferred to Osmania University in 2000. The Centre had been created in the 1960's as part of an effort to promote India/US relations as a counter to the threat of communism during the Cold War. During its final years, 150-200 US post-graduates and other scholars would come to study at the Centre.

As the director of the ASRC, Harrell was also well known for his graciousness towards staff and guests, managing the programs and hosting dinners, while also finding time to play golf and attending governmental gatherings and academic conferences throughout Asia and Africa, often lecturing on religious pluralism and toleration in the United States. His academic research interests extended to comparing missionary efforts in contemporary India, as well as

---

25. Steve Wolfgang, in discussion with author, May 28, 2021.
26. Sewell Hall, in discussion with author, May 25, 2021.
27. Paul Gideon, in discussion with author, January 23, 2023.

the study of a leading charismatic church leader of that day, D. J. S. Dinakaran, who lived in Chennai, on the east coast of India. Separate from his official work for the Centre, Harrell regularly traveled through India during this time preaching and "searching for honest men to help spread the gospel."[28]

Harrell's Fulbright trips in the 1970's and 1990's both occurred in eras when India was more hospitable to outside Christian influence than is the case in the 21st century. Since the election of Indian Prime Minister Narendra Modi in 2014 and the ascent of his Hindu nationalist government, India has often restricted organizations dedicated to the spread of Christianity. Missionaries and funding for Christian-oriented activities and organizations are now routinely blocked from entering the subcontinent.

By Harrell's own admission, the ASRC was "a fantastic job" in which he was encouraged to travel all over Asia and Africa doing the work of the Centre, especially as it related to promoting religious liberty and civil society. At the same time, he also began traveling in India working with some of the older Indian preachers whom some Americans had been working with before he arrived. However, Harrell became convinced after three to four months that many of these native evangelists were not trustworthy and were only in it for the substantial amounts of money they received from Americans. He continued for several months looking for "an honest man."[29]

After he arrived in Hyderabad in 1993, he taught at gospel meetings held by American brethren, including a meeting with Texas preacher David Watts, Sr. Watts alerted V.J. Benson to Harrell's presence, describing the American's presence by extending his arms

---

28. David Edwin Harrell, Jr., in discussion with author, January 17, 2017, New Delhi, India.

29. Ibid.

wide and stating, "He's a big man who acts like a little man." The men met while Harrell held a meeting in the city of Shantinagar, and Harrell gave Benson his card, recalling years later that Benson spoke English very well. Soon thereafter, Benson and his wife Matilda met Harrell in his office and described the work they and their family had been doing, including the church that was meeting in their home and the meeting in the village that he had recently conducted. Harrell explained that he had come to India to find good and honest men and to work with them to spread the gospel. Harrell also inquired if he could provide $400 to fund another meeting as Benson had organized before. Benson agreed. Harrell then invited Benson's family, including his parents and brother, to his home. This was the modest beginning of what would become known as the Moula Ali congregation in Hyderabad. "This church," Harrell observed, "has become a model for other places."[30]

The first class occurred in 1993 in a tent in the village of Maktheguden with about 25 people present and lasted five days, with Harrell coming to preach two of those days. During 1993-95 Harrell and Benson would also make trips into the farmlands and villages with some success, but Harrell also began to support evangelists in Hyderabad and other Telugu-speaking areas. During this year, Harrell persuaded Benson to begin preaching full-time with the church at Moula-Ali.

American evangelists like Bernard Bolton, Billy Raymer, Ken McDaniel, Gayle Towels, Gerry Sandusky, Tom Moody and others continued going to India until 1995 and held meetings at the Tourist Hotel in Hyderabad. Harrell occasionally preached at these meetings. While Benson, his father, Judson, brother Wilson and others would preach, and with Raj Kumar translating, Harrell would interview the preachers that were supported by him and

---

30. Ibid.

American churches whom Harrell had notified of the need for funding of what was usually part-time evangelistic work. Even $50 per month would significantly help an Indian evangelist's transport to different evangelistic opportunities and sometimes help avoid the need to work overtime or take a second job to support a family in increasingly expensive Indian cities.

During these years, several American churches began to support Indian evangelists, sending funds directly to them or via trusted agents who would visit India every one to two years. In addition, individual Christians in the US began to support evangelists, sometimes contributing to a non-profit organization established by Harrell for this purpose. Also, during this time, Harrell became aware of the need for church buildings in India and helped to fund approximately thirty buildings beginning with Moula-Ali and Balanagar in Hyderabad. This effort in church buildings impacted Bob Owen, a past president at Florida College, who became involved in overseas missions in Ethiopia in the 1990's and continued to support the work there for the next thirty years. Harrell had taught Owen to be careful with American dollars and to focus on providing supplemental income to foreign evangelists: "We provide partial support to over seventy different preachers in a poor country that has no middle class," observed Owen. "We also learned from Ed the value of building church buildings for growth. You're not recognized as 'real' without your own place, and through a network of individual Christians in the US one can influence Christians to give contributions to the work overseas."[31]

Harrell and V.J. Benson worked for several months in the mid-1990s in rural areas, but a "second insight" changed the work. Ed decided that instead of "running around in the small villages," they need to help start substantial congregations in the cities. By

31. Bob Owen, in discussion with the author, June 25, 2021.

the late 1990s, they had helped to start multiple congregations in Hyderabad. People would come to Bible classes throughout the week and worship on Sundays and bring their friends. This focus on large cities continued for the remainder of Harrell's life, and he would cite it as an example of being rooted in the New Testament pattern of Christian mission and evangelism, given Paul's frequent focus on the major urban populations in the ancient Mediterranean world.

After Harrell left the Centre in 1995, he continued to return to India twice a year until 2008 and then yearly until 2020. American evangelists David Bradford of Auburn, AL, and David Owen of Brandon, FL, went to India in 1996 and they were joined by Tom Kinzel, Bill Robinson, Ed's son-in-law Russ Roberts, and several others—some of whom had been involved in the work from the beginning of Ed's time in India, and many of whom remain involved in the work to the present day. It is noteworthy that when Harrell departed the ASRC in 1996, he began to study the Telugu language for about a year, tutored by native Telugu speakers in Auburn, in order to communicate more effectively with Indian preachers and to better comprehend the challenges they faced.[32] Harrell wrote several articles in *Christianity Magazine* about some significant nuances of the Telugu language, including the last of Harrell's "Rear Views" columns."[33]

---

32. David Edwin Harrell, Jr., "Telugu Idioms," *Christianity Magazine* 14.11 (November 1997): 32; "Indian Families," *Christianity Magazine* 14:2 (February 1997): 32. In one of the last issues of *Christianity Magazine*, Ed reported: "On one of my recent trips to India, I spent most of my time having one-on-one personal conversations with nearly a hundred Indian preachers. One of the advantages of being able to converse in Telugu is that it gives some insight into the level of competence and spirituality among Indian preachers. Of course, I have also been able to talk with the members of Indian congregations to assess the depth of their spiritual understanding and elicit their evaluations of their preachers." "Past, Present, and Perfect," *Christianity Magazine* 16.1 (January 1999): 6.

33. David Edwin Harrell, Jr., "Going, We Will Come," *Christianity Magazine*

In the decade following his return to residence in the US in 1996, several Christians associated with institutional Bible schools in India began to emphasize that local evangelists should not be paid by Bible schools, but only by individuals or independent congregations. This new emphasis was partly the result of contacts that Harrell and V. J. Benson had made in the large southern Indian city of Bengaluru (Bangalore), where they had come into contact and agreement with gospel preacher M. C. Gangadhar in 2004. In the subsequent year, he had introduced Harrell to several institutional preachers in the city of Chennai, on the east coast of Southern India. These preachers had come to separate from the institutional Bible colleges and their spheres of influence (and funding). The Chennai area was home to about half a dozen major Bible schools where institutional Churches of Christ in the US recruiting and training them to preach for approximately nine months before sending them out to build pyramids of influence. Some of the leading teachers from these schools were left to join the men working with Harrell and Benson and to ask if they would help them to build congregations that were independent from the influence of the Bible schools.

The situations with the Indian Bible schools varied and still differ today according to context, but often were funded by mother churches or sponsoring US churches, receiving funds from hundreds of churches in some cases. The funds are typically transferred to India through an American agent who runs a Bible school and begins what the Indians refer to as a "Raj"—a sort of mini-fiefdom or kingdom running the training of preachers in a region, their ongoing payment, and often the administration of their churches. The American in charge creates a corporate structure, with a small number of people under them, often Indians, who control the allocation of funds to other preachers and who are often referred

---

16.12 (December 1999): 32.

to by the Indians as "boss preachers." Beneath these directors there are additional layers of support, with money and acclaim flowing to those who can get converts and additional congregations. Harrell once observed that "[the Bible schools] look like a denominational missionary society funded by the 'conservative institutional' churches in the US. Many of these are part of a 'middle group' in the US between the progressives and the non-institutional churches of Christ that are still quite conservative and teach a lot of truth," Harrell observed. "Historically speaking, how this 'middle group' operates is from a determination that what they were doing with institutions in the 1950s was scriptural and they perpetuate it in India today."[34]

Harrell often observed that his efforts in India never targeted people related to the institutional Bible schools. On the other hand, if they came to classes, they learned and were captured by the idea that you didn't need to be a part of some "system" to do the Lord's work. "What you needed to do was build independent churches."[35]

In his outreach in Central and Southern India, Harrell sought to identify honest men and help to establish faithful congregations. These efforts resulted in strong relationships among Indian evangelists, including V. J. Benson's brother-in-law, Y. Surender in Hyderabad at the Balangar congregation. Each of these were evangelists and/or elders in local congregations who operated independently and gathered at meetings run by individuals or individual congregations for purposes of evangelism, edification, and preacher training.

Some of these preachers left Bible Institutes run by the American evangelist Jim Waldron, who has worked in India funded

---

34. David Edwin Harrell, Jr., in discussion with author, January 17, 2017, New Delhi, India.

35. Ibid.

by institutional Churches of Christ since the late 1980's.[36] As a result of these developments, Waldron challenged Harrell to a debate over the scriptural basis for the Bible Institutes and other church-funded institutions founded by Waldron. Harrell had never debated in his life, other than as a young man in the Naval Academy, and he resisted the engagement until Waldron became so persistent that Harrell agreed on the basis that Harrell make all the arrangements. The discussion was arranged in Bengaluru, in south-central India, on November 19, 2009, at the Christian Workers Center. Two propositions were discussed: first, "The Scriptures teach that in the matter of benevolence the church is limited to helping saints only." And second, "the Scriptures teach that one congregation may send funds to another congregation for the purpose of evangelism and edification."

In preparation for the debate, Harrell received assistance from others who had engaged such discussions in an open forum, including Benton K. Cochran, a preacher in Washington, West Virginia. The debate notes reflect a traditional approach to interpretation of the New Testament among congregational churches of Christ, with a focus on the "commandments and example of benevolence authorized for the church," and also the way that "Galatians 6:1-10 emphasizes the responsibility of the individual Christian caring for anyone in need, and not just any and all needy being cared for out of the Lord's treasury." These emphases, as well as others in Cochran's materials, were longstanding arguments for

---

36. Crossville Church of Christ, "Waldron Missions," Online at https://www.waldronmissions.org/index.htm. For Waldron's argument against the congregational, non-institutional perspective on the nature of church benevolence, see, Jim Waldron, "Beware of Forbidding Brethren," Last Accessed September 11, 2024, https://www.waldronmissions.org/Site/themed-images/pdfiles/forbidding_brethren.pdf.

church benevolence focused only on members of the church and would reappear in Harrell's presentation.[37]

The debate had a large audience, reportedly as many as 800 preachers, and had a powerful impact that continued the migration of preachers out of the institutional Churches into congregational churches with the result that they were no longer on the payroll of American-funded institutions.

Harrell began the debate with defining the question: "Do the Scriptures teach that local churches in the New Testament used their funds to provide benevolence for those other than saints?"[38] The question, he clarified, is not whether he would like to help non-Christians from the Church treasury, nor whether orphan homes and other charities are good and admirable works. The question, he adds, is not whether individual Christians should be ready to do good unto all men, nor whether helping non-saints would be good for evangelism.

Harrell then defines the universal and local meanings of "church" in the New Testament, the latter of which he defines as "the functioning unit of the body of Christ." This is set in contrast to other religious groups which tend towards denominationalism. Harrell points to passages in the New Testament where the apostle Paul describes his goal as setting in order the conduct of Christians in the church and order of worship and leadership in the local congregation. This stated concern is seen throughout Acts and the

---

37. Benton K. Cochran, "Letter to Ed and Deedee Harrell, October 13, 2009." Series 2.C.37, David Edwin Harrell, Jr. Papers, 1923-2017, Center for Restoration Studies MS #467, Abilene Christian University Special Collections and Archives.

38. "A Discussion between David Edwin Harrell Jr. and Jim E. Waldron, on November 19, 2009 at Christians Workers Center, Bangaluru, India" 4 DVD Set, produced by V. J. Benson. Series II.C.36, David Edwin Harrell, Jr. Papers, 1923-2017, Center for Restoration Studies MS #467, Abilene Christian University Special Collections and Archives.

New Testament Epistles in which there is a portrait of at least a dozen qualities of the local church, which Harrell delineates with supporting Bible passages. These qualities include providing relief for needy saints and supporting preaching. From this list of Biblical commands and examples, Harrell concludes that the Scriptures teach what we do and what we do not do in the local church. So, for example, the passages on singing in Hebrews and 1 Corinthians exemplify singing in the local church and the issue of instrumental music is a major issue, not because of the question of music, but of whether we will do only what is revealed as the Scriptures teach. In making this case against instrumental music, Harrell notes that Christian religious leaders and groups through the centuries also opposed the use of instrumental music, from the Byzantine tradition to John Calvin and the Presbyterians, to many of the Methodists, Lutherans, and Baptists including John Wesley and Charles Spurgeon.

On his last trip to India, Ed Harrell and evangelist, V.J. Benson, in Hyderabad, India, 2019.

With this more commonly accepted example in view, Harrell turned attention to two other responsibilities of New Testament churches: those regarding support of needy saints and support for preaching. His approach was to distinguish between the New Testament instructions to individuals and to the local church, which are observed not to be the same thing. Using an example with local Indian flair, he observes that an individual player is not the Indian national cricket team. Similarly, an individual Christian is not a local church, as 1 Corinthians 12:14 indicates, and these have different responsibilities. For example, individual believers are commanded by the apostle to care for the widows in their biological family, so that the church does not need to take on this responsibility. Similarly, Harrell pointed out that individual Christians and the entire church have different responsibilities for disciplining a fellow Christian in Matthew 18:16-17. Here as elsewhere in the New Testament (1 Timothy 5:16 and Acts 5:1-4), the individual's money and responsibility are distinct from the local church's money and work.

Based on this principle, Harrell looks at eight passages in which church benevolence is limited, from Acts 2 to 1 Timothy 5. "Where are the unbelievers in these examples?" Harrell asks. In every case the funding came from a church treasury and provided aid to saints and not to non-Christians. When it comes to such questions, Harrell affirms, we must obey 1 Peter 4:11 and "speak as the oracles of God." Here again Harrell the historian goes on a detour through the testimony of restorationists through the centuries, from Zwingli to the Anabaptists and Puritans to Thomas Campbell's *Declaration and Address* (1809), with its proposition that nothing be allowed in church work except what is directed by Jesus and the apostle through command or positive example. Harrell briefly cites his own historical works on the evolution of churches of Christ away from this restoration plea, including his pamphlet, *The Emergence of the Church of Christ Denomination*, and his scholarly tomes, *A Social History of the Disciples of Christ*, and *The Churches of Christ in the 20th Century*. In discussing these works and their conclusions,

Harrell shows that justification for benevolence to non-Christians occurs as an devolution away from the original restoration plea to "speak where the Bible speaks."

For the remainder of his first presentation, Harrell anticipates objections to his position. These focus on three passages: Galatians 6:10; James 1:27; and 2 Corinthians 9:13. In the first two passages, Harrell observes that neither passage references a local church, a local church treasury, or a church contributing to the relief of non-saints. Beyond the Scriptural argument, Harrell argues against the heretical teaching that congregational benevolence is a means to reach the lost. Against the argument that benevolence and entertainment aids evangelism, Harrell argues that the ends don't justify the means if the means are unscriptural. As a parallel case, Harrell cites the story of Saul and his disobedience in not destroying the Amalekites in 1 Samuel 15:13-19. Just as a sacrifice to the Lord did not justify Saul's disobedience, so too evangelism does not justify disobedience to the Word of God about church and individual benevolence.

Finally, Harrell turns to 2 Corinthians 9:13 ("they will glorify God because of ... the generosity of your contribution for them and for all others"), which Jim Waldron claims "kills [Harrell's] doctrine." Providing background, Harrell cites 1 Corinthians 16:1-3 as evidence that the collection was for the saints and involved Gentile liberality to Jews. This is further corroborated by 2 Corinthians 8:3-4, which states that the contribution to Jerusalem was a "ministering to the saints." These facts of the contribution are summarized in Romans 15:25-28, which shows it was for the poor saints which are at Jerusalem as case of Gentiles sharing with Jews. More relevant is the context of 2 Corinthians 9:13, where verses 1 and 12 identify the contribution as a "ministering to the saints" and a "filling up of the wants of the saints." In sum, statements about the Jerusalem collection are focused on the saints.

Harrell then addresses the argument that the phrase regarding the contribution in 2 Corinthians 9:13 refers to non-Christians. The key phrase is "for all others," which Harrell argues must be understood within its context. He adduces examples from Matthew 22:28 ("all" means just a woman's husbands), Matthew 21:26 ("all" means the Jews), and Acts 20:26 ("all" means those to whom Paul preached). Each of these examples show that the identity of the "all others" in 2 Corinthians 9:13 is determined by the context. Harrell shows commentators routinely agree that this "all others" is a reference to "all other Christians," thereby showing the genuineness of the Corinthian Christians' faith and fellowship with all Christians.

In the second part of the debate, Harrell took up the question of whether the Scriptures teach that one congregation may send funds to another congregation for the purpose of evangelism and edification. Against this teaching, Harrell affirmed that the Scriptures do teach that local churches supported evangelists.

Key to this case is the description of Paul's relationship to the Philippi church in Philippians 4:10-17, in which Paul affirms they "communicated with him concerning giving and receiving" (Philippians 5:15). He elaborates in the next verse: "For even in Thessalonica ye sent once and again unto my necessity." This verse is shown to accord with 2 Corinthians 11:8, which clearly states that Paul took money from churches to minister to other churches. Similarly in Acts 11:22, the Jerusalem church sends Barnabas on a trip to share a message. What emerges from these passages and others (Philippians 1:7; 2:23; 4:14-19; 2 Corinthians 11:8-9) is a New Testament pattern in which one or more churches independently supported an evangelist. Depicting this as a diagram, Harrell juxtaposes this to the model used at the origin of the Roman Catholic church, whereby multiple churches sent funds to a single sponsoring church, which in turn distributed funds to different evangelists. This would be the type of hierarchy that led to the consolidation of power in monarchial bishops and leading churches like those at Antioch, Alexandria, Carthage, Constantinople, Jerusalem, and, of course, Rome. Harrell elaborates on the fact that this sponsoring church model accounts for the situation of supporting preachers in India. This "India Pattern," he observes, is a power hierarchy that continues in the funding of "Boss Preacher Schools" in India by the American sponsoring churches. These schools are an additional layer between the American churches and the Indian evangelists, serving as a command post and conduit for funds to the Indian evangelists.

In the New Testament, therefore, Harrell can observe three models of support for evangelists and other saints in need. Before he describes these, he notes that there is a model in which an evangelist preaches self-funded. This is what is described in 1 Corinthians 9, particularly verses 12-14, in which Paul writes to the Corinthians that he did not make use of his right to get a living from the gospel. Harrell observes that the first model of Church support for an evangelist is what he had already described in Philippians 4:15, whereby a church is providing sole support for an evangelist: "And you Philippians yourselves know that in the beginning of the gospel, when I left Macedonia, no church entered into partnership with me in giving and receiving, except you only" (Philippians 4:15).

A second model is in 2 Corinthians 11:8 in which multiple churches give concurrently, but with no apparent cooperation to an evangelist: "I robbed other churches by accepting support from them in order to serve you" (2 Corinthians 11:8). And a third model is seen in 1 Corinthians 16:1-5, whereby multiple churches give concurrently not to an evangelist, but to needy saints. "Now concerning the collection for the saints: as I directed the churches of Galatia, so you also are to do. On the first day of every week, each of you is to put something aside and store it up, as he may prosper, so that there will be no collecting when I come." All these approaches, Harrell observes, are different from the "Sponsoring Church" model, whereby American churches sponsor an (often larger) distributing church to send funds to a mission director in India who further distributes funds to the director of evangelism, and a director of schools, and a director of benevolence, some of whom further distribute to preachers in the field.

Harrell concludes that the cure to these nonbiblical practices of churches sending funding to other churches and to institutions is 1 Peter 4:11: "If any man speaks, let him speak as the oracles of God; if any man minister, let him do it as of the ability which God giveth: that God in all things may be glorified through Jesus Christ, to whom be praise and dominion for ever and ever. Amen."

Two of Harrell's central convictions about the work in India are discernable in both his debate with Waldron and in his numerous *Christianity Magazine* articles on the topic. First, he observes, Indians are perfectly capable of conducting their own business and building their own churches. They do not need American or Indian supervision. This would also be a recurring theme of Harrell's teaching in India during the final years of his life. "We're not running the show," Harrell observed. "We're offering help to them."[39] Second, during the debate, Harrell noted that the Indian preachers are not "hirelings" (the word used by Jesus in John 10:12 for leaders who work purely for material reward) and that the operations of most American missionary organizations are too much driven by foreign money. Harrell observes that he is not the first to emphasize the New Testament pattern for church work and its funding. Preachers from congregational churches of Christ were in India when he came in 1976, and he worshiped with like-minded Christians for two years while he was the Director of the American Studies Research Centre (1993-1995). The real question, he finally

---

39. David Edwin Harrell, Jr., in discussion with author, January 17, 2017, New Delhi, India.

states, is "what should local New Testament churches do?" This is the decision he put to his audience to decide.[40]

In 2017, eight years after the debate, Harrell reflected on the event and acknowledged that, though he had attended a few debates in the 1950s, he had never found debating a very effective way of convincing others about your point. "But that was the way it was done because we had a debating tradition," Harrell observed. "Most debates either ended up trivializing the issues or becoming personal attacks." Harrell had tried to be sure that his debate with Waldron was different. He had not allowed it to become a personal shooting match. "I paid no attention to personal attacks," he observed.[41]

The day after the debate concluded in 2009, Harrell and Bill Robinson and several Indian translators met with "well over a hundred" of the preachers who had attended during the debate. The result of the subsequent study was the departure of a significant number of the preachers away from the institutional perspective, with many of the men choosing to cease receiving funds from the Bible Schools with which they were formally affiliated. Some of these preachers became self-funded or funded by their local work or sought out direct relationship to another local congregation or individual donor, sometimes through the assistance of Ed Harrell or his coworkers.

---

40. For the preceding account, see "A Discussion between David Edwin Harrell Jr. and Jim E. Waldron, on November 19, 2009 at Christians Workers Center, Bangaluru, India" 4 DVD Set, produced by V. J. Benson. Series II.C.36, David Edwin Harrell, Jr. Papers, 1923-2017, Center for Restoration Studies MS #467, Abilene Christian University Special Collections and Archives. Cf. *David Edwin Harrell, Jr., Reviewing the Harrell—Waldron Debate* (Hyderabad: V. J. Benson, no date): 1-8, where Harrell concludes, "If you cannot find clear Scriptural authority for a practice—reject that practice."

41. David Edwin Harrell, Jr., in discussion with author, January 17, 2017, New Delhi, India.

In the years after the debate, Harrell's annual trips increasingly involved the participation of Tom Kinzel and Russ Roberts, and expanded into other major cities, including Bangalore, Chennai, Coimbatore, Madurai, Delhi, Shillong, and Mumbai. These efforts resulted in strong relationships among Indian evangelists including Thang Guite (2010) working in Northeast India and Delhi, Roy Ebinezar (2009) in Madurai in South India, Pushparaj (2012) working in Mumbai, and Thomas David and Gopal Dass (2009) in Coimbatore. Except for two years during the COVID pandemic, the trips have continued annually to the present day, including after Ed Harrell's passing in March 2021. The fourfold purpose of the trips is stated in the annual reports.

1. To encourage and instruct Indian Christians in classes and weekend meetings.

2. To assess the potential of evangelists seeking support through personal interviews.

3. To teach and encourage preachers with the aim of grounding them in sound doctrine and teaching how to build solid, self-sufficient congregations.

4. To try to improve the ability of those supported by Americans to report on their work and to stay in touch with those in the United States who are interested in their work.[42]

These four goals highlight Harrell's basic philosophy that his and his colleagues' work in India was not about their own work, but a support of the Indians' work. The group invited each year has nothing to do with how the Indian evangelists organize and carry out their work. "[The Indians] are courteous enough to let us

---

42. Russ Roberts and Tom Kinzel, *India 2023 Trip Report*, January 3-21, 2023. Document in possession of the author.

come," Harrell observed. "They let us use their facilities and let us do our work, which is just to teach. Everything else that happens here is up them."[43] This approach continues in the present day, so that the Americans who visit are not "running the show" but are offering help to the Indian Christians in becoming financially self-sufficient and Biblically sound in their teachings and practices. Recent trips have also emphasized the nature of Biblical fellowship between Indian evangelists and supporting congregations in the United States, namely that these should be relationships that are a personal partnership for the purpose of praising and glorifying God. This is, in part, accomplished by more intentional reporting and communication between Indian evangelists and the American churches supporting them. What is resulting is a growing number of evangelists and churches that are truly congregational in their work, not ruled by institutional or other worldly interest. They are increasingly self-sufficient and able to grow in support not only for local evangelists, but for preachers who are traveling and spreading the gospel throughout India.

During one of his final trips to India, Harrell reflected on what he saw as a promising future of the work in India. As a historian, Harrell predicted that the future was bright for the Indian churches because of the societal movement out of the rural areas into the cities. He saw this as a major reason for growth. He pointed to a place like the Moula-Ali church of Christ in Hyderabad with approximately 250 members.[44] Christians there were receiving increasingly good educations and good jobs, and providing significant contributions. Harrell observed that such urban churches would be a destination for young people coming into the cities looking for work for at least the next 25 years as India continues to industrialize and grow

---

43. David Edwin Harrell, Jr., in discussion with author, January 17, 2017, New Delhi, India.

44. This is the church building depicted on this book's front cover.

as the largest country in the world. Now with over 1.4 billion people, India has over four times the population of the US in a territory a quarter of the size. "The best thing Americans can bring is not money," Harrell observed, "especially as Indians increasingly can deal with the money issues themselves. The Americans have training and skills in knowledge and teaching the Bible that are not widely present among the Indian workers, but that the Indians can quickly gain. Otherwise," Harrell concluded, "the Indians are doing it themselves."[45]

---

45. Ibid.

CHAPTER TEN

Primitivist

"When I am posing as a historian, I try not to plead any case. If I do that job well, the result may be used by a variety of polemicists and moralizers who see the past through different first-principle truths."[1]

After his retirement from Auburn and fourteen years before his death in 2021, Harrell published a fifty-page tract in 2007 called *Christian Primitivism in the Twenty-First Century*. Subtitled *Thinking "Inside the Box" About Restoring New Testament Christianity*, it would be Harrell's final publication, though he would make several academic lectures and preaching presentations in his final decade.[2] A concluding biographical sketch includes his academic career and accomplishments, but begins with the identity that would be primary for the audience of this tract: "Ed Harrell is a well-known preacher, having conducted hundreds of meetings in churches of Christ throughout the world."[3] As the

---

1. David Edwin Harrell, Jr., *Pat Robinson: A Personal, Religious, and Political Portrait* (San Francisco: Harper & Row, 1987), vii.

2. David Edwin Harrell, Jr., *Christian Primitivism in the Twenty-first Century: Thinking "Inside the Box" About Restoring New Testament Christianity* (Lakeland: Harrell/Lewis Publishing, 2007). This has been reprinted in the appendices of this book.

3. Harrell, *Christian Primitivism in the Twenty-first Century*, 362.

line suggests, this is a publication for Christians and the churches Harrell had served for over sixty years. He would present content from the booklet to congregations across the country in his final years, especially addressing the younger listeners in his audiences with the primary message of the "Thinking Inside the Box" series. This concern is reflected in the introduction of the booklet, which focuses on the "next generation" and their tendency to prefer personal religious commitment over traditional practices inherited from family. Primitivism is a tradition of seeking to believe and live as the New Testament Christians, Harrell observes, and more than a conventional legalism inherited from shallow parents—not a fundamentalism or culturally bound evangelicalism as is often charged—but rather a "profoundly Biblical, richly textured concept with deep historical roots."

In this way, the 2007 pamphlet exists as Harrell's final work towards an emerging generation of what are today called "Millennials," whom he perceives as questioning the value of the American Restoration Movement, especially in the context of 21st century world driven by digital technology, radical individualism, and growing distrust of authorities and institutions. Harrell appeals to his young audience to return to the basics of the Restoration Movement, and in doing so states why it appeals to him: "Along with generations of serious Bible-believing Christians before me, I have found no better gyroscope for life than to seek to find and follow the 'ancient order of things.'"[4] Here, for the first time in his career is an appeal for the personal value of primitivism for the next generation. Appealing to what he describes as an increasingly self-focused generation, the value of the Restoration Movement is the constancy and accuracy of the self-direction it provides to life.

---

4. Ibid., 315.

Harrell presents the three important "assumptions" of the primitivist: belief in the truth of 1) apostolic tradition, 2) a commonsense interpretation of Scripture, and 3) divine pattern in Scripture of congregational polity. The presentation of these as assumptions is remarkable, for though Harrell will take fifty pages to argue the truth of these three core principles—Apostolic Authority, Common Sense Hermeneutics, and Congregationalism—they are nevertheless presented as "assumptions" that "must seem true and reliable" in order for "the logic of trying to restore Christian communities in modern times, as in all other times" to make sense.[5]

The shift in Harrell's presentation of primitivism for the 21st century is both subtle and significant. Its criteria for judgment of truth shifts from external authorities (scripture, Christian tradition, and "common sense" reason) to the internal authority of human experience (the assumptions of "personal religious commitment" and generational "mantras" questioning received wisdom). Though Harrell, of course, appeals to the objective truth and the authority of Biblical belief and practice, his fundamental stance shifts from a modern assertion of these truths as facts, to a postmodern approach that acknowledges a questioning of the overarching story—the metanarrative—about Christian sources and their interpretation. The objective truth of the Christian Scriptures is affirmed but approached as a subjective choice of human individuals who must choose their interpretation based on personal assumptions and preferred communities and outcomes of interpretation. Here Harrell is championing Biblical primitivism in a postmodern mode, with reflection on lived experience (what people say is better because it is "outside the box") and its desired outcome (which Harrell defines as "getting it right") forming the basis for a religious commitment. Harrell acknowledges that his turn to the subjective

5. Ibid., 360.

perspective of the individual Christian is necessary if he is to overcome criticisms of Biblical primitivism:

> I concede that an emphasis on "getting it right"—on conscientiously trying to emulate the worship, organization, and work of New Testament churches—rests on important assumptions. If you do not understand and embrace these assumptions, much that is done by restorers seems to be an arbitrary trivializing of the faith. If you do not believe these assumptions, the narrow (even legalistic) exegesis of Biblical primitivists is divisive and sectarian, rooted in the traditions of a particular religious movement and outmoded hermeneutical principles. However, if the three assumptions discussed here seem true and reliable, the meticulous concern of restorers to "get it right" is an obvious and necessary consequence.[6]

Harrell's concession indicates the main target of his argument: critiques of Biblical primitivism as provincial and outmoded. The identity of these critics is revealed in his second chapter on the proposition that humans read texts and draw universal conclusions using common sense. Harrell quotes contemporary historians from the institutional Churches of Christ who express an opposing postmodern view of the American Restoration Movement.[7] According to this progressive postmodern perspective, it is no longer plausible to appeal to human reason, the facts of Scripture, and the human ability to derive universally agreed upon truths from the sacred texts of the Christian faith. Specifically, according to such Christian historians, it is no longer credible to claim, as did many interpreters in the Stone-Campbell Movement, that we know what God wants us to believe and do by identifying the direct commands, positive examples, and necessary inferences (CENI) contained in

---

6. Ibid., 316.
7. Ibid., 340-341.

Scripture. This postmodern turn among "Christian historians" is the main target of Harrell's argument for the continuing plausibility of Biblical primitivism, which is grounded in Enlightenment ideals of objective truth, universal human reason, and scientific probability, but also and more fundamentally in the "Biblical case for common sense." Drawing from the New Testament, Harrell seeks to demonstrate that Jesus and the apostles assumed that they and everyone else could commonly understand spoken and written statements, ask good questions, and arrive at conclusions and actions that were intended and approved by God. Harrell's examples range from the parable of the Good Samaritan in Luke 10, to the instructions of Paul in 1 Corinthians 9, to the account of the purpose of miracles in Hebrews 2. In each case, Harrell observes, the Biblical hermeneutic is straightforward: "If you ask a good question about God's will, the way to find the answer is to listen to all that the Scriptures reveal on that matter."[8]

By critiquing the subjectivism and relativism of postmodernism from within a postmodern frame, Harrell stands as a bridge figure between the rationalism and biblicism of the 19th and early 20th century American Restoration Movement and the postmodernism of the cultured and elite Christian historians who he cites as dismissing this modern worldview from within a late 20th and early 21st century mindset. Harrell is not naïve to the sources of modernity and postmodernity. The sources of subjectivistic postmodernity (e.g., the emotional appeal of Pentecostalism around the globe) and the failed progress of hierarchical structures (e.g., the decline of mainline Protestantism) are described through his scholarship on the religious South. And in his own personality he bridged the modern and postmodern worldviews by combining a modernist certainty in Biblical facts and postmodern openness to different viewpoints than his own. It was a combination of convicted

---

8. Ibid., 349.

primitivism and compassionate pluralism that his colleagues observed in his own life.[9] Ten years before writing the booklet on primitivism, Harrell reflected to an academic audience on how his life in the late 20th century had impacted his approach to truth: "My exposure to the world has caused the things that I'm not sure about, or that I'm less sure about. It doesn't bother me to say that I'm less likely to be judgmental and I commend courteous, patient dialogue, and diligent care for the souls of others—a witness of our own faith that has a ring of integrity."[10]

In *Christian Primitivism in the Twenty-first Century*, Harrell reflects this courteous, patient, dialogical approach to truth while not hedging on his witness to the truth. His appeal is aware of the critical deconstruction that the restoration plea had undergone in the previous fifty years, even citing at length some of the most acidic claims for his readers to grapple with.[11] What Harrell comes to, however, is a focused reaffirmation of the same truths from a more expansive vantage point. Though he does not name this new stance towards the time-honored truths of restorationism (besides terming it "Biblical primitivism"), it is akin to what others have called a "second naivete," which is a progression of faith moving past naïve certainty about Biblical truth through a critical distancing from Biblical truth claims caused by the pluralism and secularism of

---

9. Beth Barton Schweiger, "Conclusion," 103.

10. David Edwin Harrell, Jr., *"How My Mind Has Changed/Stayed the Same,"* Christian Scholar's Conference, 1991. "Ed Harrell July 1991 CSC" Audiotape, Box 31, David Edwin Harrell, Jr. Papers, 1923-2017, Center for Restoration Studies MS #467, Abilene Christian University Special Collections and Archives, Brown Library.

11. For example, "the traditional hermeneutic of command, example, and necessary inference is not found in the Old and New Testament but is grounded in the human history of Reformed theology ..." (Micheal W. Casey, *The Battle over Hermeneutics in the Stone-Campbell Movement, 1800-1870* (Lewiston: The Edwin Mellen Press, 1998), 268. Cited by Harrell, *Christian Primitivism in the Twenty-first Century*, Appendix 3, 287.

our postmodern era, and back to a chastened affirmation of Biblical primitivism (in a second, critiqued, and self-consciously committed naivete) as the best approach to believing and living a Biblical pattern for following God because it is probably true.[12] Harrell's critique of his fellow church historians is that, in their progressive accommodation of the dominant culture, they have become stuck in the disorientation of postmodern critiques of the American Restoration Movement, and have not passed through to a stance that recognizes the true probability of Biblical primitivism's core truth claim: the apostolic documents provide a pattern of Christian saving belief and authorized church action that can be understood and assented to by everyone with the knowledge that God gives us commonly, as long as this common sense is not distorted or disabled.

Harrell thus operates with what others have termed a Christian "critical realism" that both vigorously asserts that timeless objective truth exists in the pattern of teachings in the New Testament documents, but asserts it with a humility about the extent to which we can fully grasp that objective reality.[13] As a result of this humility, Harrell places his confidence not in the complete and incorrigible accuracy of his primitivist conclusions (e.g., he provides a list of

---

12. What is described here in Harrell's presentation of Biblical faith is a progression sometimes referred to as the "hermeneutical arc," which interprets authoritative texts (and other powerful life experiences) along a journey, passing from a first naivete, to a critical distancing from preliminary understandings, to a second naivete that recovers the original belief but from a wiser, more chastened perspective. On the concept of a "second naivete," see Paul Ricoeur, *Symbolism of Evil* (Boston: Beacon Press, 1967), 350-356; John Dominic Crossan, *Semeia 4: Paul Ricoeur on Biblical Hermeneutics* (Missoula: Society of Biblical Literature, 1975), 7, 19.

13. Cf. Lesslie Newbigin, *Proper Confidence: Faith, Doubt, and Certainty in Christian Discipleship* (Grand Rapids: Eerdmans, 1995); cf. Shawn Brace, "Why Critical Realism?" Last accessed July 2, 2024, https://shawnbrace.substack.com/p/why-critical-realism. .

what he thinks the Bible teaches churches should do collectively but invites corrections and additions), but in the call of God in Scripture to be faithful disciples, reading the Word, reflecting on it in pursuit of unity with other Christians, and seeking to "get it right" individually and collectively. We do this, Harrell observes, because that is what our gracious and loving God has given us to do as free and forgiven followers of Christ. As in his writings about Christian fellowship a decade earlier, Harrell's argument for Biblical primitivism emphasizes the process of pursing Biblical truth more than the propositions to be defended, though he acknowledges that the pursuit and premises are both important.

In *Christian Primitivism in the Twenty-first Century*, Harrell does not elaborate on the nature of God as a source of his confidence in Biblical primitivism, but he does elaborate on human freedom as a motivation. Harrell encourages readers to not succumb to the fashionable mode of "looking outside the box," but to press against both postmodern dismissals of primitivism and modern distortions of primitivism in Pentecostalism and Amish culture, which do not ask the right questions as they are signaled in the Scriptures.[14] Readers may question his assumptions, but he encourages them to evaluate both his and their own assumptions, seeking the best direction in the "religious marketplace." This high valuation of human freedom leads him to assert that his readers should choose a faith, not under the weight of received tradition or out of dogmatic coercion or "faddish truths," but what is "grounded in the Scriptures" and a "powerful message."[15] This is a concern for freedom of thought and choice, rooted in the Restoration Movement, that Harrell had frequently affirmed:

There is a freedom on both ends of the restoration

---

14. Harrell, *Christian Primitivism in the Twenty-first Century*, 345-346.
15. Ibid., 362.

movement. Once one renounces whatever denominational status he might have, whatever desire for position, or property or jobs that institutions might offer, then there is a certain freedom of conscience to say what you will. I think I feel that. I would not be willing to subject myself to any other kind of Christian relation. It is a strong undenominational sense that I have.[16]

The primitivist's appeal to Scripture apart from human dogma (whether protestant or postmodern) and denomination is, upon Harrell's reading, an expression of human freedom. In his sermons in the early 2000's on the topic of primitivism, Harrell would often witness to the power of religious freedom in primitivism and the impact it had on others. In one sermon illustration, for example, Harrell would tell of his encounter with a fellow professor, Michael O'Brien, during his time at the University of Arkansas, who initially thought Harrell eccentric because of his Christian faith. After some conversation, Harrell concluded: "I am a Christian, I feel, almost without any brief for historic Christianity. I am a Christian who would only hold a brief for just trying to be a simple New Testament Christian." Harrell relates that his fellow professor thought about it for a minute and replied, "Ah, that's interesting. If one must be a Christian, that would be a good kind to be."[17]

The story illustrates Harrell's approach to witnessing to the truth by seeking to obey the Bible and appeal to it in simplicity over against the corrupting influences of human traditions and philosophies. Another common illustration during Harrell's preaching about primitivism and being "inside the box" was his story of the time he and another academic colleague, Sam Hill, shared a breakfast conversation at an annual meeting of the

---

16. Harrell, Jr., *"How My Mind Has Changed/Stayed the Same," Christian Scholar's Conference, 1991. "Ed Harrell July 1991 CSC" Audiotape.*

17. Ibid.

Southern Historical Association in 1982. Hill suggested that he and Harrell compress their respective philosophies of life into one word. Hill replied with "meaning;" Harrell said, "obedience."[18] This focus on personal submission to God was often observed by his colleagues in higher education as an unusual trait; Harrell himself at times contrasted his Christian obedience to his academic career in a way that struck his hearers as paradoxical. As Harrell expressed it, he was an intellectual who was suspicious of intellectuals, in part because of this historical work detailing the sources and outcomes of human ingenuity and institutions.

> My experience with the wider world has had an influence,
> The thing that has kept me on the course is an enduring anti-
> intellectualism. I would like to find another phrase for it,
> because I am an academic and I have a respect for learning,
> but I also have a strong sense of the limitations of learning.
> I used to teach a course in intellectual history and surveyed
> what people have believed. There is a presumptuousness to
> our belief.

Sometimes telling the joke about the signed graffiti discovered in Europe–"The earth is flat, Class of 1491"–Harrell conveyed his conviction that human theories and theologies tend to be trendy, speculative, and even pompous. "I don't take our intellectual life as seriously as many of us do," he once quipped to an academic audience. "I'm interested and informed by it, but I will not be ruled by it. My own religious ideas, what I'm sure about–I'm still just as sure as I ever was."[19]

---

18. Samuel S. Hill, "David Edwin Harrell, Jr.: American Religious Historian," 3-14 in *Recovering the Margins of American Religious History*, edited by B. Dwain Waldrep & Scott Billingsley (Tuscaloosa, Al: University of Alabama Press, 2010), 7.

19. Harrell, *"How My Mind Has Changed/Stayed the Same,"* July 1991 Audiotape.

For some audience members and readers, Harrell's categorical assertion of certainty about his religious beliefs might easily have struck an amusing and perhaps even offensive chord. But different from the blind dogmatists or doctrinaire literalist, Harrell viewed his Biblical primitivism, not as rooted in a life of smug academic ideology or comfortable theological creedalism, but in the messy zeal of a disciple's quest to explore his Master's directions and to emulate His life as laid out in the New Testament. The key distinction here is between the Christian life as orthodoxy and orthopraxy. Harrell resisted as pursuit of God's way a reciting of the right words or statements of beliefs, though he saw the need for such secondarily. But he saw the essence of the Christian life as having the right loyalty to Jesus and pursuit of this love of God in all his life. The right way was a free pursuit of seeking to know, live, and share the teachings of Jesus and His apostles. This lifetime, dogged pursuit of Biblical primitivism and New Testament Christianity was well summarized in the quote of his own words during the eulogy at his funeral: he sought, simply, to be "an explorer in search of Zion."[20]

---

20. Russ Bowman, in discussion with author, 3/20/21. In the graveside service, March 18, 2021, Russ Bowman quoted line from Harrell's essay: "To be a restorer has always meant to be an explorer in search of Zion bound to grope in our own human and cultural maze," Harrell, "Epilogue," 244.

CHAPTER ELEVEN

Postlude

> "Ed's attitude was to get it right
> but to give people time to get it
> right."[1]

Ed Harrell explained the historical heritage and contemporary theological stance of congregational churches of Christ in a way that shed new light on both their present faith and the future possibilities for the movement. Harrell explained the development of religious movements as a cyclical process of change from "a sect to a denomination" in both the 19th century Disciples of Christ and the 20th century Churches of Christ.[2] Up until his adoption and popularization of social historians of religious movements (Ernst Troeltsch, Max Weber, and H. Richard Niebuhr), the primary understanding of "sect" in the American Restoration Movement was as a reference to the "denominations," which were synonymous with religious divisions caused by human traditions and worldly churches. This definition of "sect" is seen in a declaration by an early 20th century ecumenical leader among the Disciples of Christ: "Henceforth let no man glory in his denomination; that is sectarianism: but let all men glory in Christ and practice brotherhood

---

1. Lynn Dowdy, in discussion with author, 12/28/2020.

2. For a synopsis of Harrell's view of the "sect" and "denomination" and the process from the former to the latter, see the opening section ("Sociological Patterns and the Sect-To-Denomination Process") of his booklet, Emergence of the "Church of Christ" Denomination," pages 289-91 in Appendix 1 of this book.

with men; that is Christianity."[3] Standing on the shoulders of other scholars, Harrell's unique contribution was to distinguish "sects" from "denominations" in the context of the American Restoration Movement.[4] The "sect" was the original contrarian group that truly and sacrificially sought to return to the Scriptures. The "denomination" was the sect that had matured into a compromise with the world. In this compromise, the denomination was akin to the state-oriented church, like the Lutherans, Anglicans, and Roman Catholics, wherein individual conscience and resistance against culture and clergy are controlled by bureaucratic institutions (leading to separation of believers from Christian work), sacerdotalism (leading to separation of believers from Christian leadership), and sacramentalism (leading to separation of believers from God's Word and power).[5] Thus, unlike previous scholars in the Restoration Movement, Harrell describes a type of religious group that was self-conscious in its radical adherence to Scripture and in its separation from other churches and from the culture. To describe this peculiar group, he adopted the traditional designation of "sect." The

---

3. Peter Ainslie, *If Not a United Church, What?* (New York: Fleming H. Revell, 1920), 103; cf., James D. Bales, *Soils and Seeds of Sectarianism* (Kansas City: Old Paths Book Club, 1947), 2: "We want to know what the seeds of sectarianism are in order that we may explain to sincere people, who are entangled in denominational doctrines, what has taken place in order to help them to study intelligently their own doctrine in the light of the word of God."

4. For a more recent and balanced overview of the literature on sects and sectarianism, see Robert H. Gundry, *Jesus and the Word according to John the Sectarian* (Grand Rapids: Eerdmans, 2002). Another important study of the social history of the Disciples of Christ, published before Harrell's dissertation is that of Oliver Read Whitley, *Trumpet Call of Reformation* (St Louis: Bethany Press, 1959).

5. For similar distinction between church and sect see the observations of Ernst Troeltsch originally published in 1912 and translated in *The Social Teaching of the Christian Church*, Volume 2 (Louisville: Westminster/John Knox, 1992), 991-1013. For a critique of sacramentalism from a restorationist perspective see John B. Weaver, "Baptism As Sacrament And/Or Command" (2016). *ACU Lectureship and Summit Audio Collection* 5264 https://digitalcommons.acu.edu/sumlec_audio/5264.

churches of Christ in the American Restoration Movement began as a "sect" and many ended up as denominations, often more interested in maintaining orthodoxy and managing organization than in spreading the gospel and supporting local Christians and neighbors.[6] It would become a predominant understanding of the history of the 19th century Disciples of Christ and the 20th century Churches of Christ, recovering the concept of "the sect" as a designation of the original, authentic Christian *ethos* or way of life.[7]

Harrell's sociological use of the term "sect" also reframed the historical account of the divisions in the Restoration Movement so that these divisions were seen from the perspective of the minority, dissenting tradition, i.e., the Churches of Christ in the late 19th century and the congregational churches of Christ in the mid-20th century. Seen within the "sect-to-denomination" framework, the less compromising and more distinctive minority group is better understood not as the upstart and divisive group, but as the more original and potent movement that is developed and diluted by the denominationalizing tendency to accommodate the secular culture and domesticate Christ's church into more of a human club of historically associated churches and cultivator of religious business ventures that take their cues from the ecumenical world of nongovernmental organizations (NGOs). To be sure, the majority group's rhetoric often argued against this characterization, seeking to claim more aged and original precursors for its denominational ideology.

---

6. The managerial emphasis of the denominational mindset is foundational to Harrell's account of B. C. Goodpasture, in David Edwin Harrell, Jr., "B.C. Goodpasture: Leader of Institutional Thought," 249: "B. C. Goodpasture fits neatly into a sociological model of second-generation religious leaders."

7. The sociological model undergirds a number of recent accounts of the history of the Churches of Christ, including Douglas A. Foster, *Will the Cycle Be Unbroken: Churches of Christ Face the 21st Century* (Abilene: ACU Press, 1994), 1-16.

This was seen, for example, in the arguments among institutional Churches of Christ, namely that "anti" concerns and division over church funding of businesses to provide benevolence and education was an innovative concern created by non-institutional figures like Roy Cogdill and Yater Tant.[8] A second rhetorical strategy was the branding of separatist, contra-cultural positions as "sectarian" by more progressive interpreters. Returning to the earlier association of "sect" with the dividedness of religious denominations, but ironically applying the term to groups that were overtly "undenominational," critics of the more exclusive and reactionary groups deployed the term "sectarian" as a negative term, highlighting the often uncompromising and oppositional criticisms that the "anti" groups leveled against progressive departures from the New Testament teaching and practice, e.g., instrumental music, egalitarian gender roles, and accommodative sexual ethics.[9] Under Harrell's brush, therefore, the picture of what it is to be a "sect" comes full circle from designating departures from the original faith ("the sectarian denominations"), to positively describing adherents of this NT patterns ("a religious sect of peculiar people"), to a slur against such conservative perspective by those seeking to move beyond it ("those sectarian antis"). Harrell's interpretation is persuasive because it is predictive. He shows that one should expect this evolution in the way reforming movements begin as outsiders, become insiders to an exacting ideology and community of true believers, and face ostracization by members of the original movement that move beyond the original plea.

---

8. This argument was variously deployed in the 1990 Dallas Meeting, "The Dallas Meeting | 1990 | Uniting Institutional & Non-Institutional churches of Christ," YouTube video, https://www.youtube.com/watch?v=pcOTk15eGaA.

9. E.g., Douglas A. Foster, *Will the Cycle Be Unbroken?* 48-49. Foster also cites (p. 21) a 1994 conservative newspaper article accusing ACU of departing from the faith and how it was termed an example of "sectarian hatred" by Darryl Tippens, "Vicious Hatred Helps No One," *Abilene Reporter-News* (February 23, 1994): 8A.

A developmental understanding of sectarianism is also helpful because it provides an interpretive lens for understanding Harrell's own religious commitments and communications during the disagreements over MDR and the boundaries of Christian fellowship among preachers in the congregational churches of Christ. The key difference between these intragroup debates and the institutional division was the cause of the disagreement: the former debate over MDR was among sectarians, disagreeing over interpretations of Matthew 19, for example, and its implications for individual Christian unity, but essentially united in their commitment to voluntary, exclusivist, and counter-cultural stances on congregational doctrine and individual Christian ethics. No one in the MDR debate doubted, for example, that a church could and should divide over unbiblical practices of worship and over unvarnished accommodation of worldly standards for Christian conduct, e.g., relaxing opposition to divorce, a woman's role in the family and church, and active engagement in evangelism and care of the needy. In all these ways, those engaged in the disagreements over Homer Hailey and related issues exhibited their membership in a sect: a purposefully separatist and distinctive association of individuals who rejected widely respected religious leaders and required proof of commitment to the Biblical faith, which was the priority in life, broaching no compromise with unbiblical teaching and no accommodation of secular culture. This was the mindset of the peculiar "fanatic" and "literalist" first trumpeted by Harrell in his 1966 Reed Lecture and subsequently championed throughout his life as the way of the true believer committed to the restoration principle. His repeated affirmations of a "common mind" among those involved in the MDR debate is best understood as a psychological description of the sectarian social group. And so, Harrell's emphasis on a process of returning to the Scriptures for discernment in how to overcome doctrinal differences is often punctuated by assertion of his own harsh posture in defining Biblical truth and his complete unwillingness to kowtow to the cultural trends of the day, especially as related to divorce of married couples. By contrast, Harrell argues, the split over institutionalism occurred when some Christians began to have more allegiance to a bigger and more prestigious group of churches (namely, the institutional Churches of Christ) and less allegiance to a principled approach of reading and applying Scripture for what it tells, shows, and implies about we should do in serving Christ. Stated differently, the institutional division was between sectarians and denominationalists, between separatists and accommodationists, between an otherworldly approach to Christian community and an increasingly this-worldly mindset and hermeneutic. The two Christian communities and their respective hermeneutics had diverged, and the institutionalism debate was a doctrinal symptom of a more fundamental sociological and spiritual division that had already occurred coming out of the post-WWII boom in American society.

Beyond describing Harrell's own approach to Christian faith, we have seen that his clarification of the meaning of "sect" was intended as instruction for younger Christians seeking to be true believers. In conclusion, one can identify at least three ways Harrell's sociological redefinition of the "sect" gave direction to Christians seeking to find and share Biblical faith in the present day.

First, Harrell's work leads to a new recognition that "sect" is a Biblical term for a community that seeks unity following Christ, but nevertheless leads to accusations of being divisive. This is rooted in the use of the Greek term *heiresin* (translated "sect" but literally meaning "choice") in the Acts of the Apostles. In his address to the governor Felix in Acts 24, Paul is accused by the high priest's spokesman of being "one who stirs up riots among all the Jews throughout the world and is a ringleader of the sect of the Nazarenes" (Acts 24:5). In his defense, Paul denies that he was trying to be divisive but "that according to the Way, which they call a sect, I worship the God of our fathers, believing everything laid down by the Law and written in the Prophets ...." Paul's explanation illustrates how an outsider term like "sect" can designate a true reality among God's people, namely that there is a way of thinking and acting prescribed by God and chosen by believers over against nonbelievers. This choice and its distinctiveness will often lead to separation from others and negative accusations. Indeed, as the Jews in Rome would later admit to Paul, his "sect" was "everywhere spoken against" (Acts 28:22).

Clearly, the term "sect" is not the approved term for designating the Christian "Way" in the Bible, and Harrell does not present it as such in his writings. But in its repeated use in Acts, the term serves as a linguistic bridge to the non-Christian world's designations of groups like the Sadducees (Acts 5:17) and Pharisees (Acts 15:5), both of which are understandable as stringent groups within a religion, as is evident in the way Paul described his relationship to the Pharisees: "according to the strictest party (*heiresin*) of our religion I have lived as a Pharisee" (Acts 26:5). One value of this linguistic bridge is that it allows for critical comparison to other religious groups (sects) that have similarly distinctive characteristics (e.g., voluntary, exclusive, separatist, and countercultural), while not losing the ability to claim uniqueness for one of them—"the Way" as defined by God's word (as Paul did in Acts 24). As we have seen, Harrell made a career of building this bridge between, 1) secular comparisons of sectarian religious groups and 2) his own observance of a singularly true way of being Christian, rooted in the New Testament. His readers could use the category of "sect" as both explanation for the distinctive characteristics of New Testament Christianity and as warrant for continuing to speak with conviction about a strict and demanding Christian faith in the face of attacks on this faith as judgmental and divisive. The conflict produced by true Christian conviction is not evidence of its falsehood but of the effects caused by a singular and exacting way of religious life, aka "a sect."

Second, understanding the sectarian nature of New Testament Christianity helps to reverse the negative charge of being an "anti," rendering it a positive attribute. As Harrell wryly phrased it, he was an "anti anti." That is someone who used the pejorative phrase to indicate a convicted stand for truth. Like the Biblical "sect," the "anti" position is not primarily opposed to any human group, but is opposed to beliefs and practices that oppose Biblical teachings—it is "anti" to those who are "anti" to Scripture. Adherence to the narrow way of following Jesus inherently opposes the many who will not walk with Him, and so the sect is essentially oppositional in its stand for the truth. As sociologist Bryan Wilson observes, "Sects are movements of religious protest."[10] And the protest of the New Testament Christian "anti" is against the world in all its pride and progressive disguise. "Sectarians define themselves over against the world, unbelievers," observes Wilson. "They form themselves into an antisociety that uses an antilanguage."[11] Harrell's emphasis on the congregational churches of Christ as "a peculiar people" purposefully avoiding pretensions to worldly power and prestige provided his generation with a clarification that the marginalized nature of their churches was not simply a consequence of their doctrinal and sociological positions, but a choice that was made by humble hearts seeking otherworldly goals. As we have sought to show, the spirituality of this sect was often one of kenotic self-emptying, which sought God's Way above their own preferences or the progressive trends of more worldly churches and Christians.

Third, Harrell's adoption of the "sect" as a framework for describing the historical development of the churches of Christ underscored the challenge of maintaining this identity in the world. These churches must purposefully maintain themselves,

---

10. Bryan Wilson, *Religious Sects: A Sociological Study* (New York: McGraw-Hill, 1970), 7.

11. Ibid., 56.

not as a group, but as a choice for Christ against culture. "So, let's remember that what we begin with," Harrell concluded about his landmark pamphlet on *The Church of Christ Denomination*. "And what we are left with after denominational groups appear, is the undenominational church of Jesus Christ–no group."[12] This paradoxical formulation, the "no group" group, encapsulates the challenge facing the members of a restorationist movement who seek to perpetuate a common understanding of Scripture in the world without making it about the group. As Harrell knew well, theologians like H. Richard Niebuhr concluded that sects necessarily underwent transformation with the birth of a second generation.[13] The second generation would presumably be less committed to voluntary adherence, simply inheriting their sectarian persuasion. As we have seen, Harrell raised concerns about the evidence of this shift among the younger preachers of his day, but never moved into campaigning against the signs of a "new apostasy," though others would reasonably criticize him for this moderation and the degree to which he left open the door to uncertainty and differences in interpretation of Scripture. Harrell's approach to cultivating a principled sectarian mindset was more pastoral than polemical, reiterating the premises upon which the next generation(s) would need to maintain the quest for primitive Christianity, and emphasizing restoration as a lifelong process of Bible study, spiritual discernment, and Christian fellowship focused on the power and oracles of God (1 Peter 4:11). If the sect is to persist as a sect, Harrell concludes, its members must continue to assert a strong countercultural position, demanding exacting tests of their own young people, and hold themselves aloof from the

---

12. David Edwin Harrell, Jr., "Emergence of the Church of Christ Denomination Update," *Vanguard* 5.2 (January 25, 1979): 14.

13. H. Richard Niebuhr, *The Social Sources of Denominationalism* (New York: Holt, 1929), especially chapters 2 and 3 on "The Churches of the Disinherited." Cf. Bryan Wilson, *Religious Sects*, 233.

wider society.[14] This is seen most poignantly in Harrell's biography of Homer Hailey and his tract on "Thinking Inside the Box," which were overt attempts to socialize the next generation to a particular set of values. His hope was that these works might help produce high integrity, strong moral dispositions, and heightened sense of responsibility in the next generation.

Harrell had learned from his father the value of an older generation pouring its love and insights into their sons and daughters. His pivotal years as a young scholar among older mentors like James R. Cope and Clinton Hamilton had taught the value of socialization into the dispositions and responsibilities of the restorationist. And the arc of his mature work as a historian demonstrates an abiding appreciation for the practical lessons taught by attention to the marginalized Christian sect, including its beliefs and practices related to community improvement, race relations, and Biblical interpretation. In a less publicized way, his preaching, missionary work, and writing in religious publications show a disciplined attention to the need for simplicity and humility in maintaining obedience to God's word and opposition to the world's wisdom and pleasures, even as one's own education and wealth increase. In these ways, much of the spiritual journey of Ed Harrell's life is familiar territory for New Testament Christians in the 21st century and helps them on the way to Zion.

---

14. In his work "The Protestant Sects and the Spirit of Capitalism," the German sociologies Max Weber provides the classic case for the ability of a sect to cultivate and perpetuate an ethos, or way of believing and behaving, that endures beyond the first generation. His famous argument is that the Puritans maintained an ascetism before God that translated into a way of living with other people that prized thrift and dedication to work (a "protestant work ethic") that led to the spirit of capitalism in the modern era; in H. H. Gerth and C. Wright Mills, *From Max Weber: Essays in Sociology* (New York: Oxford, 1946), 302-322, especially 321. Cf. Bryan Wilson, *Religious Sects*, 233.

APPENDICES

Emergence of the "Church of Christ" Denomination

David Edwin Harrell, Jr.

Originally Published by Harwell/Lewis Publishing Company in 1962 and reprinted with a preface in 2005.
Reprinted with permission.

2005 Preface

This tract was published first in 1962. I had recently received my Ph.D. from Vanderbilt University and begun teaching history at East Tennessee State University. My first book, *Quest for a Christian America*, had just been published by the Disciples of Christ Historical Society. In the years since its publication, this brief tract has been read by tens of thousands of people, but it has now been out-of-print for a number of years.

Have you ever read something you wrote 45 years ago? From a literary point of view, it can be a pretty humbling exercise. I was full of spit and vinegar and had a penchant for superlatives that has diminished through the years. Happily, my writing style has become less flowery, and I am now less impressed by the opinions of the conclusions of "eminent" historians and sociologists. I have continued to study restoration history, and in a pretty extensive list of books and articles I have fleshed out (and in some cases modified slightly) some of the conclusions stated in the tract.

I considered revising and rewriting the original text of this tract to bring it into line with some of the nuances that I have subsequently published during a long career as a professional historian. But I decided that this tract had such integrity in its own right that it deserved to be preserved in the form in which it was originally published. Furthermore, the general outline of the three-way division in the churches of Christ outlined here has proven to be prophetically correct. The years from 1950 to 2005 have seen churches of Christ divided into three wings that are separated by both doctrinal and sociological tensions. In my writings I have labeled these three wings of the movement "Non-Institutional churches of Christ," "Institutional Churches of Christ," and "Progressive Churches of Christ." The predictions and descriptions in The Emergence of the "Church of Christ" Denomination deserve a continued hearing at the beginning of the 21st century.

Several recent writers have speculated that my sociological interpretation of the restoration movement—stated openly for the first time in this tract—was tied to my identification with the non-institutional wing of the movement. That is chronologically inaccurate. My views about the nature of the division within the movement were formed very early during my days as a student at Vanderbilt. At the time, I was a recent graduate of David Lipscomb College and was fully engaged with institutional churches. Many of the doctrinal issues being debated at the time seemed peripheral to me (though they were not), but as I began reading the literature of religious sociology, I became increasingly uncomfortable with the observable changes taking place in churches of Christ. It was that uneasiness that led me first to listen with some sympathy to Biblical arguments against institutionalism and social gospel practices.

Many readers of this tract will know that I recently wrote an extensive treatment of the twentieth century history of the churches of Christ: *The Churches of Christ in the Twentieth Century: Homer Hailey's Personal Journey of Faith* (Tuscaloosa: University of Alabama Press, 2000). That book looks at the changes predicted here in much greater detail. In addition, I have recently written a study pamphlet giving my current views on the twentieth century divisions in the churches of Christ, Three Churches of Christ Face the 21st Century, that should be published soon.

David Edwin Harrell, Jr.
P.O. Box 3397
Ponte Vedra, FL 32004
November 2005

Emergence of the "Church of Christ" Denomination

The struggles of recent years have certainly taught us that the necessary ingredients for maintaining the purity of the faith are knowledge of the Bible and the courage to stand upon it. There is only one way to test a question, only one way to decide an issue, and that is by the authority of the Scriptures. The time and effort expended by faithful gospel preachers in open-minded study and unintimidated preaching on the current issues is the source of most of the good accomplished in the last few decades. I recognized that this is where the battle is fought; I hope that I have contributed to the cause.

It is true, however, that sometimes we can better understand the specifics of a subject if we have a view of the broader setting. Sometimes one can be so intent on a befuddling specific that he loses sight of the obvious. There is meaning in the truism that some cannot see the forest for the trees.

Within this context an historical and sociological study of the restoration movement offers some insights into the past and present problems of the church. This is not to say that one's faith should rest on historical foundations; it should be rooted in the Word of God. But good history, unbiased and objective, can tell us something about ourselves, and those who differ from us.

My book, *Quest for a Christian America*, which recently was published by the Disciples of Christ Historical Society, is a study of the first half-century of the restoration movement from an historical and sociological point of view. It is an honest effort at objective scholarship and has been received as such by the academic world. Some of the most prominent scholars in the country have reviewed the book in the leading historical journals. They have not always given the book unstinted praise, but they have generally been very kind, and all have accepted it as an honest, scholarly, and objective contribution to the literature of American history. I have, as an historian should, simply made an effort to tell the story of what early Disciples thought and did with regard to social issues. I think they were sometimes right; I think they were sometimes wrong; as an historian I simply did not judge.

I do believe, however, that there is a moral in the story that I told. It is my intention to clarify that moral as I see it, in this booklet. But before I lapse into polemics, let me simply state some facts that are apparent to every historian of the restoration.

The better scholars in the universities in the United States are not unaware of the problems and divisions that have taken place within the Disciples movements. As a matter of fact, religious divisions have long been a subject of interest to historians and sociologists of religion and these scholars have carefully catalogued the nature of these divisions. The classic pattern involved in a religious division is known as the "sect-to-denomination" process.

I
Sociological Patterns and the Sect-To-Denomination Process

As briefly stated by Ernst Troeltsch, an eminent German historian, all new and fervent religious groups emerge as "sects." Troeltsch called the church of the first century a "sect." "Sects," according to Troeltsch and hundreds of others who have built on his work, have certain definable traits. Their members believe they have "the truth," they are strict morally, they believe themselves to be "the church," they are fervent, and exhibit other similar characteristics. While one is under no obligation to accept the name "sect," there is no question that my religious convictions belong in the conservative realm that sociologists describe with this term. I am not a member of a "sect," I am a Christian and a member of "the church." But it is precisely this attitude which, to the modern scholar, means "sectarianism."

"Denomination" is the term used by sociologists to describe the other classic religious form in the United States. "Denominations" have a variety of distinguishable characteristics. They are tolerant of other "churches," they generally accept the moral standards of the society in which they exist, they are less dogmatic, less active, and more interested in the world around them.

Sociologists have long recognized that "sects" tend to evolve into "denominations." Countless groups which had their origins as conservative and exclusive churches have evolved in the course of a few generations into liberal and tolerant denominations. Of course, there is usually a small element in any division which clings to the old conservative convictions, refuses to make the transition to liberalism, and usually is forced to separate itself. Sometimes a group will make only a partial transition toward true denominationalism, accepting some changes in its traditional beliefs but unwilling to make the full evolution. Sociologists classify these groups as "institutionalized sects."

While this explanation could be vastly extended, it is enough to say that scholars have carefully catalogued these types of religious reactions and have also made some provoking studies on the nature of these divisions. The different types of religious bodies attract different sociological and psychological types. "Sects" have a tendency to attract lower economic groups, the troubled, and people who feel a deep psychological need for a fervent and spiritually-oriented religion. Denominations, on the other hand, appeal to the complacent, satisfied, the wealthier and more sophisticated people. While there are many individual exceptions to these generalizations, there is no question that they can be substantiated by facts.

The "sect-to-denomination" process, which is recurrent in American religious history, is an easily explained phenomenon once these facts are understood. A religious group that begins as the fervent offspring of poor but honest people can change quite decisively in a few generations' time. The successful grandchildren and great-grandchildren that have far exceeded their forbearers financially, educationally, and socially are not likely to want the same kind of worship, the same kind of preachers, or the same kind of gospel that their ancestors loved. So they change the church. The "denomination" is the type of religious expression that suits their sociological and psychological needs.

All of this has a rather deterministic sound. It clearly implies that only certain types of people are attracted to pure and fervent religion. Someone asked me a few months ago if I was not saying in my book that if you were not poor you could not be a Christian. A liberal Churches of Christ historian accused me of saying that the only reason the conservative brethren rejected the instrument was because they were too poor to afford it. That is patently false. But what is true, and what is easily demonstrated by historical scholarship, is that the rich and the sophisticated tend to want a different kind of religion from the poor and the humble. Of course there are individual exceptions; nor does this deny that they all may act on honest convictions. But who can deny that the humble and the proud are apt to hold to different convictions? The clear pattern is there.

This is no news to the Christian. The New Testament is literally loaded with the sociological message. Again and again Jesus said that His message was peculiarly directed to the poor (Luke 6:20-26; Mark 10:23-27; Matthew 11:4-5). James clearly states the case: "Hearken, my beloved brethren, hath not God chosen the poor of this world rich in faith, and heirs of the kingdom which he hath promised to them that love him?" (James 2:5). In 1 Corinthians 1:26 the Apostle Paul includes not only wealth but also success and sophistication as barriers to spiritual success: "For ye see your calling, brethren, how that not many wise men after the flesh, not many mighty, not many noble, are called."

God has clearly revealed that His message would be influenced by social conditions. That such has been the case is a matter of record. The examination that follows of the nineteenth- and twentieth-century divisions of the church are, I believe, from a scholarly and historical point of view, unimpeachable. One might not like the consequences, but I do not see how he can avoid them, or ignore them.

II
The Success and Division of the
Nineteenth-Century Restoration Movement

Using the terminology of modern religious sociologists and historians, the early nineteenth century religious movement led by Alexander Campbell and Barton Stone was a "legalistic sect." The church was intolerant, dogmatic, fervent, and spiritually oriented; it had its early appeal mainly among the common people and the psychologically aggressive. The claim to uniqueness of the early Disciples was based on their search for New Testament Christianity based on a legalistic and literalistic approach to the Scriptures.

The story of the success of this early aggressive movement is well known. The church experienced a startling growth. By 1850 the Disciples had become the sixth largest religious group in the nation and the largest religious body of American origin. But this growth was not accomplished without the generation of internal tensions and already by 1860 there were serious doctrinal differences among the church leaders. In the years after the Civil War these differences hardened and deepened and led eventually to a three way schism in the movement.

The theological issues involved in the division of the movement have long been subject to discussions by historians and other scholars. The most serious problems were the use of instrumental music in worship, organized missionary societies, the pastor system, and eventually, such issues as acceptance or rejection of higher Biblical criticism, and open membership. I do not intend to trace the development of these theological differences. Suffice it to say here that by the end of the nineteenth century the movement had divided around three groups of doctrinal standards.

The most conservative element in the church had able spokesmen in David Lipscomb and his powerful paper the *Gospel Advocate*, as well as a whole crop of hard-nosed preachers scattered from Tennessee to Texas. The most progressive element in the church was moving rapidly by 1900 to a liberal point of view on all major doctrinal issues. The early liberal movement had been led by the St. Louis editor, James Harvey Garrison, and by 1900 was being spearheaded by a core of brilliant young scholars associated with the University of Chicago. A sizeable portion of the movement straddled the middle-of-the-road on these doctrinal issues. Many of the most important post-Civil War Disciples leaders, including James W. McGarvey, Moses Lard, and Isaac Errett, accepted the organ or missionary society or both while persistently refusing to follow the mushrooming liberal movement in other areas. This doctrinal tri-section led to (1) the twentieth century church of Christ, and (2) the cooperative and (3) independent Disciples of Christ.

While a good deal has been written about the doctrinal controversies which led to the schisms in the restoration movement, very few scholars have realized the enormous importance of sociological pressures in prompting and forming the divisions. I believe that economic, psychological, and sectional motives were paramount in the nineteenth century divisions. In fact, I have written a good deal in the past few years pointing out the importance of these factors. I want to make my position perfectly clear. I have been accused of saying that the only basis for the division in the church over the organ was that those who were too poor to afford one opposed its introduction and those who were wealthy enough to own one defended it. This is not what I have said by any means. I believe that men on both sides of the controversy acted in good faith and with the firm conviction that they could scripturally fortify their position. But this does not alter the fact that the division of the church can be defined in terms of sociological classes as well as in terms of doctrinal differences—and I suspect that this is a more meaningful division.

III
The Sectional and Sociological Dimensions of Nineteenth Century Divisions

That the schism of the restoration movement in the nineteenth century was a division into sociological groups is a matter of simple fact. A study of census returns makes the point obvious. According to the religious census of 1916, the Disciples of Christ had a membership of 1,226,000 while the Churches of Christ had only 317,000 members. In the former slave states, however, Disciples membership totaled only 485,000, over half of which was in the border states of Kentucky and Missouri. On the other hand, nearly 250,000 of the Churches of Christ's members were in the former slave states. In Tennessee, the Disciples listed 21,500 members while the Church of Christ claimed 63,500.

[See David Edwin Harrell, Jr., "The Sectional Origins of the Churches of Christ," Journal of Southern History, XXX (August, 1964), 261-277; "The Disciples of Christ and Social Force in Tennessee, 1860-1900," East Tennessee Historical Society Publications (1966); "Disciples of Christ Pacifism in Nineteenth Century Tennessee, Tennessee Historical Quarterly, XXI (September, 1962), 263-274.]

In short, the most conservative element of the church centered in the lower South, the former states of the Confederacy. The middle-of-the-roaders found their strongest support in the border area of Kentucky, Missouri, West Virginia, and East Tennessee. The liberal stream in the movement was most successful in the North. Some of the more perceptive church leaders of the day recognized that the division taking place was decidedly sectional in character. David Lipscomb was repeatedly accused of trying to draw the Mason-Dixon line through the church. And it was true that many Southern church leaders did associate digression with the North and conservatism with the South. The caustic T. R. Burnet, condemning the formation of the state missionary society in Texas in 1892, said: "The brethren are following northern ideas and northern men, and patterning after sectarian plans and models, and have given up the Bible model."

The late nineteenth-century division of the church of Christ, then, was essentially a sectional division. Of course, there were thousands of individual exceptions, but this was the general pattern. The interesting question raised by this is: Why did most southerners believe that the organ was wrong and most northerners believe that it was right? One may assume that they were honest in their convictions, that the doctrinal problems involved were significant, but it does appear that some other factors must have been involved.

The three great sections in post-Civil War United States (the South, Border areas, and the North) also represented three economic and sociological groups. The population of the South remained rural and economically depressed after the war. It was among this sociological class that the conservative plea of the restoration movement continued to thrive. Outside of the South the only areas where the conservative position held its own were in some of the economically depressed farming sections of the Midwest. The areas of the South where the conservatives failed to win the doctrinal battle were largely in the middle class congregations of the Southern cities. In short, that element which was receptive to conservative pleas and uncompromisingly rejected all innovations was the most depressed class in the movement.

On the other hand, the liberal wing in the church was strongly urban. It was led by the preachers of the growing cities of the Midwest and Kentucky. Disciples in these areas had grown rich and fat in the nineteenth century. The liberal movement grew in almost a precise ratio to the growth of sophistication of the membership of the churches. In short, that element in the movement which was most receptive to "progress," that element which first introduced the organ, which pushed for changes in the organizational structure in the church, and which accepted the findings of modernistic scholarship, was the most economically and psychologically stable element in the church.

Those who were middle-of-the-roaders doctrinally represented an economic class somewhere between these extremes. The most notable doctrinal moderates were Kentuckians. The moderate movement got strong support from the neat and respectable rural churches in Kentucky and the Midwest. These churches were neither so economically depressed as those of the South nor so sophisticated as the growing congregations in the cities. Neither was the doctrine they accepted as extreme as that of either of the other groups.

What this demonstrates is that while the nineteenth century division of the restoration took place over doctrinal problems, it was rooted in deep economic differences in the membership of the movement. By 1900, there were serious class differences within the movement and the church divided along class lines.

What had happened was that the Disciples of Christ had undergone the "sect-to-denomination" evolution—at least a segment of the movement had completed the transition. The group had passed through the same transition common to all religious movements. Three incompatible classes had emerged within the church.

By 1900, the sociological unity of the church had vanished. The old conservative values of the early movement were simply no longer an acceptable expression of Christianity to the more sophisticated elements in the church.

As wealthier, more educated and more socially established elements in the church emerged, they simply formulated a more denominational expression of Christianity. By 1900, the liberal element of the Disciples of Christ was well on its way to becoming a prominent American denomination. On the other hand, there remained in the church in 1900 a sociological class of fervent people who could only be satisfied with the same old vital, aggressive emphasis common to the founders of the movement. They refused to evolve into a denomination and retained the strict standards which fitted their emotional religious needs.

IV
Growth and Division in Churches of Christ in the Twentieth Century

It is enough to simply point out that the peacemakers in the middle-ofthe-road were simply another sociological group. They made a part of the transition to denominationalism but stopped short of the full process. Doctrinally, they reached a hybrid position of partial acceptance of denominational standards and partial retention of the old legalistic standards. In short, they became an "institutional sect." This was the point in the transition which suited their sociological needs. They were also a hybrid sociological class—at a kind of halfway house between rural poverty and urban sophistication. In sum, they also had their own unique religious needs which were met by the unique solution of the institutional sect.

As these sociological changes took place within the movement—as the movement came to include vastly different kinds of people—it was inevitable that a schism take place. The simple fact of the matter was that the people within the church no longer wanted the same kind of Christianity. This was the basic issue—what doctrinal problems arose to divide over were inconsequential. When this basic transition had taken place issues were bound to arise. The doctrinal clashes could have taken place in a hundred different areas. As it happened, the first innovations injected by the liberals in the movement were instrumental music and organized missionary societies. But they were only the first; many others followed; many others were bound to follow. Instrumental music and organized societies were in essence the accidental basis of the doctrinal division in the movement. They certainly were not the cause of the schism. The cause was that the church had grown to include incompatible kinds of people.

Of course, most of the people involved in the long and bitter controversy in the church little understood the deeper tensions within the movement. Some were not totally unaware of the class divergence underlying the doctrinal problems. In 1897, Daniel Sommer wrote a very perceptive analysis of the pressures leading to the schism:

As time advanced such of those churches as assembled in large towns and cities gradually became proud, or at least, sufficiently world-minded to desire popularity, and in order to attain that unscriptural end they adopted certain popular arrangements such as the hired pastor, the church choir, instrumental music, manmade societies to advance the gospel, and human devices to raise money to support previously mentioned devices of similar origin. In so doing they divided the brotherhood of disciples, and thereby became responsible for all the evils resulting from the division which they caused. (*Octographic Review,* XL, October 5, 1897, 1).

Sommer had placed the responsibility for the division at the doorsteps of the upper-class city churches —precisely where it belonged. But such understanding was rare. Especially liberal leaders in the movement were unwilling to admit that they had become too sophisticated for the old principles of the fathers.

As a result, the controversy was largely a doctrinal struggle. Most of the debates centered, for several decades, on the attempts of each side to scripturally document its position; Each side was also profoundly interested in rallying the testimony of the early leaders of the movement to the support of its position.

This was an uneven and unrealistic struggle from the beginning. Within the context of a literalistic interpretation of the scriptures, it was no contest. The innovations which became issues in the controversy were simply not justifiable in terms of a literalistic interpretation of the scriptures. The best a liberal literalist could do was obfuscate, muddle, or evacuate. This is not to say that there was no defense for liberalism. There is, and later liberal Disciples leaders find and use rationalism and liberal Biblical interpretation as their rationale. But the point is, there is no case for liberalism within the context of Biblical literalism and this is where most early Disciples liberals felt compelled to fight. They lost. I say it not because I think they were wrong, but because any objective witness of the struggle would say they lost. You can't accept the Book of Mormon and defeat a Mormon; you can't use papal proclamations to beat a Roman Catholic; and you can't be a Biblical liberal and fight a legalist.

I suppose it ought to be parenthetically asked: If they lost, why did the majority of the people follow them? The answer is simply that who wins or loses an argument has very little to do with the convictions of the listeners. The listeners generally believe what they want to believe and in the nineteenth century controversy most members of the Disciples wanted to be denominationalists.

Not only was there no realistic clash between the groups within the context of a literalistic interpretation of the scriptures, neither was there any question about which of the elements was heir to the traditions of the early movement. The early movement would be classified by every religious sociologist as a "sect," and when the split came the conservatives were clearly the spiritual sons of the early leaders of the movement. This question is not important to us doctrinally, but it is interesting, and in every church controversy it is broadly disputed. But the question is not even debatable. Both sides quoted Alexander Campbell, Walter Scott, and Barton Stone during the controversy on specific issues. But whatever they might have said on specific issues, they were by nature fanatical literalists. By 1900, they would have only fit within one segment of the church—the church of Christ.

But back to the main question. The battle between the divergent elements within the church was fought on the unrealistic and meaningless battleground of scriptural literalism. This raises the further interesting question of why the liberal element joined the battle on these uneven and unrealistic terms.

One obvious answer is that they did not know (as many of the conservatives did not know) that this was not the real point of controversy. It was not until the twentieth century that a sizeable number of liberal leaders recognized the fact that they had abandoned their allegiance to scriptural literalism and restoration. It was easy for a man who wanted a more progressive and denominational religion, and yet at the same time wanted to believe that he still held to his old-time convictions, to satisfy himself with fuzzy rationalizations. Some very unconvincing arguments can convince us to believe what we already believe. The transition into a denomination is a complex one. It takes time and it often takes place subtly—even though the change is basic and dramatic. A man in the midst of the change often fails to recognize it. If he is perceptive enough to recognize it, he must have the additional ingredient of courage and moral honesty to admit it. It takes at least one generation to make the change and at least one more generation to understand and admit the change.

But there was another important reason why early liberal leaders in the church refused to admit that they were changing the fundamental direction of the movement during the nineteenth century. By 1875, the divergent elements within the church were engaged in mortal battle for the loyalty of local congregations. A successful liberal leader must move with calculated caution.

Many church members in the fifty years from 1860 to 1910 traveled the slow road to denominationalism that would have been repelled by a rapid and conscious transition. It was certainly the part of wisdom for the progressive leader to move slowly. Many a liberal Disciples leader during these crucial years underplayed the magnitude of the transition in his own personal conviction for the benefit of the less perceptive general body of members. Whether this policy is vicious and dishonest, or enlightened and shrewd, depends pretty largely upon which side the viewer is on.

This, then, is a sociological interpretation of the late nineteenth century division in the Disciples of Christ. It was a division which followed the well established patterns of "sect-to-denomination" evolution based on diverging class interests.

This evolution reached a rather satisfactory and stable conclusion by about twenty years ago. The church of Christ remained at that date firmly conservative in emphasis, united around the old plea of restoration of the ancient order. The Disciples had reached a point of fairly stable denominationalism. What conservatism remained in the Disciples movement was shed in the independent-cooperative division of the early twentieth century. Liberal Disciples today, by and large, are proud to have made the transition to denominationalism, and have gained new insight into the meaning of the restoration movement. A liberal Disciple today would not think of holding a scriptural debate on instrumental music—or anything else. He understands he does not stand on the same platform as the early nineteenth century reformers. I think most would freely admit that the church of Christ does. The Disciples of Christ have an entirely new set of justifications for their existence. In short, in the perspective of some thirty or forty years it is relatively easy for the historian to draw meaningful conclusions. With the passing of time it has also become easy for the interested groups to understand and appreciate what has happened.

V

Growth and Division In Churches of Christ In the Twentieth Century

Within the framework of the definitions of modern historians and sociologists, the late-nineteenth-century religious movement led by David Lipscomb and others of like mind was also a "legalistic sect." Doctrinally, the church was intolerant, highly moralistic, and insistent on strict adherence to certain doctrinal standards. Psychologically, the members of the church were aggressive, dogmatic, and deeply religious. Economically, the church appealed largely to the lower classes of the South and other areas influenced by migration from the South.

From the standpoint of the historian, the growth of the church of Christ during the first half of the twentieth century has been extraordinary. With limited financial resources, a total lack of inter-congregational organizational structure, and a seemingly unimpressive leadership, the group nevertheless emerged as one of the most rapidly growing religious bodies in the nation. But the growth of the church in the twentieth century (as had been the case in the nineteenth century) was accompanied by the rise of serious internal tensions. The nineteenth-century story of success and schism was being vigorously reenacted by 1940.

The doctrinal issues which have emerged within the church of Christ within the past few decades are well known. They include basic differences on questions of church work and organization. The propriety of church-sponsored organizations such as orphan homes, schools, and hospitals; the proper limitations of multi-church activities; and the proper function of the church in the broad area of social action are fundamental problems which have caused deep cleavages in the unity of the church.

New doctrinal issues continue to arise, and some people yet remain uncommitted to any point of view, but by and large the opposing positions have become recognizable and stable. Three major doctrinal emphases are clearly discernible. The most conservative element in the church rejects all such schemes as "innovation." The future historian will associate this position with a number of conservative religious papers, including the Gospel Guardian. Of course, there is considerable variety within the conservative camp; religious conservatism is a haven for rank individualists of every stripe. The most progressive element in the church is led by *Mission Magazine* and *Christian Chronicle* and the liberal educational institutions associated with that segment of the movement. The liberal Church of Christ controls nearly all of the institutions created in the twentieth century and progressive church leaders have demonstrated an amazing ingenuity in hatching new projects. A somewhat hazy middle-of-the-road approach is followed by the editor of the Firm Foundation and, apparently, a sizeable group of moderates within the church.

It is enough to establish the existence of three segments within the movement. Most of those who read this article will be familiar with the doctrinal position and the apologetics of each group. After several decades of heated debate, an apparently irreversible rupture has taken place, isolating the more conservative element from the other two. Even an amateur prophet could predict that the partnership between the other two groups will become an increasingly uneasy one.

But now to my point. It is one thing to understand the theological problems involved in the present controversy in the church and another thing entirely to assume that all of the problems are based in theological differences. Sociological factors are involved in the present controversy (as they always are in religious divisions) and the situation in the church comes into much clearer focus when viewed from this direction.

Unfortunately for the historian, statistical information about the present schism in the church is not available, and it probably will be some time before data does come to hand. But I believe that it is obvious that the current division in the movement is essentially a class rupture. By and large, the conservative doctrinal view is most successful among the poorer economic groups within the church. On the other hand, the liberal position is most firmly entrenched among the wealthier and more sophisticated congregations and has its greatest appeal to this class of people. There are many exceptions to this generalization, as there were many exceptions in the nineteenth century division, but this does not impair the basic economic pattern present in both of the controversies.

I believe there is also a clear psychological pattern in the present division. Those who have the most fervent religious psychologies are almost invariably in the conservative camp. Most of the "fanatics," the individualists, the "eccentrics" in the church are "antis." Not all conservatives are "eccentrics" by any means, but most of the people who are deeply and intensely concerned about their religion are conservatives. On the other hand, the liberal point of view attracts the contented and the complacent. If the conservative plea attracts those whose zeal might lead them to extremes, the liberal plea finds its most devoted supporters among those who want the easiest and least bothersome religion they can find.

The sociological unity which existed within the church of Christ around the turn of the century simply no longer exists. As the sociological and psychological complexion of the movement changed, the theological unity which had characterized the churches in the early part of the century was bound to give way.

What had happened by the middle of the twentieth century was· simply the completion of the "sect-to-denomination" cycle again—the familiar process constantly at work in American religious history. In the course of the half-century since 1900 one segment of the membership of the church had grown wealthier, better educated, and more sophisticated. This new generation of "Church of Christers" (largely children and grandchildren of the pioneers who lived around the turn of the century) reached the sociological status which demanded a more denominational expression of Christianity. By 1960, the most liberal element within the church was well on its way into the mainstream of American denominationalism.

On the other hand, in this schism, as in the divisions of the past, it was not the entire church which made the transition. A substantial minority—the fervent and generally the less affluent classes—retained the old attitudes about religion. They yet refuse to make the transition and remain committed to the conservative theological standards which fit their religious presuppositions.

The division of the mid-twentieth century has its sociological and theological middle ground as did the break of the last century. Theologically, this middle group is willing to make only a part of the transition to denominationalism. They will probably evolve (or at least many of them will) into an "institutionalized sect"—partially accepting denominational standards and partially clinging to the conservative plea of the past. This is the theological compromise which meets the needs of the middle class sociological group.

To a professional historian, there is considerable evidence that such a sociological transition is underway in the church of Christ today. Liston Pope, an eminent sociologist of religion, has provided an interesting list of criteria for measuring the progress of a religious group toward denominationalism. Pope suggests twenty-one changes which take place during the evolution. Some of them are inapplicable to a group with the emphasis of the restoration movement, but several of them are highly suggestive. Of course, some of these transitions do not involve matters that are inherently right or wrong, but taken together they are symptoms of a dramatic change indeed.

"From propertyless to property-owning membership." This is the basic economic change that takes place as a religious group makes its move toward a more sophisticated religious expression. That much of the membership of the church of Christ has made this change to economic comfort and stability is apparent to the casual observer. It would be naive to assume that this economic shift has had no impact on the thought of the movement.

"From economic poverty to economic wealth, that is, value of church property, minister's salary." The erection of costly and elaborate buildings has been one of the most prominent visible changes in the church since World War II. The unpretentious, inexpensive, sometimes ugly, little building on the wrong side of town has repeatedly given way to the "as good as the Methodists" status symbol. Many liberal ministers have shared in the rise in economic prosperity; they are far from a deprived but fervent band of evangelists.

"From cultural periphery toward the cultural center of the community." Much of the church has moved from a critical, or at least skeptical, attitude toward the values of the society around it to a general acceptance of that culture. Within the past few years such typical representatives of the culture as politicians, business wizards, athletes, and movie stars have become the most-advertised members of the church of Christ. In the early days of the movement they would certainly have been hidden, and probably disowned.

"From a community excluding 'unworthy members' to an institution embracing all who are socially compatible." Again the application is obvious. It is common knowledge that a "socially acceptable" member would never be disciplined in one of the sophisticated churches of the brotherhood today. The very principle of discipline has been abandoned by a large segment of the church.

"From an unspecialized, unprofessional ministry to a professional ministry." The acceptance of the idea of the clergy is well advanced in the liberal element of the church of Christ. Specialized education has become a prerequisite for preaching in most of the congregations. Whatever they may be called, the equivalents of denominational seminaries are in existence.

"From emphasis on evangelism to emphasis on religious education." The church has become increasingly less zealous and less effective in evangelization. On the other hand, the more socially acceptable emphasis on "Christian education" is growing into a highly specialized business.

"From stress on future in the next world to primary interest in this world." This is the denominational basis for the social gospel movement. Much of the doctrinal clash within the church today centers around the expanded activities of the denominational element into the area of social service and activities.

Several of the other changes listed by Pope lend themselves to obvious comparisons: "From non-cooperation with other churches to cooperation;" "From fervor in worship to restraint;" "From a high degree of congregational participation to delegation of responsibility to a few." Finally, one other interesting item: "From persecution to success and dominance psychology." The conservative has a combative mind that is out of step with most of the world. The "on the march," "million dollar," spectacular approach of the liberal today fits into an entirely different category. He has a denominational psychology.

This is sufficient to indicate to the unbiased mind that a large segment of the church of Christ is well along the path toward denominational status. The evolution that is taking place is essentially a sociological one. It is the result of the changing character of the membership of the church. The cultured element in the movement has simply begun the search for a more sophisticated type of religion.

As the kinds of people who were members of the church began to diversify, it was inevitable that theological "issues" would arise between the sociological groups. What those issues happened to be is really accidental. The church is not really dividing over the relationship of the local congregation to an orphan home. The orphan home "issue" and all the other issues are only tangentially involved. It could have been something entirely different; other areas of friction will surely arise in the future. The church is dividing because there are two basic kinds of people within the movement who are demanding two very different kinds of religion.

Many, I suppose most, of the people involved in the present schism are unaware of this basic conflict. The debate has largely been confined to scriptural argument or theological questions. In a way, this is inevitable; sound gospel preachers must defend the truth with the Word. And they have. In truth, however, this whole Biblical clash has been unrealistic. It is unrealistic because it is simply no contest. Within the framework of a literal approach to the Scriptures, within the context of the search for the ancient order, there simply is no justification for the liberal movement within the church of Christ. This is not to say that there is no intellectual justification for liberalism in religion. I do not believe the argument of the liberal, but he has a rational defense for his behavior; he simply cannot defend his liberalism and try to cling to a conservative Biblical faith. A liberal platform on a conservative foundation is a pyramid of paradoxes. The efforts of modern "Church of Christers" to fight denominational battles with legalistic weapons are ludicrous. I believe that every objective observer today would say that such efforts by liberals are just as ridiculously misguided as were those of the liberal Disciple fifty years ago.

Neither is the battle over the church fathers a realistic one. It is true that both sides can quote David Lipscomb with relation to the "issues," as both sides quoted Alexander Campbell during the nineteenth-century controversy. But this is not the point at all. The point is: David Lip comb was a literalistic conservative, as were James A. Harding and J. D. Tant and Benjamin Franklin and Alexander Campbell and Barton Stone. Those in the conservative element of the church are clearly the heirs of the heritage of the past. This is not justification of either side—it is a simple statement of historical fact. One who does not understand this simply does not understand the past—or the present.

Why do the leaders of the denominational element of the church of Christ fail to recognize the nature of the controversy? I believe the answer is simple. It is the same answer to the same question asked about the church leaders a half a century ago. It is the answer that explains the behavior of nearly all liberal religious leaders in the early stages of denominational development.

In the first place, many of the liberal leaders of the church do not understand that they have made a basic transition. Thousands of preachers who are well on their way to the acceptance of a denominational point of view do not realize that they are no longer committed to the old conservative approach. As I have suggested before, men can utilize some very unconvincing rationalizations to demonstrate the correctness of their own views. The liberal movement has some talented rationalizers and obscurantists. They are in the same position that James H. Garrison was in some sixty years ago when he wrote *The Old Faith Re-stated*. Garrison had moved far beyond the "old faith," and had encouraged those who had gone even farther than he had, but he still felt the necessity of anchoring his faith in Biblical authoritarianism. It was a natural desire, but a foolish one. It still is.

While most of the liberal leaders in the church today do not realize the nature of the change taking place, many do understand the denominational cycle. There are many preachers in the church of Christ today who are consciously liberal enough that twenty years ago they would have left the church. But the young liberal does not leave the church now as he used to do. He does not because he understands the fundamental denominational tendency of the church. And yet those who do understand the nature of the division are not usually very vigorous in stating their liberal views. They are deterred by the practical necessity of not allowing the leadership of the church to move too far in advance of the body of members. In the battle for local churches denominational leaders must be careful not to move so rapidly that they offend the moderate members. Many "Church of Christ preachers" find it necessary to be as deceptive about their true convictions as does a liberal Methodist pastor in a rural church. In short, to be very blunt, the only two ways that I know of to account for the actions of modern liberals in the movement are ignorance and dishonesty.

It would be foolish for me to argue that my convictions have not influenced my conclusions. I believe that the old faith is good; I believe that the legalistic plea for the restoration of the ancient order of things is valid; and I believe that the denominational evolutions of the nineteenth and the twentieth centuries are inconsistent, unscriptural, and sinful. These are my beliefs; they are not above attack; I stand ready to be corrected if they are wrong. I believe that there is a legitimate ground for discussion among the three elements in the church today on whether denominationalism is good or bad, or whether some sort of compromise with it is necessary. In fact, this is the issue.

The fact that the church of Christ is divided into conservative and denominational factions is not a partisan question. It is not even debatable. This is a good, sound, inescapable historical conclusion.

Every secular scholar who has studied the current status of the church of Christ understands that the movement is in the process of a "sect-to-denomination" evolution. My good friend who teaches American social and intellectual history at a university where I taught for five years (a man whose religious convictions, if any, are very vague) teaches in his basic classroom courses that this is the current status of the church of Christ. All of my scholarly colleagues who are vaguely interested in religious history or sociology understand the present situation in the church. Hundreds of reputable scholars in hundreds of distinguished educational institutions would consider this an elementary observation. I have repeatedly developed this theme in lectures before scholarly groups and in articles published by distinguished academic journals. This interpretation has been presented not only in my book, which was published by the Disciples of Christ Historical Society and which has been reviewed by an eminent corps of historians, but in some of the most important professional journals in the country. No historian or no editor has questioned the basic interpretation. It would be questioning the obvious.

There has been a kind of intellectual snobbery throughout the present controversy in the church. By the very nature of the sociological character of schism, most of the "doctors," most of the educational centers, and most of the sophisticated people have been concentrated in the liberal camp. An underlying assumption among the liberals throughout the whole controversy has been that these "intellectuals" must have a better grasp of the issues than their less impressive antagonists. In fact, with many, this assumption reaches the proportions of an all encompassing argument.

The truth is that these pseudo-intellectuals are virtually alone in their contention that they have made no basic shift in religious emphasis. I do not believe that there is a reputable scholar in the country who would not consider their protestations the ridiculous aberrations of blinded religionists. Everyone knows the situation in the church of Christ today except the liberal "intellectuals." Scholars, informed people in other religious groups, and anyone else who understands religious sociology and history can see the clear symptoms of a denominational evolution in the church. Any member of a liberal church who really wants to know where he stands religiously does not have to ask an anti—he can ask almost anybody—except his preacher. The smug liberal "Church-of-Christer intellectual" does not have the support of modern scholarship; he is exposed by it. And when he denies his exposure, he becomes the laughingstock of the real intellectual community.

The time will come, no doubt, when the leaders of the denominational movement within the church will accept the responsibility and credit for their liberal leadership. The time may not be too far distant when considerable numbers of Churches of Christ will be proud of their denominational status. When that time comes, a whole new set of religious values will become the intellectual justification for a denominational Church of Christ. The same intellectual assumptions that undergird the Methodist or Christian church will be adequate props for the newly-oriented Church of Christ. A realistic balance in the present controversy will be reached only when the liberals make this adjustment toward honesty.

Finally, the old seed remains. The fertile idea of "restoration" is as challenging to those people who are of a mind to accept it as it ever was. I have no doubt that it retains the same extraordinary and expansive spiritual force which it has twice demonstrated in the recent history of this nation. I am just as certain that success will ever bring with it problems, tensions, and schisms. Before we finish the work, we can look forward to the struggle of the future. It may be the struggle of my old age, or it may be the struggle of my son or grandson—but if the Lord does not come, it will. It would be trite and anticlimactic to say "history repeats itself." Perhaps it would be proper simply to conclude: "there is nothing new under the sun."

"Peculiar People: A Rationale for Modern Conservative Disciples"

Reed Lectureship, 1966

David Edwin Harrell, Jr.

Originally Published by The Disciples of Christ Historical Society
Reprinted with permission.

In his book, *The Small Sects in America*, Elmer T. Clark asserts that it is "a peculiar type of mind which is convinced that God is interested in whether his worshipers sing with or without instrumental accompaniment" (p. 16). I once wrote that I thought it was "a peculiar type of mind" which thinks it is "a peculiar type of mind" which is convinced that instrumental music is sinful. But I agree with Clark's judgment. It is a "peculiar type of mind" which believes that God cares whether people sing with or without instrumental music. It is the mind of a legalistic fanatic. I would not think of trying to avoid any of the harsh consequences of such a religious posture. Obfuscation or a lack of candor would surely defeat the purpose of this lecture series.

I am a Biblical literalist. I mean by that simply that I believe in a literal and narrow interpretation of the Bible as the Word of God. My aim is the exact restoration of the ancient order of things. It is an article of my faith that the Bible should be, can be, and is literally understandable and that it should lead all men to the same conclusions. I am concerned about all sorts of problems which most people consider irrelevant to Christianity. Baptism for the remission of sins, the proper time for taking the Lord's Supper, the biological qualifications of elders, distinctions between individual and congregational activities, and hundreds of similar questions, seemingly technical in nature, are crucial in my faith. I can spend a challenging evening with one of my brethren discussing an issue which has never occurred to many people and would be considered inconsequential by nearly everyone. This is not all that Christianity means to me, but it is an important part of the whole. It would be naive to think that this attitude is anything but "peculiar" in modern sophisticated society.

I am also a fanatic of sorts. I am not a dangerous enthusiast. Most members of the Churches of Christ share the American heritage of freedom of religious expression and are fully committed to religious toleration. But I have my zealot side. Any man who believes that he can find literal truth in the Scriptures must also believe that those who do not find the same truth are wrong. What follows is that such people are sinful. The next logical conclusion is that they will go to hell. The most onerous charge levelled against those who are members of the Churches of Christ is that they are bigots. It is frequently assumed that they believe that all who do not accept the truths which they find in the Bible will be lost. All members of the Churches of Christ do not have such an attitude, but I do. This does not imply that I would restrict anyone's right to believe as he pleases; I hold no brief for persecution. The essence of the philosophy of toleration is a willingness to defend a man's right to free expression even when one has deep convictions to the contrary. But I do recognize that the logical consequence of a legalistic concept of truth—the kind of mind which would cause one to quibble about instrumental music—is the condemnation of those who refuse to accept the revelation.

This doctrinal stance places obvious limitations on a speech on the relation of "my group" to the "Church Universal." From my theological point of view, the group to which I belong is the church universal. This narrow view is not a new attitude in American religious history, nor is it unique to the Churches of Christ today. Members of the Churches of Christ did not invent the idea of being God's "peculiar people," but they are surely some of the staunchest advocates of the concept.

Before examining my rationale for this position, I shall acknowledge the vast diversity of thought that exists within the Churches of Christ today. What I believe does not represent a "Churches of Christ platform." There is currently a very liberal and ecumenical-minded element within the church. The recent book, Voices of Concern, is some indication of the growing liberal concern within the Churches of Christ. Of course, many liberals find that the most satisfying course for them is to leave the narrow confines of the church and search for religious meaning in more tolerant environs. This has been especially true until the very recent past. Some of the ablest leaders of the Disciples of Christ have come out of the Churches of Christ. To a lesser extent the conservative church has contributed outstanding men to other religious communions. It is significant that more and more liberal preachers are choosing to remain in the church. Liberal sentiment has grown strong enough that they see some hope of influencing the church from within.

A great many other members of the Churches of Christ are much more slowly making feeble steps toward a rapproachment with the main stream of American protestantism. Opposition to instrumental music, missionary societies, and "mixing with the sects" has become so creedalized that it is difficult to abandon these positions quickly. But dissatisfaction with these old dogmas is growing. Many sophisticated members of the Churches of Christ are embarrassed by the old commitments. They would like to abandon the harsh legalism of the past, and, in time, they will. Today these timid liberals have a good deal more in common with the cooperative Disciple spirit than with the conservative theology I described at the beginning of this lecture.

Still, Biblical legalism is typical of the thought of many members of the Churches of Christ. These conservatives do not all agree among themselves on particulars, but they do agree that all should be guided by the literal truths of the Bible. Without question, this is also one of the historic poles of emphasis within the Disciples of Christ movement. The early twentieth century leaders of the Churches of Christ are classic examples of Biblical legalists. It is fitting that such an attitude should be represented in this lecture program. Our common heritage was the incubator that hatched it, whether one likes it or not. One would miss the fascinating diversity of the Disciples mind if he overlooked the fanatical legalist.

This kind of faith has been an important ingredient in American history. It is a harsh theology, rooted in harsh times. The concept of simple truths, simply arrived at by common people, was in the air in the early nineteenth century. Most Americans had positive ideas about right and wrong and most of them were convinced that these absolute values were easily identifiable. They discarded theological complexities, distrusted sophistication and "show," and had implicit faith in the literal truth and simple clarity of the Bible. They considered the promise of salvation from this bleak and stern world the greatest of all blessings. The eternal damnation of those who refused the truth was dutifully accepted and frequently preached. This was the message of a society girded for war; it gave men courage in the face of fear, certainty in place of doubt, and comfort in the presence of abundant tribulation.

The historical pertinence of the faith of the legalistic fanatic, in the Disciples tradition, and in others, is simply that this commitment met the needs of thousands of souls in their bewildering human experience. The conservative rationale also contributed some admirable qualities to the American character. Authoritarian faith brought order into a rowdy and unruly society. It nurtured the cult of the will, the virtues of middle-class respectability, and the necessity of self-control and individual responsibility. Professor Ralph Barton Perry has written of the Puritans, who were as certainly a part of the family tree of the Disciples as the liberal minds of the Enlightenment: "From this school of discipline came men who were notable for doing what they soberly and conscientiously resolved to do, despite temptations and obstacles—such men as William the Silent, ... Oliver Cromwell, ... and our New England ancestors. The Puritans imprinted on English and American institutions a quality of manly courage, self-reliance, and sobriety. We are still drawing upon the reserves of spiritual vigor which they accumulated" (*Puritanism and Democracy*, p. 268). But I would not commend my faith on the basis of such relative values. One might easily make a list of seemingly harmful consequences of authoritarian religion. The contribution of the conservative faith in the Disciples tradition is simply that it met the spiritual needs of our fathers and grandfathers; it gave an anchor to cling to and an ethic to live by to the saints of old.

The legalism of nineteenth-century Disciples thought was blunted by a concomitant emphasis on the union of all Christians. The Enlightenment idea that "natural" truths existed and that they were self-evident and rational provided a base for the Disciples principle of restoration. The companion idea to that of natural law was the assumption that in time all men, because of their reasonable nature, would arrive at, and unite on, the truth. So it was with the Disciples philosophy of union. Disciples did not espouse a detached hope for union; they believed that Christian union was an inevitable consequence of the restoration of the ancient order of things. The two went together. The literal dogmatism of the nineteenth-century Disciple may seem less objectionable to a modern liberal because it was mixed with a millennial anticipation of ultimate union—in the early years of the movement, the anticipation of a very imminent union. Restoration was not an end in itself; it was a means of accomplishing the union of Christians. On the other hand, the nineteenth-century Disciples just as firmly believed that the end could be accomplished by no other means. In short, the early leaders of the Disciples were more than legalists. They were optimistic legalists, Enlightenment legalists, men with a plan of world-wide impact and universal application.

The traumatic experience of second-generation Disciples history is the result of the crushing disillusionment that follows the collapse of this dream. The naive optimism of early Disciples history vanished in the years after the Civil War. Post-war leaders were not 'embued' [sic] with a millennialistic anticipation of victory; they lost their confidence in the dual plea for restoration and union. The plea was simply impractical. It became perfectly obvious to anyone who was willing to face reality that all people were not going to accept the Disciples platform of church order. Some preachers still mouthed the dual slogans but they no longer had the faith in fulfillment which had marked the hope of the first generation. And so, the Disciples came to the parting of the ways. Discerning men chose which plea expressed their faith; less discerning souls gravitated to the emphasis that suited their needs.

The question which I must deal with tonight is: What is the pertinence of restoration legalism in modern society? What does the old faith have to contribute in this day? Stripped of its naive Enlightenment optimism, frustrated in its idealistic hope for union, what justification remains for authoritarian legalism? Perhaps the modern world will find less use for it. When old Increase Mather was near the end of his many years, a friend wrote and asked if he were still in the land of the living. "No, Tell him I am going to it," he said to his son, "this Poor World is the land of the Dying." (quoted in Vernon Louis Parrington, *Main Currents in American Thought*, Vol. I, p. 116) The "Great Society" may not have as much use for conservative faith as did frontier society.

Biblical literalism still offers a way to come to terms with life, however— even in the modern world. Acceptance of authoritarian truth as a solution to the knotty problems of death, frustration, and suffering has satisfied many fine minds in the past. Francis Bacon, an honored and trusted advisor to early restoration leaders, came to terms with the spirit of the Enlightenment by the formulation of a doctrine of "double truth." He held that philosophy should be kept separate from theology. The purpose of philosophy was practical: to give men mastery over the forces of nature by means of scientific discoveries and inventions. Theology consisted of that which is known by revelation. There was no necessary continuity between the two, indeed, one might seem contradictory of the other. Bertrand Russell describes Bacon's attitude thus: "Indeed he held that the triumph of faith is greatest when to the unaided reason a dogma appears most absurd" (*A History of Western Philosophy*, p. 542).

There are certain advantages in such a schizoid view of truth. In a world of scientific relativism, of political uncertainty, of social injustice, and individual brutality, it is no small comfort to be able to turn to a citadel of truth. Of course, absolute allegiance to an authoritarian standard may have harmful effects unless one accepts a double standard of truth. Reason is the guide to truth in this world. If we cannot discover it in the neat and simple laws of nature that men once sought, we will simply have to deal with this world with the pragmatic rational capacity which we possess. But to be sure the problems of this life must be solved with the faculties of the human mind. If a man needs to know more, if he needs answers to questions which the reason cannot, by its human limitations, solve, then he must turn to revelation.

An understanding of "double truth" is implicit in much of the thinking of the nineteenth-century restoration movement. Many of the early reformers carefully sorted the religious from the social in their thinking and insisted that one was the domain of revelation and the other of reason. Their reluctance to issue religious proclamations on social subjects was rooted in this distinction in levels of truth. One could disagree with his brother about the pragmatic truths of this world, but not about the revealed truths of the spiritual realm.

To me, this remains the most compelling insight in the conservative Disciples mind. I am utterly repelled by the rallying of God to the support of worldly causes. God has been on every side of every social issue I have ever studied; He has participated in every war on every side; He is a Democrat and a Republican, high tariff and low tariff, a fascist and a communist. I distrust the man who has a plan from God for every social ill. I trust my reason more. On the other hand, an absolutist God with heavenly truth plays an important role in my scheme of things. One might argue that there is no need for such an impractical and remote God, a God who is confined to the unknowable and, to some, the unnecessary. And for some this may be true, but I do need Him. On the other hand, if all that God has to do with is this world, I do not need him.

It seems to me, then, that there is no essential relation between the mind of man and the faith of man in this life. One might believe in the ultimate harmony of things and recognize the probability of present contradiction. One's faith is, indeed, a blind leap. My profane but compelling friend Sigmund Freud has accused all religious men of behaving "in some respects like the paranoiac, substituting a wish-fulfillment for some aspect of the world which is unbearable" to us. All religions are "mass-delusions" designed to lighten the unbearable psychological burden of being (*Civilization and Its Discontents*, p. 23). He continues: "At such a cost—by forcible imposition of mental infantilism and inducing a mass-delusion—religion succeeds in saving many people from individual neuroses.... When the faithful find themselves reduced in the end to speaking of God's 'inscrutable decree/ they thereby avow that all that is left to them in their sufferings is unconditional submission as a last-remaining consolation and source of happiness. And if a man is willing to come to this, he could probably have arrived there by a shorter road" (Ibid. p. 27)."

I agree; religion is delusion. It is "the substance of things hoped for, the evidence of things not seen." It is an admission of human fallibility, an acceptance of defeat, a surrender to the overpowering compulsion to know the unknown, a tranquilizer to still the fear of death, a prop to hold man up in the face of tragedy and adversity; it is an expression of man's unreasonable insistence that his life must have some higher meaning than that of the other animals around him. There are many forms of the delusion. But whatever the form, they have in common the universally applicable: "If a man is willing to come to this ...."

The form that a man's faith takes is determined by a tenuous complex of causes. Basically, religion is a psychological response. Different types of people have different types of religious needs. The problems of life affect us in different ways. We see ourselves differently, and we view the world from a variety of vantage points. And so our religious outlooks are diverse. Professor J.

"Peculiar People: A Rationale for Modern Conservative Disciples"

Milton Yinger writes: "These who feel it [psychological frustration] most acutely may struggle with it in religious terms. For a few—the mystics, the ascetics, the prophets—[religion] became the dominant preoccupation of life." (*Religion, Society and the Individual*, p . 79)

Such reasoning easily runs into a kind of psychological determinism. With the reservation that I believe that this idea can be reconciled with a doctrine of free will, I accept the conclusion. I believe that "not many wise, not many noble, not many mighty after the world are called." The Churches of Christ is a gathering of certain psychological types, as is every other religious communion. Modem Disciples conservatism is rooted in the same psychology that Ralph Barton Perry describes as being typical of medieval Christianity: "These high truths are accessible, not through reason, but through faith and revelation: like salvation, they are a gift of God to such men as are, through the cult of humility, fit for their reception" (*Puritanism and Democracy*, p. 85). The cult of humility is central in the thought of the modern conservative. Of course, the humiliation of one's self does not fit the psychological inclinations of every man, but it fits some.

The psychology of humility is obviously related to the society which breeds it. Poverty, sorrow, and hardship breed intense religious psychologies. On the other hand, economic stability and comfort tend to produce complacent religious psychologies. I believe that this is the kind of determinism that Jesus had in mind when he warned of the dangers of riches. There is no question in my mind but that this is the nature of the sociological division of the Disciples in the nineteenth century. This is also the basis of the twentieth century rifts within both the Disciples of Christ and the Churches of Christ. Legalistic fanaticism remains the religious expression of the psychologically fervent, religiously intense, and socially and economically dispossessed.

What is the pertinence of the Churches of Christ in modern society? What contribution can legalistic conservatism make to modern man? The answer is simply that this religious expression meets the needs of some people. It meets my needs. I think that I have some understanding of why I accept Biblical literalism. I understand the sociological and psychological sources of my faith. But that does not minimize the fact that I do believe. I recognize the encounter when my faith conflicts with the best calculations of human reason; I think I am rarely blind to the obvious. But to me, and to those who share my faith, such clashes are totally irrelevant. I choose to believe and I do believe.

I understand that not everyone has these same inclinations. I believe that the individual who rejects the truth which is clear to me will be lost. That is where my faith leads me and I would not try to avoid the conclusion. But rationally I understand the motives that lead other men in other directions. Clearly, many people will never accept the truth which I accept. I have often said that I do not conceive of the mission of an evangelist as badgering those who have no inclination to accept his faith. His mission is to find those who are of a mind to share his mind. The gospel of evangelization is not the compelling of the unwilling but the search in your times for those who will, in your way, seek the Lord. My religious quest is to find those who would be "peculiar people."

My faith, and the traditional legalism of the members of the Churches of Christ, has nothing to offer "Christianity" in the broad sense of the term. Theologically, I have nothing in common with a modern liberal. We have two totally different religious minds. I am much closer to a Primitive Baptist, or a Seventh-Day Adventist, or a medieval Roman Catholic than I am to a liberal Disciple. As a historian, I hope that I understand his mind, but I do not share it. Reconciliation is inconceivable.

The only common ground which gives meaning to this lecture series, from my point of view, is the one that this building symbolizes and that this society is a tangible expression of. We have a common interest in the contradictory figures of the past from whom, curiously enough, we all learned our lessons. It is fitting that we meet here to discuss the paradoxes of the past, the diversity of the harvest, the perplexing meaning of the Disciples heritage.

This interest in our past will not be without its rewards. The result will not be union; my 'obstinancy' [sic] will certainly preclude that. But it might be understanding. As an immortal soul, my deepest hope is the attainment of salvation through literal obedience to the Word of God. As a mortal man, I believe the greatest achievement in life is the gaining of an understanding of one's self and of those who differ from you. I do not believe that we shall ever reach accord in things spiritual, but if we could attain the lower good of understanding why, the insight would serve us well in our struggle in this life.

Christian Primitivism in the Twenty-first Century: Thinking "Inside the Box" About Restoring New Testament Christianity

David Edwin Harrell, Jr.

Originally Published by Harwell/Lewis Publishing Company
Reprinted with permission.

Introduction

The belief that local churches can be and should be uniform in organization, worship and work in every age, sometimes referred to as "restorationism" or "primitivism," has been challenged throughout Christian history and has been seriously questioned in recent years by many people inside the Disciples of Christ/Churches of Christ ("Stone-Campbell") restoration movement. Inevitably, and properly, many second and third generation Christians who have grown up in churches of Christ feel that they must ponder the basis of their personal religious commitment rather than accept the traditional practices handed down to them. Unfortunately, their speculations often carelessly confuse the inadequacies and inconsistencies they have observed in the personal and institutional behavior of past generations with the grand and ancient ideal of living as primitive New Testament Christians. The stylish mantra of late urges the next generation to "think outside the box." I am convinced that a large percentage of the people who voice such challenges have very little understanding of what is "inside the box." The box of New Testament primitivism contains far more than seemingly legalistic arguments about instrumental music and sponsoring churches—though those discussions are necessarily a part of the agenda of anyone seriously committed to following Biblical patterns. But the idea of restoring New Testament churches, of modeling ourselves on primitive Christians, is a profoundly Biblical, richly textured concept with deep historical roots. After fifty years of studying and writing religious history, I have looked inside many "boxes." Along with generations of serious Bible-believing Christians before me, I have found no better gyroscope for life than to seek to find and follow the "ancient order of things."

In this brief study, I suggest three concepts that are fundamental to the idea of restoring New Testament churches. I concede that an emphasis on "getting it right"—on conscientiously trying to emulate the worship, organization, and work of New Testament churches—rests on important assumptions. If you do not understand and embrace these assumptions, much that is done by restorers seems to be an arbitrary trivializing of the faith. If you do not believe these assumptions, the narrow (even legalistic) exegesis of Biblical primitivists is divisive and sectarian, rooted in the traditions of a particular religious movement and outmoded hermeneutical principles. However, if the three assumptions discussed here seem true and reliable, the .meticulous concern of restorers to get it right is an obvious and necessary consequence.

In the three sections that follow, these three principles will be discussed in the light of Scripture, historical precedent, and common sense.

PROPOSITION 1: Regarding Apostolic Authority

Restorationist, primitivist religious thinking assumes that the Apostles were given specific authority to define doctrine and set in order churches. This authority was perpetuated in the inspired writings of the New Testament.

PROPOSITION 2: Regarding Common Sense Hermeneutics

Restorationist, primitivist religious thinking assumes that human beings, through the use of a common sense possessed by all, have the ability to read texts and reach common conclusions about meanings. This empirical, logical type of thinking is the basis for all public (as opposed to private and subjective) human understanding.

PROPOSITION 3: Regarding Local Churches (Congregationalism)

Restorationist, primitivist religious thinking assumes that the practices of local churches in New Testament days rested on apostolic authority and that the ordering of churches was intentionally designed by God to promote uniformity (catholicity) among Christians.

PROPOSITION 1
Defining the Issue: Apostolic Authority

Restorationist, primitivist religious thinking assumes that the Apostles were given specific authority to define doctrine and set in order churches. This authority was perpetuated in the inspired writings of the New Testament.

I
THE BIBLICAL CASE FOR APOSTOLIC AUTHORITY

The Apostles were chosen by Jesus to be the revealers of his will. Their actions and teachings were not arbitrary or incidental; they were intentional and authoritative. The practices they ordained were in accord with Divine will. It was on this foundation that the church was built. This image is both a symbolic and a practical description of how New Testament churches developed in history. They were "ordered" by apostolic authority. Thus, the directions given by the apostles to local churches were uniform, and they were binding. This being the case, every instruction given to local churches, and every example of their conduct, was a matter of apostolic precedent. [Unless noted, citations are from the King James Version. Bold type for emphasis has been inserted by the author.]

1. The Apostles were commissioned by Jesus to complete the work of revealing God's plan.

   John 14:25-26: These things have I spoken unto you, being yet present with you. (26) But the Comforter, which is the Holy Ghost, whom. the Father will send in my name, **he shall teach you all things**, and bring all things to your remembrance, whatsoever I have said unto you.

   Acts 1:1-2: The former treatise have I made, 0 Theophilus, of all that Jesus began both to do and teach, (2) Until the day in which he was taken up, after that **he through the Holy Ghost had given commandments unto the apostles whom he had chosen**,...

2. The apostles were "credentialed" for the work of revelation, being qualified by their association with Jesus to be witnesses of his resurrection. Paul was zealous in defending his apostolic credentials because of the authority vested in that office.

   Acts 1:13-26: And when they were come in, they went up into an upper room, where abode both Peter, and James, and John, and

---

apostolos

ap-os'-tol-os A delegate; specifically an *ambassador* of the Gospel; officially a *commissioner* of Christ ("apostle"), (with miraculous powers): - apostle, messenger, he that is sent. (James Strong, *Greek Dictionary*)

Andrew, Philip, and Thomas, Bartholomew, and Matthew, James the son of Alphaeus, and Simon Zelotes, and Judas the brother of James .... (21) **Wherefore of these men which have companied with us all the time that the Lord Jesus went in and out among us, (Z.2) Beginning from the baptism of John, unto that same day that he was taken up from us, must one be ordained to be .a witness with us of his resurrection**.

1 Cor. 9:1: **Am I not an apostle?** am I not free? have I not seen Jesus Christ our Lord? are not ye my work in the Lord?

2 Cor. 12: 11-12: I am become a fool in glorying; ye have compelled me: for I ought to have been commended of you: for in nothing am I behind the very chiefest apostles, though I be nothing. (12) **Truly the signs of an apostle were wrought among you in all patience, in signs, and wonders, and mighty deeds.**

3. In the New Testament, revelation is inseparably connected with the apostles (and those strongly related to them, including Mark and Luke).

Eph. 3:2-6: If ye have heard of the dispensation of the grace of God which is given me to you-ward: (3) How that by revelation he made known unto me the mystery; (as I wrote afore in few words, (4) Whereby, when ye read, ye may understand my knowledge in the mystery of Christ) (5) **Which in other ages was not made known unto the sons of men, as it is now revealed unto his holy apostles and prophets by the Spirit**; (6) That the Gentiles should be fellow heirs, and of the same body, and partakers of his promise in Christ by the gospel:

2 Pet. 3:1-4: This second epistle, beloved, I now write unto you; in both which I stir up your pure minds by way of remembrance: (2) **That ye may be mindful of the words which were spoken before by the holy prophets, and of the commandment of us the apostles of the Lord and Saviour:** (3) Knowing this first, that there shall come in the last days scoffers, walking after their own lusts, (4) And saying, Where is the promise of his corning? for since the fathers fell asleep, all things continue as they were from the beginning of the creation.

Acts 2:41-42: Then they that gladly received his word were baptized: and the same day there were added unto them about three thousand souls. (42) And they **continued stedfastly in the apostles' doctrine** and fellowship, and in breaking of bread, and in prayers.

4. The church was built on the foundation of apostolic authority.

> Matthew 18:18: Truly I say to you, **Whatever you shall bind on earth shall occur, having been bound in Heaven**; and whatever you shall loose on earth shall occur, having been loosed in Heaven. (Modern King James Version)

> Eph. 2:19-22: Now therefore ye are no more strangers and foreigners, but fellow citizens with the saints, and of **the household of God; (20) And are built upon the foundation of the apostles and prophets, Jesus Christ himself being the chief corner stone;** (21) In whom all the building fitly framed together groweth unto an holy temple in the Lord: (22) In whom ye also are builded together for an habitation of God through the Spirit.

> 2 Thessalonians 2:15: Therefore, brethren, stand fast, and hold the traditions which ye have been taught, whether by word, or our epistle.

5. Local churches were "ordered" by the instructions of the apostles.

> 1 Corinthians 7:17: But as God has distributed to each one, as the Lord has called each one, so let him walk. And so I **ordain** in all churches.

> 1 Corinthians 4:16-17: **Therefore I beseech you, be imitators of me.** (17) For this cause I have sent Timothy to you, who is my beloved son

---

diatasso

dee-at-as'-so To arrange *thoroughly*, that is, (specifically) *institute, prescribe*, etc.: - appoint, command, give, (set in) order, ordain. (James Strong, *Greek Dictionary*)

> and faithful in the Lord, **who shall remind you of my ways which are in Christ, as I teach everywhere in every church.**

> 1 Corinthians 11:16: But if anyone seems to be contentious, we have no such custom, **nor the churches of God.**

> 1 Corinthians 11:33-34: So that, my brothers, when you come together to eat, wait for one another. (34) But if anyone hungers, let him eat at home, so that you do not come together to condemnation. **And the rest I will set in order when I come.**

> 1 Corinthians 16:1: Now concerning the collection for the saints, **as I have given order to the churches of Galatia, even so do ye.**

1 Timothy 3:14-15: These things write I unto thee, hoping to come unto thee shortly: (15) But if I tarry long, **that thou mayest know how thou oughtest to behave thyself in the house of God, which is the church of the living God**, the pillar and ground of the truth.

Titus 1:2-5: In hope of eternal life, which God, that cannot lie, promised before the world began; (3) But hath in due times manifested his word through preaching, which is committed unto me according to the commandment of God our Saviour; (4) To Titus mine own son after the common faith: Grace, mercy, and peace from God the Father and the Lord Jesus Christ our Saviour. (5) **For this cause left I thee in Crete, that thou shouldest set in order the things that are wanting, and ordain elders in every city, as I had appointed thee**:

II

THE HISTORICAL RECORD AND THE PRINCIPLE OF APOSTOLIC AUTHORITY

From the earliest days of Christian history, apostolic authority became the most persistent source of authority for those seeking uniformity of practice and teaching in the early churches. Before the end of the first century (before the New Testament itself had been finished), heresy abounded and churches were awash in controversy and corruption. Three basic authority systems emerged to support competing doctrinal claims. Gnosticism, apostolic succession, and apostolic authority offered distinct rationales for justifying religious practices. These systems more of less mirror modern alternatives. Most ante-Nicene writers, even those who embraced modern heresies acknowledged the authority of the teaching of the apostles. The quest for codification of apostolic teaching led to the collection of the New Testament canon.

In early Christian history, three clear methods for establishing authority emerged.

Gnosticism: "Derived from the Greek for 'knowledge,' ... the term 'Gnosticism' covers a number of religious and quasiphilosophical movements that developed in the religious pluralism of the Hellenistic world and flourished from the second to the fifth centuries A.D .... It refers to a 'revealed knowledge' available only to those who have received the secret teachings of a heavenly revealer. All other humans are trapped in ignorance of the true divine world .... " [Pheme Perkins in Everett Ferguson, ed., *Encyclopedia of Early Christianity* (New York: Garland Publishing, Inc., 1990), p. 371].

Subjective authority (present throughout history in a variety of forms) offers justification for thousands of systems of religious teaching and practice. Throughout history, countless systems of thought have been based on various forms of "Gnostic," private, subjective, knowledge—in the last three centuries such movements as Postmodernism, Transcendentalism, Romanticism, Mysticism, and Pentecostalism are examples. Private knowledge, when offered as a basis for truth claims, has been and is the source of confusion, extremism, and division.

Apostolic Succession: "Doctrine that ministry in the church derives from the apostles in historical continuity .... Irenaeus of Lyons drew on the idea of the succession of bishops to formulate an orthodox response to the Gnostic claim. of a secret tradition...." [Everett Ferguson in *Encyclopedia of Early Christianity*, p. 76].

The institutional organization of religious groups is pretty uniformly triggered by a desire to control heretical teaching. The emergence of the Roman Catholic Church (and the many other institutional forms of general church organization that have no precedent in the first century church) empowered the historical church to deal with heresy through the formulation of creeds and the punishment of heterodoxy.

Apostolicity: In the first and second centuries the issue of apostolic authorship became the primary test used to determine the "canonicity" of the books of the New Testament. The inclusion of books in canonical listings, and the exclusion of other books, rested largely on their clear identification with an apostle. Non-apostolic books were accepted more slowly and required apostolic justification. Mark and Luke's writings "were given apostolic authority on the basis of their association with Peter and Paul, respectively." [Arthur J. Patzia, *The Making of the New Testament* (Leicester: Apollos, 1995), p. 104]. Late inclusions in the canon, such as Hebrews and Jude, were acknowledged as a part of the New Testament only after there was wide acceptance of their apostolic authorship. The general acceptance of the New Testament canon was a final confirmation that apostolic authority was the "rule" for the churches.

III
APOSTOLIC AUTHORITY IN THE EARLY CHURCH

1. The New Testament writers appealed for uniformity of teaching based on the message that had been delivered.

    Colossians 2:6-8: **As ye have therefore received Christ Jesus the Lord, so walk ye in him**: (7) Rooted and built up in him, and stablished in the faith, as ye have been taught, abounding therein with thanksgiving. (8) Beware lest any man spoil you through philosophy and vain deceit, after the tradition of men, after the rudiments of the world, and not after Christ.

2 Thessalonians 2:15: Therefore, brethren, stand fast, and **hold the traditions which ye have been taught, whether by word, or our epistle.**

1 John 1:5: **This then is the message which we have heard of him,** and declare unto you, that God is light, and in him is no darkness at all.

1 Timothy 6:3: If any man teach otherwise, and consent not to wholesome words, **even the words of our Lord Jesus Christ,** and to the doctrine which is according to godliness;

2. Early Christian literature is filled with appeals to apostolic authority. The citations below are a sampling. These Ante-Nicene (pre-325AD) writers frequently cited apostolicity as the standard to determine sound teaching and practice. Even as creeds, councils and hierarchical organizations appeared in the early church, the foremost authority for establishing orthodoxy was the teaching of the apostles.

Clement of Rome: Little is known about Clement (who in Roman Catholic tradition is regarded as the fourth Pope), but he seems to have been a presbyter in the church in Rome and his letter to the Corinthians, generally known as First Clement, was widely circulated among early Christians. First Clement (circa 94-100 A.D.) is one of the oldest extant Christian documents outside of the writings in the New Testament. It was written from Rome to the church in Corinth. In this early writing there is no hint of "apostolic succession." Rather, Clement's comments on "bishops and deacons," noted in the closing segment of the quote that follows, concur with the teachings in the New Testament.

1 Clement 7:1-3: "These things, dearly beloved, we write, not only as admonishing you, but also as putting ourselves in remembrance. For we are in the same lists, and the same contest awaiteth us. **Wherefore let us forsake idle and vain thoughts; and let us conform to the glorious and venerable rule which hath been handed down to us;** and let us see what is good and what is pleasant and what is acceptable in the sight of Him that made us.

1 Clem 42:1-5: **The Apostles received the Gospel for us from the Lord Jesus Christ; Jesus Christ was sent forth from God.** So then Christ is from God, and the Apostles are from Christ. Both therefore came of the will of God in the appointed order, Having therefore received a charge, and having been fully assured through the resurrection of our Lord Jesus Christ and confirmed in the word

of God with full assurance of the Holy Ghost, they went forth with the glad tidings that the kingdom of God should come. So preaching everywhere in country and town, they appointed their firstfruits, when they had proved them by the Spirit, to be bishops and deacons unto them that should believe. And this they did in no new fashion; for indeed it had been written concerning bishops and deacons from very ancient times; for thus saith the scripture in a certain place, I will appoint their bishops in righteousness and their deacons in faith. [J. B. Lightfoot translation, www.earlychristianwritings.com].

Origen (185-254): Born in Alexandria, Egypt, his life is one of the best documented of the early Christian writers. Origen was a voluminous writer; one contemporary estimated that he wrote 6,000 volumes. Much of his writing survives. The brief quotation that follows was cited in an instructive article written by Jack P. Lewis.

> **"That alone is to be accepted as truth which differs in no respect from ecclesiastical and apostolic tradition."** [See, Jack P. Lewis, "Silence of Scripture in Reformation Thought," *Restoration Quarterly*, Second Quarter, 2006, pp. 73-90].

Polycarp of Smryna (69-155): Little is known about Polycarp, but his letter to the Philippians probably dates from the middle of the second century. According to tradition, he was a disciple and student of the Apostle John.

> *Letter to the Philippians*; "Chapter VI—The Duties of Presbyters and Others: "And let the presbyters be compassionate and merciful to all, bringing back those that wander, visiting all the sick, and not neglecting the widow, the orphan, or the poor, but always "providing for that which is becoming in the sight of God and man ..... **Let us then serve Him in fear, and with all reverence, even as He Himself has commanded us, and as the apostles who preached the Gospel unto us, and the prophets who proclaimed beforehand the coming of the Lord [have alike taught us].** Let us be zealous in the pursuit of that which is good, keeping ourselves from causes of offence, from false brethren ..." [Roberts-Donaldson English Translation, www.earlychristianwritings.com].

Cyril of Jerusalem (315-386): Cyril was a learned bishop in Jerusalem. Cyril's lectures provide insight into the continuing emphasis on apostolicity in the early post-Nicene period.

> *Catechetical Lectures*, Lecture 4:17: "This seal have thou ever on thy mind; which now by way of summary has been touched on in its heads,

and if the Lord grant, shall hereafter be set forth according to our power, with Scripture proofs. **For concerning the divine and sacred Mysteries of the Faith, we ought not to deliver even the most casual remark without the Holy Scriptures: nor be drawn aside by mere probabilities and the artifices of argument.** Do not then believe me because I tell thee these things, unless thou receive from the Holy Scriptures the proof of what is set forth: for this salvation, which is of our faith, is not by ingenious reasonings, but by proof from the Holy Scriptures. But take thou and hold that faith only as a learner and in profession, which is by the Church delivered to thee, and is established from all Scripture. For since all cannot read the Scripture, but some as being unlearned, others by business, are hindered from the knowledge of them; in order that the soul may not perish for lack of instruction, in the Articles which are few we comprehend the whole doctrine of Faith ..... And for the present, commit to memory the Faith, merely listening to the words; and expect at the fitting season the proof of each of its parts from the Divine Scriptures .... **Behold, therefore, brethren and hold the traditions which ye now receive, and write them on the table of your hearts.** [Translation from the Catholic Encyclopedia, www.newadvent.org].

IV
APOSTOLIC AUTHORITY IN PRE-REFORMATION AND REFORMATION THOUGHT

The history of Christianity is filled with heterodox groups, some of them large enough to be persecuted by the state churches, and to leave behind some record of their beliefs and practices, including the Bogomils, Cathars, and Albigensians beginning in the tenth century. It seems entirely probable that other, smaller, non-Catholic bodies existed. It is futile to try to trace an orthodox, scriptural trail of faith through the centuries, but the existence of these "heretical" groups establishes two important principles. First, local and regional groups of Christians throughout the centuries divorced themselves from "Catholic" or other national religious groups and followed independent courses. Second, these movements uniformly justified their independence by appealing to apostolic authority. [A Roman Catholic website that provides a useful listing of major schisms through the centuries, "Christian Heresies," is found at www.religion-cults.com/heresies/. More extensive information on these movements can be found at links suggested at this site.] Martin Luther's momentous challenge to Roman Catholic authority in 1517 launched the Protestant Reformation. The Reformation was a broad and diverse movement that is generally divided into four streams, each with its own distinct history. The most moderate reforms were instituted by Luther; the center of the Reformation was led by Ulrich Zwingli and John Calvin and was generally known as the Reformed movement; the "radical reformation" is generally associated with the Anabaptists who called for adult baptism, separation of church and state, and independent local congregations. The English reformation was influenced by all of these streams, but it had a unique history of its own. The wing of the English reformation that most influenced American churches was the Puritan movement. For our purposes, it is enough to note that all of these reforms embraced apostolic authority. Their appeals to New Testament authority evidence the historical continuity of the idea. Listed below are a few statements coming from the various wings of the Reformation.

1. Historical descriptions of the heterodox groups of Pre-Reformation years generally emphasize their dependence on apostolic authority. Noted below are brief descriptions of two of the more prominent movements of the late Middle Ages written by Stuart Murray Williams. [These sketches, and many others, may be found on the very useful website, www.anabaptistnetwork. com.]

The Waldensians, 1174-1560:

"(1) .... Waldensians preached a simple message of repentance, individual responsibility and holy living. They 'criticised' [sic] the corruption of the clergy and denied that such men should be trusted. Instead they endorsed lay Bible study. **The movement was marked by deep love for the Bible and passionate desire to understand and obey it. They were committed to a 'believers' church ecclesiology, where the local congregation ordered its life together, and they were determined to submit to Biblical authority alone.** (2) Church structure. There was emphasis on the priesthood of all believers, men and women. The role of the preachers was crucial for the movement, but these leaders were not ordained, nor generally regarded as belonging to a separate class of Christians, not ranked in any kind of hierarchy .... Those who were not preachers remained in their homes and jobs, devoting time to Bible study and nurturing their faith in secret. They collected support for the preachers, ran training schools in their homes and, where they could, tried to draw others into the movement."

John Wycliff (1329-1384) and the Lollards:

"(2) **Lollards used their new English versions of the Bible to** contrast the simplicity of the early church with the formalism and complexity of contemporary church life. They rejected anything they perceived as superstitious rather than authentically Christian, including doctrines such as purgatory and transubstantiation and practices such as prayers for the dead. They rejected pilgrimages as a waste of time and a money-making scheme for the priests. Simple rational explanations held greater appeal for them than elements of mystery and symbolism. (3) The priesthood of all believers. The distinction between clergy and laity was crucial in the established churches, with the laity being largely passive. But Lollards rejected this distinction, and their anti-clerical stance found a ready welcome among many who were already critical of a privileged and corrupt clergy .... **The true church was a congregation of true believers.** Although there are instances of Lollard groups ordaining their own priests, generally they were committed to the priesthood of all believers, with lay people involved in all aspects of religious life, including preaching, hearing confessions informally, and officiating at the Eucharist. (4) The sacraments. **Lollards stressed a common sense approach to faith and applied this to issues such as communion, where it seemed obvious that the bread remained bread, whatever the metaphysical explanations behind the traditional dogmas.** Transubstantiation was regarded as a recent and perverted development contrary to the teachings of the orthodox creeds."

2. Martin Luther (1483-1546) introduced the German Reformation. It was anchored by the principle of Sola Scriptura ("by Scripture alone"). While the reforms of the Lutheran reformation fell short of those urged by other Reformation leaders, his commitment to the principle of apostolic authority was the alarm that set off the broad movement known as the Reformation. When confronted with a demand to recant his teachings at the Diet of Worms in 1521, he made the following oft-published reply.

"Unless I am convicted by scripture and plain reason—I do not accept the authority of the popes and councils, for they have contradicted each other—**my conscience is captive to the Word of God**, I cannot and I will not recant anything for to go against conscience is neither right nor safe. God help me. Amen."

3. Ulrich Zwingli (1484-1531) of Zurich was the most consistent Reformation advocate of Biblical primitivism. Virtually every Reformation writer vigorously embraced the principle of apostolic authority, but they differed significantly in their application of the principle. Few were more unswerving

than Zwingli.

"Away with human ceremonies and regulations, **we want only the Word of God.**" (1523)

"This church imposes no laws on the conscience of people without the sanction of the Word of God, and **the laws of the Church are binding only in so far as they agree with the Word'** (1528)

"XLIX. Those who model their teachings upon the pattern of the Scriptures cannot be said to teach according to the whims of their own feelings, but those who go to work without resting on the authority of the sacred writings, contrary to Paul's directions to Timothy .... [II Tim. 3:14] Timothy had learned from Paul, and Paul from Christ, but both had been led by the same spirit into the knowledge of holy things .... **Those who give assent unto flesh and blood, regulate their teachings according to their own sweet will; those who give assent unto the spirit of God sweetly breathing from the Holy Scriptures and ever freshly blooming, regulate their teaching according to the thought and purpose of God.** And He is by no means of recent origin, for the prophet called him the Ancient of days.... They therefore, who refer all things to His purpose, and examined all things by the standard of His thought, do not set up a new standard, but go back to the old, old one, as Jeremiah also urges [vi., 16] 'stand ye in the ways, and see, and ask for the old paths, where is the good way, and walk therein .... ' You see that rest will be found in the old standard, not in the new one, to which you cling so obstinately, meanwhile accusing of innovations those who for this one thing alone urge war upon you and your likes, they want to abrogate innovations too freely introduced and to restore the old by right of recovery, as it were." ["Defence Called Archeletes" published in 1522 in Zurich. Samuel Macauley Jackson, ed., *The Latin Works and the Correspondence of Huldreich Zwingli*, Vol. 1 (New York and London: G. P. Putnam's Sons, 1912), pp. 270-271] .

4. The Anabaptist movement, a term that describes the diverse radical wing of the Reformation, was united by a commitment to adult baptism, the independence of local churches, and appeals to apostolic authority. It was a uniformly restorationist and primitivist movement.

Bernard Rothmann (1495-1535) was a leader of the church in Munster, Germany, who embraced adult baptism by immersion as the proper New Testament practice. The following quote is from a meeting of Protestant leaders known as the Munster Colloquy (1533):

> **"It is essential that everything required or desired by men should be done in the name and at the command of God through the positive word of God as Peter affirms** [I Pet. 4:11]. And certainly we should discontinue everything else that God has not expressly commanded."

5. The English Reformation and Puritanism [Two excellent sources of information on the English Reformation are www.exlibris.org and www. puritantsm.online.fr]. The citations that follow may be found on the latter site.

John Hooper (1495-1555): Puritan Bishop of Gloucester who was martyred during the reign of Queen Mary. Hooper spent two periods of exile in Europe where he became an ardent disciple of the Zwingli's ideas.

> "Nothing should be used in the church which has not either the express Word of God to support it, or otherwise is a thing indifferent in itself, which brings no profit when done or used, but no harm when not done or omitted."

John a Lasco (1499-1560): Leader of the Reformation in Poland who preached for more than a decade in the Stranger's Church in London. Of noble birth, he was deeply influenced by Zwingli's ideas.

> "There is one way of safety if we altogether turn to repentance: believe the gospel of Christ, walk in innocence of life, and retain nothing in the church which does not either have the express word of God, or else take its infallible origin from that source."

Richard Baxter (1615-1691): One of the most influential English Puritan preachers and writers.

> "What man dare go in a way which has neither precept nor example to warrant it...? For my part, I will not fear that God will be angry with me for doing no more than He has commanded me, and for sticking close to the rule of His word in matters of worship; but I should tremble to add or diminish."

Westminster Confession—1646: This was the most important Englishlanguage creedal statement of the Reformation period.

Chapter I "Of the Holy Scriptures:"

VI. The whole counsel of God concerning all things necessary for His own glory, man's salvation, faith and life, is either expressly set down in Scripture, or by good and necessary consequence may be deduced from Scripture: unto which nothing at any time is to be added, whether by new revelations of the Spirit, or traditions of men ....

VII . All things in Scripture are not alike plain in themselves, nor alike clear unto all: yet those things which are necessary to be known, believed, and observed for salvation are so clearly propounded, and opened in some place of Scripture or other, that not only the learned, but the unlearned, in a due use of the ordinary means, may attain unto a sufficient understanding of them.

V

THE AMERICAN EXPERIMENT IN PRIMITIVISM

Most of the settlers who came to America in the seventeenth century were thoroughly versed in Puritan religious ideas. The assumption that the church should be restored to its apostolic purity was widely accepted throughout the colonies. Indeed, this primitivist assumption deeply influenced the political life of the nation as well as the religious life. I made that point in a closing address at a conference on religious primitivism held at Abilene Christian University in the 1980s: "One indelible impression I take away from this conference is that the restoration ideal has been a powerful motif. In fact, it may be the most vital single assumption underlying the development of American Protestantism. Equally important, the restoration ideal continues as one of the most compelling ideas in modern Christianity." [David Edwin Harrell,Jr., "Epilogue," in Richard T. Hughes, ed., *The American Quest for the Primitive Church* (Urbana: University of Illinois Press, 1988), p. 239.] Noted below are a few samples of the continuing emphasis on apostolic authority from the early Puritan settlers in America to the leaders of the early nineteenth century American restoration movement that used the names Christian Church, Churches of Christ and Disciples of Christ. The statements of Thomas and Alexander Campbell and of Barton W. Stone noted below are remarkable not because they are sharp departures from earlier assumptions about apostolic authority, but because they are restatements of principles long present in the Christian tradition. These classic American restoration documents are transparently continuous with the past (as all of the present is continuous with the past).

1. American Puritans established independent congregations (generally called "Church of Christ); the work and worship of these churches, they insisted, must be justified by apostolic authority. Below are two of the early congregational "covenants."

Salem Covenant of 1629:

> We covenant with the Lord and one with another and doe bynd our selves in the presence of God, to walke together in all his waies, **according as he is pleased to reveal himself unto us in his blessed word of truth.**

The Watertown Covenant, July 30, 1630:

> For in the End of the Day, after the finishing of our Publick Duties, we do all, ... Promise, and enter into a sure Covenant with the Lord our God, and before him with one another, by Oath and serious Protestation made, **to renounce all Idolatry and Superstition, Will-Worship, all Humane Traditions and Inventions whatsoever, in the Worship of God**; and forsaking all Evil Ways, do give ourselves wholly unto the Lord Jesus, to do him faithful Service, **observing and keeping all his Statutes, Commands, and Ordinances, in all Matters concerning our Reformation; his Worship, Administrations, Ministry, and Government; and in the Carriage of our selves among our selves, and one another towards another, as he hath prescribed in his Holy Word.** Further swearing to cleave unto that alone, and the true Sense and meaning thereof to the utmost of our Power, as unto the most clear Light and infallible Rule, and All-sufficient Canon, in all things that concern us in this our Way. [These two documents may be found on www.puritanism.online.fr]

2. The Disciples of Christ/Churches of Christ Restoration Movement: Cited below are excerpts from four basic documents from the nineteenth century reforms led by Thomas and Alexander Campbell and Barton W. Stone. The appeals to apostolic authority in these documents were not innovations; they were continuous with the long Christian acceptance of the writings of the New Testament as the proper standard of authority for all Christians. [These documents, and many other restoration movement publications, may be found at www.mun.ca/rels/restmov].

Thomas Campbell, *Declaration and Address,* 1809:

DECLARATION

AND

ADDRESS

OF THE

CHRISTIAN ASSOCIATION

OF

WASHINGTON.

WASHINGTON, (Pa.)

PRINTED BY BROWN & SAMPLE.

AT THE OFFICE OF "THE REPORTER."

1809

PROP. 1. THAT the church of Christ upon earth is essentially, intentionally, and constitutionally one; consisting of all those in every place that profess their faith in Christ and obedience to him in all things according to the scriptures, and that manifest the same by their tempers and conduct, and of none else as none else can be truly and properly called christians.

2. That although the church of Christ upon earth must necessarily exist in particular and distinct societies, locally separate one from another; yet there ought to be no schisms, no uncharitable divisions among them. They ought to receive each other as Christ Jesus hath also received them to the glory of God. And for this purpose, they ought all to walk by the same rule, to mind and speak the same thing; and to be perfectly joined together in the same mind, and in the same judgment.

3. **That in order to this, nothing ought to be inculcated upon christians as articles of faith; nor required of them as terms of communion; but what is expressly taught, and enjoined upon them, in the word of God. Nor ought anything be admitted, as of divine obligation, in their church constitution and managements, but what is expressly enjoined by the authority of our Lord Jesus Christ and his Apostles upon the New Testament church; either in express terms, or by approven precedent ....**

With a direct reference to this state of things; and, as we humbly think, in a perfect consistency with the foregoing explanations, have we expressed ourselves in page 10th; wherein **we declare ourselves ready to relinquish, whatever we have hitherto received as matter of faith or practice, not expressly taught and enjoined in the word of God; so that we, and our brethren, might, by this mutual condescension, return together to the original constitutional** unity of the christian church; and dwell together in peace and charity.

Thomas Campbell, On Religious Reformation (Richmond, Va., 1832), p. 6:

3.   **That in order to this, nothing ought to be inculcated upon christians as articles of faith; nor required of them as terms of communion; but what is expressly taught, and enjoined upon them in the word of God. Nor ought anything be admitted, as of divine obligation in their church constitution and managements, but what is expressly enjoined by the authority of our Lord Jesus Christ and his apostles upon the New Testament church; either in express terms, or by approved precedent.**

4.   That although the scriptures of the Old and New Testament are inseparably connected, making together but one perfect and entire revelation of the Divine will, for the edification and salvation of the church; and, therefore, in that respect cannot he separated; yet as to what directly and properly belongs to their immediate object, the New Testament is as perfect a constitution for the worship, discipline, and government of the New Testament church, and as perfect a rule for the particular duties of its members, as the Old Testament was for the worship, discipline, and government of the Old Testament church, and the particular du" ties of its members.

Barton Stone (1772-1844) *The Last Will and Testament of the Springfield Presbytery*:

OBSERVATIONS

ON

CHURCH GOVERNMENT,

BY THE

PRESBYTERY OF SPRINGFIELD.

TO WHICH IS ADDED,

THE LAST WILL AND TESTAMENT

OF THAT REVEREND BODY

WITH A PREFACE AND NOTES, BY THE EDITOR.

Prepare ye the way of the Lord—make straight in the desert

a highway for our God.

Christian Primitivism in the Twenty-first Century:

The word of our God shall stand forever.

ISAIAH.

1808.

Item. We will, that candidates for the Gospel ministry henceforth study the holy scriptures with fervent prayer, and obtain license from God to preach the simple Gospel, *with the Holy Ghost sent down from heaven*, without any mixture of philosophy, vain deceit, traditions of men, or the rudiments of the world. And let none henceforth *take this honor to himself, but he that is called of God, as was Aaron*. [21]

Item. We will, that the church of Christ assume her native right of internal government—try her candidates for the ministry, as to their soundness in the faith, acquaintance with experimental religion, gravity and aptness to teach; and admit no other proof of their authority but Christ speaking in them. *We will* that the church of Christ look up to the Lord of the harvest to send forth labourers into his harvest; and that she resume her primitive right of trying those *who say they are Apostles) and are not*.

Item. We will, that each particular church, as a body, actuated by the same spirit, choose her own preacher, and support him by a free will offering without written call or *subscription*—admit members—remove offences; and never henceforth *delegate* her right of government to any man or set of men whatever.

*Item. **We will, that the people henceforth take the Bible as the only sure guide to heaven; and as many as are offended with other books, which stand in competition with it, may cast them into the fire if they choose: for it is better to enter into life having one book, than having many to be cast into hell.***

Item. We will, that preachers and people, cultivate a spirit of mutual forbearance, pray more and dispute less; and while they behold the signs of the times, look up and confidently expect that redemption draweth nigh.

Alexdander Campbell, *The Christian System in Reference to the Union of Christians and a Restoration of Primitive Christianity* (Bethany, W. Va., A.

Campbell, 18.39), p. 111:

> **The second proposition, viz.-*That the word or testimony of the Apostles is itself all-sufficient, and alone sufficient, to the union of all Christians,* cannot be rationally doubted by any person acquainted with that testimony, or who admits the competency of their inspiration to make them infallible teachers of the Christian institution.** And, indeed, all who contend for those human institutions called creeds, contend for them as necessary only to the existence of a party, or while the present schisms) contentions, and dissensions exist. Therefore, all the 'defences' [sic]of creeds, ancient and modern, while they assert that the Bible alone is the only perfect and infallible rule of faith and morals; not only concede that these symbols called creeds, are imperfect and fallible,—but, also, that these creeds never can achieve what the Bible, without them, can accomplish.

V
SUMMARY

1. The authority of the apostles to bind the will of God on earth, and to "order" the churches, is clearly taught **in the New Testament**. The principle of apostolicity was set in place by Jesus and repeatedly claimed by the apostles themselves. The apostolic role in revealing God's plan, and in laying the foundation for the church, is clearly stated in scripture. Nowhere was this authority more frequently asserted in the scriptures than in the apostolic prerogative to give instructions to local churches.

2. **In early Christian history** establishing apostolic authority was critically important because of the need to refute heretics and to establish uniformity of practice in the churches. Some false apostles claimed continuing revelation based on Gnostic revelations, but such "private" leadings created division and extremism. The doctrine of apostolic succession vested authority in bishops as the successors of the apostles. This concept was first used by second century Gnostics to justify their revelations, but was later developed as a cornerstone of Roman Catholicism beginning with the teachings of Irenaeus (ca.115-ca. 202). [See Everett Ferguson, "Apostolic Succession," in Ferguson, ed., *Encyclopedia of Early Christianity*, pp. 76-77.] However, the belief that the inspired teachings of the apostles (apostolicity) provided instructions for the universal faith and the ordering of the church, was the most broadly accepted source of authority throughout the early centuries of Christian history.

3. During **the Middle Ages and in Pre-Reformation period**, many non-Roman Catholic forms of Christianity existed and left behind historical records. No doubt, many others vanished leaving no trace. While many groups reached bizarre and erroneous conclusions, the existence of these heterodox movements confirms two important conclusions about this shadowy historical period. (1) The appeal to apostolic authority was the standard for calls for reform and restoration. Except in those heretical movements that claimed supernatural revelation (a form of Gnosticism) apostolicity was the authority relied on to counter creedal and institutional authority and nonbiblical traditionalism. (2) These movements illustrate the degree to which local churches, and regions, were capable of acting independently in their organization and worship. The idea that churches could model themselves on the New Testament clearly had a life throughout these centuries.

4. **The Reformation began** in 1517 when Martin Luther challenged Roman Catholic authority when he nailed 95 theses to the church door in Wittenberg. The Reformation was anchored on a single principle—Sola Scriptura (by Scripture alone). Every wing of the Reformation—Lutheran, Calvinist, Anabaptist, and English—issued clear calls for a return to apostolic authority. Among the early reformers, Ulrich Zwingli of Zurich had the clearest vision of restoring primitive Christianity and the congregation in Zurich, and many others in Switzerland and elsewhere, made extraordinary reforms in their practices.

5. Within **the English and Scottish Reformation**, Puritanism was the strongest primitivist movement in that wing of the Reformation. Few English-language statements regarding the authority of the Scriptures are clearer than that found in the Westminster Confession of Faith which was published in 1636. The Puritan commitment to apostolic authority led to the establishment of many independent congregations and movements to restore the purity of congregational organization and worship.

6. **The American experiment in Primitivism** began with the founding of the first settlements and churches in the 17th century. The early Puritan settlers established independent local churches committed to following New Testament patterns. The ideas voiced by such figures as Thomas Campbell in The Declaration and Address in 1809 and Barton W. Stone in The Last Will and Testament of the Springfield Presbytery in 1808 were continuous with the tradition of earlier reformers in calling for a return to .apostolic authority. Few of the reforms they called for were original or unique, and the basis for these reforms, a demand for apostolic sanction for all teaching

and practice, was a reassertion of one of the most fundamental ideas in Christian history.

VI
CONCLUSION

Restorationist, primitivist religious thinking assumes that the Apostles were given specific authority to define doctrine and set in order churches,

This authority was perpetuated for later generations in the inspired writings of the New Testament.

Far from being an arbitrary or recent assumption, apostolic authority is one of the most fundamental themes running through Christian history. A belief in apostolicity is profoundly Biblical and deeply rooted in the thinking of centuries of serious Christians. It is frivolous and ahistorical to dismiss "apostolic authority" because it is "inside the box." It is, indeed, a concept that has been inside the box of Christian thought from the beginning, and it is one that deserves respect, study, and emulation.

PROPOSITION 2
Defining the Issue:
Common Sense Hermeneutics

Restorationist, primitivist religious thinking assumes that human beings, through the use of a common sense possessed by all, have the ability to read texts and reach universal conclusions about meanings. This empirical, logical type of thinking is the basis for all public (as opposed to private and subjective) human understanding.

I
POSTMODERNISM—MODERN GNOSTICISM

History is filled with subjectivist intellectual movements that claimed special intuitive insights and questioned the quest for systems of rational truth that could be shared by all human beings. In recent years, certain academic disciplines—particularly literary criticism and some other areas of the humanities and social sciences—have been influenced by a subjectivist movement called "postmodernism." Broadly defined, "postmodernism" is "a theory that involves a radical reappraisal of modern assumptions about culture, identity, history, or language" [*Merriam-Webster Dictionary Online*, www.m-w.com/dictionary/postmodern/]. Below is a fuller, literary definition offered by Professor L. Kip Wheeler:

> **POSTMODERNISM:** A general (and often hotly debated) label referring to the philosophical, artistic, and literary changes and tendencies after the 1940s and 1950s up to the present day. We can speak of postmodern art, music, architecture, literature, and poetry using the same generic label. The tendencies of postmodernism include (1) a rejection of traditional authority, (2) radical experimentation—in some cases bordering on gimmickry, (3) eclecticism and multiculturalism, (4) parody and pastiche, (5) deliberate anachronism or surrealism, and (6) a cynical or ironic self-awareness (often postmodernism mocks its own characteristic traits). In many ways, these traits are all features that first appeared in modernism, but postmodernism magnifies and intensifies these earlier characteristics. It also seems to me that, while modernism rejected much of tradition, it clung to science as a hopeful and objective cure to the past insanities of history, culture and superstition. Modernism hoped to tear down tradition and longed to build something better in its ruins. **Postmodernism, on the other hand, is often suspicious of scientific claims, and often denies the possibility or desirability of establishing any objective truths and shared cultural standards. It usually embraces pluralism and spurns monolithic beliefs, and it often borders on solipsism.** While modernism mourned the passing of unified cultural tradition, and wept for its demise in the ruined heap of civilization, so to speak, postmodernism tends to dance in the ruins and play with the fragments [*Literary Vocabulary*, we.b.c.n.edu/kwheeler/lit_terms.html].

As noted by Professor Wheeler, postmodernism questions the existence of "objective truths and shared cultural standards," and it enthrones personal feeling and intuition. It is, in short, a modern "Gnosticism'" in which private leadings and feelings give insights unattainable by observation and rational thinking. Indeed, "objective truth" is not possible.... While the accomplishments of science are difficult to dismiss, hardcore postmodernists are not reluctant to dismiss science and the scientific method. All in all, it is an elitist fad that, hopefully, seems to be on the wane in American academia.

II

POSTMODERNISM AND A NEW HERMENEUTIC FOR THE RESTORATION MOVEMENT

Using postmodern assumptions, at the end of the twentieth century a variety of academics within the American restoration movement challenged the "possibility or desirability of establishing any objective truths." The error of Biblical primitivism, they argue, is that it assumes that objective truth can and should be sought. They insist that the interpretative assumptions of the restoration movement, labeled the "Baconian hermeneutic," were based on an outmoded "Enlightenment" system of thought. They seem to suggest that it must be replaced by a vague, subjective, solipsistic system of private, "feel-good" religion. Welcome to the chaos of postmodernism. These postmodern critics reserve special derision for the idea that one can reach valid Biblical conclusions based on "command, example, and necessary inference."

Below are several quotations from books written by professors at Abilene Christian University and Pepperdine University that state the case against traditional primitivist hermeneutics.

"A cultural shift in the West is occurring. It gives no evidence of being a passing fad. Its roots lie early in the twentieth century and its effects should be felt for generations to come. The gains and methods of science will not be lost in the coming centuries. **But, there is considerable evidence that people are beginning to view knowledge and the world differently**" [Jeff W. Childers, Douglas A. Foster, and Jack H. Reese, *The Crux of the Matter* (Abilene: ACU Press, 2001), pp. 50-51].

"That they [nineteenth-century restoration leaders] allowed Scripture to play such a role is praiseworthy. **Their confidence in the ability of human reason to arrive at interpretations everyone would accept has turned out to be problematic**, yet they demonstrated a humble and right attitude when they deliberately put themselves under Scripture and fearlessly began to examine everything by it." [*Ibid.*, p. 60].

"For the practitioner of restoration theology in the Stone-Campbell movement, the most serious question this study raises is the validity of the rationalistic restoration hermeneutic. Two challenges face the tradition. **The entire Enlightenment project and its epistemological foundationalism are under attack and have been discredited in many academic circles. The normative vocabulary of American Common Sense philosophy has also been discredited.** Given the extent that restoration hermeneutics is grounded in the Enlightenment and the normative language of Common Sense, can an alternative restoration hermeneutic be constructed? [Michael W. Casey, *The Battle Over Hermeneutics in the Stone-Campbell Movement; 1800,1870* (Lewiston: The Edwin Mellen Press, 1998), p. 268].

"**The second challenge is that the traditional hermeneutic of command, example, and necessary inference is not found in the Old and New Testament, but is grounded in the human history of Reformed theology, Scottish Common Sense philosophy and logic, and the nineteenth century American culture.** It is not a 'divine' hermeneutic insulated from the 'chaos' of history. If the idea of restoration theology is to remain viable ... what should the hermeneutic be? This is the most serious challenge facing the tradition today. A failure to address this question means that the tradition is now dead, having rejected its purpose and goals" [*Ibid.*, pp. 268-269].

Notice the assumptions embedded in these quotations:

1. According to the authors of *The Crux of the Matter*, modern people have come to "view knowledge and the world differently" and the idea that human beings can reach common interpretations through "human reason' has turned out to be "problematic." Thus, it seems, human beings are trapped in a subjectivist postmodern world where it is impossible to reach common conclusions. The authors do acknowledge that "the gains and methods of science" will probably survive the postmodern onslaught, but religious people will have to find another way of reaching truth.

2. Professor Casey's assertions are bolder. He believes that "the entire Enlightenment project and its epistemological foundationalism have been discredited in many academic circles" and that the "restoration hermeneutic" (command, example, and necessary inference), rooted in the Scottish Common Sense intellectual system, is neither philosophically defensible nor Biblical. Thus, without a new hermeneutic, Biblical primitivism is an exhausted movement.

These critiques of "common sense" reasoning are discussed in the following sections:

1. *Section III* offers a brief overview of the accomplishments of the Enlightenment era and the enduring impact of the period on modern thought. The assertion that the new hermeneutical discoveries of the last half of the twentieth century (postmodernism) wiped away the intellectual accomplishments and insights of the centuries preceding is academic elitism and arrogance in its rankest and most absurd form. The enormous contributions of Enlightenment thinkers, including the development of the scientific method, are firmly in place in most academic disciplines, unfazed by the avante garde subjectivism that often captures the artistic disciplines.

2. **Section IV** examines "common sense" as a description of the innate intellectual potential shared by all human beings. The ability to observe the world around us and make reasonable decisions based on our perceptions was described, not discovered, by Enlightenment thinkers. Can a different hermeneutic be devised to lead us, as Professor Casey asks? Of course, one can act impulsively without observation or follow his or her subjective, personal leadings. But those options were hardly new at the end of the twentieth century. Millions of people have been "Gnostics" in every age.

3. **Section V** explores the Biblical case for common sense hermeneutics. Casey's assertion that "the traditional hermeneutic of command, example, and necessary inference is not found in the Old and New Testament, but is grounded in the human history of Reformed theology, Scottish Common Sense philosophy and logic, and the nineteenth century American culture" is a loaded statement. If one means by stich an assertion that the Bible is not a text on hermeneutics, the statement is correct. If, however, one means that the Bible does not manifest an understanding and use of common sense reasoning, the statement is nonsensical.

4. **Section VI** argues that the critical interpretative issue faced by Christians is not hermeneutics, it is rather learning to ask good questions. We learn what God wants done (as we learn what the government or our parents want done) by putting together all of the information available to us through the use of our common sense. If we are wise, we use our common sense to make good decisions.

III

FRANCIS BACON AND ENLIGHTENMENT THOUGHT

Romans 1:19-20: For what can be known about God is plain to them, because God himself has made it plain to them. (20) For since the creation of the world his invisible attributes—his eternal power and divine nature—have been understood and observed by what he made,

so that people are without excuse. (ISV)

The Enlightenment is a term used to describe the extraordinary intellectual period (sometimes the early years are known as the Age of Reason) beginning in the sixteenth century. It was marked by dramatic changes in political, religious, and scientific thought. The Enlightenment was preceded by the Renaissance and Reformation; it witnesses an explosion in scientific advancement. In part, the new mindset of the Enlightenment period was a continuation of the Reformation's rejection of the superstition and mysticism of earlier centuries. Francis Bacon was one of the giant intellects of the early Enlightenment; his exploration of the "inductive method" influenced Isaac Newton (1642-1727) and became foundational in scientific development. The principles of the "Baconian hermeneutic" were also considered fundamental by religious leaders in the centuries that followed; many regarded Bacon as a hero because his emphasis on careful and rational observation helped rid the world of the superstition and subjectivism.

Francis Bacon (1561-1626): Bacon's private life was less than admirable, but he is held in the highest esteem by intellectual historians. One English biographical dictionary writes: "The intellect of Bacon was one of the most powerful and searching ever possessed by man, and his developments of the inductive philosophy revolutionised the future thought of the human race." [John W. Cousins, ed., *A Short Biographical Dictionary of English Literature* (London: J.M. Dent & Company, 1910)]. His most important book, Novum Organum, published in 1620, explored the scientific method and inductive reasoning. At the simplest level, Bacon argued that truth claims should be based not on speculation—either philosophical or subjective—but on objective and unbiased observation and a rational testing of the results of experimentation. One encyclopedia defines the scientific method thus: "A body of techniques for investigating phenomena and acquiring new knowledge, as well as for correcting and integrating previous knowledge. It is based on gathering observable, empirical, measurable evidence, subject to the principles of reasoning" [www. wikipedia.org]. In short, the inductive method involves (1) asking a pertinent question; (2) collecting all of the information available (for instance, commands and examples); (3) drawing conclusions based on your investigation (through logic and "necessary inference"); and (4) testing one's conclusions by comparing them to the evidence.

Thomas Bayes (171J2-1761) and Probability Theory: Many other monumental scientific breakthroughs came during the Enlightenment years. One of the more interesting contributors to the thought of the period was a mathematician named Thomas Bayes. His theory of probability, published posthumously in *Philosophical Transactions of the Royal Society of London* in 1764, remains an important mathematical formula for determining the likelihood that a conclusion is true. The theorem is the fundamental mathematical law governing the process of logical inference—determining what degree of confidence we may have, in various possible conditions, based on the body of evidence available. The formula is still widely used in such fields as economics.

> **A Baysean Excursion**: The viability of the tools of interpretation that were explored and advocated during the Enlightenment period was showcased in a recent conference of religious scholars at Yale University. In 2002, the New York Times reported on a paper presented by Oxford University Professor Richard Swinburne which used the Baysean theorem to explore the probability of the existence of God. His paper outlined the conclusions he reached after 25 years of feeding information into the Baysean formula:

> > *"Thanks to the efforts of Mr. Swinburne and a handful of other nimble scholarly minds ... religious belief no longer languishes in a state of philosophical disrepute. Deploying a range of sophisticated logical arguments developed over the last 25 years, Christian philosophers have revived faith as a subject of rigorous academic debate, steadily chipping away at the assumption—all but axiomatic in philosophy since the Enlightenment—that belief in God is logically indefensible." [Emily Eakin, "So God's Really in the Details," New York Times, May 11, 2002, pp. A1 7, 19].*

Professor Swinburne concluded that the probability of the existence of God, according to the Baysean equation, was 97%.

IV
COMMON SENSE

> Acts 17:11: These were more noble than those in Thessalonica, in that they received the word with all readiness of mind, and searched the scriptures daily, whether those things were so.

> John 5:39: Search the scriptures; for in them ye think ye have eternal life: and they are they which testify of me.

Common sense, in its broadest definition, is simply the knowledge every individual learns through direct encounter with the world around him or her. All of us innately and instinctively use "the scientific method" when we make rational decisions based on the information we receive through our senses. And all of us also make "probability" judgments; we look at the evidence available to us (in Baysean fashion) and decide what action is most likely true. The *Cambridge Dictionary* makes clear the universal nature of common sense:

> "**common sense** noun: the basic level of practical knowledge and judgment that we all need to help us live in a reasonable and safe way .... " [www.dictionary.cambtidge.org].

The following quotations from *New Scientist* magazine flesh out the dimensions of human intelligence:

> "SOME things are just obvious. We all know that people don't walk on their heads, for example, or that if you go out in the rain you're likely to get wet. It's common sense ....
>
> "Spare a thought, then, for those trying to design computers that have common sense. It took each of us humans many years to build up a portfolio of wisdom about the way the world works. When a baby repeatedly knocks over towers of bricks it may look like a futile activity, but what the child is really doing is exploring the world and filling its brain with fundamental rules. By the age of 3, it will have acquired more common sense than the most sophisticated computer. This is the big headache for artificial intelligence (AI) researchers: they can design a computer that might beat Garry Kasparov at chess, but you couldn't have an intelligent conversation with it because it has no grasp of ordinary life...."

Admittedly, common sense sometimes gets clouded by prejudice, emotion, and culture.

> "Some things that seem obvious to one person may seem obscure to another if they are from another culture, religion, or background. Common sense is not always common to everyone. This is especially true when beliefs play a strong part in how people perceive things. It may seem obvious to me that a drought was caused by a random change in weather patterns, but to someone who believes in supernatural beings it could seem just as obvious that it's because they've displeased the rain god. Einstein summed it up this: 'Common sense is the collection of prejudices acquired by age 18.'... The latest neuroscience shows we base our judgments on gut feeling and emotion rather than a rational assessment of the facts?" [From issue 2547 of *New Scientist* magazine,

15 April 2005, p. 54].

In short, human beings instinctively, from birth to death, accumulate evidence (based on stated laws and examples) and make decisions. At best, our common sense operates with Baconian objectivity and at worst we make irrational judgments based on false information and untested feelings. Usually, our actions are based on years of instruction, observation, and testing. We behave sensibly because of the things we have learned and because of the things we can clearly infer from this experiential knowledge (sounds like command, example, and necessary inference). Of course, sometimes we cannot be sure. Then we make probability decisions (in Baysean fashion), deciding about what is the safest course of action.

V

THE BIBLICAL CASE FOR COMMON SENSE

To say that the Baconian hermeneutic (that is, scientific thinking, empirical investigation and rational thought, or non-technically, "common sense") is not present in the Old and New Testaments is an odd statement, indeed. The Scriptures consistently assume that the directions given by God, and the lessons learned by observing the history of obedience and disobedience will be appropriated by the common sense of human beings.

The Hermeneutic of Jesus: On a number of occasions, Jesus addressed hermeneutical questions in a non-technical, common sense manner. The conclusion of the tenth chapter of Luke offers a clear-cut hermeneutical exchange. In giving charge to the 70 disciples He sent out to prepare the way for Him, Jesus acknowledged that the message they preached would not be universally accepted:

> Luke 10:21: In that hour Jesus rejoiced in spirit, and said, I thank thee, O Father, Lord of heaven and earth, that thou hast hid these things from the wise and prudent, and hast revealed them unto babes: even
>
> so, Father; for so it seemed good in thy sight.

While the disciples pondered this statement about "understanding," Jesus taught a lesson about hermeneutics. It was embodied in what is generally called the parable of the good Samaritan, a story that is an excellent reminder of the meaning of brotherly love. But the passage at the end of Luke 10 is primarily about Biblical interpretation—it is about hermeneutics.

The Question:

> Luke 10:25: And, behold, a certain lawyer stood up, and tempted him,
> saying, Master, what shall I do to inherit eternal life?

All of life is about asking questions and getting answers. Many of our questions are frivolous, or have no certain answers (do I look better in blue or brown?), but others are critically important. The lawyer who encountered Jesus in Luke 10:25 asked a transparently important question, although he seemingly was not interested in knowing the answer. What follows is a hermeneutical exchange about how to find the answer to a good question.

The Answer:

> Luke 10:26-28: He said to him, what is written in the law? How readest
> thou? (27) And he answering said, Thou shalt love the Lord they God
> with all they heart, and with all thy soul, and with all they strength,
> and with all they mind; and they neighbour as thyself. (28) And he said
> unto him, Thou hast answered right; this do, and thou shalt live.

If you want to know what behavior God expects of you, Jesus answers, you read His instructions. Had God given directions on the matter of how to "inherit eternal life?" Indeed, He had, and the lawyer knew precisely what God had said. So, Jesus responded, the questioner's problem was not hermeneutical; his problem was not "knowing," but "doing."

The Postmodernist Dilemma:

> Luke 10:29: But he, willing to justify himself, said unto Jesus, And who
> is my neighbour?

Surely, it is not that easy. Such an answer sounds almost "scientific," or, one might say "Baconian." And such tidy reasoning often restricts our conduct in personally undesirable ways. So, the lawyer replies, such rational appeals to evidence must surely be blurred by the inexactness of words and our inability to communicate precise meanings. What does "neighbour" mean? It sounds good to say we must do what the Scriptures teach, but can we really understand?

The Common Sense Answer:

> Luke 10:30-37: And Jesus answering said, A certain man went down
> from Jerusalem to Jericho, and fell among thieves, which stripped him

of his raiment, and wounded him, and departed, leaving him half dead. (31) And by chance there came down a certain priest that way: and when he saw him, he passed by on the other side. (32) And likewise a Levite, when he was at the place, came and looked on him, and passed by on the other side. (33) But a certain Samaritan, as he journeyed, came where he was: and when he saw him, he had compassion on him, (34) And went to him, and bound up his wounds, pouring in oil and wine, and set him on his own beast, and brought him to an inn, and took care of him. (35) And on the morrow when he departed, he took out two pence, and gave them to the host, and said unto him, Take care of him; and whatsoever thou spendest more, when I come again, I will repay thee. (36) Which now of these three, thinkest thou, was neighbour unto him that fell among the thieves? (37) And he said, He that shewed mercy on him. Then said Jesus unto him, Go, and do thou likewise.

This parable of the good Samaritan is a common sense hermeneutical answer to a loaded question. There is no sophistry in the answer, no appeals to logical models, no thecnical explanations, just an appeal to a common sense shared by all human beings. Our experience teaches us quite clearly what it means to be a good neighbor. The issue, Jesus reaffirms, is not "knowing" what is pleasing to God, but "doing" it.

Common Sense Reading of the Scriptures:

Hebrews 7:13-14: For he of whom these things are spoken pertaineth to another tribe, of which no man gave attendance at the altar. (14) For *it is* evident that our Lord sprang out of Judea; of which tribe Moses spake nothing concerning priesthood.

Like many other Biblical passages, the argument in Hebrews chapter seven regarding the priesthoods of Melchisedec and of Christ assumes the basics of common sense reasoning. The author does not set out to establish or codify a hermeneutical system, he rather uses self-evident, common sense principles to establish his teaching on the priesthood. He appeals to direct instruction, the "example" of the Jewish priesthood, and the limitations imposed by silence— all common sense principles that need no explanation. Common sense is not something to be proven, it is something assumed.

VI

ASKING GOOD QUESTIONS

In Luke chapter 10 the lawyer asked a good question. He simply needed to investigate God's instructions and obey them. On the other hand, it is possible to ask questions that are not relevant. Our responsibility is to determine **what** God intends to bind. Such decisions are not subjective, they must be based on a common sense reading of the Scriptures. If we ask good questions, **how** to find the answers is not a mystery, nor do we need to be versed in philosophical discussions of hermeneutics.

Where should we worship? Consider the encounter between Jesus and the Samaritan woman recorded in John chapter 4.

The Question:

John 4:19-20: The woman saith unto him, Sir, I perceive that thou are a prophet. (20) Our fathers worshipped in this mountain; and ye say, that in Jerusalem is the place where men ought to worship.

The Answer:

John 4:21-24: Jesus saith unto her, Woman, believe me, the hour cometh, when ye shall neither in this mountain, nor yet at Jerusalem, worship the Father. (22) Ye worship ye know not what: we know what we worship: for salvation is of the Jews. (23) But the hour cometh, and now is, when the true worshippers shall worship the Father in spirit and in truth: for the Father seeketh such to worship him. (24) God *is* a Spirit: and they that worship him must worship *him* in spirit and in truth.

Where to worship was a pertinent question under the law, but Jesus informed the woman that under His law the father's concern was **how** His children worshipped, not **where** they worshipped. Specifically, this passage makes clear that where we assemble for Christian worship is not bound and that the examples we find in the New Testament are not intended to govern our conduct. More broadly, the encounter teaches us that we must ask proper questions of the Scriptures. Many Biblical primitivists attempt to restore practices that God did not intend to be models for modern Christian behavior.

Restoring Spiritual Gifts—the Pentecostal Dilemma:

Hebrews 2:3-4: How shall we escape, if we neglect so great salvation; which at the first began to be spoken by the Lord, and was confirmed unto us by them that heard him; (4) God also bearing them witness, both with signs and wonders, and with divers miracles, and gifts of the Holy Ghost, according to his own will?

Pentecostals embrace a Biblical primitivism focusing on a restoration of the spiritual gifts that the Scriptures tell us were intended to confirm the revelation of the "great salvation" announced in the last days. The gifts of the Holy Spirit accomplished that purpose. I believe, based on my reading of the Scriptures, that asking how spiritual gifts should be used in the present-day church is not a proper question. They were never intended for that purpose.

Restoring First Century Lifestyles—the Amish Dilemma:

1 Corinthians 9:20-22: And unto the Jews I became as a Jew, that I might gain the Jews; to them that are under the law, as under the law, that I might gain them that are under the law; (21) To them that are without law, as without law, (being not without law to God, but under the law to Christ,) that I might gain them that are without law. (22) To the weak became I as weak, that I might gain the weak: I am made all things to all men, that I might by all means save some.

Few Christians have been more committed to the idea of returning to primitive Christianity than the Amish and similar groups with origins in the Anabaptist wing of the Reformation. The problem with such restoration movements is not that they misinterpret the scriptures, but they ask wrong questions. Nothing in the New Testament implies that Christians would dress and look the same in every society and in every age. On the contrary, Christians were urged to live righteously within any culture, while not participating in its wickedness.

VII
SUMMARY

1. Recent attacks on the "Baconian hermeneutic" have been deeply influenced by postmodernism, a modern recycling of subjective thinking that looks very much like a latter-day Gnosticism. Every age has such anti-rational movements. For those who do not like authority, or who disapprove of the limits imposed by authority, it is useful to assert that there is no common truth.

2. It is ironic that the central culprit in the attacks on restoration thinking

(including the concepts of command, example, and necessary inference) is the Enlightenment, the extraordinary era of discovery and reason that laid the foundation for modern science. While one may not be interested in the hermeneutical theories of Francis Bacon, or the probability formula of Thomas Bayes, it is absurd to dismiss the insights and accomplishments of these intellectual giants on the basis of the sloppy subjectivism of postmodernism. The scientific method that calls for observation, drawing objective and rational conclusion, and testing the results is healthy and well at the beginning of the 21st century.

3. Interpreting the world around us is a matter of common sense. All human beings make judgments based on observation and rational testing. One does not need to understand any hermeneutical model to use his or her powers of observation and logical reasoning. Throughout our lives we learn by instruction, example, and inferences. We also make probability judgments based on the accumulation of convincing evidence.

4. The Biblical hermeneutic is simple and direct. If you ask a good question about God's will, the way to find the answer is to listen to all that the Scriptures reveal on that matter.

5. If these assumptions are correct, interpreting the Scriptures is a straightforward matter of using our common sense in the same way that we use it throughout life to make decisions. When you ask an important question, yon act on the basis of the best evidence you can gather. The issue, then, is whether we are asking good questions.

VIII
CONCLUSION

The final section of this study will ask whether God intended to order local churches so that they looked alike in all societies and in all ages. If that was God's intent, we should use our common sense to collect and act on all of the available information. So, if it is correct to assume that the apostles were authorized to set God's plan in order, and to assume that understanding their directions is a matter of using the tools of common sense shared by all human beings, two questions remain: (1) what does the Bible teach us about the organization, worship, and work of local churches, and (2) why should we think it matters?

PROPOSITION 3

DEFINING THE ISSUE: CONGREGATIONALISM

Restorationist, primitivist religious thinking assumes that the practices of local churches in New Testament days rested on apostolic authority and that the ordering of churches was intentionally designed by God to promote uniformity (catholicity) among Christians.

What did New Testament churches look like? Did the apostles intend to "order" the organization, worship and work of local churches? If these are good questions, we should seek the answers by accumulating all of the authoritative information we can find. If New Testament churches were, by God's intent, uniform (catholic) in practice, the means of reproducing them in succeeding generations is simple, There is no hermeneutical dilemma about how to do it. The methods we use are no different from those we would use to recreate any historical institution, event, or era. Like all restoration enterprises, the methods we use may seem legalistic., technical, and narrow. All serious primitivist efforts—religious or secular—may be described in those terms.

It seems fair to begin this chapter with a listing of the pertinent information I have gleaned from the New Testament about the organization, worship, and work of local churches. Other passages could be cited, but representative citations are noted beside each entry. I claim no infallibility for my list, though I am willing to give reasons for the items on it. Most of what is there, I learned from others. However, I should make it clear that I am not wedded to my list. On the other hand, I am deeply committed to the principles that compel the making of such a list and that justify the methods used to compile it. We shall return to the list at the end of this section.

A NEW TESTAMENT LOCAL CHURCH

1.   An organization—Phil. 1:1; Acts 14:23; I Tim. 3:1ff; Titus 1:.5ff

2.   An assembly—Heb. 10:25; I Cor. 11:15

3.   Taught—Acts 20:7; I Cor. 14:15

4.   Prayed—Acts 12:5; I Cor. 14:19

5.   Sang—Eph. 5:19; Col. 3:16

6.   Lord's Supper on 1st Day—Acts 20:7; I Cor. 11:20

7.   Gave on the 1st Day—I Cor. 16:1, 2; Acts 2:44-45

8.   Had a Common Treasury—Acts 5:1-4

9.   Relieved Needy Saints—Acts 4:34-35; 11:29-30; I Cor. 16:1

10. Supported Preaching—II Cor. 11:8; Phil. 4:15-16

11. Disciplined Unruly Members—I Cor. 5:1-5

I

A STRATEGY FOR CHRISTIAN UNITY

Few principles are more clearly stated, or more obviously violated, than the New Testament exhortation to unity of faith and practice. Religious demographer David B. Barrett's World Christian Encyclopedia currently lists more than 33,830 separate religious bodies—all claiming to be Christian [see www.adherents. com]. Is there a remedy for this chaotic and scandalous desecration of the name Christian? The answer calls for the acceptance of a common source of authority and submission to it.

1. Jesus prayed for unity among His disciples so that His message would not be damaged:

    John 17:23 I am in them, and you are in me. May they be completely one, so that the world may know that you sent me and that you have loved them as you loved me. (ISV)

2. Congregational unity was commanded:

    1 Corinthians 1:10: But I exhort you, brothers, by the name of our Lord Jesus Christ, that you all speak the sarne thing and that there be no divisions among you; but that you be perfectly joined together in the same mind and in the same judgment.

3. Local churches modeled on one another (based on the teachings they received by apostolic authority):

    1 Thessalonians 2:13-14: For this cause also thank we God without ceasing, because, when ye received the word of God which ye heard of us, ye received it not as the word of men, but as it is in truth, the word of God, which effectually worketh also in you that believe. (14) For ye, brethren, became followers of the churches of God which in Judea are in Christ Jesus: for ye also have suffered like things of your own countrymen, even as they have of the Jews, ...

4. In the book of I Corinthians, Paul repeatedly states that he gave uniform instructions to all of the churches:

    I Cor. 4:17: For this cause have I sent unto you Timotheus, who is my beloved son, and faithful in the Lord, who shall bring you into remembrance of my ways which be in Christ, as I teach every where in every church.

I Cor. 7:17: But as God hath distributed to every man, as the Lord hath called every one, so let him walk. And so ordain I in all churches.

I Cor. 11:16: But if any man seem to be contentious, we have no such custom, neither the churches of God.

I Cor. 16:1: Now concerning the collection for the saints, as I have given order to the churches of Galatia, even so do ye.

5.   Churches were "ordered" by apostolic authority (see Proposition 1, Section I, Nos. 4 and 5). That claim is perhaps most clearly stated in the Apostle Paul's statements to Timothy and Titus following his instructions to them about the appointing of elders and deacons:

1 Timothy 3:14-15: These things write I unto thee, hoping to come unto thee shortly: (15) But if I tarry long, that thou mayest know how thou oughtest to behave thyself in the house of God, which is the church of the living God, the pillar and ground of the truth.

Titus 1:2-5: In hope of eternal life, which God, that cannot lie, promised before the world began; (3) But hath in due times manifested his word through preaching, which is committed unto me according to the commandment of God our Saviour; (4) To Titus, mine own son after the common faith: Grace, mercy, and peace, from God the Father and the Lord Jesus Christ out Saviour. (5) For this cause left I thee in Crete, that thou shouldest set in order the things that are wanting, and ordain elders in every city, as I had appointed thee:

6.   The desire for catholicity—that is common teaching and practice—was the driving force behind both the defining of the canon (positively) and the early formulation of creeds, the convening of councils, and the early institutionalization of the universal church (negatively). *The Apostles' Creed* (2nd century) is generally regarded as the most ancient baptismal formula used in the early churches. It is still recited in many churches today. Among the basic assertions in it, found in many of the documents of early Christianity, is the intended catholicity (uniformity) of the church.

I believe in God the Father Almighty, Maker of heaven and earth. And in Jesus Christ his only Son our Lord; who was conceived by the Holy Ghost, born of the Virgin Mary, suffered under Pontius Pilate, was crucified, dead, and buried; he descended into hell; the third day he rose again from the dead; he ascended into heaven, and sitteth on the right hand of God the Father Almighty; from thence he shall come to judge the quick and the dead. I believe in the Holy Ghost; **the holy** catholic Church; **the communion of saints**; the forgiveness of sins; the resurrection of the body; and the life everlasting. AMEN.

II

THE GRANDEUR OF THE CHURCH IN GOD'S PLAN

No one can respectfully read the New Testament text without grasping the grandeur of the church headed by Jesus Christ. Those who blithely dismiss the "organized church" show, either carelessly or arrogantly, a regrettable disrespect for Biblical revelation.

1. The church in Ephesians: Considered below are a few selections from the book of Ephesians. Admittedly, most of the book of Ephesians deals with the church in its grand universal sense, but each local congregation is a part of that magnificent and divine building—as is every Christian.

    Ephesians 1:22-23: And hath put all things under his feet, **and gave him to be the head over all things to the church, (23) Which is his body, the fulness of him that filleth all in all**.

    Ephesians 2:19-22: Now therefore ye are no more strangers and foreigners, but fellow citizens with the saints, and of **the household of God**; (20) And are built upon the foundation of the apostles and prophets, Jesus Christ himself being the chief corner stone; (21) In whom all the building fitly framed together groweth unto an holy temple in the Lord: (22) **In whom ye also are builded together for an habitation of God through the Spirit**.

    Ephesians 3:9-11,21: And to make all men see what is the fellowship of the mystery, which from the beginning of the world hath been hid in God, who created all things by Jesus Christ: (10) **To the intent that now unto the principalities and powers in heavenly places might be known by the church the manifold wisdom of God,** (11) According to the eternal purpose which he purposed in Christ Jesus our Lord: ... (21) **Unto him be glory in the church by Christ Jesus throughout all ages**, world without end. Amen.

    Ephesians 4:11-16: **And he gave some, apostles; and some prophets; and some evangelists; and some pastors and teachers**; (12) For the perfecting of the saints, for the work of the ministry, for the edifying of the body of Christ: (13) Till we all in the unity of the faith, and of the knowledge of the Son of God, unto a perfect man, unto the measure of the stature of the fullness of Christ: (14) That we henceforth be no more children, tossed to and fro, and carried about with every wind of doctrine, by the sleight of men, and cunning craftiness, whereby they lie in wait to deceive; (15) But speaking the truth in love, may grow up into him in all things, which is the head, even Christ: (16) From whom the whole body fitly joined together and compacted by that which every joint supplieth, according to the effectual working in the measure of every part, maketh increase of the body unto the edifying of itself in love.

Ephesians 5:23-26: For the husband is the head of the wife, **even as Christ is the head of the church: and he is the saviour of the body.** (24) Therefore as the church is subject unto Christ, so let the wives be to their own husbands in every thing. (25) Husbands, love your wives, even as Christ also loved the church, and gave himself for it; (26) That he might sanctify and cleanse it with the washing of water and by the word ....

2. God's intent for His coming kingdom was made know by His meticulous foreshadowing of things to come. The book of Hebrews repeatedly calls our attention to the (to coin a word) INTENTIONALITY of everything God did in leading us into a kingdom that cannot be shaken.

Hebrews 12:18-29: For ye are not come unto the mount that might be touched, and that burned with fire, nor unto blackness,, and darkness, and tempest, ... (22) **But ye are come unto mount Sion, and unto the city o f the living God, the heavenly Jerusalem, and to an innumerable company of angels, (23) To the general assembly and church of the firstborn, which are written in heaven, and to God the Judge of all, and to the spirits of just men made perfect, (24) And to Jesus the mediator of the new covenant, and to the blood of sprinkling, that speaketh better things than that of Abel.** (25) See that ye refuse nor him that speaketh. For if they escaped not who refused him that spake on earth, much more shall not we escape if we turn away from him that speaketh from heaven: (26) Whose voice then shook the earth: but now he hath promised, saying, Yet once more I shake not the earth only, but also heaven. (27) And this word, Yet once more, signifieth the removing of those things that are shaken, as of things that are made, that those things which cannot be shaken may remain. (28) **Wherefore we receiving a kingdom which cannot be moved, let us have grace, whereby we may serve God acceptably with reverence and godly fear:** (29) For our God is a consuming fire.

Hebrews 8:5: Who serve unto the example and **shadow of heavenly things**, as Moses was admonished of God when he was about to make the tabernacle: for, **See, saith he, that thou make all things according to the pattern shewed to thee in the mount**.

Hebrews 10:1: **For the law having a shadow of good things to come**, and not the very image of the things, can never with those sacrifices which they offered year by year continually make the comers thereunto perfect.

Hebrews 7:14: For it is evident that our Lord sprang out of Juda; **of which tribe Moses spake nothing concerning priesthood**.

Acts 7:44: Our fathers had the tabernacle of witness in the wilderness, as he had **appointed**, speaking unto Moses, **that he should make it according to the fashion that he had seen**.

III
CONGREGATIONALISM IN HISTORY

In Chapter 1 of this pamphlet I suggested that the ideal of independent local churches, organized and functioning according to the pattern of congregations in the New Testament, survived as an idea throughout Christian history. Often these heterodox reforms were seriously flawed (their lists did not look much like mine), but the ideal of restoration remained a powerful force in the presence of powerful and frequently repressive efforts to institutionalize and organize the universal church.

By the time the American restoration movement was launched in the early nineteenth century, with its appeal for a return to the "ancient order of things," the principle of establishing local churches based on New Testament patterns was well established. I cite again a few examples from early American Puritan sources that show a clear grasp of both the concept of New Testament congregationalism and the common sense methodology for carrying out this "search for the ancient order of things."

1. The *Salem Covenant* (1629) is a statement of congregational organization typical of those drafted by early Puritan settlers in America. In these documents, they agreed to gather as independent groups of Christians guided only by the Scriptures.

    We covenant with the Lord and one with another and doe bynd our selves in the presence of God, to walke together in all his waies, according as he is pleased to reveal himself unto us in his blessed word of truth.

2. The *Watertown Covenant* (July 30, 1640) is a somewhat fuller statement of congregational intent:

    For in the End of the Day, after the finishing of our Publick Duties, we do all, ... Promise, and enter into a sure Covenant with the Lord our God, and before him with one another, by Oath and serious Protestation made, to renounce all Idolatry and Superstition, Will-Worship, all Humane Traditions and Inventions whatsoever, in the Worship of God; and forsaking all Evil Ways, do give ourselves wholly unto the Lord Jesus, to do him faithful Service, observing and keeping all his Statutes, Commands, and Ordinances, in all Matters concerning our Reformation; his Worship, Administrations, Ministry, and Government; and in the Carriage of our selves among our selves, and one another towards another, as he hath prescribed in his Holy Word. Further swearing to cleave unto that alone, and the true Sense and meaning thereof to the utmost of our Power, as unto the most clear Light and infallible Rule, and All-sufficient Canon, in all things that concern us in this our Way.

3. The Platform of *Church Discipline*, drafted in 1649 by the Puritans of New England as a statement of those things they had "gathered out of the Word of God," was meticulously documented with scriptural citations. All in all, such Puritan documents look much like my list describing a local church.

    CHAPTER I.

    Of the form of Church-Government; and that it is one> immutable> and prescribed in the Word of God.

    Ecclesiasticall Polity or Church Government (1), or discipline is nothing els, but that Forme & order that is to he observed in the Church of Christ vpon earth, both for the Constitution of it, & all the Administrations that therein are to bee performed .... The partes of Church-Government are all of them exactly described in the word of God (5) being parts or means of Instituted worship according to the second Commandement: & therefore to continue one & the same, vnto the apearing of our Lord Iesus Christ as a kingdom that cannot be shaken, untill hee shall deliver it up unto God, enen the Father. Soe that it is not left in the power of men, (6) officers, Churches, or any state in the world to add, or diminish, or alter any thing in the least measure therein ....

Notes

1. Ezek. 43, 11 Col 2, 5 I Tim. 3, 15

2. Hebr 3, 5, 6

3. Exod 25 40

4. 2 Tim 3 16

5. I Tim 3 15 I Chron 15 13 Ex 20 4 I [T]im 6 13 v 16 Heb 12 27 28 I Cor, 15 22

6. Deut 12 32. Ezek 43 8. I Kings 12. 31 32 33

7. I Kings 12 v: 28 29 Isai 29 13.

8. Col 2 22 23 Acts 15 28

9. Matt 15 9 I Cor 11 23 c 8 34.

10. I Cor 14 26 I Cor 14 40 I Cor 11 14 I Cor 11 16 I Cor 14 12 19 Acts 15 28.

5 The state the members of the militant visible church walking in order, was either before the law, Oeconomical, that is in families [patriarchal]; or under the law, National: or, since the comming of Christ, only congregational: ... Therfore neither national, provincial, nor classical.

6 A Congregational-church, is by the institution of Christ a part of the Militant-visible-church, **consisting of a company of Saints by calling, united into one body, by a holy covenant, for the publick worship of God, & the mutuall edification one of another, in the Fellowship of the Lord Iesus.**

IV
CAN PRIMITIVIST CONGREGATIONALISM SURVIVE IN MODERN SOCIETY?

Evidence abounds in the modern world that the idea of Christian primitivism is as compelling as ever. "Independent" and "nondenominational" congregations have covered the American landscape, filled with people perplexed by the inconsistencies and self-serving agendas of denominational hierarchies. Most such groups offer little to those seeking a return to apostolic authority, though many modern voices are calling for a return to serious Biblical study. Religion scholars and journalists have noted the trend.

1. In a 1993 article exploring the reasons why Protestant churches grow or decline, three prominent professors of religious studies wrote: "In our study, **the best predictor of church participation turned out to be belief—orthodox Christian belief**, and especially the teaching that a person can be saved only through Jesus Christ." [Benton Johnson, Dean R. Hoge and Donald A Luidens, "Mainline Churches: The Real Reason for Decline," *First Things*, March, 1993, pp. 13-18]

2. An article published on March 6, 2003 in the *Christian Science Monitor*, written by Jane Lampman, was provocatively titled: "A Return to Primitive Christianity in a Modern Age." She wrote: "As many seekers have set off in recent years to pursue spirituality outside the bounds of organized religion, another trend has quietly emerged within and across Christian denominations: a return to orthodoxy .... It is perhaps most visible in the least expected place—the liberal mainline churches—where many 'renewal' groups are taking an assertive stance, **seeking to replace what they consider secularized theology and political activism with Biblical authority and evangelical fervor.**"

3. In a book published in 2003, Professor Thomas Oden of Drew University urged a return to "classic Christianity" based on a willingness to "think with the early church about the sacred text." He noted a growing desire to think again about the "Christian tradition as defined by the sacred texts of scripture, the ecumenical councils of the first five centuries, and the teachings of the 'fathers of the first millennium.'" Such a step, he warned, would require a willingness "to say 'no' to false doctrine." Nonetheless, Oden noted, a search for and commitment to authority is a marked trend in the modern religious environment: "There is an avid new interest in setting boundaries fr Christian teaching." [*The Rebirth of Orthodoxy: Signs, of New Life in Christianity* (San Francisco: Harper & Row, 2003)].

In short, there is ample evidence that there is a hunger in modern society for authority, which the apostles offer us in the New Testament, and for community, which is what is provided in New Testament congregations.

V
SUMMARY

1. 1. What can we learn from the New Testament about the organization, work, and worship of first century churches? Is this a good question? If it is, the source of authority is clear and our common sense ability to collect information demands simply that we read and conscientiously go about

trying to follow as closely as possible the pattern we find.

2. The New Testament urges the unity of Christians based on apostolic authority. In particular, the churches were instructed to be uniform in practice. Apostolic directions to the churches were not arbitrary or elective, they were intentional and binding. Thus, the information we glean that tells what New Testament churches were instructed to do, and what they did, provides an apostolic pattern for local churches. The need for uniform practice in the churches (for "catholicity") was a repetitious theme in early Christian writing.

3. The grandeur of the church in God's eternal scheme is a major theme in the Scriptures. Everything that God ordained in the establishment of his "everlasting kingdom" was done by Divine intent. It was presumptuous to ignore God's instructions in those things that foreshadowed the coming of Christ and His church and it would be even more foolish to assume that God did not establish all things precisely as He intended when the churches were ordered by apostolic authority.

4. There is much precedent in history for Christians going about building independent local churches (for practicing congregationalism). The American Puritans provide a recent example. The method they used is instructive. They committed themselves to follow apostolic authority and they sought to pattern themselves after the congregations of the New Testament. These were serious Bible students, who were prepared to give an answer for their every act and belief. That is the common commitment of all Christian primitivists.

5. While Christian primitivism aims to please God and not men, it is nonetheless true that over and over in history the idea of returning to apostolic authority and restating the purity of the early church has been welcomed by those despairing of the shortcomings of institutional religion. The message is as vital as ever at the beginning of the twenty-first century. It is shameful that many who are heirs of the message have come to doubt it, or to tire of it, at a time when many are trying to find a way back to the simplicity of primitive Christianity.

VI

CONCLUSION:
APOSTOLIC AUTHORITY, COMMON SENSE BIBICAL IN-
TERPRETATION, AND CONSTRUCTING NEW TESTAMENT

CHURCHES

The logic of trying to restore Christian communities in modern times, as in all other times, rests on certain assumptions.

PROPOSITION 1: REGARDING APOSTOLIC AUTHORITY

Restorationist, primitivist religious thinking assumes that the Apostles were given specific authority to define doctrine and set in order churches. This authority was perpetuated in the inspired writings of the New Testament.

Lip service is widely given to the **authority of the apostolic teaching**, and to the New Testament, but the depth of that commitment often seems shallow when compared to the intense hunger for the Scriptures that characterized devout Christians in earlier times. Christian primitivism demands that we study the Scriptures diligently, honor their authority absolutely, and seek to conform to every instruction given for the salvation of mankind and the perpetuation of the faith in the church of Jesus Christ.

PROPOSITION 2: REGARDING COMMON SENSE HERMENEUTICS

Restorationist, primitivist religious thinking assumes that human beings through the use of a common sense possessed by all, have the ability to read texts and reach common conclusions about meanings. This empirical, logical type of thinking is the basis for all public (as opposed to private and subjective) human understanding.

Challenging the ability of human beings to understand the Scriptures has been as consistent in Christian history as has been the Biblical injunction to follow them. The study of how we understand in common (hermeneutics) offers insights into the ways that common sense works. The great hermeneutical leaps forward that came with the clarification of inductive reasoning and the scientific method remain useful models, but, in the end, they do little more than describe the inherent human capacity to observe, think about, and test information. The Bible does not teach hermeneutics, it presumes that we will use our capacity to receive instruction, observe examples, and draw sensible conclusions. Common sense is a Biblical assumption.

It is important to remember that most of our disagreements in matters of Biblical interpretation stem not from our inability to draw conclusions about how data should be processed, but by what questions we are trying to answer.

Why are some Biblical examples binding and others not? Why, for instance, is the time of the taking of the Lord's Supper in Acts 20:7 (the first day of the week) considered binding, but not the location (an upper room)? One does not need to do hermeneutical somersaults to answer such a question. There are no legalistic or arbitrary rules that must be applied. The answer is that primitivist Christians though the centuries have read the New Testament and concluded that the apostles intended to bind the time of assembling to eat the Lord's Supper and that they had no intention of binding the place where that was to be done. If one feels strongly compelled to argue the contrary (I am not aware of any serious such discussions in Christian history), the issue could be engaged. But the point of such a discussion would not be hermeneutical (when is an example binding) but rather the pertinence of the question being asked.

PROPOSITION 3: REGARDING LOCAL CHURCHES (CONGREGATIONALISM)

Restorationist, primitivist religious thinking assumes that the practices of local churches in New Testament days rested on apostolic authority and that the ordering of churches was intentionally designed by God to promote uniformity (catholicity) among Christians.

Most scholars agree that the early Christians met in local churches organized with elders and deacons. It is clear that the concept of independent congregations worshipping and working in the ways described in the New Testament has been a live idea throughout Christian history. It is a habit of the human mind to long for the pristine purity of earlier times. How to do it seems clear. One must acknowledge an authority and, applying the common sense given by God, seek to find and test all of the instruction available. If you want to know how to become a Christian (a good question), read the New Testament, write down every piece of information you find (command, example, inference), and go and do what you find. If you want to know how to build a New Testament church (a good question), read the New Testament, write down all the information you can find, and go and do it.

A NEW TESTAMENT LOCAL CHURCH

1. An organization—Phil. 1:1; Acts 14:23; I Tim. 3:1ff; Titus 1:.5ff

2. An assembly—Heb. 10:25; I Cor. 11:15

3. Taught—Acts 20:7; I Cor. 14:15

4. Prayed—Acts 12:5; I Cor. 14:19

5. Sang—Eph. 5:19; Col. 3:16
6. Lord's Supper on 1st Day—Acts 20:7; I Cor. 11:20
7. Gave on the 1st Day—I Cor. 16:1, 2; Acts 2:44-45
8. Had a Common Treasury—Acts 5:1-4
9. Relieved Needy Saints—Acts 4:34-35; 11:29-30; I Cor. 16:1
10. Supported Preaching—II Cor. 11:8; Phil. 4:15-16
11. Disciplined Unruly Members—I Cor. 5:1-5

There is nothing petty or arbitrary about the enterprise of seeking to be primitive Christians in the twenty-first century. Nor is the idea based on an outmoded system of thought that has somehow been discredited by academics in the past fifty years. The idea of building New Testament churches today, grounded in the Scriptures and committed to obedience) can be, and should be, a powerful message in the religious marketplace.

That is what is "inside the box" of Christian primitivism. Consider it well before buying faddish "truths" that look very much like the intellectual rubble of Christian history.

Biographical Sketch

Ed Harrell is a well-known preacher, having conducted hundreds of meetings in churches of Christ throughout the world. In recent years, he has worked extensively with Christians in India. He served as one of the editors of Christianity Magazine for sixteen years. He has spoken on numerous lectureship programs, including the annual lectures at Florida College, Abilene Christian University, and Pepperdine University. He currently serves as an evangelist and elder in the South Jacksonville Church of Christ in Jacksonville, Florida.

Harrell spent fifty years teaching history at East Tennessee State University, the University of Oklahoma, the University of Georgia, the University of Alabama in Birmingham, the University of Arkansas, and Auburn University. In 2005, he retired from Auburn and now holds the title Daniel Breeden Eminent Scholar in the Humanities Emeritus. He received a B.A. degree from David Lipscomb College in 1954 and M.A. and Ph.D. degrees from Vanderbilt University in 1958 and 1962. He has written seven books on American religious history, including *The Churches of Christ in the Twentieth Century: Homer Hailey's Personal*

Journey of Faith (University of Alabama Press, 2000), *All Things Are Possible: The Healing and Charismatic Revivals in Modern America* (Indiana University Press, 1975), *Oral Roberts: An American Life* (Indiana University Press, 1985) and *Pat Robertson: A Personal, Religious, and Political Portrait* (Harper & Row, 1987). He is co-editor of "Minorities in Modern America," a series published by Indiana University Press, and a series entitled "Religion and American Culture" by the University of Alabama Press. He is the author of over fifty articles in scholarly publications. He is co-author of a college-level textbook on American history, *Unto a Good Land: A History of the American People* (Wm. B. Eerdmans Publishers, 2005).

Harrell has won many professional honors and awards. He was a Senior Fulbright Lecturer in Allahabad, India and has twice been a Resident Fellow of the Institute for Ecumenical and Cultural Research, St. John's Abbey, Collegeville, Minnesota. In 1995 Harrell completed a two-year Distinguished Fulbright appointment as Director of the American Studies Research Centre in Hyderabad, India. In that position he coordinated more than 50 international conferences in Asia and Africa on American society and received an ambassadorial citation for "his outstanding contributions to strengthening scholarly understanding of the United States in India." In 2003 he was honored in a special session at the meeting of the American Academy of Religion and in 2005 he received a similar honor at the meeting of the American Church History Society.

Recognized as an authority on religion and politics in America, Harrell has appeared on many network television news programs such as Good Morning America, Nightline, CBS News, NBC News, Fox News, and CNN News, and has been quoted in hundreds of American and international publications including *Time, Newsweek, U.S. News & World Report, The Economist, The Nation,* the New York *Times,* and the London *Times.*

[Personal contact info excluded]

INTERVIEWS

1.   Harrell, Jr., David Edwin. . January 17, 2017

2.   Harrell, Jr., David Edwin. . May 20, 2019

3.   Harrell, Deedee. . November 16, 2020

4.   Lyerley, Pokey. . November 24, 2020

5.   Dowdy, Lynn Warren. . December 28, 2020

6.   Dowdy, Glenn. . December 28, 2020

7.   Lewis, Brent. . February 26, 2021

8.   Hall, Sewell. . May 25, 2021

9.   Wolfgang, Steve. . May 28, 2021

10.   Earnhart, Paul. . May 28, 2021

11.   Wolfgang, Bette, . May 28, 2021

12.   Owen, Bob. . June 25, 2021

13.   Wolfgang, Steve, . July 1, 2021

14.   Hall, Bill. . July 5, 2021

15.   Billingsley, Scott. . July 19, 2021

16.   Bowman, Dee. . July 25, 2021

17.   Halbrook, Ron. . October 17, 2022

18.   Willis, Mike. . October 17, 2022

19.   Wolfgang, Steve, . October 17, 2022

20.   Benson, V. J. . January 22, 2023

21.   Gideon, Paul. . January 23, 2023

22.   Calton, Bill. . November 12, 2023

23.   Adams, Wilson. . June 20, 2024

24.   Adams, Wilson. . June 25, 2024

25.   Holder, David. . July 28, 2024

BIBLIOGRAPHY

Adams, Connie. "Appraising 'A Reappraisal and Warning.'" *Searching the Scriptures* 21 (June 1980): 123-125.

—————. "Warnings Assessed—Again." *Searching the Scriptures* 21 (September 1, 1980): 207.

—————. "Watch Which Dogs?" *Guardian of Truth* (February 6, 1997): 67-68.

—————. "The Harrell Booklet on the Bounds of Christian Unity." *Truth Magazine* 42.7 (April 2, 1998): 195-196.

—————. "Introduction. In Understanding the Controversy." In *Understanding the Controversy Over Divorce-Remarriage*, Romans 14, and Fellowship. Bowling Green: *Guardian of Truth*, 1998.

—————. "Editorial Left-overs." *Truth Magazine* 44.17 (September 7, 2000): 3.

—————. "Harsh Treatment at Florida College." *Truth Magazine* 45.11 (June 7, 2001): 8.

Adams, James W. "False Conclusions from Just Principles." *Gospel Guardian* (June 1, 1976): 220-221.

—————. "False Conclusions from Just Premises." *Gospel Guardian* (June 1, 1976): 220-221.

—————. "Speak for Yourself John." *Gospel Guardian* (January, 15, 1978), 28-29.

—————. "Johnny-Come-Lately-Sommerites." *Gospel Guardian* (February 1, 1978): 52-53.

—————. "Every Way of Man is Right In His Own Eyes." *Gospel Guardian* 30.10 (May 15, 1978): 220-221.

—————. "Splendid Murder." *The Apostolic Messenger* (July

1989): 3.

Adams, Wilson. "Email to editors of Christianity Magazine and Guardian of Truth, January 14, 1999." Series 2.E.1. David Edwin Harrell, Jr. Papers, 1923-2017. Center for Restoration Studies MS #467. Abilene Christian University Special Collections and Archives. Brown Library.

Ainslie, Peter. *If Not A United Church, What?* New York: Fleming H. Revell, 1920.

Allen, Dennis G. and Gary Fisher, eds. *Is It Lawful? A Comprehensive Study of Divorce.* Auburn, MI: Allan and Fisher, 1989.

Allen, Roland. *Missionary Methods: St. Paul's or Ours?* London: R. Scott, 1912.

Auburn University. "UAB Historian Harrell Named Breeden Scholar," *AU Report* 23.13 (April 19, 1990), 1.

――――――. "Americanists Course Rotation." Series II.G.12. David Edwin Harrell, Jr. Papers, 1923-2017. Center for Restoration Studies MS #467. Abilene Christian University Special Collections and Archives. Brown Library.

Baker, William R., ed. *Evangelicalism & The Stone-Campbell Movement.* Abilene: ACU Press, 2006.

Balbag, Simeon A. "Letter to Brother Ed Harrell, June 10, 1981." Series 2.I.1. David Edwin Harrell, Jr. Papers, 1923-2017. Center for Restoration Studies MS #467. Abilene Christian University Special Collections and Archives. Brown Library.

Bales, James D. Soils and Seeds of Sectarianism. Kansas City: Old Paths Book Club, 1947.

――――――. Not Under Bondage (Searcy: J.D. Bales, 1979).

Baxter, Batsell Barrett. Questions and Issues of the Day in the Light of the Scriptures. Nashville, 1963.

Belknap, Jeff. "An Examination of Ron Halbrook's Charts." Last updated January 26, 2006. Last accessed August 30, 2024. https://www.mentaldivorce.com/mdrstudies/AnEximinationOfRonHalbrooksCharts.htm.

──────. "Ron Halbrook's Letter to J. T. Smith in 1993." Last updated January 26, 2006. Last Accessed November 17, 2024. https://www.mentaldivorce.com/mdrstudies/RonHalbrooksLetterToJTSmithIn1993Examined.htm.

Benson, V. J. "A Discussion between David Edwin Harrell Jr. and Jim E. Waldron, on November 19, 2009 at Christians Workers Center, Bangaluru, India." 4 DVD Set. Produced by V. J. Benson. Series II.C.36. David Edwin Harrell, Jr. Papers, 1923-2017. Center for Restoration Studies MS #467. Abilene Christian University Special Collections and Archives. Brown Library.

Birdwell, Jr. O.C. "2001 Florida College Lectures." *Truth Magazine* 45.11 (June 7, 2001): 6.

Blumhofer, Edith L. *Restoring the Faith: The Assemblies of God, Pentecostalism, and American Culture.* Champaign, IL: University of Illinois Press, 1993.

Boles, H. Leo. "Voices from the Past: Church Cooperation." *Truth Magazine* 1.3 (December 1956): 8-9.

Bonner, David. "Biggest Departure Now!!" *Torch* 24.12 (December 1989): 5-7.

Bowman, Dee. "What it Means to Love God," *The Bible Standard* 1.1 (November 5, 1972): 1-2.

──────. "Going too far (The Other Way)." *The Bible Standard* 1.5 (January 5, 1973): 57-58.

──────. "Wrong Tendencies and Broadway's Out-of-the-church Religion." *The Bible Standard* 1.12 (April 20, 1973):

138-40.

————. Personal journal entry, dated Jan 22, 1981.

————. Personal journal entry, dated July 19, 1983.

Bozeman, Theodore Dwight. "Biblical Primitivism: An Approach to New England Puritanism," in *The American Quest for the Primitive Church*. Edited by Richard T. Hughes. Urbana: University of Chicago Press, 1988.

————. *To Live Ancient Lives: The Primitivist Dimension in Puritanism*. Chapel Hill: University of North Carolina Press, 1988.

Brace. Shawn. "Why Critical Realism?" Last accessed July 2, 2024. https://shawnbrace.substack.com/p/why-critical-realism.

Campbell, J. Herman."When Unity Ceases—No. 3," *Gospel Guardian* 1.21 (September 29, 1949): 5.

Carlisle, Roy M. "Letter to Patricia Newforth about Harrell project on Oral Roberts, December 10, 1985." Series I.N.28. David Edwin Harrell, Jr. Papers, 1923-2017. Center for Restoration Studies MS #467. Abilene Christian University Special Collections and Archives. Brown Library.

Casey, Michael W. *Saddlebags, City Streets, and Cyberspace: A History of Preaching in the Churches of Christ*. Abilene: ACU Press, 1995.

————. *The Battle over Hermeneutics in the Stone-Campbell Movement, 1800-1870*. Lewiston: The Edwin Mellen Press, 1998.

Cavender, Bill. "Donnie Rader's Resignation." Email dated October 03, 2005. Last accessed August 4, 2024. https://www.mentaldivorce.com/mdrstudies/DonniesResignation.htm.

Cedar Park Church of Christ. *Toward a Better Understanding: The Burnet Meeting, February 2000*. Last modified July

17, 2002. Accessed July 26 2024. Internet Archive, https://web.archive.org/web/20020609130628/http://www.cedarparkchurchofchrist.org/tabu/index.html.

Chappelear, Floyd. *Sentry Magazine* 1.1 (January 31, 1974): 3-4.

—————. "Editorial." *Sentry Magazine* 1.3 (March 31, 1975): 2-3.

—————. "Editorial." *Sentry Magazine* 1.7 (July 31, 1975): 2-3.

—————. "Florida College, another view." *Sentry Magazine* 1.9-10 (Sep-Oct 1975): 10-12.

Clark, Elmer T. *The Small Sects in America*. Nashville: Abingdon, 1965.

Cochran, Benton K. "Letter to Ed and Deedee Harrell, October 13, 2009." Series 2.C.37. David Edwin Harrell, Jr. Papers, 1923-2017. Center for Restoration Studies MS #467. Abilene Christian University Special Collections and Archives. Brown Library.

Cogdill, Roy E. "The Called out Body." In *The New Testament Church*. Lufkin: Gospel Guardian, 1959.

Cook, Paul. "Letter to Ed Harrell, September 25, 2008." Series 2.A.47. David Edwin Harrell, Jr. Papers, 1923-2017. Center for Restoration Studies MS #467. Abilene Christian University Special Collections and Archives. Brown Library.

Cope, James R. "The Preceptor." *The Preceptor* 1.1 (November 1951): 2-3.

—————. "Consistency and Character." *The Preceptor* 1.2 (December 1951): 4.

—————. "Majorities and Manners." *The Preceptor* 1.4 (February 1952): 4-5.

—————. "The Church and Community Agencies." *The*

Preceptor 1.5 (March 1952): 5.

——————. "The Problem of Institutionalism (No.1)." *The Preceptor* 2.6 (April 1953): 4-5.

——————. "The Problem of Institutionalism (No.6)." *The Preceptor* 2.10 (August 1953): 8-9.

——————. *Where Is the Scripture?* Temple Terrace, FL, 1964.

Cox, Brady Kal, "Postwar Churches of Christ Mission Work: The Philippines as a Case Study" (2018). Digital Commons @ ACU. *Electronic Theses and Dissertations*, Paper 78. https://digitalcommons.acu.edu/etd/78.

Cox, Harvey. "All Things Are Possible." *New York Times Book Review* (February 22, 1976): 2.

——————. "Proposal for a Biography of Ian Paisley, [1987]." Series I.N.2. David Edwin Harrell, Jr. Papers, 1923-2017. Center for Restoration Studies MS #467. Abilene Christian University Special Collections and Archives. Brown Library.

Craig, R. L. "Everyone is Right?" *The Bible Standard* 1.6 (January 20, 1972): 61-62, 66.

Crossan, John Dominic. *Semeia 4: Paul Ricoeur on Biblical Hermeneutics*. Missoula: Society of Biblical Literature, 1975.

Crossville Church of Christ. "Waldron Missions." Online at https://www.waldronmissions.org/index.htm.

Curry, Jr., Melvin D. "Being a Sojourner and Pilgrim in this World." *Christianity Magazine* (May 1998): 12.

——————. "Follow after Things Which Make Peace," Truth Magazine (January 4, 1979): 28–30. Last Accessed online December 12, 2024, https://www.truthmagazine.com/archives/volume23/TM023010.html."

Dark, Harris J. "Congregational Independence." *The Preceptor* 1.2 (December 1951): 22-23

Davison, Fred, "Notice of Appointment for the Academic Year." Series 1.D.1. David Edwin Harrell, Jr. Papers, 1923-2017. Center for Restoration Studies MS #467. Abilene Christian University Special Collections and Archives. Brown Library.

Dawson, Samuel G. "Fellowship on Marriage, Divorce, & Remarriage." Last Accessed September 10, 2023. https://www.samuelgdawson.com/uploads/1/1/5/5/115526689/fellowship_on_mdr.pdf.

Diestelkamp, Leslie. "Flee From It." Gospel Guardian 1.21 (September 29, 1949): 3.

Donovon, Timothy. "Letter to David E. Harrell, February 4, 1981," Series I.F.10. David Edwin Harrell, Jr. Papers, 1923-2017. Center for Restoration Studies MS #467. Abilene Christian University Special Collections and Archives. Brown Library.

Dossett, Burgin. "Confirmation of 1966-67 employment." Series 1.B.2, David Edwin Harrell, Jr. Papers, 1923-2017. Center for Restoration Studies MS #467. Abilene Christian University Special Collections and Archives. Brown Library.

Dowdy, Harold. "Dr. David Edwin Harrell, Sr." *Christianity Magazine* 7.2 (February 1990): 49.

Dowdy, Harold. *Shooting Creek Parables*. Connie Lewis Hill, 2018.

Duffield, Jr., Ollie. "The Outlet of the Heart." *Truth Magazine* 1.6 (March 1957): 14-15.

Earnhart, Paul. "Watch Them Dogs." *Christianity Magazine* 13.7 (July 1996): 10.

————."When Christians Disagree." Last updated April 2022. Last Accessed November 18, 2024. https://

www.cedarparkchurchofchrist.org/resources/
articles/2022/04/04/when-christians-disagree.

Echols, Bill. "Humility." *Truth Magazine* 2.2 (May 1958): 20-21, 23.

Ed Harrell Memorial. "Ed Harrell Online Memorial Service- March 20, 2021." YouTube Video, 2:06. March 30, 2021. https://www. youtube.com/watch?app=desktop&v=cXJXDvpzLM4.

Ellis, Kent. "A Generation that Knew Not." *The Bible Standard* 1.4 (December 20, 1972): 39-4.

Ferris, Ray. "What is 'Autonomy'?" *Truth Magazine* 1.5 (February 1957): 6-7, 19.

Flynt, Wayne. "Forward." In *Recovering the Margins of American Religious History*. Edited by B. Dwain Waldrep and Scott Billingsley. Tuscaloosa: University of Alabama Press, 2010.

—————. "David Edwin Harrell Jr.: Restoration Activist, Christian Globalist, Social Historian, Rigorous Mentor." In Recovering the Margins of American Religious History. Edited by B. Dwain Waldrep & Scott Billingsley. Tuscaloosa: University of Alabama Press, 2010.

Foster, Douglas. *Will the Cycle be Unbroken?* Abilene: ACU Press, 1994.

Frazier, Kenneth. "As the Oracles of God." *Sentry Magazine* 1.7 (July 31, 1975): 6.

Gardner, Terry J. *The Original Gospel Guardian (1935-1936) and The Bible Banner (1938-1949) Indexed by Author and Subject Complied by Terry J. Gardner with A Biographical Sketch of the Life of Cled E. Wallace.* Indianapolis, Indiana: Terry Gardner, 1994.

Garrison, Winfred E. *Religion Follows the Frontier*. New York: Harper & Brothers, 1931.

Gerth, H. H. and C. Wright Mills. *From Max Weber: Essays in*

Sociology. New York: Oxford, 1946.

Givens, Donald R. "Slay the Sinful Self." *The Bible Standard* 1.2 (November 20, 1972): 16.

──────. "Putting Self in God's Place." *The Bible Standard* 1.5 (January 5, 1973): 52.

Goff, James R. "Elijah's Never-Failing Cruse of Oil: David Harrell and the Historiography of American's Pentecostals." In *Recovering the Margins of American Religious History*. Edited by B. Dwain Waldrep and Scott Billingsley. Tuscaloosa: University of Alabama Press, 2010.

Gospel Advocate. "Minister Wanted" Advertisement. *Gospel Advocate*, 137.5 (May, 1995): 60.

Greer, Keith M. "Quarreling Brethren: Discouragement to a Young Preacher." *Truth Magazine*, 41.3 (Dec. 4, 1997): 21-22.

──────. "Romans 14—Where Are We Heading?" Last accessed September 13, 2024. https://www.knollwoodchurch.org/yr2001/h01_heading.html.

Gundry, Robert H. *Jesus and the Word according to John the Sectarian*. Grand Rapids: Eerdmans, 2002.

Haile, Tim. "A Review of Tom Roberts' Book: 'The Church is the Pillar and Ground of Truth' (1 Timothy 3:15)." Last accessed August 21, 2024. https://www.biblebanner.com/articles/general/roberts.htm.

Hailey, Homer. "Dependent Children." *Gospel Guardian* 1.28 (November 17, 1949): 5.

──────. "The Silver Thermometer." *The Preceptor* 1.2 (December 1951): 8-9.

──────. "Attitudes." *The Preceptor* 1.8 (June 1952): 10.

──────. "Italy and Incense." *The Preceptor* 2.12 (October

1953): 2.

—————. "Dear Brother Brashears." Letter dated January 5, 1957. Series II.A.1, David Edwin Harrell, Jr. Papers, 1923-2017. Center for Restoration Studies MS #467. Abilene Christian University Special Collections and Archives. Brown Library.

—————. "Sermon at El Cajon, CA, Feb 25. 1988—A.M. Session." Series 2.D.1. David Edwin Harrell, Jr. Papers, 1923-2017. Center for Restoration Studies MS #467. Abilene Christian University Special Collections and Archives. Brown Library.

—————. "Letter to Ron Halbrook, May 4, 1988." Box 28. David Edwin Harrell Jr. Papers 1923-2017. Center for Restoration Studies MS #467. Abilene Christian University Special Collections and Archives. Brown Library.

—————. "Letter to Ed Harrell, February 28, 1991." Series 2.A.28. David Edwin Harrell, Jr. Papers. 1923-2017. Center for Restoration Studies MS #467. Abilene Christian University Special Collections and Archives. Brown Library.

Hafley, Larry Ray. "The Church vs Denominationalism." *The Bible Standard* 1.2 (November 20, 1972): 17.

Halbrook, Ron. "Letter to Homer Hailey, April 15, 1988." Box 28. David Edwin Harrell Jr. Papers 1923-2017. Center for Restoration Studies MS #467. Abilene Christian University Special Collections and Archives. Brown Library.

—————. "To Set the Record Straight: Recent Studies With Homer Halley On Divorce And Remarriage." *Guardian of Truth* 32.22 (November 17, 1988): 689-91.

—————. Trends Pointing Toward a New Apostasy. Bowling Green: *Guardian of Truth*, 2000 (1992).

—————. "Romans 14 Abused to Accommodate False Doctrine."

Guardian of Truth 36.1 (January 2, 1992): 27-32.

————. "The Continuing Battle Over Divorce & Remarriage." *Guardian of Truth* 37.10 (May 20, 1993): 16-19.

————. "Gospel Preaching, Gospel Preachers, Gospel Papers: The Heritage of the Guardian of Truth." *Guardian of Truth* 39.14 (July 20, 1995): 433-436.

————. "Are We Doomed to Divide Over Every Difference on Divorce and Remarriage? (2)" *Guardian of Truth* 40.17 (September 5, 1996): 16-18.

————. Understanding the Controversy Over Divorce-Remarriage, Romans 14, and Fellowship. Bowling Green: *Guardian of Truth*, 1998.

————. "False Teachers: Ron Halbrook's Rebuttal to Bob Owen." *Toward a Better Understanding: The Burnet Meeting, 2000.*" Last modified July 17, 2002. Accessed August 4, 2024.

————. "Why Halbrook Fellowships Smith, Rader, and Other Faithful Men in Spite of Some Differences." *Gospel Truths* 12.4 (April, 2001). Last updated November 1, 2008. https://www.truthmagazine.com/why-halbrook-fellowships-smith-rader-and-other-faithful-men-in-spite-of-some-differences.

Hall, Gardner. "Letter to Ed Harrell, Feb 27, 1991." Series 2.A.28. David Edwin Harrell, Jr. Papers, 1923-2017. Center for Restoration Studies MS #467. Abilene Christian University Special Collections and Archives. Brown Library.

————. *Conviction vs Mercy: Merging the Two to Deal with Modern Spiritual Challenges*. Port Murray, NJ: Mount Bethel Publishing, 2013.

————. "Sewell Hall: A Combination of Convictions and Forbearance." Unpublished Manuscript.

Hall, Sewell. "Email to Ed Harrell and Paul Earnhart, September 4, 2002." Series 2.D.4. David Edwin Harrell, Jr. Papers, 1923-2017. Center for Restoration Studies MS #467. Abilene Christian University Special Collections and Archives. Brown Library.

——————. Tribute to Ed Harrell. "Ed Harrell Online Memorial Service- March 20, 2021." YouTube Video. March 30, 2021. https://www.youtube.com/watch?app=desktop&v=cXJXDvpzLM4.

Hardeman, N. B. "Spending the Lord's Money." *Gospel Advocate* 92 (May 29, 1947): 372.

——————. "The Banner Boys Become Enraged." *Firm Foundation* 64:43 (October 28, 1947): 1.

Hardin, John C. "Rock Fights, Quarantines, and Confessionals: B. C. Goodpasture, the *Gospel Advocate*, and Keeping Order in Churches of Christ." In *Recovering the Margins of American Religious History*. Edited by B. Dwain Waldrep & Scott Billingsley. Tuscaloosa: University of Alabama Press, 2010.

Harrell, Jr., David Edwin. "Letter to Earle H. West, dated December 20, 1957." David Edwin Harrell, Jr. Papers, 1923-2017. Center for Restoration Studies MS #467. Abilene Christian University Special Collections and Archives, Brown Library.

——————. "Thoughts on Dishonesty." *Gospel Guardian* 11.20 (September 24, 1959): 312-314.

——————. "The Social Gospel." *Florida Christian College Lectures, March 23, 1960. Box 24. David Edwin Harrell, Jr. Papers, 1923-2017*. Center for Restoration Studies MS #467. Abilene Christian University Special Collections and Archives, Brown Library.

—————. "The Social Gospel." *Gospel Guardian* 12.15 (August 18, 1960): 225.

—————. "The Faith versus Intellectualism." 1961 Florida College Lectures. Manuscript copy, 1-7. David Edwin Harrell, Jr. Papers, 1923-2017. Center for Restoration Studies MS #467, Abilene Christian University Special Collections and Archives. Brown Library.

—————. "The Sectional Pattern: The Divisive Impact of Slavery on the Disciples of Christ." *Discipliana* 31 (March, 1961): 26-28.

—————. "The Faith Versus Intellectualism - (I)." *Gospel Guardian* 13.1 (May 4, 1961): 1,12. Available online at https://www.wordsfitlyspoken.insearchoftruth.org/gospel_guardian/v13/v13n1p1,12.html.

—————. "The Faith Versus Intellectualism - (II)." *Gospel Guardian* 13.2 (May 11, 1961): 1, 12.

—————. Letter to Dr. J. Wesley Hoffman, dated May 12, 1961. David Edwin Harrell, Jr. Papers, 1923-2017. Center for Restoration Studies MS #467. Abilene Christian University Special Collections and Archives. Brown Library.

—————. "Brothers Go to War." *World Call* 43 (October, 1961): 6-15.

—————. *Emergence of the "Church of Christ" Denomination*. Lakeland: Harwell/Lewis Publishing Company, 2005 (1962).

—————. "The Fervent Frontier: Religion in the Trans-Appalachian West, 1790-1820." *Watauga Review* 1 (Fall, 1962): 28-36.

—————. "Disciples of Christ Pacifism in Nineteenth Century Tennessee." *Tennessee Historical Quarterly* 21 (September,

1962): 263-274.

—————. "The Sectional Origins of the Churches of Christ." *Journal of Southern History*, 30 (August, 1964): 261-277.

—————. "The Disciples of Christ and the Single Tax Movement," *Encounter* 26 (Winter, 1964): 261- 277.

—————. Letter to Dr. Joseph H. Parks, dated November 17, 1964. David Edwin Harrell, Jr. Papers, 1923-2017. Center for Restoration Studies MS #467, Abilene Christian University Special Collections and Archives. Brown Library.

—————. "The Disciples of Christ and Social Force in Tennessee, 1865-1900." *The East Tennessee Historical Society's Publications*, 38 (1966): 30-47.

—————. "Sin and Sectionalism: A Case Study of Morality in the Nineteenth Century South." *Mississippi Quarterly*, 19 (Fall, 1966): 157-170.

—————. "The Emergence of the Church of Christ Denomination." *Gospel Guardian* 18.40, 41, 42 (February 16, 23 and March 2, 1967).

—————. "The Agrarian Myth and the Disciples of Christ in the Nineteenth Century." *Agricultural History* 41 (April, 1967): 181-192.

—————. "Pardee Butler: Kansas Crusader." *Kansas Historical Quarterly*, 34 (Winter, 1968).

—————. "Some Practical Observations on the Middle of the Road." *Gospel Guardian* 20 (September 5, 1968): 273-278.

—————. "Description of Research Plans to Dean McWhorter, March 25, 1969," Series I.D.1. David Edwin Harrell, Jr. Papers, 1923-2017. Center for Restoration Studies MS #467. Abilene Christian University Special Collections and Archives. Brown Library.

————."James Shannon." *Missouri Historical Review*, 63 (January, 1969): 135-170.

————. "Peculiar People: A Rationale for Conservative Christian Disciples," In *Disciples and the Church Universal*. Authored by Robert O. Fife, David Edwin Harrell, and Ronald E. Osborn. Nashville: Disciples of Christ Historical Society, 1967.

————. "Disciples and the Church Universal—A Postscript." *Discipliana* 27.4 (January 1968): 75-76.

————. *Quest for a Christian America 1800-1865: A Social History of the Disciples of Christ, Volume 1*, reprinted edition. Tuscaloosa: University of Alabama Press, 2003 (196_).

————. *White Sects and Black Men in the Recent South*. Nashville: Vanderbilt, 1971.

————. "Letter to Carl Vipperman, January 5, 1972." Series I.F.1, David Edwin Harrell, Jr. Papers, 1923-2017. Center for Restoration Studies MS #467. Abilene Christian University Special Collections and Archives. Brown Library.

————. "Letter to George E Passey." I.F.3 Series, David Edwin Harrell, Jr. Papers, 1923-2017. Center for Restoration Studies MS #467. Abilene Christian University Special Collections and Archives. Brown Library.

————. "Letter to Dale, August 21, 1972." Series 2.A.10. David Edwin Harrell, Jr. Papers, 1923-2017. Center for Restoration Studies MS #467. Abilene Christian University Special Collections and Archives. Brown Library.

————. "Letter to James R. Cope, September 12, 1972." Series 2.A.10. David Edwin Harrell, Jr. Papers, 1923-2017. Center for Restoration Studies MS #467. Abilene Christian

University Special Collections and Archives. Brown Library.

——. "Letter to Brother Graves, November 1972." Series 2.A.10. David Edwin Harrell, Jr. Papers, 1923-2017. Center for Restoration Studies MS #467. Abilene Christian University Special Collections and Archives. Brown Library.

——. "Letter to Paul Andrews, November 1, 1972." Series 2.A.10. David Edwin Harrell, Jr. Papers, 1923-2017. Center for Restoration Studies MS #467. Abilene Christian University Special Collections and Archives. Brown Library.

——. "Letter to Gene Holder, July 25, 1973." Series 2.A.11. David Edwin Harrell, Jr. Papers, 1923-2017. Center for Restoration Studies MS #467. Abilene Christian University Special Collections and Archives. Brown Library.

——. *Sources of Division in the Disciples of Christ, 1865-1900: A Social History of the Disciples of Christ, Volume 2*, reprinted edition. Tuscaloosa: University of Alabama Press, 2003 (1973).

——. "Three-year research report, March 13, 1973." Series I.F.3. David Edwin Harrell, Jr. Papers, 1923-2017. Center for Restoration Studies MS #467. Abilene Christian University Special Collections and Archives. Brown Library.

——. *All Things are Possible: The Healing & Charismatic Revivals in Modern America*. Bloomington: Indiana University Press, 1975.

——. "Research Report, 1975." Series I.F.4. David Edwin Harrell, Jr. Papers, 1923-2017. Center for Restoration Studies MS #467. Abilene Christian University Special Collections and Archives. Brown Library.

——. "Religion: Symptom and Source of Change in Appalachia." In *Appalachia: Family Traditions in*

Transition. Edited by Emmett M. Essin. Johnson City: East Tennessee State University Research Advisory Council, 1975.

—————. "From Consent to Dissent: The Emergence of the Churches of Christ in America." *Restoration Quarterly* 29 (Second Quarter, 1976): 98-111.

—————. "This Land Is Filled With Sorrow." *Vanguard* 3.10 (March 26, 1977): 240.

—————. "Don't Fish in the Ganges." *Vanguard* 3.18 (September 22, 1977): 419.

—————. "The Significance of Social Force in Disciples History." *Integrity* IX (October, 1977): 67-73.

—————. "Love it or Leave it." *Vanguard* 3.21 (November 11, 1977): 10.

—————. "Emergence of the Church of Christ Denomination Update." *Vanguard* 5.2 (January 25, 1979): 1, 14-15.

—————. "Something Permanent." *Vanguard* 5 (March 8, 1979): 193.

—————. "The American Dutch Reformed Chinese." *Vanguard* 5 (March 22, 1979): 121.

—————. "Disciples Motto." *Vanguard* 5 (June 1, 1979): 106.

—————. "Fundamentalism Again." *Vanguard* 5 (August 1, 1979): 241, 254.

—————. "The People of God—Their Attitude Toward the Social Order." *Vanguard* 5 (September 1, 1979): 327.

—————. "David and Susan and Orville and Debbie." *Vanguard* 5 (November 1, 1979): 339.

—————. "It Might Have Been." *Vanguard* 6 (February 1, 1980): 40.

—————. "Eightfold Path of Buddhism." *Vanguard* 6 (March 1, 1980): 54.

—————. "Letter to Virginia Hamilton, May 16, 1980," Series I.F.6. David Edwin Harrell, Jr. Papers, 1923-2017. Center for Restoration Studies MS #467. Abilene Christian University Special Collections and Archives. Brown Library.

—————. "Pain of Sin." *Vanguard* 6 (June 1, 1980): 137.

—————. "The Philippines—A Warning Repeated." *Searching the Scriptures* 21 (June 1980): 209-211.

—————. "Wrong Attitudes Beget Wrong Practices." *Vanguard* 6 (August 1, 1980): 173.

—————. "The Church and Human Pride." *Vanguard* 6 (Sept 1, 1980): 335.

—————. "Fashions Change—Morals Don't." *Vanguard* 6 (November 1, 1980): 356.

—————. "Javanese Tongue Speaking." *Vanguard* 7 (February 1, 1981): 40.

—————. "On the March." *Vanguard* 7 (March 1, 1981): 63.

—————. "B.C. Goodpasture: Leader of Institutional Thought." In *They Being Dead Yet Speak, Florida College Lectures*. in Edited by Melvin D. Curry. Temple Terrace: Florida College, 1981.

—————. "Introduction," In *Varieties of Southern Evangelicalism*. Edited by David Edwin Harrell, Jr. Macon: Mercer University Press, 1981.

—————. "Letter to Virginia Hamilton, 22 February 1983." Series I.F.9. David Edwin Harrell, Jr. Papers, 1923-2017. Center for Restoration Studies MS #467. Abilene Christian University Special Collections and Archives. Brown Library.

————. *Oral Roberts: An American Life*. San Francisco: Harper & Row, 1985.

————. "Waiting." *Christianity Magazine* 3.4 (April 1986): 32.

————. "Letter to Editor, Newsweek, 444 Madison Avenue, New York, NY. 10022." Typewritten letter dated July 13, 1987. David Edwin Harrell, Jr. Papers, 1923-2017, Center for Restoration Studies MS #467. Abilene Christian University Special Collections and Archives. Brown Library.

————. *Pat Robinson: A Personal, Religious, and Political Portrait*. San Francisco: Harper & Row, 1987.

————. "Epilogue." In *The American Quest for the Primitive Church*. Edited by Richard T. Hughes. Urbana: University of Chicago Press, 1988.

————. "The Evolution of Plain-Folk Religion in the South, 1835-1920." In *Varieties of Southern Religious Experience*. Edited by Samuel S. Hill. Baton Rouge: Louisiana State University Press, 1988.

————. "Homer Hailey: False Teacher?" *Christianity Magazine* 5.11 (November 1988): 326.

————. "The Bounds of Christian Unity (1)" *Christianity Magazine* 6.2 (February 1989): 38.

————. "The Bounds of Christian Unity (2)." *Christianity Magazine* 6.3 (March 1989): 70.

————. "The Bounds of Christian Unity (3)." *Christianity Magazine* 6.4 (April 1989): 134.

————. "Letter to the Breeden Scholar Search Committee, August 3, 1989." Series I.G.2. David Edwin Harrell, Jr. Papers, 1923-2017. Center for Restoration Studies MS #467. Abilene Christian University Special Collections and

Archives. Brown Library.

—————. "The Bounds of Christian Unity (16)." *Christianity Magazine* 7.5 (May 1990): 134.

—————. "A Response by Ed Harrell." *Guardian of Truth* 34.15 (August 2, 1990): 455-456.

—————. "Dear Brent, Dee, Paul, and Sewell." Letter dated August 15, 1990. Series 2.A.27. David Edwin Harrell, Jr. Papers, 1923-2017. Center for Restoration Studies MS #467. Abilene Christian University Special Collections and Archives. Brown Library.

—————. "Letter to the Christianity Magazine Editors, October 30, 1990." Series 2.F.8. David Edwin Harrell, Jr. Papers, 1923-2017. Center for Restoration Studies MS #467. Abilene Christian University Special Collections and Archives. Brown Library.

—————. "Letter to Tom Roberts, November 24, 1990." David Edwin Harrell, Jr. Papers, 1923-2017. Center for Restoration Studies MS #467. Abilene Christian University Special Collections and Archives, Brown Library.

—————. "Ed Harrell's 3rd Response to Dudley Ross Spears." Last accessed August 31, 2024. https://www.biblebanner. com/ga_art/rom14/eh2drs3.htm.

—————. "How My Mind Has Changed/Stayed the Same." Christian Scholar's Conference. 1991.

—————. "Ed Harrell July 1991 CSC" Audiotape, Box 31, Tape 69, David Edwin Harrell, Jr. Papers, 1923-2017. Center for Restoration Studies MS #467. Abilene Christian University Special Collections and Archives, Brown Library.

—————. "Letter to Homer Hailey, February 28, 1991." Series 2.A.29. David Edwin Harrell, Jr. Papers, 1923-2017. Center for Restoration Studies MS #467. Abilene Christian University Special Collections and Archives. Brown Library.

————. "Rear Views: How My Mind Has Changed." *Christianity Magazine* 8.10 (October 1991): 32.

————. "Rear Views." *Christianity Magazine.* 10.5 (June 1993): 32.

————. "Oral Roberts: Religious Media Pioneer." In *Communication and Change in American Religious History.* Edited by Leonard Sweet. Grand Rapids: Eerdmans, 1994.

————. "Pentecost at Prime Time." *Christian History*, 15.1 (January, 1996): 52-54.

————. "Rethinking the History of Churches of Christ: Responses to Richard Hughes." *Restoration Quarterly* 38.1 (1996): 5-10.

————. "Indian Families." *Christianity Magazine* 14:2 (February 1997): 32.

————. "Telugu Idioms." *Christianity Magazine* 14.11 (November 1997): 32.

————. "Bipolar Protestantism: The Straight and Narrow Ways." In *Re-forming the Center: American Protestantism, 1900 to the Present.* Edited by Douglas Jacobsen and William Vance Trollinger, Jr. Grand Rapids: Eerdmans, 1998. "Past, Present, and Perfect." Christianity Magazine 16.1 (January 1999): 6.

————. "Letter to Mike Willis, undated." Series 2.F.8. David Edwin Harrell, Jr. Papers, 1923-2017. Center for Restoration Studies MS #467. Abilene Christian University Special Collections and Archives. Brown Library.

————. "Divorce and Fellowship." Discussion Presentation at

the 1999 Florida College Lectureship, 12-13. Series II.G.38. David Edwin Harrell, Jr. Papers, 1923-2017. Center for Restoration Studies MS #467. Abilene Christian University Special Collections and Archives. Brown Library.

—————. "Going, We Will Come." *Christianity Magazine* 16.12 (December 1999): 32.

—————. *The Churches of Christ in the 20th Century: Homer Hailey's Personal Journey of Faith.* Religion and American Culture. Tuscaloosa: The University of Alabama Press, 2000.

—————. "A Primitivist Life: Embracing Objective Truth and Biblical Primitivism." [Unpublished manuscript]. David Edwin Harrell, Jr. Papers, 1923-2017. Center for Restoration Studies MS #467. Abilene Christian University Special Collections and Archives. Brown Library.

—————. "Peculiar People." [Manuscript Copy]. David Edwin Harrell, Jr. Papers, 1923-2017, Center for Restoration Studies MS #467. Abilene Christian University Special Collections and Archives. Brown Library.

—————. "Recovering the Underside of Southern Religion." In *Autobiographical Reflections on Southern Religious History.* Edited by John B. Boles. Athens, GA: University of Georgia Press, 2001.

—————. "Homer Hailey's Personal Journey of Faith - Part 1." Audio recording. February 20, 2001. https://texashistory. unt.edu/ark:/67531/metapth791513/. Accessed August 27, 2024. University of North Texas Libraries. The Portal to Texas History. https://texashistory.unt.edu. Crediting Abilene Christian University Library."Homer Hailey's Personal Journey of Faith - Part 3." Audio recording, February 20, 2001. https://texashistory.unt.edu/ark:/67531/ metapth792899/m1/. accessed August 26, 2024. University of North Texas Libraries. The Portal to Texas History. https://texashistory.unt.edu. Crediting Abilene Christian University Library.

—————. "Letter to Tommy and Wicky Poarch, March 3, 2001." Series 2.A.38. David Edwin Harrell, Jr. Papers, 1923-2017, Center for Restoration Studies MS #467, Abilene Christian University Special Collections and Archives, Brown Library.

—————. "Healers and Televangelists After World War 11." In *The Century of the Holy Spirit*. Edited by Vinson Synan. Nashville: Thomas Nelson, 2001.

—————. "Taped Sermon on Nehemiah 8, From Lessons from Restoration History, Kirkland WA May 13-14, 2005." Series 3.31.76. David Edwin Harrell, Jr. Papers, 1923-2017. Center for Restoration Studies MS #467. Abilene Christian University Special Collections and Archives. Brown Library.

—————. "Letter to Berry Kercheville, August 24, 2006." Series 2.A.44. David Edwin Harrell, Jr. Papers, 1923-2017. Center for Restoration Studies MS #467. Abilene Christian University Special Collections and Archives. Brown Library.

—————. *Christian Primitivism in the Twenty-first Century: Thinking "Inside the Box" About Restoring New Testament Christianity*. Lakeland: Harrell/Lewis Publishing, 2007.

—————. *Reviewing the Harrell—Waldron Debate*. Hyderabad: V. J. Benson, no date [2009].

—————. "Talk to Grandkids." Digital audio recording. July 2012. Recording in possession of author.

—————. "The Price of Sin: 'By His Wounds Ye Are Healed.'" In *Of First Importance: He Died and Was Buried—Studies in the Crucifixion of Jesus*. Florida College Annual Lectures Book. Temple Terrace, FL: Florida College Press, 2012.

———. "Eulogy for Harold Glenn Dowdy." August 3, 2015. David Edwin Harrell, Jr. Papers, 1923-2017. Center for Restoration Studies MS #467. Abilene Christian University Special Collections and Archives, Brown Library.

Harrell Jr., David Edwin and Edwin S. Gaustad, et. al. *Unto a Good Land: A History of the American People*. Grand Rapids: Eerdmans, 2005.

Harrell Jr, David Edwin and Tommy Poarch. "The Philippines—A Reappraisal and A Warning." *Searching the Scriptures* 21 (June 1980): 125-128.

Harrell, Edward Jerome. History of The Harrell Family. Unpublished manuscript, n.d.

Hatch, Nathan O. *The Democratization of American Christianity*. New Haven: Yale, 1989.

Henkels, Wicky. "Letter to March Pitzer, January 6, 2000." Series 2.G.12, I.F.3. David Edwin Harrell, Jr. Papers, 1923-2017. Center for Restoration Studies MS #467. Abilene Christian University Special Collections and Archives. Brown Library.

Hicks, John Mark. "Stone-Campbell Hermeneutics VI—Appreciation and Critique." Personal Blog, June 1, 2008. Online at http://johnmarkhicks.wordpress.com/2008/06/01/stone-campbell-hermeneutics-vi-appreciation-and-critique/.

Hill, Samuel S. "David Edwin Harrell Jr. American Religious Historian." In *Recovering the Margins of American Religious History*. Edited by B. Dwain Waldrep and Scott Billingsley. Tuscaloosa: University of Alabama Press, 2010.

Hooper, Robert E. *A Distinct People: A History of the Churches of Christ in the Twentieth Century*. West Monroe: Louisiana: Howard Publishing, 1993.

Hooper, Robert E., Jim Turner, and Willard Collins. *The People*

Person. Nashville: 20th Century Christian, 1986.

Hughes, Richard. *Reviving the Ancient Faith: The Story of Churches of Christ in America*. Grand Rapids: Eerdmans, 1988.

—————. "David Edwin Harrell, Jr. and the History of the Stone-Campbell Tradition." In *Recovering the Margins of American Religious History*. Edited by B. Dwain Waldrep and Scott Billingsley. Tuscaloosa: University of Alabama Press, 2010.

—————. *Myths America Lives By: White Supremacy and the Stories That Give Us Meaning*. Champaign, Ill.: University of Illinois Press, 2018.

Hughes, Richard and Leonard C. Allen. *Illusions of Innocence: Protestant Primitivism in America, 1630-1875*. Chicago: University of Chicago, 1988.

Hughes, Richard T. and James L Gorman. *Reviving the Ancient Faith: The Story of Churches of Christ in America*. 3rd ed. Grand Rapids: Eerdmans, 2024.

Humble, Bill. "Restoration and Reaction." *The Preceptor* 2.10 (August 1953): 6-7.

Jacksonville Journal. "Germany Surrenders Unconditionally," *Jacksonville Journal* 58.202, May 7, 1945.

Jacobsen, Douglas and William Vance Trollinger, Jr., eds. *Re-forming the Center: American Protestantism, 1900 to the Present*. Grand Rapids: Eerdmans, 1998.

Jenkins, Ferrell. "The 'Days' of Genesis 1." Florida College Lectures. February 8, 2000. Last accessed August 4, 2024. https://bibleworld.com/daysgen1.pdf.

Jenkins, Jesse G. "Romans 14." *Toward a Better Understanding: The Burnet Meeting, February 2000*. Last Accessed August 8, 2024. https://web.archive.org/web/20020718003231/http://

www.cedarparkchurchofchrist.org/tabu/romans_jenkins. htm.

Jenkins, Philip. *The Next Christendom: The Coming of Global Christianity*. London: Oxford, 2011.

Kimbrough, Earl. "Landmarks of the Lord's Church (No. 3)." *Truth Magazine* 2.10 (July 1958): 21-23.

Kingry, Jeffrey. "Know When to Drop a Subscription." *Sentry Magazine* 1.1 (January 31, 1974): 3-4.

————. "Is Florida College a Seminary?" *Sentry Magazine* 1.9-10 (Sep-Oct 1975): 5-8.

Lambert, C. O. "The Problem of Organized Cooperation." *Gospel Guardian* 2.3 (Mar-Apr 1936): 32-33.

Lard, Moses. "Pioneer Preaching in the West." *Apostolic Times* 3 (February 1872): 346.

Lewis, John T. "Bible Colleges As I See Them." *Gospel Guardian* 2.4 (May 1936): 4.

Linn, Eldridge B. "Let Him Deny Himself." *Gospel Guardian* 1.34 (January 5, 1950): 3.

Lipscomb College, "Winner of the Prater Greek Medal" Lipscomb New Bureau Release, Nashville Tennessee, June 10, 1954.

Little, Wallace H. "'The Philippines—A Reappraisal and a Warning'— My Reply." *Searching the Scriptures* 21 (September 1, 1980): 211-215.

Locke, F. F. "Do Justly, Love Mercy, Walk Humbly." *Searching the Scriptures* 11.6 (June 1961): 7-8.

Marquis Who's Who. *Who's Who in America, 1990-1991*. Wilmette: Marquis Who's Who, 1990.

Martin, Don. "'Is Fellowship a 'Brotherhood' Issue?' - a Review." Last Accessed August 10, 2024. https://www.bibletruths.

net/Archives/BTAR116.htm.Harrell Jr., "The Bounds of Christian Unity (2)." *Christianity Magazine* (March 1989): 70.

—————. "Who is a False Teacher?" [2000] Last accessed July 29, 2024. https://www.bibletruths.net/Archives/BTAR108. htm.

—————. "An Exchange on Unity in Diversity." Accessed August 4, 2024. https://www.bibletruths.net/Archives/BTAR210. htm.

—————. "A Commendable Resignation." Last updated Thursday, January 26, 2006. Last accessed August 4, 2024. https://www.mentaldivorce.com/mdrstudies/ ACommendableResignation-DMartin.htm.

—————. "Mike Willis Responds!" Last accessed August 4, 2024. https://www.bibletruths.net/Archives/BTAR348.htm.

—————. "Exchange started by Pat Donahue with Mike Willis." Page updated January 26, 2006. Last Accessed August 4, 2024. https://www.mentaldivorce.com/mdrstudies/ ExchangeStartedByPatDonahueWithMikeWillis.htm.

Mayberry, Mark. "FC Lecture 2001." Created October 31, 2008. Last accessed August 20, 2024. https://www.truthmagazine. com/fc-lecture-2001.

—————. "The Changing Face of Denominationalism." *Truth Magazine* 67.2 (February 2023): 4-5.

—————. "Editorial: Progressive Perverseness." *Truth Magazine* 68.2 (February, 2024): 3-13.

Marty, Martin E. "Primitivism and Modernization: Assessing the Relationship." In *The Primitive Church in the Modern World*. Edited by Richard T. Hughes. Urbana: University of Illinois, 1995.

Mayo, Nathan. "The seventh census of the state of Florida, 1945: Taken in accordance with the provisions of chapter 22515 Laws of Florida, Act of Legislature of 1945." (1946), *Florida Heritage* 79. https://stars.library.ucf.edu/floridaheritage/79.

McLoughlin, William. *Revivals, Awakenings, and Reform.* Chicago: University of Chicago Press, 1980.

Meyers, Robert. *Voices of Concern; Critical Studies in Church of Christism.* Mission Messenger, 1966.

Miller, James P. "Changing with the Times." *Searching the Scriptures* 1.7 (July 1960): 4.

Montgomery, Nancy. "Who's Who, Abilene Christian High School." *The Periscope* (November 1, 1946).

Needham, James P. *A Review of Batsell Barrett Baxter's Tract: "May the Church Scripturally Support a College?"* Orlando, FL: Truth Magazine Bookstore [reprint], 1970.

——————. "Don't Criticize Me Until You've Walked a Mile in My Shoes." *Torch* 24.12 (December 1989): 8-10.

Newbigin, Lesslie. *Proper Confidence: Faith, Doubt, and Certainty in Christian Discipleship.* Grand Rapids: Eerdmans, 1995.

Niebuhr, H. Richard. *The Social Sources of Denominationalism.* New York: Holt, 1929.

Norred, C. A. "A Homily on Benevolences." *Gospel Guardian* 2.3 (Mar/Apr 1936): 39.

Ogden, Art. "The Fellowship of Churches." *Gospel Truths Magazine* (February 1991): 13-14.

O'Neal, Thomas G. "Tom O'Neal's Letters Exposing Jeff Belknap's Binding of MDR Scruples." Last accessed August 30, 2024. https://www.biblebanner.com/articles/mdr/tgon2jb1.htm.

Otey, W. W. "From the Written Record—Brother Brewer's Memory."

Gospel Guardian 5.34 (January 7, 1954): 11.

──────. "What Will You Leave?" *Gospel Guardian* 1.37 (January 26, 1950): 1.

Owen, Bob. "We Differ, Can We Fellowship." PM Sermon, and Q&A Period. Concord, NC. February 19, 1995. https://soundteaching.org/fellowship/owen3.htm.

──────. "Local Church and Salvation." Bible class at Concord, NC. February 19, 1995. Last accessed August 7, 2024. https://soundteaching.org/fellowship/owen2.htm.

──────. "Local Congregational Fellowship." Sermon at Temple Terrace Church of Christ, Temple Terrace, FL. March 28, 1996. Last accessed August 7. 2024. https://soundteaching.org/fellowship/owen4.htm.

──────. "False Teaching and False Teachers." *Toward a Better Understanding: The Burnet Meeting, February 2000*. Last modified July 17, 2002. Accessed July 27, 2024. https://web.archive.org/web/20020717114053/http://www.cedarparkchurchofchrist.org/tabu/false_owen.htm.

──────. "False Teachers: Bob Owen's Rebuttal to Ron Halbrook." *Toward a Better Understanding: The Burnet Meeting, February 2000*. Last modified July 17, 2002. Last accessed July 26, 2024. https://web.archive.org/web/20020717114053/http://www.cedarparkchurchofchrist.org/tabu/false_owen.htm.

Owen, George Earle. "Disciples and the Universal Church—A Review." *Discipliana* 27.3 (October, 1967): 50-53.

Patton, Don. "Romans 14—Fellowship." Longview, TX. April 12, 1990. Last accessed July 27, 2024. https://soundteaching.org/fellowship/patton2.htm.

──────. "Exegesis of Romans 14." Preachers' Study - Grand

Prairie, TX (November 10, 1994). Last accessed August 7, 2024. https://soundteaching.org/fellowship/patton5.htm.

Patton, Marshall E. "Divorce and Remarriage." *Searching the Scriptures* (January 1977): 249-51.

Perry, Ralph Barton. *Puritanism and Democracy.* New York: *Vanguard* Press, 1944.

Phillips, H. E. "Editorial." *Searching the Scriptures* 11.10 (Oct 1961), 2.

Pope, Kyle. "A Conscience without Offense toward God and Man" *Focus Online* (February 4, 2014): https://focusmagazine. org/a-conscience-without-offense-toward-god-and-man. php.

Progressive Primitivist, "The Dallas Meeting | 1990 | Uniting Institutional & Non-Institutional Churches of Christ | Day 1." YouTube video. Last accessed September 9, 2024. https://www.youtube.com/watch?v=pcOTk15eGaA.

—————. "Divorce & Remarriage and Fellowship Discussion | Florida College 1991 | Dr. Ed Harrell & Mike Willis." Last Accessed August 4, 2024. https://www.youtube.com/ watch?v=x3rF_-mLM6g.

Rader, Donnie V. "What God Has Joined Together—Jesus on Marriage." Lecture given at Florida College (February 8, 2001). Last updated October 31, 2008, last accessed August 4, 2024, https://www.truthmagazine.com/what-god-has-joined-together-jesus-on-marriage.

Ramsey, Johnny. "Plain Preaching." *Truth Magazine* 1.9 (June 1956): 16-17.

Ricoeur, Paul. *Symbolism of Evil.* Boston: Beacon Press, 1967.

Roberts, J.W. "What is the Social Gospel?" *Gospel Advocate* 101.27 (July 2, 1959): 419-420.

Roberts, Russ and Tom Kinzel. *India 2023 Trip Report*. January 3-21, 2023.

Roberts, Tom. "Romans 14: Satan's Trojan Horse for Fellowship With Error." *Guardian of Truth* 39.4 (February 16, 1995): 14-17.

—————. "Response to Don Patton." *Guardian of Truth*, 39.4 (February 16, 1995): 23-27.

—————. "Liberty in Christ: An Analytical Exegesis of Romans 14:1 - 15:7." Last Accessed Sept 13, 2024. https://soundteaching.org/fellowship/fellowship7.htm.

—————. "Speaking Smooth Things About ... Romans 14 and Fellowship." *Truth Magazine* 42 (1998). https://www.truthmagazine.com/speaking-smooth-things-about-romans-14-and-fellowship.

—————. "Fellowship," *Toward a Better Understanding: The Burnet Meeting, February 2000*. Last Accessed August 8, 2024. Internet Archive. https://web.archive.org/web/20020717111339/http://www.cedarparkchurchofchrist.org/tabu/fellow_ha.htm.

—————. "Fellowship: Tom Roberts Rebuttal to Harry Pickup, Jr.," *Toward a Better Understanding: The Burnet Meeting, February 2000*. Last Accessed August 8, 2024. http://www.cedarparkchurchofchrist.org/tabu/fellow_roberts_rebuttal.htm.

—————. "The Church is The Pillar and Ground of Truth." In *Great Truths from Historic Controversies: Truth Magazine Annual Lectures, June 22-25, 2009*. Edited by Mike Willis. Bowling Green, KY: Guardian of Truth Foundation, 2009.

Robertson, Thomas Allen. "The Christian Church—How They Got That Way." *Gospel Guardian* 1.1. (May 5, 1949): 5.

Russell, Bertrand. *The History of Western Philosophy*. New York: Simon and Schuster, 1945.

Schweiger, Beth Barton. "Conclusion: The Very Civil Convictions of Ed Harrell." In *Recovering the Margins of American Religious History*. Edited by B. Dwain Waldrep and Scott Billingsley. Tuscaloosa: University of Alabama Press, 2010.

Shepherd, James Walter. *The Church, the Falling Away, and the Restoration*. Nashville: *Gospel Advocate*, 1929.

Shipps, Jan. "The Reality of the Restoration and the Restoration Ideal in the Mormon Tradition," in *The American Quest for the Primitive Church*. Edited by Richard T. Hughes. Urbana: University of Chicago Press, 1988.

Strauss, William and Neil Howe. *Generations: The History of America's Future, 1584 to 2069*. New York: Harper Perennial, 1991.

Short, Howard E. Letter to David Edwin Harrell, Jr, dated October 25, 1965. David Edwin Harrell, Jr. Papers, 1923-2017. Center for Restoration Studies MS #467. Abilene Christian University Special Collections and Archives. Brown Library. Brown Library.

Shouse, Roger. *A History of Publications Among Brethren in the Churches of Christ*. Greenwood, IN: Roger L. Shouse, 1991.

—————. "Brotherhood Papers," *Christianity Magazine* (January 1993): 9.

Smith, Elias. The Herald of Gospel Liberty 1.1 (September 1, 1808): 1-4. Available online at https://digitalshowcase.oru.edu/hsbooks/3. Last accessed January 5, 2024.

Smith, J. T. "Brethren Do Strange Things." *Torch* 23.5 (May 1988): 7.

—————. "Homer Hailey's Teaching on Divorce and Remarriage." *Torch* 23.6 (June 1988) 21-22.

————. "Did I Misrepresent Homer Hailey." *Torch* 23.8 (August 1988): 2-8.

————. "Finis." *Torch* 24.12 (December 1989).

Smith, Truman. "Neo-Institutionalism." [2001]. Last accessed August 30, 2024. https://www.knollwoodchurch.org/yr2001/106_neo_inst.html.

Smitherman, David. "The Work of the Local Church?" *The Bible Standard* 1.5 (January 5, 1973): 53.

Spears, Dudley Ross. "In Response to Ed Harrell—#2." Last accessed July 29, 2024. https://www.biblebanner.com/ga_art/rom14/drs2eh2.htm.

————. "In Response to Ed Harrell—#3." Last accessed July 29, 2024. https://www.biblebanner.com/ga_art/rom14/drs2eh3.htm.

Stocks, Bond. "Why Christ was Persecuted." *The Preceptor* 13.2 (December 1951): 12-13

Strauss, William and Neil Howe. *The Fourth Turning: What the Cycles of History Tell Us About America's Next Rendezvous with Destiny*. New York: Crown, 1997.

Swingley, Lillian to Mr. Ed Harrell. Card dated October 27, 1961. David Edwin Harrell, Jr. Papers, 1923-2017. Center for Restoration Studies MS #467. Abilene Christian University Special Collections and Archives, Brown Library.

Tant, Fanning Yater. "Jim Cope and Florida Christian College." *Gospel Guardian* 1.5 (June 2, 1949): 2.

————. "The Overflow: The Bartlesville School." *Gospel Guardian* 1.21 (September 29, 1949): 8.

————. "The Overflow: New Policy for Abilene Christian College?" *Gospel Guardian* 1.28 (November 17, 1949): 1.

————. "Editorial: Not Alone—We Hope." *Gospel Guardian* 1.49 (April 20, 1950): 2.

Thomas, J. D. *We Be Brethren: A Study in Biblical Interpretation.* Abilene: Biblical Research Press, 1958.

Tippens, Darryl. "Vicious Hatred Helps No One." *Abilene Reporter-News.* February 23, 1994: 8A.

Trimble, Bill. "Report on Visit to Ed Harrell, HIST 3670 Contemporary History, October 9, 2001." Series I.G.21. David Edwin Harrell, Jr. Papers, 1923-2017. Center for Restoration Studies MS #467. Abilene Christian University Special Collections and Archives. Brown Library.

Tripathi, C. B. "Letter to David E. Harrell, May 15, 1986." Series I.F.12. David Edwin Harrell, Jr. Papers, 1923-2017. Center for Restoration Studies MS #467. Abilene Christian University Special Collections and Archives. Brown Library.

Troeltsch, Ernst. *The Social Teaching of the Christian Church, Volume 2*. Louisville: Westminster/John Knox, 1992.

Turner, Robert F. "Attitudes Toward Current Issues." *Truth Magazine* 1.9 (June 1957): 2, 17-18. Accessible online at https://www.truthmagazine.com/archives/volume1/TM001078.htm. Last accessed January 5, 2024.

Ussery, Jamie to Dr. D. E. Harrell, Letter dated June 10, 1954. David Edwin Harrell, Jr. Papers, 1923-2017. Center for Restoration Studies MS #467. Abilene Christian University Special Collections and Archives, Brown Library.

Vinson, Jr., Bryan. "Is There a Need for 'Truth'?" *Truth Magazine* 1.2 (November 1956): 2.

Vinson Jr., Bryan. "I recommend ...." *Truth Magazine* 1.11 (August 1957): 2, 13.

Wacker, Grant. "Playing for Keeps: The Primitivist Impulse in Early

Pentecostalism." In *The American Quest for the Primitive Church*. Edited by Richard T. Hughes. Urbana: University of Chicago Press, 1988.

————. "Preface." In *Recovering the Margins of American Religious History*. Edited by B. Dwain Waldrep and Scott Billingsley. Tuscaloosa: University of Alabama Press, 2010.

Waldrep, B. Dwain and Scott Billingsley, eds. *Recovering the Margins of American Religious History: The Legacy of David Edwin Harrell, Jr.* (Tuscaloosa: University of Alabama Press, 2012).

Waldron, Jim. "Beware of Forbidding Brethren." Last Accessed September 11, 2024, https:/ www.waldronmissions.org/ Site/themed-images/pdfiles/forbidding_brethren.pdf.

Walker, D. Ellis to Elvis Huffard, Letter dated October 26, 1951. David Edwin Harrell, Jr. Papers, 1923-2017. Center for Restoration Studies MS #467. Abilene Christian University Special Collections and Archives. Brown Library.

Wallace, Cled E. "Getting Me Straightened Out." *Gospel Guardian* 1.42 (DATE): 1

————. "What the New Testament Teaches." *Gospel Guardian* 1.48 (April 13, 1950): 1.

————. "Tricks of Pride." *Gospel Guardian* 1.13 (August 4, 1949): 1.

Wallace, Jr., Foy E. "The Gospel Guardian." *Gospel Guardian* 1 (October 1935): 1-2.

————. "Editorial." *Bible Banner* (July 1938): 2-3.

————. "The Issues Before Us." *Gospel Guardian* 1.1. (May 5, 1949): 3.

————. "Compendium of Issues." *Torch* 1.1. (July 1950): 4-22.

—————. "Comment." *Torch* 1.1 (July 1950): 29.

Wallace, G. K. "Orphan Homes." *Gospel Guardian* 1.28 (November 17, 1949): 1.

—————. 'The Difference Between the Christian Church and the Church of Christ II." *The Preceptor* 2.1 (November 1952): 8.

Warner, W. Lloyd. *Social Class in America: A Manual of Procedure for the Measurement of Social Status.* New York: Harper & Row, 1960.

Weaver, John B. *Plots of Epiphany: Prison-Escape in Acts of the Apostles.* Beihefte zur Zeitschrift für die neutestamentliche Wissenshaft und die Kunde der älteren Kirche 131. Berlin: Walter de Gruyter, 2004.

—————. "Theological Libraries and The Next Christendom: Connecting North American Theological Education to Uses of the Book in the Global South." *Theological Librarianship* 1.2 (Winter 2008): 38-48.

—————. "Baptism As Sacrament And/Or Command" (2016). *ACU Lectureship and Summit Audio Collection* 5264. https://digitalcommons.acu.edu/sumlec_audio/5264.

—————. "The Bible in Digital Culture." In *Oxford Handbook of the Bible in America.* Edited by Paul Gutjahr. New York: Oxford University Press, 2017.

—————. "Transforming Practice: American Bible Reading in Digital Culture." In *The Bible in American Life.* Edited by Philip Goff, et. al. New York: Oxford University Press, 2017.

—————. "David Edwin Harrell Jr. and Journalism Among Congregational Churches of Christ." February 6, 2024. YouTube video. Last accessed September 9, 2024. https://www.youtube.com/watch?v=s2XDGJfj7Dw.

West, Earl Irvin. *The Search for the Ancient Order: A History of the Restoration Movement*. 4 Volumes. Indianapolis: Religious Book Service, 1949-1974.

──────. "Learning a Lesson from History—No. 2." *Gospel Guardian* 1.41 (February 23, 1950): 4.

──────. Letter to D. E. Harrell Jr. and Howard White, dated January 1958. David Edwin Harrell, Jr. Papers, 1923-2017. Center for Restoration Studies MS #467. Abilene Christian University Special Collections and Archives, Brown Library.

White, Howard. Letter to D. E. Harrell Jr., dated January 1958. David Edwin Harrell, Jr. Papers, 1923-2017. Center for Restoration Studies MS #467. Abilene Christian University Special Collections and Archives, Brown Library.

Whitley, Oliver Read. *Trumpet Call of Reformation*. St Louis: Bethany Press, 1959.

Wickerham, Coulter and David Holder. "Intro Part 1." [Interview of Five Editors of Christianity Magazine.] YouTube video. February 10, 2009. https://www.youtube.com/watch?v=R-dL2GdZhIk&t=62s.

──────. "Intro Part 2." YouTube video. February 10, 2009. https://youtu.be/LG64Zi8zUVY.

──────. "Intro Part 4." YouTube video. February 10, 2009. https://www.youtube.com/watch?v=7xpdXiqu3kA.

──────. "Intro Part 7." YouTube video. February 10, 2009. https://youtu.be/Nwu2NX61CXU?si=iWfyc6MGA4A4kJGf&t=170.

──────. "Intro Part 13." YouTube video. February 10, 2009. https://www.youtube.com/watch?v=ZwaYTtDOjxk.

Willis, Cecil. ""White Sects and Black Men." *Truth Magazine* 16.16 (February 24, 1972): 3-5.

————. "New Papers Galore." *Truth Magazine* 18.6 (December 12, 1974): 82-87. Online at: https://www.truthmagazine. com/new-papers-galore. Last accessed July 24, 2024.

Willis, Mike. "When Apostasy Occurs." *Guardian of Truth* 34.8 (April 19, 1990): 226, 246-248.

————. "Ed Harrell on Divorce and Remarriage." *Guardian of Truth* 34.8 (April 19, 1990): 227.

————. "What Saith the Scriptures? Divorce and Remarriage and Fellowship." Speech Delivered at Florida College (5 February 1991).

Wilson, Bryan. *Religious Sects: A Sociological Study*. New York: McGraw-Hill, 1970.

Wilson, Charles Reagan. "David Edwin Harrell Jr. and the Broadening of Southern Religious Studies." In *Recovering the Margins of American Religious History*. Edited by B. Dwain Waldrep and Scott Billingsley. Tuscaloosa: University of Alabama Press, 2010.

Wolfgang, Steve. "Speech Delivered at the Nashville Meeting: History and Background of the Institutional Controversy (1)." *Guardian of Truth* 33.7, (April 6, 1989): 208-211.

————. "History and Background of the Institutional Controversy (3)." *Guardian of Truth* 33.9 (May 4, 1989): 272-275. Online at: https://www.truthmagazine. com/archives/volume33/GOT033130.html#N_4_. Last accessed on February 3, 2024.

————. "History and Background of the Institutional Controversy (4)." *Guardian of Truth* 33.2 (January 19, 1989): 49-51.

————. "Marriage, Divorce and Remarriage in Church History." *Guardian of Truth* 34.1 (January 4, 1990): 27,

29-3.

————. "Ed Harrell as Preacher and Public Historian." Unpublished paper presented at the Christian Scholars' Conference. David Lipscomb University. Nashville, 2022.

Zeller, Benjamin E. "American Postwar 'Big Religion': Reconceptualizing Twentieth-Century American Religion Using Big Science as a Model." *Church History* 80.2 (June 2011): 321-351.

Index

Guardian of Truth
(See *Truth Magazine*)

H

Hailey, Homer
44, 54, 121, 127, 128, 130,
145, 168-192, 195-197, 203-
204, 206-208, 210, 212, 214,
217-218, 225-226, 228-229,
231-232, 234, 279, 284
Halbrook, Ron
164, 176, 178, 179, 184, 185,
193-194, 206, 214, 223, 232
Hall, Sewell
5, 143, 144, 149, 150, 151, 152,
159, 160, 162, 164, 166, 180,
186, 190, 191, 213, 227, 235,
238, 240, 245
Hamilton, Clinton
43, 183, 188, 284
Harrell Sr., David Edwin
30, 169
Hughes, Richard
4-6, 9, 34, 72, 101-103, 131,
173

I

Individual vs. Group
50, 54, 64, 74, 83, 126, 170,
182-183, 194, 211, 215,
218-226, 229, 240, 250-253,
255-256
Institute for Ecumenical and
Cultural Research
84, 86, 91
Institutional Churches of Christ
5, 45, 47, 54-55, 58, 111, 115-
116, 122, 126, 130, 144, 158,
159, 172, 199, 207, 239, 241,
250, 252-253, 267, 278, 280

Institutionalism
38, 40, 41, 45, 49, 52, 110, 117,
119, 120, 122, 124, 125, 126,
133, 134, 135, 138, 139, 140,
151, 165, 183, 198, 199, 213,
223, 241, 280
Intellectualism
60, 61, 273

J

Jacksonville, Florida
19-24, 27, 46, 160-161

K

Kenotic spirituality
134, 139-140, 183, 282

L

Lewis, Brent
49, 147, 154, 159-163, 167
Lipscomb College
28-30, 38, 40, 42, 75

M

Marriage, Divorce, and Remarriage (MDR)
19, 138, 171, 174-179, 183-185,
187, 190, 192, 195, 202-204,
206-207, 216-217, 229
Mental divorce
205, 206, 207
Miller, James P.
129
Moula Ali Church
247

N

Niebuhr, H. Richard
30, 275, 283

V

W

Made in the USA
Columbia, SC
08 March 2025

54807842R00237